Bon Appetit!

Martha Johnson

Raleigh House

COOKBOOK

Martha Johnson

Dedication and Thanks

This book is dedicated, with love, to my Mother, Flora Best Robinson, who not only taught me how to cook but showed me also the love and joy cooking brings. I wish she had written a cookbook.

My sincere thanks to my family and friends for their encouragement and willingness to try the many recipes I tested.

My thanks to Mike Christenson and Lewis Matteson, my computer mentors, for their patience and invaluable help.

Raleigh House

Many of my customers and friends were interested in the history of Raleigh House.

First of all, it was named for my husband, Raleigh White Johnson. He was born in Temple, Texas. His mother named him for the physician who delivered him, Doctor Raleigh White, a co-founder of the Scott and White hospital in Temple.

Raleigh and I were married in 1925, when I was only 20 years old. We had 26 happy years together, then he died suddenly of a heart attack. Our son and daughter were both married. My home and family had been my only interest. However, I loved to cook and that led me into a whole new way of life.

I had always taken an active part in the kitchen of our church. At this time, the new Fellowship Hall had just been completed. It had a beautiful all electric, stainless steel kitchen with commercial equipment. The Women's Association of our church had served meals to community organizations such as the Red Cross, Y.M.C.A. and other church groups to help raise their budget. Now, with the new kitchen, we stepped up our catering. It was a challenge and, in meeting that challenge, we learned about our new equipment and the preparing of food in quantity. This experience was very valuable to me in establishing Raleigh House and I have always been very grateful to my church.

I visited in Kerrville and loved the Hill Country, and decided to move there in 1955. My Kerrville friends asked me to "do a little catering" to keep my hand in. By the following June, I found myself in the restaurant business in response to urging from some of the camps and motels in the area and also my new-found friends. I knew absolutely nothing about the restaurant business, but with a nucleus of experienced staff and lots of hard work and long hours on my part, we survived that first summer. Thus began 34 wonderful years.

Many of my customers ate with me each year I was open. Some who had brought their children to camp in the early years, came back with their grandchildren who were at camp, to eat at Raleigh House. My customers and my family were great "ego" boosters. I should explain that I was open only during the summer months. I wanted to have time to be with my family and the now increasing number of grandchildren. I now have 19 great grandchildren with a 20th due soon after this book comes out.

One of the bonuses of owning Raleigh House was the advantage of joining groups of restauranteurs for trips to Europe, the Scandinavian countries, the Orient and one trip around the world, which included Egypt, India, the Holy Land, Lebanon and Thailand among others. On this last trip, a group from Kraft Foods were with us. It was interesting to see the recipes and their comments in the Kraft Food advertisements in the months after we returned. I had an opportunity to attend the Cordon Bleu and La Varenne cooking schools in Paris. On these trips, we also had the opportunity to observe at many chef's schools, even one in Japan. Dinners were given in our honor. Altogether, they were delightful, informative experiences. However, one of my customers cautioned me to have a good time, but not to change my menu!

Some of the recipes are my mother's and aunt's, many are from my co-workers of my church and members of my family who all like to cook, and some are my original ones. Some are easy, some complicated; some expensive, some economical. I guess it is a kind of potpourri. This book was written with love and many fond memories. I hope you will enjoy it as much as I have enjoyed writing it. Bon Appetit!

Table of Contents

Appetizers
& Soups

Mushroom Turnovers

Recipe can be doubled. These are very good, so make plenty.

Crust:
3   (3 ounce) packages cream
      cheese, room temperature
½   cup (1 stick) butter or
      margarine, softened

1½ cups flour

Mix cheese and butter, add flour and work until smooth. Chill 30 minutes. Roll dough ⅛" thick, on lightly floured board. Cut into 2½" rounds. Reroll trimmings. Put 1 teaspoon filling in center of each round. Fold over and crimp edges.

Filling:
3   tablespoons butter
1   medium onion, chopped
½   pound fresh mushrooms
      washed and chopped
¼   teaspoon thyme

½   teaspoon salt
Dash pepper
2   tablespoons flour
¼   cup heavy cream

Heat the butter in a heavy saucepan, add the onion, cook about 3 minutes, then add the mushrooms and cook an additional 2 minutes. Remove from heat, add thyme, salt, dash pepper and 2 tablespoons flour. Mix then add the cream. Put 1 teaspoon filling in the center of each round, fold over and crimp the edges with a fork. These can be frozen at this point. If not, cook in a 400 degree oven for 15 minutes or until light brown. Serve hot.

Yield: 25 to 30

Tipsy Mushrooms

¼   cup butter (½ stick)
1   clove garlic, minced
¼   cup Vermouth

1   teaspoon Italian seasoning
1   pound fresh button
      mushrooms

Combine butter and garlic in a glass measure and microwave on high 2 minutes. Add vermouth and seasoning. Place mushrooms in a 1 quart casserole. Pour butter mixture over mushrooms. Cover and microwave on high 3 minutes. Do not overcook as mushrooms will shrink. Makes about 40 appetizers. Serve with toothpicks.

Yield: 35 to 40

Kelly Plumb's Cheese Bread

Kelly was an excellent cook in the Hill Country. She lived in Hunt and entertained graciously.

2   **large loaves of sandwich
bread**

Take crusts off of bread. Stack 3 slices on top of each other, cut into quarters. Keep stacks separate. Continue until all bread is prepared. Spread each square of bread with cheese mixture, stack another square on top, spread it and stack the third one on top. Ice the whole stack with the cheese mixture. Stick a toothpick in each stack to hold it together. Set on cookie sheet and continue stacking and spreading until all the stacks of 3 squares are iced.

You may either store in the refrigerator, covered, if you are using the next day, or leave on the cookie sheets and freeze. Place in covered containers or boxes until needed. Bake on lightly greased cookie sheets in a 350° oven about 20 minutes or until puffed and lightly browned. Serve warm.

Cheese Mixture:

1 **pound butter, do not substitute**	1½ **teaspoon Worcestershire sauce**
4 **jars Old English cheese spread**	**Dash cayenne pepper**
1 **teaspoon Tabasco sauce**	½ **teaspoon dried dill weed**
1 **teaspoon onion powder**	1 **teaspoon Beau Monde seasoning**

Place all the above ingredients in mixer bowl, Cream well. Finish according to above directions. This should be enough filling to ice 2 loaves of bread.

Yield: 50 squares

This can be frozen. Place iced squares on a cookie sheet; freeze, then wrap or place in plastic bags. If frozen, allow extra baking time.

Chili Cheese Dip

This is a quickly made dip for any time, but especially if you need a dip in a hurry.

2 **pound package Velveeta cheese**	1 **cup Wolf Brand chili without beans**

Break Velveeta into pieces and place it and the chili in top of a double boiler. Place over boiling water and cook, stirring constantly, until cheese is melted and mixture is well blended. Serve in a chafing dish with corn chips or nachos.

Yield: about 6 cups

Broccoli Soup

This is a recipe of my own. I make it often with either broccoli or spinach. It can be served hot or cold. If served cold a dollop of sour cream is good. I keep some on hand to drink, sans cream, before a meal to keep me from eating high calorie snacks.

1 (10 ounce) package frozen chopped broccoli or spinach	½ cup powdered low-fat milk
2½ cups water	Salt, pepper and nutmeg to taste

Place frozen broccoli or spinach and water in a saucepan with ½ teaspoon salt. Bring to a boil and cook just until broccoli is thawed. Place in blender container with liquid. You may have to divide it in two sections if blender is not large enough. Blend, then add the powdered milk, ¼ teaspoon nutmeg and blend again. Taste for seasoning. If made in two sections, combine soup in a bowl, then taste for seasoning. Serve hot or cold. Serve either in mugs or, if you are having company, serve in the coffee cups of your best china, as an appetizer.

Yield: About 3½ cups

I sometimes serve it in the living room before dinner as an appetizer. Mrs. Culmore's cheese balls are delicious with it.

Mrs. Culmore's Cheese Balls

Mrs. Culmore was a faithful active member of the kitchen committee at my church in Houston many years ago. We served these at Raleigh House for many years, until we could not keep up with the demand.

1 cup margarine	½ teaspoon paprika
1 cup grated very sharp cheese	2 dashes Tabasco
2 cups unsifted flour	4 teaspoons Worcestershire

Have cheese and margarine cold. Cut margarine in slices and place in mixer bowl, add rest of ingredients. Mix until well combined, but not too long as mixture has a tendency to become sticky. Pinch off dough to make a 1 inch ball. Roll between palms of hands and place on ungreased cookie sheet. Bake at 300 degrees until light brown on bottom and firm to the touch. Store in covered container.

Yield: 25 to 30 balls

These freeze well.

Chilled Avocado Soup

This soup can also be served hot.

2	large avocados, sliced	Salt and white pepper to taste
1	cup cream, half and half or heavy cream	Sour cream for garnish (optional)
1	teaspoon grated onion	
4	cups chicken broth, homemade or canned	

Place all ingredients except salt and pepper in food processor. Process until mixture is smooth. Taste for seasoning. Transfer soup to a container and chill for 3 hours. To serve ladle into pretty cups or mugs. A dollop of sour cream may be added, if desired.

Yield: 6 to 8 servings

Chunky Beef Soup

This is a hearty, satisfying soup.

1 (14 ounce) can whole tomatoes, drained but save juice
4 medium potatoes, diced
2 green peppers, finely diced
4 large carrots, diced
3 tablespoons butter or margarine
1½ cups chopped onions
2 cloves garlic, minced
2 pounds of round or top sirloin steak cut into ½ inch cubes

2 tablespoons flour
2 tablespoons paprika
3 tablespoons tomato paste
4 (14 ounce) cans of beef broth or equivalent of homemade
1 bay leaf
Salt and freshly ground pepper to taste
Sour cream
Grated parmesan cheese

Cook onions in butter in heavy large stockpot over medium heat, until limp. Remove with a slotted spoon and set aside. Cook beef in same stockpot, until brown on all sides. Add flour and paprika. Cook, stirring, for 3 minutes. Remove from heat. Add tomato paste and stir until smooth. Break up tomatoes and add them and their juice, then add the garlic, onions, beef broth, vegetables and bay leaf. Add salt and pepper, bring to a boil, then simmer for 30 to 45 minutes. As with any soup, flavor improves if served the second day. When serving, top with a dollop of sour cream and grated Parmesan cheese.

Yield: About 14 cups

I usually make it a day ahead. Reheating the next day improves the flavor.

Beef Pasta Soup

This is my version of ground beef soup.

2   pounds very lean ground beef
1   cup water
2   medium onions, chopped
4   cloves garlic, minced or ½ teaspoon garlic powder
26 ounces mixed frozen vegetables
6   ounces small elbow macaroni or pasta of your choice
2   (1 pound) cans of whole tomatoes, broken up with juice

1   teaspoon dried thyme, crumbled
1   teaspoon dried sweet basil, crumbled
2   teaspoons salt
1 to 2 teaspoons pepper
8   cups water
3   tablespoons instant beef boullion

Cook ground beef and onion in a little olive oil until browned. Add 1 cup water. Break loose any brown particles in bottom of pot. Add rest of ingredients. Bring to a boil, then cover and simmer about 40 minutes. Taste for seasoning. Serve with grated Parmesan cheese and Italian bread.

Yield: 8 to 10 servings

I happened to have on hand some pasta salad mix. I used a 32 ounce package instead of the vegetables listed. The mix had red and yellow peppers, broccoli, carrots and small curly pasta. There are other varieties, too. Use whichever you like.

Green Chili Dip

This is a good dip to serve with a Mexican supper.

1   cup grated sharp cheddar cheese
½   cup mayonnaise

¼   cup sour cream
4   ounce can chopped green chilis, very well drained

Mix the cheese, mayonnaise and sour cream in a blender. Blend until smooth. Remove to a bowl and gently fold in green chilis. Serve with toasted tortillas or nacho chips.

Yield: About 2 cups

You may want to add only half of the chilis until you taste for seasoning.

Cream of Broccoli Mushroom Soup

This is a richer and more elaborate version of broccoli soup.

6	tablespoons butter (¾ of a stick)	2	(10¾ ounce) cans chicken broth
¼	pound fresh mushrooms, sliced	1½	cups half and half
2	(10 ounce) packages chopped broccoli, thawed and drained, reserving liquid		Pinch garlic powder, not garlic salt
1	medium onion, sliced		Pinch dried dillweed
2	green onions, white top only, minced		Salt and freshly ground pepper to taste

Melt 2 tablespoons butter in large skillet over medium high heat. Add mushrooms and sauté until tender. Remove from skillet, using slotted spoon, and set aside. Melt remaining 4 tablespoons butter in same skillet. Add sliced onions and green onions and sauté over medium heat until tender. Do not let brown. Add broccoli and cook 2 minutes. Transfer ⅓ of the broccoli mixture to a blender. Add ⅓ of the broth and ⅓ of the broccoli liquid and purée. Pour into large saucepan. Repeat with remaining broccoli mixture, broth and liquid. Stir in half and half, garlic powder, dill weed and sautéed mushrooms. Bring to a simmer, stirring frequently, Reduce heat to low and simmer 10 minutes, stirring occasionally. Season with salt and pepper and serve.

Yield: 6 to 9 servings

This should be served in cream soup dishes since it is thicker than a previous recipe.

Sherried Mushrooms

This appetizer should be served at the table as a first course. It is quite rich. I like to serve an intermezzo between it and the entree. My favorite is a tart lemon or raspberry sherbet served in a half lemon rind on an ivy leaf.

1	pound fresh mushrooms	¾	teaspoon salt
4	tablespoons (½ stick) butter or margarine	¼	teaspoon pepper
2	tablespoons flour	1	cup half and half
		1½	tablespoons dry sherry

Rinse and pat dry mushrooms. Then cut in half if medium size, in fourths if large. Melt butter in skillet, add mushrooms and sauté about 5 minutes. Stir in flour, salt and pepper. Remove from heat and gradually stir in half and half. Return to heat and simmer slowly until thickened slightly. Add sherry. Heat and serve over toast points or on a round of pastry.

Yield: 4 to 6 servings

Baked Potato Soup

This is my version of a soup I ate in a restaurant. I particularly liked the toppings served with it which makes it a one dish meal. Sexton and Minor make the chicken base.

6	(¾ stick) tablespoons butter or margarine	2	cups chicken broth or 2 cups hot water with 1 tablespoon chicken base, not chicken boullion.
2	tablespoons grated onion		
8	level tablespoons flour		
⅛	teaspoon pepper	2	cups leftover baked potatoes cut into small cubes
1	teaspoon salt		
3	cups hot milk		

Make a buerre manié by creaming the butter and flour together. Heat milk in saucepan, add buerre manié in small pieces, stirring constantly, then add chicken broth and cook over medium heat, stirring, until thickened. Sauté onion in small skillet with an additional tablespoon butter and add to creamed mixture. Add baked potatoes, mix and taste for seasoning. Serve in bowls topped with bacon, chopped green onion and grated cheese. I serve additional toppings in bowls on the tables so guests can add, if they like.

Yield: 6 to 8 servings

It was simple to make at Raleigh House as we usually had leftover baked potatoes. Do not use boiled potatoes. They do not have the flavor of baked ones. Next time you are serving baked potatoes, put some extra in the oven for a pot of soup.

Mushroom Spinach Appetizers

This is an easy appetizer as it is served cold.

50	medium sized fresh mushrooms, wash, saving stems	1	cup mayonnaise
		1	(5 ounce) can water chestnuts, drained well and chopped
1	(10 ounce) package frozen chopped spinach, thawed and squeezed dry		
		1	envelope Knorr's vegetable soup mix
1	cup sour cream		

Wipe mushrooms and remove stems. Chop stems and set aside. Combine spinach, sour cream, mayonnaise, water chestnuts, soup mix and chopped mushroom stems. Stuff mushrooms. Put in refrigerator in a covered container overnight. Serve cold.

Yield: 50 servings

Vegetable Chowder

2½ cups water
2   cups diced peeled potatoes
¾   cup diced green onions
½   cup celery, diced
2   teaspoons salt, divided
¼   cup (½ stick) butter or
    margarine
¼   cup flour
2   cups milk
1½ teaspoons Worcestershire

¼   teaspoon freshly ground
    pepper
1   (1 pound) can of tomatoes,
    broken up with juice
4   ounces grated Parmesan
    cheese
4   ounces grated processed
    yellow cheese
1   tablespoon minced parsley

Bring water to a boil in large saucepan over high heat. Add potatoes, onions, celery and 1 teaspoon salt. Return to boiling, reduce heat to medium-low. Cover and simmer until vegetables are tender. Melt butter in medium saucepan over medium-low heat. Remove from heat and add flour. Add milk, Worcestershire, remaining 1 teaspoon salt, and pepper. Return to medium-low heat and cook, stirring, until thickened. Stir in cooked vegetable mixture, add tomatoes, Parmesan, processed cheese and parsley. Heat and serve in deep bowls.

Yield: 4 servings

Church Bouillion

I named it thus because we used to serve it from electric roasters at church dinners — kind of a substitute for the cocktail hour. It is also a welcome gift to anyone "under the weather." It is very easy to prepare.

46 ounce can V8 juice
2   cans of water
3   tablespoons Worcestershire
    sauce
2   teaspoons pepper

1½ teaspoons salt or salt to
    your taste.
15 beef bouillion cubes, broken
    up

Place all ingredients in large stock pot. Bring to a boil and let simmer about 20 minutes. Taste for seasoning. Serve in cups.

Note: For 6 cups bouillion, use 2 cups V8, 4 cups water, 1 tablespoon Worcestershire, 6 bouillion cubes, and salt and pepper to taste. Makes 6 cups.

Yield: About 18 cups

This recipe can become jellied bouillion by adding one envelope of unflavored gelatin dissolved in 2 tablespoons water. Heat 2 cups of the bouillion and add to the softened gelatin. Stir until gelatin is dissolved, then chill. Recipe can be increased.

Miniature Quiche

You may want to at least double this recipe as they disappear fast.

Pastry:

1	stick butter or margarine	1¼	cups flour
4	ounces cream cheese, room temperature	¼	teaspoon salt

Combine butter and cream cheese. Mix well. Stir in flour and salt. Divide into 36 balls. Place a ball into each cup of 3 (1 dozen size) miniature muffin pans, that have been sprayed with a vegetable spray. Press into bottom and sides to make tart shells. Set in refrigerator while making filling.

Filling:

1	cup (4 ounces) grated cheddar cheese	2	eggs, beaten
2	tablespoons finely chopped green onions	½	cup half and half
1	teaspoon dried tarragon, crumbled	¼	teaspoon salt
		¼	teaspoon pepper
		⅛	teaspoon nutmeg
			Dash Tabasco

Combine eggs, half and half, salt, pepper, ground nutmeg and a dash of Tabasco. Mix well. Add rest of ingredients. Spoon into pastry shells, filling ¾ full. Bake at 350 degrees about 25 to 30 minutes or until just set. Serve hot.

Yield: 36 Quiche

These may be frozen after cooking by placing on cookie sheets to freeze then placing in a box with a tight cover. However, place them in a pre-heated 350 degree oven in the frozen state to reheat.

Avocado Dip

1	cup mashed avocado pulp		Dash Worcestershire sauce
8	ounces cream cheese, room temperature	¼	cup very finely chopped green onions
3	tablespoons lemon juice	1	teaspoons salt

Gradually add the avocado to the cream cheese, blending until smooth. Add the lemon juice, Worcestershire sauce, onions and salt. Mix until thoroughly blended. Place in a bowl on a tray and surround with crackers.

Yield: 1½ cups

Oysters Octavio

This is my daughter-in-law's recipe. She serves them in ramikins in the living room before dinner accompanied with squares of French bread for getting every bit of the delicious sauce.

24 to 36 oysters		2	dashes Worcestershire
2	cloves garlic, ¼ ounce		sauce
1	stick unsalted butter	2	dashes Maggi sauce
2	ounces grated Parmesan	1	teaspoon vermouth
	cheese	1	teaspoon Pernod
Dash salt and pepper			
1	teaspoon parsley flakes,		
	crumbled		

Crush garlic in garlic press. Make a paste of the butter, and garlic. Add parsley, then add salt, pepper, Worcestershire sauce and Maggi sauce. Next add the Vermouth and Pernod. Place 3 or 4 oysters into ramikins or oyster shells and cover with the garlic butter. Sprinkle with the Parmesan cheese and bake at 350° until bubbly. Serve immediately with oyster forks and French bread cubes.

Yield: 6 to 9 servings

Escargots in Mushroom Caps

This recipe adds Grand Marnier or Vermouth on top of the escargots.

24	large canned snails, washed	2	cloves garlic, minced
	and dried	½	teaspoon salt
24	large mushroom caps	Pepper to taste	
3	tablespoons butter	⅛	teaspoon ground nutmeg
1	teaspoon lemon juice	3	tablespoons soft, fresh
2	sticks unsalted butter, do		breadcrumbs,toasted
	not substitute	2	tablespoons Grand Marnier
⅓	cup fresh parsley, minced		or dry Vermouth
2	green onions, minced		

Melt the 3 tablespoons butter in pan and sauté mushrooms until lightly browned, but not softened. Remove from pan and drain. Mince by hand or in a food processor, the parsley, salt, pepper, green onions and garlic. Cream together the butter, nutmeg and parsley mixture. Fill mushroom caps with butter mixture, reserving 4 teaspoons. Place a snail in each and cover with the reserved teaspoons butter. Sprinkle the toasted bread crumbs over mushrooms. Spoon Grand Marnier or Vermouth over each and bake in a pre-heated 400° oven about 10 minutes or until bubbly. Serve with French bread.

Yield: 4 servings

Oyster Soup

The addition of the cheese to this soup makes it extra good. This is an excellent first course, either served in the living room before dinner or at the table.

12	ounces oysters, undrained	¼	cup butter, melted
½	cup finely chopped carrots	½	cup flour
½	cup finely chopped celery	4	cups whole milk
3½	cups chicken broth, canned or homemade	1	cup sharp cheddar cheese, grated
½	cup finely chopped onion	½	teaspoon pepper

Drain oysters, reserving ½ cup liquid. Coarsely chop oysters, set aside. Combine carrots, celery, chicken broth and oyster liquid in a large, heavy saucepan. Bring to a boil, then reduce heat and simmer until vegetables are crisp tender. Sauté onions in butter until tender but not brown. Add flour and cook, stirring, until mixture is thickened. Cook 1 more minute, stirring constantly. Gradually add milk, then stir in broth mixture, grated cheese and pepper. Add salt, if needed. Stir over very low heat until cheese is melted. Add chopped oysters and simmer about 8 minutes or just until edges of oysters begin to curl. Serve hot.

Yield: 9½ cups

Stuffed Baby Brie en Croute

This is another recipe for Brie cheese, one of my favorite cheeses

1	wheel (1 pound, 1 ounce) baby brie, chilled	1	sheet Pepperidge Farm frozen puff pastry
4	thin slices baked ham	1	egg beaten with 1 tablespoon water
8	thin slices pastrami		

Using a large sharp knife, cut chilled brie horizontally into 3 layers. Arrange baked ham on bottom layer. Place middle layer of brie on top and layer with pastrami. Top with last piece of brie. Cover and chill.

Thaw pastry for 20 minutes; unfold and roll on a lightly floured board to a 14" square. Trim to a 14" circle (reserve trimmings). Unwrap brie and place in center of pastry; brush pastry edges with egg wash. Fold pastry over brie, trimming edges as necessary to enclose cheese. Place on baking sheet, seam-side down; brush with more egg mixture. Garnish with pastry trimmings; brush with egg wash and bake at 375° for 25 minutes or until pastry is puffed and golden brown. Remove from oven and transfer to a wire rack to cool for at least 30 minutes before serving. If too hot, brie will be very runny. This is also good served cold.

Yield: 6 to 8 servings

Pesto Pinwheels

1 sheet Pepperidge Farm frozen puff pastry thawed according to package directions	½ cup grated Parmesan cheese
⅓ cup pesto sauce, store-bought or homemade	1 egg beaten with 1 teaspoon water

Roll thawed pastry into a rectangle 14″ × 11″. Spread evenly with the pesto sauce and sprinkle with Parmesan cheese. Starting at the long edge, roll up pastry like a jelly roll. Press in edges. Cut roll into ⅜″ thick slices. Place on lightly greased baking sheet, cut-side down, and brush with egg mixture. Be careful not to let egg wash roll down the sides or rolls will stick to the pan. Bake at 400° for 8 to 10 minutes, or until golden brown. Transfer to a wire rack and serve while warm.

Yield: about 35 pinwheels

Lamb Balls

A tangy first course, good any time.

1 pound ground lamb	2 teaspoons salt
1 cup dry bread crumbs	½ teaspoon pepper
2 eggs, beaten	⅓ cup minced onion
1 cup water	Pinch dried Marjoram, crumbled

Mix the lamb, bread crumbs, eggs, water, salt, pepper, marjoram and minced onion. For easier handling, place in refrigerator 1 hour before shaping. Shape into balls of about 1 inch. Brown on all sides in some fat in a skillet, use a wooden spoon or spatula for turning. When done, place in chafing dish or food warmer. Stick toothpicks in balls. Place honey mustard sauce in a bowl for dipping.

Sauce:

½ cup honey	½ cup prepared mustard

Mix and serve.

Yield: about 25 balls

Lillian's Pickadillo

I first ate this at a picnic supper at a ranch near Fredericksburg. The hostess graciously gave me the recipe.

2	large finely chopped onions	2	(10 ounce) cans tomatoes
2	tablespoons bacon		with green chilis, undrained
	drippings	2	teaspoons sugar
2	pounds lean ground beef	1	cup raisins
2	cloves minced garlic		Salt, if needed
2	teaspoons ground cloves		Corn chips, tostados or
2	teaspoons cinnamon		homemade bread
2	teaspoons ground cumin		
1½	cups chopped toasted		
	pecans		

Brown onion in bacon drippings or butter in a large pan. Add beef and brown, discarding excess fat. Add garlic, cloves, cinnamon, tomatoes, chilis and sugar. Simmer, covered, approximately an hour, stirring occasionally. Add raisins and cumin and simmer 20 minutes. Add pecans and simmer, covered, another 10 minutes. Salt to taste. Serve hot.

Yield: 2 quarts

This can be a side dish or served from a chafing dish with corn chips or tostados.

Slim Tuna Chowder

If you do not have the water-packed tuna on hand, you may use the oil-packed by putting it in a colander and running hot water over it. My mother used to do this whenever she used tuna for a salad. It makes a much milder dish, less calories.

2	cups V8 juice	1	tablespoon Worcestershire
2	cups water	½	teaspoon pepper
4	cloves garlic, minced	1	potato (at least 8 ounces),
¼	teaspoon dried oregano,		peeled, quartered then cut
	crumbled		into thin strips
¼	teaspoons dried sweet basil,	1	(7 ounce) can water-packed
	crumbled		tuna, undrained

Place V8 juice and water in a saucepan. Add garlic and herbs, potatoes and Worcestershire. I add the salt and pepper to taste when ready to serve. Simmer, covered, until potatoes are tender, then flake tuna and add to pot. Simmer 20 more minutes, stirring occasionally.

Yield: About 8 cups

Quiche Lorraine for a Crowd

This is a handy recipe to have for entertaining. It is cut into 1½ inch squares, so is easy to handle for a cocktail hour. It is also quicker to make than several smaller quiche.

Pie crust for 3 pie shells		**4**	**cups light cream**
1	**pound sliced bacon**	**1½**	**teaspoons salt**
2	**cups finely chopped onions**	**¼**	**teaspoon nutmeg**
3	**cups grated Swiss cheese**	**¼**	**teaspoon pepper**
	(12 ounces)		**Dash cayenne pepper**
6	**eggs**		

Roll out pastry to a 18″ × 15″ rectangle. Use to line a 15½″ × 10½″ × 1″ jelly roll pan. Flute edge. Refrigerate.

Fry bacon until crisp, drain, then crumble. Sauté onion in two tablespoons bacon drippings. Sprinkle cheese over bottom of pastry shell, sprinkle bacon and onion over cheese. Beat eggs with cream, salt, nutmeg and pepper. Mix well. Bake 35 to 40 minutes in a pre-heated 375° oven, or until knife inserted in middle comes out clean. Cut into 1½″ squares for 45 cocktail servings. Serve warm.

Yield: 45 cocktail, 24 appetizers

Creamy Mushroom Filling

I was taught to crumble dried herbs between the palms of my hands over the other ingredients. The warmth of your hands brings out their flavor.

2	**tablespoon butter**	**¼**	**cup sour cream**
8	**ounces fresh mushrooms,**		**Salt and freshly ground pepper**
	washed and chopped		**to taste**
¼	**cup finely chopped onion**		
¼	**teaspoon dried thyme**		
	leaves, crumbled		

Sauté mushrooms and onion in the butter; cook, stirring, until mushrooms are softened. Remove from heat; cool, then stir in thyme, sour cream and salt and pepper to taste. Refrigerate until served.

Yield: About 1½ cups

This mixture can be put on toast rounds or used as a dip with crackers.

Mother's Vegetable Soup

Mother always had this soup simmering on the back of the stove for supper on Mondays, washday.

4	pounds of soup bones	¼	teaspoon dried thyme, crumbled
2	pounds coarsely ground lean beef	1	bay leaf
1	cup chopped onion	½	teaspoon pepper
1	cup diced raw potato	2	tablespoons instant beef boullion
1	cup diced carrots		
1	cup sliced celery	1	pound can golden whole kernel corn, undrained
2	(16 ounce) cans whole tomatoes, cut coarsely with juice	1	pound can cut green beans, undrained
5	cups water and stock combined	1	pound can green peas, undrained
2	teaspoons salt		
¼	teaspoon dried basil, crumbled		

The day before making the soup, cover the soup bones with water, bring to a boil then lower heat and simmer for 1 hour. Let bones cool in stock, then remove. Strain the stock and measure it. Put it in a covered container and refrigerate.

Next day, skim fat off stock reserving about 3 tablespoons. In a large heavy stockpot, lightly brown beef and onion in beef fat. Add enough water to stock to make 5 cups and pour into meat mixture. Add potatoes, carrots, celery, tomatoes, herbs and seasonings. Bring to a boil and simmer about an hour or until vegetables are very tender. Add rest of ingredients and heat through. If soup seems too thick, add a little more water and taste for seasoning. Remove bay leaf before serving.

Yield: 15 cups

Minestrone

I first ate this soup at a restaurant in Nice, France, many years ago. The pesto served with it was the ultimate touch.

Pesto:

1	cup olive oil, divided	¾	cup fresh basil
¼	cup fresh basil	¾	cup fresh parsley
¼	cup fresh parsley	¾	cup grated Parmesan
4	cloves garlic		cheese
½	cup walnuts		

Place ½ cup oil with the ¼ cup basil, ¼ cup parsley and the garlic in a blender. Blend until puréed. Then add the remaining ½ cup of oil by driplets. Blend until thick, then add rest of basil, parsley, nuts and Parmesan cheese. Blend until smooth. Refrigerate in a covered container.

Soup:

2	cups white navy beans	2	small zucchini, diced
2	quarts water	2	medium size potatoes,
2	teaspoons salt		peeled and diced
½	teaspoon pepper	3	tablespoons minced parsley
4	tablespoons olive oil	2	teaspoons dried rosemary,
4	cloves garlic, minced		crumbled
2	onions, diced	1	teaspoon dried oregano,
3	stalks celery, diced		crumbled
4	quarts beef stock	4	whole cloves
4	tablespoons tomato paste	4	ounces small pasta
2	cups carrots, diced	3	cups cabbage, shredded

Soak beans in water overnight. In the morning, add salt. Bring to a boil and simmer slowly until beans are tender. Add more water, if necessary, so beans are covered. Heat olive oil in a heavy saucepan and sauté garlic, onion, potatoes and celery. When these are yellow, add carrots and zucchini. Sauté until crisp tender. Do not add cabbage and pasta, they are added at end of cooking time. Add beef stock. Put half of the cooked beans in blender or food processor and blend until smooth, then add whole beans, mashed beans, their liquid, cabbage and pasta to stock mixture. Simmer for 10 minutes or until pasta is done. Season to taste. Serve with pesto or grated Parmesan cheese, never both. As with all soups, flavor improves the second day.

Continued on next page

Beef Stock:

5   pounds beef ribs or soup   5   quarts water
    meat

The day before you are making the soup, place meat and water in large stock pot and bring to a boil, then simmer about 1½ hours. Cool and refrigerate. Next day, bring to a boil, remove meat and bones. Strain and add to soup.

Yield: About 18 cups

The pesto can be added to each bowl of soup when served. I like to offer it to guests from a bowl so they can help themselves.

Polly's Fish Chowder

Polly was a dear friend of mine, She and her sister Trudie were both good cooks. The amount of garlic, 4 cloves, is correct.

3   tablespoons flour
3   tablespoons butter
1   (1 pound 13 ounce) can
    tomatoes broken up with
    juice
½   cup chopped celery
4   cloves garlic, minced
1   large onion chopped

2   pounds cod, pollock or
    other firm-fleshed white fish
2   cups diced potatoes
1   tablespoon Worcestershire
1   quart water
Salt and pepper to taste
Dash Tabasco

Lightly brown flour in butter. Lower heat and add onion. Cook gently until onion is tender. Add tomatoes, celery, garlic and water. Simmer slowly for 20 minutes, add potatoes. Cut fish into 1 inch cubes and add to soup mixture. Simmer slowly for 30 to 40 minutes. More water maybe added, if needed. Taste for seasoning.

Yield: 6 generous servings

I usually use cod for this chowder. Pollock or any firm white fish may be used.

Helpful Hint: *Always sauté chopped onions and celery in butter before adding them to a recipe unless otherwise instructed.*

Ruth's Pineapple, Green Pepper Dip

Recipe may be cut in half for smaller quantity

16   ounces cream cheese, room,
    temperature
16   ounce can crushed
    pineapple, drained
¼   cup chopped green pepper

2   teaspoons chopped green
    onions
2   teaspoons Lawry's seasoned
    salt
1   cup chopped pecans

Mix all ingredients together except chopped pecans. Stir in pecans. Serve with crackers of your choice.

Yield: 5¼ cups

Cream and Bacon Dip

4   slices bacon
8   ounces cream cheese, room
    temperature
1   cup sour cream
¼   cup finely minced celery

2   tablespoons finely minced
    onion
¼   cup chopped pecans
½   teaspoon salt, if needed

Cook bacon until crisp, then crumble fine. Mix cream cheese and sour cream in a bowl until smooth. Stir in onion, celery, pecans, bacon and salt, if needed. refrigerate until ready to serve.

Yield: 2½ cups

Marjorie's Taramasalata

Tarama may be obtained in the gourmet section of food stores. It is carp roe.

4   ounces tarama
2   level tablespoons onion,
    minced
Juice of one lemon

2½   slices white bread,
    homemade style or French,
    crusts removed
½   cup olive oil

Place tarama, onion, and lemon juice in blender. Dip bread in hot water, then squeeze dry and break into pieces. Add to tarama mixture and blend. Add the olive oil in driblets and blend until no trace of oil remains. Spoon into a plate or bowl. Garnish with chopped parsley and Greek olives. Serve with French bread.

Yield: about 2 cups

In Greece, this dish is sometimes made with mashed potatoes instead of the bread.

Scallops au Gratin

This one of my family's favorite appetizers. It is some trouble to make but can be made the day before and heated. It can also be frozen, however, put in oven before completely thawed. Allow extra time for heating.

¾	cup dry vermouth	¼	bay leaf
½	teaspoon salt	2	tablespoons minced shallots
Pinch pepper			or green onions

Simmer above ingredients in a stainless steel or enameled saucepan for 5 minutes. Set aside.

1	pound washed scallops
½	pound fresh mushrooms, washed and sliced

Cut scallops in slices, if large. Add them and the mushrooms to the wine mixture. Add enough water to barely cover. Simmer, covered, for exactly 5 minutes. Remove scallops and mushrooms and set aside. Reserve liquid.

Sauce:

3	tablespoons butter, do not substitute	2	egg yolks
4	tablespoons flour	½	cup whipping cream
¾	cup whole milk		Salt and pepper to taste
			Lemon juice

Boil liquid until it measures 1 cup. Cook flour and butter together for two minutes, stirring. Mix the boiling liquid with the milk and slowly blend with the flour mixture. Boil one minute. Beat the egg yolks and cream together, then add hot sauce slowly, beating well. Put back into saucepan and boil one minute. Season with salt and pepper and lemon juice. If too thick, add a little more whipping cream. Add ⅔ of the sauce to scallops and mushrooms, then divide them between 6 buttered scallop shells. Cover with rest of the sauce and top each with 1 tablespoon grated imported Swiss cheese and divide 1½ tablespoons butter bits on top of cheese. Heat in a 375° oven or under broiler until bubbly and lightly browned. Serve with French bread.

Yield: 6 servings

This is very rich. I always follow it with an intermezzo, a small serving of tart sherbet, preferably homemade. Lemon or raspberry are good.

Herb Cheese Spread

Serve this with plain crackers.

8	ounces cream cheese, room temperature	1	teaspoon finely chopped parsley
¼	cup lightly salted butter or margarine, room temperature	¼	teaspoon pepper
		½	teaspoon minced garlic
		¼	teaspoon salt

Place cheese, butter, parsley and pepper in a small bowl. Beat in an electric mixer at medium speed about 2 minutes until light and fluffy. With the blade of a heavy knife, mash garlic and salt to a purée and add to cheese mixture. Beat again until well blended. Line a 10 ounce dessert dish or souffle dish with plastic wrap and scrape cheese mixture into it. Smooth top of cheese. Place in refrigerator for 2 hours or more. To serve, uncover cheese; unmold onto serving plate and serve with crackers.

Yield: 1¼ cups

Spinach Torta

This is an Italian dish with rice, spinach, cheese and nuts. It is easy to make and not too expensive.

¾	cup uncooked long grained rice	1	cup grated Parmesan cheese
10	ounce package frozen chopped spinach, thawed and squeezed dry	1	teaspoon salt
		⅛	teaspoon pepper
5	eggs	2	tablespoons olive oil
15	ounces Ricotta cheese	¼	cup packaged bread crumbs
		⅓	cup sliced almonds

Cook rice according to package directions. Beat eggs slightly in large bowl. Reserve 3 tablespoon of the egg. Add rice, spinach, Ricotta cheese, Parmesan cheese, salt and pepper. Stir well. Brush bottom and sides of a 13″×9″×2″ baking pan with olive oil, sprinkle with bread crumbs. Spoon spinach mixture in and smooth surface. Brush top with reserved beaten egg; sprinkle with almonds. Bake at 350° for 30 minutes or until firm. Remove pan to wire rack; cut into 1½ inch squares, Transfer to warm serving platter. Note: baked torta may be held in the refrigerator for one or two days. Reheat at 350°. Baked torta can also be frozen. However, cut before freezing.

Yield: About 60 1½ inch squares

Spinach Soup

I prefer to use a chicken base in this recipe. Sexton and Minor are two brands I use. This product has a true chicken flavor and is not as salty as boullion cubes. However, chicken boullion cubes may be used.

6   cups water
6   teaspoons chicken base, Sexton's or Minor's
10   ounces frozen chopped spinach, thawed and drained
10   ounces frozen chopped broccoli, thawed and drained
1   medium carrot, peeled and sliced thin
2   ribs celery, with strings removed and thinly sliced
½   cup minced onion
Pepper and salt to taste

Heat water to boiling, add chicken base or boullion, mix, then add carrot, celery, and onion. Cover, and simmer for 20 minutes, then add broccoli and spinach. Simmer 10 minutes. Do not overcook as broccoli and spinach tend to lose their bright green color if cooked too long. Place in blender or food processor and process until you have a smooth purée. Taste for seasoning. Heat and serve.

Yield: 6 servings

Zucchini Cream Soup

This is a delicious first course or can be served for a luncheon with sandwiches.

3   cups thinly sliced zucchini
½   cup water
3   teaspoons chicken base, not chicken boullion
1   tablespoon minced onion
1   teaspoon minced parsley
2   tablespoons butter
2   tablespoons flour
1   teaspoon salt
¼   teaspoon white pepper
½   teaspoon Accent (optional)
¼   teaspoon Bouquet Garni
1   cup whole milk
½   cup light cream

Mix chicken base and water in heavy saucepan, add zucchini and onion and cook until tender. Place in blender or food processor and purée, then add parsley. Place back into saucepan. In a saucepan or skillet, melt the butter, remove from heat and mix in flour and seasonings, then add milk and light cream and blend well. Return to heat and cook, stirring constantly with a wire whip, until thickened. Add to zucchini mixture and taste for seasoning. Serve hot.

Yield: 4 servings

Mrs. Lindemann's Shrimp Gumbo

I ate this at a supper in the Lindemann's summer home on Clear Lake near Houston many years ago. The menu was a delicious slaw, cold boiled crab, this shrimp gumbo and plenty of crusty French bread along with beer or a drink of your choice. Delicious!

1 pound lean bacon, chopped or cut into small pieces with shears	6 ounce can tomato paste
	1 cup chopped celery
	½ a lemon, sliced very thin
1 pound onions, chopped	3 tablespoons Worcestershire
2 (10 ounce) packages of frozen sliced okra, thawed	Salt and pepper to taste
	3½ quarts water (14 cups)
1 pound can tomatoes undrained	3 pounds raw, cleaned shrimp
	¾ cup uncooked rice

Place bacon in a heavy 2½ gallon stock pot. Cook over low heat until crisp. Remove from bacon grease and set aside. Cook onions in same pot and bacon grease until they are limp but not brown. Thaw okra in microwave in its box with about 6 slits in it. Place in food processor and purée with on and off bursts. This is very important. Add to stock pot along with reserved bacon,tomatoes, tomato paste, celery, Worcestershire, lemon slices and water. Let come to a boil, then simmer for 2 hours. Do not add shrimp and rice until 30 minutes before serving. Add salt and pepper to taste.

Yield: 8¼ quarts

The recipe has been in my files for over fifty years. I use my food processor to mash the okra. Mrs. Lindemann did it by hand. I also use frozen okra instead of canned. Just defrost the okra and purée in the processor.

Carrot Pecan Spread

This mixture is also good as a sandwich spread, but use thinly sliced whole wheat bread. Even people who do not like carrots like this. I am always asked the ingredients when I serve it.

2 cups peeled carrots, cut into pieces	Mayonnaise, not salad dressing
	White pepper
1 cup pecans	

Place carrots and pecans in food processor with the metal blade. Process until finely ground. Turn into a bowl and add enough mayonnaise to make a spreading consistency, Add white pepper to taste. Spread on whole wheat crackers.

Yield: 3 cups

Spinach Tarts

You may buy tart shells or make them with your favorite pie crust recipe. Bake them with centers weighed down with foil filled with dried beans or uncooked rice. Bake at 375° for 5 minutes, remove foil and beans and bake until very light brown.

2   (10) ounce packages frozen chopped spinach, thawed, and squeezed dry
2   tablespoons frozen or fresh chives, chopped

Salt and pepper to taste
1   cup grated cheddar cheese
1   (8 ounce) package cream cheese, room temperature
8   baked 3" tart shells

Heat spinach in saucepan with a little water for only 3 minutes, drain. While spinach is still warm, blend in cream cheese, chives, onion, salt and pepper until smooth. Place in tart shells. Top with cheddar cheese and bake at 375° 10 to 15 minutes or until piping hot.

Yield: 8 servings

Chicken Tortilla Soup

1   tablespoon olive oil
1   large onion, chopped
1   (4 ounce) can green chilis, diced
1   teaspoon chili powder
1   teaspoon ground cumin
1   large garlic clove, minced
½   teaspoon dried oregano, crumbled
⅛   teaspoon cayenne pepper, optional
6   cups chicken broth, homemade or canned

1   (16 ounce) can tomatoes, chopped, juices reserved
12 ounces boneless, skinless chicken breasts, cut into ½ × 1½" strips
1   cup frozen corn, thawed and drained
⅓   cup chopped cilantro
5   ounces Monterey Jack cheese, grated (1½ cups packed)
Tortilla chips, broken into large pieces

Heat oil in heavy large saucepan over medium-low heat. Add onion and sauté until limp. Add chilis, chili powder, cumin. garlic, oregano and cayenne. Stir 1 minute. Mix in stock and tomatoes and their juice. Bring mixture just to a boil. Add chicken and simmer until cooked through about 3 minutes. Add corn and simmer 1 minute. Mix in cilantro, season with salt and pepper. Ladle into bowls and sprinkle each serving with grated cheese and chips. Pass additional cheese and chips.

Yield: 4 servings

Mushroom Spread

This spread is served warm on crackers.

4	slices bacon	1	(8 ounce) package cream
8	ounces fresh mushrooms,		cheese, cubed
	chopped (about 3 cups)	2	teaspoons Worcestershire
1	medium onion, minced		sauce
1	garlic clove, minced	1	teaspoon soy sauce
2	tablespoons flour	½	cup sour cream
⅛	teaspoon freshly ground	1	teaspoon fresh lemon juice
	pepper		Assorted crackers

Cook bacon in large skillet over medium heat until crisp. Drain and transfer to a small bowl, crumble and set aside. Pour off all but 2 tablespoons drippings from skillet. Add mushrooms, onion and garlic to skillet and sauté over medium heat until liquid evaporates. Stir in flour and pepper and mix well, add cream cheese, Worcestershire and soy sauce, and continue cooking until cheese is melted. Blend in sour cream, lemon juice and bacon and cook until heated through; do not boil. Serve warm with crackers of your choice.

Yield: About 2½ cups

Sausage Balls in Chili Con Queso

These go well with a Mexican supper.

4	pounds sausage, medium
	hot or whatever your taste
	dictates

Make into 1½" balls and bake in a 325° oven until done. Drain well on paper towels. Set Aside.

Chili Con Queso:

2	pounds velveeta cheese	2 to 3 tablespoons chili powder
1	can tomatoes and green		or to your taste
	chilis	½	clove garlic, crushed

Mix all ingredients together in top of a double boiler. Set over boiling water and stir until cheese is melted and ingredients are well blended. Place sausage balls in chafing dish and pour hot sauce over. Heat. Serve with toasted tortillas or chips. Provide toothpicks for dipping.

Yield: about 80 balls

Almond Mushroom Pate

¼	small onion	Dash white pepper	
1	small clove garlic, peeled and halved	12	ounces cream cheese, room temperature
½	pound fresh mushrooms, halved	1	tablespoon dry sherry
2	tablespoons butter	1	tablespoon heavy cream
¼	teaspoon salt	⅔	cup coarsely chopped blanched, toasted almonds
⅛	teaspoon dried tarragon leaves, crushed		

In food processor with metal blade, process onion and garlic with on and off bursts until coarsely chopped. Melt butter in medium skillet; add onion, garlic, mushrooms, salt, tarragon and pepper. Cook, stirring constantly, until most of the liquid is evaporated. Add cream cheese, mushroom mixture, sherry and cream. Process until smooth. Chill. Make a ball of the pate on a serving plate, press the coarsely chopped toasted, blanched almonds on ball. Serve with crackers or melba toast.

Yield: 1½ cups

Mushrooms with Pecans

Pick out a two-bite sized button mushroom to fill for appetizers.

2	pounds button mushrooms, washed and stems removed, save stems	1	cup chopped pecans
		1	teaspoon salt
¼	cup finely chopped onion	1	tablespoon ketchup
¼	cup butter	1	tablespoon lemon juice
1	cup fresh soft breadcrumbs	4	strips bacon, diced

Chop stems of mushrooms and sauté with onion in butter. Add crumbs and nuts and cook 2 minutes. Add lemon juice, ketchup and salt. Stuff mushroom caps. Sprinkle bacon over top. Place in a buttered shallow baking dish and bake in a 350 degree oven 15 to 25 minutes or until lightly browned. Time of cooking depends on size of mushrooms. Serve hot.

Yield: 30 to 40

I have filled large mushrooms and used them as a garnish on an entree of roast beef or steak.

Avocado Green Goddess Dip

This recipe was given to me by David Moncrief, a well known caterer in Houston. It is so simple to make and so-o-o good.

1   cup avocado pulp   Green Goddess Salad Dressing
8   ounces cream cheese,
     softened

Blend together the cream cheese and avocado pulp in a bowl. Add enough green Goddess Salad Dressing to make dip consistency. Serve with crudites.

Yield: About 1¼ cups

Brie en Croute

This is a spectacular hors d'oeuvres, particularly if you decorate it.

1   package (2 sheets)   2   pound wheel of Brie cheese
     Pepperidge Farm frozen   1   egg beaten with 1
     puffed pastry, thawed   tablespoon cold water for
     according to package   egg wash
     directions

Place wheel of cheese on pastry sheet to measure. Remove and roll sheet so that there will be a margin of 1½ inches around the cheese. Trim to a circle with scissors. Save trimmings for decoration. Roll second sheet the same size. Place one circle on cookie sheet and put wheel of cheese on it. Fold up margin around cheese and brush with egg wash making sure that none rolls down on cookie sheet as it will make pastry stick. Prick top circle a few times with a fork and place on top of cheese, pressing edge firmly onto rolled up edge of bottom pastry.

Brush top and sides with egg wash. Cut out decorations of flowers, leaves or whatever and place them on top, then brush them with egg wash. Refrigerate until ready to bake. Bake in a 375° oven about 25 minutes or until golden brown. Place on serving tray and wait about 30 minutes before serving with a basket of crackers or slices of small French bread. This can also be served cold.

Yield: 25 or more servings

This can be made early in the day and refrigerated until needed.

Agnes' Cheese Olive Snacks

These are great to keep on hand in the deepfreeze for emergencies.

6 English muffins, split	1½ cups chopped ripe olives
2 cups grated Cheddar cheese	1 cup mayonnaise
1½ cups chopped pimento olives	1 teaspoon salt
	1 teaspoon pepper

Mix all the above ingredients together and spread on muffin halves. Cut each muffin half into 6 wedges. Put on cookie sheets and freeze, then put in baggies. When ready to use, bake at 375° 10 to 12 minutes or until piping hot. Serve hot.

Yield: 36 servings

Brie with Pecans

2 pound wheel Brie cheese	1 cup unsalted butter
1 cup sliced almonds or pecan pieces	

Melt butter in small heavy skillet. Add nuts and cook over very low heat, stirring, until nuts are lightly toasted. Place Brie in ovenproof shallow dish, pour nuts and butter over and bake at 350° until Brie is melted. Serve with crackers.

Yield: 15 to 24 servings

Brie with Fruit

1 pound Brie cheese	Fresh fruit of your choice
French bread	

Cut the Brie into 6 or 8 wedges. Cut French bread in wedges on the diagonal. Place wedge of cheese on each wedge of bread. Broil until top is lightly browned. Serve on a plate with fresh fruit for an appetizer.

Yield: 8 servings

Cocktail Meat Balls

These meat balls are not pre-cooked. They are simmered in a sweet-sour sauce and served with a mustard sauce similar to the Chinese sauce. I often serve in a wok instead of a chafing dish. You may do as you wish.

2	pounds ground ham	1	cup milk
1	pound ground pork	½	teaspoon salt
3	eggs, beaten		
1	cup unseasoned fine bread crumbs		

Mix all ingredients with a fork. Do not use mixer as it will make meat too solid. Roll into 1″ balls and simmer in sauce.

Sweet-Sour Sauce:

4	cups dark brown sugar	2	cups white vinegar
4	cups water		

If you have a large stockpot, you can combine all ingredients. If not, divide ingredients into 2 smaller saucepans. Mix well and bring to a boil. If using the 2 pots, divide meat balls between them, if not, put all the balls in the one large pot. Simmer on top of the stove, uncovered, for 1 hour. Serve with some of the sauce in wok or chafing dish accompanied with the mustard sauce in a bowl for dipping. Have toothpicks on hand for dipping.

Mustard Sauce:

2	ounce can Coleman's dry mustard	½	cup granulated sugar
½	cup white vinegar	1	egg, beaten

Mix mustard and vinegar together and let stand overnight. Next day in a small heavy saucepan, add sugar and egg to the mustard mixture and cook over low heat, stirring constantly, until sauce boils and thickens.

Yield: About 50 meat balls

Make plenty as these disappear fast.

Patti's Spanish Leek Torte

This dish can serve as an appetizer or main dish and can be served hot or cold.

2	cups cooked long grain rice	1	(10 ounce) package frozen chopped spinach, thawed and squeezed dry
1	stick butter or margarine, melted		
1	pint small curd cottage cheese	1	cup finely sliced hard salami, cut into pieces
1	envelope Knorr Leek Soup Mix	2	cups grated Romano cheese
1	teaspoon each garlic powder, pepper and onion powder	12	large eggs, divided

In large bowl, mix rice, butter, cottage cheese, salami, soup mix, spinach, onion powder, garlic powder and pepper. Beat 9 eggs and add to mixture. Mix well.

Generously butter bottom of a 16″ × 11″ × 1″ cookie sheet. Sprinkle half of the cheese over bottom. Carefully pour the rice mixture in and spread until smooth. Beat remaining 3 eggs and spread over top. Sprinkle remaining cheese on top and bake, uncovered, at 325° about 45 minutes or until knife inserted in the middle comes out clean.

Yield: 1 jellyroll pan

This can be prepared ahead, refrigerated and baked the next day.

David's Escargots

The garlic butter is my grandson's recipe, a short cut to most recipes.

24	canned snails, rinsed and drained	½	teaspoon garlic powder, not garlic salt
1	stick unsalted butter, softened		Dash pepper
1½	teaspoon dried parsley flakes, crumbled		Dash nutmeg

Cream butter with parsley flakes, garlic powder, pepper and nutmeg in a small bowl. Place a little of the garlic butter in the bottom of snail shells, insert snails and cover with rest of butter. Place in snail baking dishes, 6 to a serving, and bake at 350° until bubbly and piping hot. Serve with plenty of French bread to sop up the delicious juices.

Yield: 4 servings

Escargots Raleigh

The escargots are placed in mushrooms instead of shells.

24	canned snails, washed and drained	1	teaspoon snipped chives
2	sticks unsalted butter, room temperature	1	teaspoon snipped parsley
		24	(1½ inch) mushrooms, stems removed
2	garlic cloves, mashed	3	tablespoon additional butter
¼	teaspoon nutmeg		

Cream the 2 sticks of butter with the garlic, nutmeg, chives and parsley. Set aside. Brown mushrooms in the 3 tablespoons butter over high heat, then transfer the caps, hollow side up, to a baking dish just large enough to hold them in one layer, or place in 6 individual casseroles. Sprinkle lightly with salt and pepper and place a drained snail in the hollow of each one. Top the stuffed mushrooms with the garlic butter.

Bake them in a pre-heated 375° oven for 5 to 8 minutes or until just bubbly. Serve with French bread.

Yield: 6 servings

Red Cross Hors d' Oeuvres

We were served this appetizer at a dinner we attended during World War II. The hostess was a volunteer worker for the Red Cross. She named it thus because it could be prepared quickly for guests after a day at the Red Cross.

12	ounces cream cheese with chives (If the cheese with chives is not available, add some chopped chives or use it plain.)	6	ounce can sliced mushrooms, saving juice
			Saltine crackers

Mix cream cheese in a bowl until creamy, then add mushrooms with enough mushroom juice to make of spreading consistency. Top crackers with generous spoonful of mixture and serve. I have never used any crackers but the saltines, which was what my hostess used.

Yield: 2 cups

This mixture also makes a delicious sandwich filling on thinly sliced white bread.

Kathryn's Spinach Pastry Triangles

I always make the full recipe as these freeze well and are delicious when baked after freezing.

3   (10 ounce) packages frozen chopped spinach, thawed and squeezed dry

2   eggs, beaten

½   cup Ricotta cheese, broken up or small curd cottage cheese can be substituted

¾   cup Feta cheese, broken up

6   ounces cream cheese at room temperature, broken up

½   cup grated Parmesan cheese

¼   cup finely chopped green onion

2   level tablespoons dried dill weed

3   packages (6 sheets) Pepperidge Farm frozen puff pastry, thawed according to package directions.

2   eggs beaten with 2 tablespoons cold water for egg wash

Mix all ingredients except the puff pastry and egg wash, in a large bowl. Set aside.

Return 1 sheet of the puff pastry to the freezer. Roll each sheet of pastry into a square approximately 14″. Cut into 16 squares, 4 cuts down and 4 cuts across. Place about 2½ teaspoons of the spinach filling on one corner of the square, leaving a small margin. Brush margin with egg wash, fold over the other corner of the square to make a triangle. Press edges together with a fork to seal. Brush tops of triangles with egg wash making sure that none rolls down on the cookie sheet as it will make pastry stick. If not baking right away, place triangles in refrigerator as pastry rises better when cold. Continue with rest of puff pastry and filling. Bake on ungreased cookie sheets at 350° until light brown. Serve hot.

If freezing, place on cookie sheets until frozen, then store in baggies, securely tied. Remove from freezer. Bake as above.

Yield: 80 triangles

There will be 1 sheet of the puffed pastry left over. Leave it in the package and do not let it thaw. There are recipes on the package that you can use it for.

Cream of Corn Soup

3	cups whole milk	½	cup heavy cream
1	(1 pound) can creamed yellow corn	1	teaspoon chopped fresh or frozen chives (optional)
1	tablespoon minced onion	1	teaspoon chopped parsley
2	tablespoons butter		Salt and white pepper to taste
3	tablespoons flour	1	small red pepper, chopped (optional)
1	egg		

Combine milk and corn in top of double boiler. Sauté onion in butter a few minutes, do not brown. Add flour. Add to corn mixture and cook, stirring, over boiling water 15 to 20 minutes until slightly thickened. Mash through strainer. Refrigerate in covered container, if not serving right away. Just before serving, add the egg beaten with the cream, then the chives and parsley. Add salt and pepper to taste. Reheat in double boiler and serve hot in cream soup bowls. Garnish with red pepper, if desired.

Yield: 6 to 8 servings

Crustless Ham Quiche

These Quiche freeze well as there is no crust to get soggy. They are also very good.

1	cup alphabet noodles, cooked al dente	2	eggs
¼	pound sliced ham	½	cup heavy cream
¼	pound sliced Swiss cheese	½	cup milk
3	green onions	1	teaspoon salt
			Pinch of ground nutmeg

Use muffin cups, 1 dozen size and 1¼" diameter at the bottom. You will need 3 pans making 36 quiche. Grease pans generously with shortening. Chop ham, cheese and onion finely. I use the food processor. Mix with cooked noodles. Divide the mixture among the muffin cups. Beat eggs slightly in medium-size bowl. Stir in cream, milk, salt and nutmeg. Spoon over ham mixture, dividing evenly among them. Bake at 350° about 30 minutes or until firm. Ease out of pans gently, using a table knife around edges. Serve hot.

Yield: 36 Quiche

Freeze in a single layer on baking sheet, then store in a sealed plastic bag, Defrost on a greased baking pan and heat at 350° until hot.

Breads

Raleigh House Blueberry Muffins

This recipe was given to me by "Mrs. B" the mother of a neighbor of my son's. The 2 heaping teaspoons of baking powder attest to the age of the recipe. I have never been able to duplicate the texture with standard measurements.

1	cup sugar	¾	teaspoon salt
⅔	cup shortening	1	cup milk
3	eggs	1	cup or more of blueberries,
3	cups flour		fresh, frozen or canned
2	heaping teaspoons baking powder		

Cream sugar and shortening well, add eggs one at a time, beating after each addition. Sift dry ingredients and add to sugar mixture alternately with milk, beating after each addition. Drain canned blueberries. If frozen blueberries are used, add in the frozen state. Fold blueberries in batter just enough to distribute them evenly. Keep in covered container in refrigerator. This batter will keep in the refrigerator up to 4 weeks and can also be frozen.

Yield: 3 dozen

These were very popular at Raleigh House especially by the children and their fathers.

Spiced Carrot Muffins

These are moist and delicious as well as healthful.

½	cup brown sugar, packed	1	teaspoon cinnamon
⅓	cup vegetable oil	½	teaspoon ground nutmeg
1	egg	1	teaspoon baking powder
1¼	cups shredded carrots	¼	teaspoon baking soda
1	cup all-purpose flour	¼	teaspoon salt

Mix sugar and oil in medium-size bowl. Beat in egg; stir in carrots. Sift dry ingredients, then stir in just until moistened. Do not overmix. Either grease or spray muffin cups with vegetable spray. Fill cups half full. Bake at 375° until they test done in middle.

Yield: 1 dozen

These can be microwaved by cooking on high in microwave muffin pan until edges are firm but centers are soft. Rotate after 1 minute.

Trudie's Crullers

These are made with a cream puff base and are light and delicious. I have made them for coffees. Serve warm.

¼	cup sugar	1	cup hot water
1	teaspoon salt	1	cup flour, sifted
1	tablespoon grated orange rind	3	eggs
¼	cup shortening		Sugar glaze

Put sugar, salt, orange rind and shortening in a medium saucepan. Add hot water and bring to a boil. Add flour all at once, stirring constantly, until mixture leaves side of the pan and forms a ball, and until a spoon pressed into the center leaves a clear impression. Remove from heat and add eggs, one at a time, beating well after each addition. Beat until mixture adheres to spoon when held upside down. Cut 3 inch squares of foil or waxed paper. You will need 10 squares, oil each square. Using a cookie press or pastry tube, form dough into rings, placing a ring on each square. Let stand 15 minutes. Fry in 375° deep fat. Hold square close to fat and slip cruller in. As soon as cruller rises to the surface, turn with a spoon. Be careful not to pierce it in turning. Fry until golden brown.

Glaze:

¾	cup powdered sugar	3 to 4 teaspoons water
½	teaspoon vanilla	

Mix sugar, vanilla and 3 teaspoons water. If not thin enough, add 1 more teaspoon water. Either dip top of crullers in glaze, then turn right-side up or spread glaze over crullers. Place on waxed paper until glaze hardens.

Yield: 10 crullers

Helpful Hint: *Bread: Make instant garlic butter by puréeing a half pound of softened butter with 1 or 2 peeled garlic cloves in a blender. Divide in half, wrap and freeze. Use for garlic bread or for sautéeing.*

Kâtés Drop Scones

When I was about ten years old, we had a Scottish neighbor. She always had tea every afternoon. I loved being asked in to share. She served these scones, home-made cookies and shortbread.

1	egg and one egg yolk	3	ounces cold unsalted butter,
½	cup milk		cut up
2	cups all-purpose flour	¼	cup white raisins
3	teaspoons baking powder	¼	cup chopped pecans
¼	cup sugar	1	tablespoon sugar
¼	teaspoon salt		

Preheat oven to 425°. In a small mixing bowl, lightly beat the egg and egg yolk. Add the milk and set aside. Sift the flour, baking powder, sugar and salt into a large mixing bowl. Cut in the cold butter with two knives or pastry blender, until mixture resembles coarse meal. Add raisins and pecans and stir to distribute evenly. Form a well in center and add egg-milk mixture. Stir with a fork just until dry ingredients disappear. Do not overmix. Drop rounding tablespoons of the batter onto a greased or parchment lined cookie sheet. Lightly sprinkle top with the additional tablespoon sugar. Bake for 15 minutes at 425°.

Yield: 24 to 30

These freeze well. Can be served hot or cold. I prefer them hot.

Helpful Hint: *You can freeze egg whites in cube trays, one section for each white. When solid, remove from trays and store in plastic bags. They keep for months. Bring to room temperature and use as you wish.*

Filled Orange Muffins

These muffins are a conversation piece when served for lunch.

½	stick butter	3	teaspoons baking powder
¼	cup sugar	⅔	cup milk
2	eggs, well beaten	½	teaspoon salt
2	cups flour		

Cream butter, sugar, and eggs in mixer until fluffy. Sift dry ingredients together and add to creamed mixture alternately with the milk, beginning and ending with flour. Spoon into greased or sprayed muffin tins, filling only half full. Put 1 teaspoon of the following filling into each, then add enough more batter to fill tins ⅔ full. Bake at 375° about 20 minutes or until they are firm in middle.

Filling:

3	tablespoons orange marmalade or pineapple preserves	4	tablespoons flour
4	tablespoons brown sugar, packed	1	tablespoon melted margarine
		1	tablespoon cream

Combine all ingredients and use as directed.

Yield: 2 dozen

Libby's Chocolate Crescents

My granddaughter is learning to cook. These are a good imitation of the French Croissants.

8	ounce package of refrigerated crescent rolls	1	egg, slightly beaten
4	tablespoons margarine, melted	3	tablespoons sliced almonds
4	ounces sweet baking chocolate		Powdered sugar

Heat oven to 375°. Separate dough into 8 triangles; press each to slightly enlarge. Spread melted margarine on each. Break or cut chocolate in small pieces. Do not worry if it breaks in irregular shapes. Place an equal amount of chocolate on the large side of each triangle, roll up to point of triangle. Place point-side down on lightly greased cookie sheet. Curve into a crescent shape. Brush with beaten egg being careful not to let any egg run down onto pan. Sprinkle with almonds. Bake at 375° until golden brown, about 11 to 13 minutes. Cool. then sprinkle with powdered sugar.

Yield: 8 rolls

Grandmother's Gingerbread

My grandmother lived in a white cottage with a garden of old-fashioned flowers. On Sunday night, she would make a large pan of gingerbread which we ate hot with sweet butter while sitting at a beautiful old cherry table in her large homey kitchen.

½	cup sugar	2½	cups flour
1	teaspoon cinnamon	1	egg
1	teaspoon ginger	½	cup oil
½	teaspoon cloves	1	cup molasses
½	teaspoon salt	1	cup hot water
1½	teaspoon baking soda		

Sift dry ingredients onto a piece of waxed paper, then sift again into an ungreased 9″ × 13″ × 2″ baking pan. Make 2 wells in dry ingredients. Place oil and egg in one and the molasses in the other. Beat the egg and oil slightly with a fork, then pour 1 cup hot water over all. Mix with a fork or wire whip until no dry ingredients can be seen. Be sure to get in corners. Bake in a 350° oven 30 to 35 minutes or until done in center when tested.

Yield: 12 to 15 pieces

The ingredients are the same except for the substitution of oil for the shortening. I have changed the method of mixing, which does away with washing bowl and utensils.

Metro Muffins

This recipe makes an exceptionally tender, light muffin.

¼	cup sugar	1	egg, well beaten
1½	cups flour	¾	cup milk
3	teaspoons baking powder	¼	cup (½ stick) margarine,
1	teaspoon salt		melted
1	cup quick oatmeal	¼	cup molasses

Sift dry ingredients into medium-size bowl; stir in oatmeal. Combine milk, egg, melted margarine and molasses in small bowl then add, all at once, to dry ingredients, stirring only enough to combine. Do not use mixer as overmixing tends to make muffins tough. Grease muffin tin, divide batter in muffin cups, filling ⅔ full. Bake in a pre-heated oven at 400° about 20 minutes or until done in center. You may put 1 teaspoon raisins or chopped nuts on top of each muffin before cooking, if desired.

Yield: 12 muffins

Aunt Carrie's Oatmeal Muffins

1 cup quick oatmeal	1 cup flour
1 cup buttermilk	1 teaspoon baking powder
2 eggs, beaten	½ teaspoon baking soda
½ cup firmly packed brown sugar	½ teaspoon salt
½ cup vegetable oil	¾ cup raisins

Combine oats and buttermilk in a large bowl. Let stand for an hour. Add sugar, eggs and oil and mix well with a fork. Sift flour, baking powder, soda and salt onto a square of waxed paper. Add to buttermilk mixture, stirring again with a fork just until dry ingredients are moistened. Do not use an electric mixer. Add raisins. Spoon into greased muffin cups filling ¾ full. Bake in a pre-heated 400° oven about 20 minutes or until done in the center.

Yield: 18 muffins

Felma's Strawberry Bread

I like this recipe because it can be made the year round with frozen strawberries.

3 cups flour	2 (10 ounce) packages frozen strawberries, thawed
2 cups sugar	
3 teaspoons baking powder	1¼ cups vegetable oil
3 teaspoons cinnamon	4 eggs, well beaten
1 teaspoon salt	1 cup chopped pecans

Mix dry ingredients in a bowl. Make a hole in center and pour in liquid ingredients: oil, strawberries and eggs. Mix thoroughly with a spoon, then fold in nuts. Pour into 2 greased and floured loaf pans. Bake in a pre-heated oven at 325° for 1 hour or until done in center when tester is inserted.

Yield: 2 loaves

This bread will keep several weeks in the refrigerator and can also be frozen.

Helpful Hint: *Shortbread: Instead of rolling out shortbread, place dough in miniature muffin pans. It is a nice change of shape and so easy. Make it the same thickness you would when rolling.*

Six Weeks Bran Muffins

This recipe was from the Texas Department of Agriculture. It is one of my favorites. The dough will keep in the refrigerator for 6 weeks.

1 (15 ounce) box Post's raisin bran
3 cups sugar
5 cups flour
5 teaspoons soda
2 teaspoons salt
4 eggs, beaten
1 cup shortening, melted and cooled
1 quart buttermilk or sour milk

In a very large mixing bowl, place raisin bran, sugar, flour, soda and salt. Mix buttermilk and melted shortening, then add beaten eggs. Mix, then pour over dry ingredients and combine with a wooden spoon or spatula. Place in a covered container in refrigerator for up to 6 weeks. Use as desired. To bake muffins, fill greased tins ⅔ full and bake in a pre-heated 400° oven 15 to 20 minutes, or until firm in center.

Yield: About 6 dozen muffins

Be sure to use a very large bowl for final mixing.

Refrigerator Gingerbread Muffins

This recipe was given to me 35 years ago by a new friend in the Hill Country.

1¼ cups shortening
1 cup molasses
½ teaspoon salt
1 cup sugar
1 cup buttermilk
4 cups flour
4 eggs
2 teaspoons soda
2 teaspoons ginger
1 teaspoon cinnamon
¼ teaspoon allspice

Cream sugar, shortening and salt. Add eggs, one at a time, beating well. Add molasses, beat well. Dissolve soda in buttermilk and add to mixture. Sift flour and other dry ingredients together and add. Mix just until dry ingredients are combined. Fill greased muffin pans ⅔ full and bake in a pre-heated 400° oven until done in center.

Yield: About 2½ dozen

This batter will keep in the refrigerator for 4 weeks.

Speedy Muffins

These muffins are quickly mixed and have a good texture. They taste like a baked doughnut and are great for breakfast. Recipe can be doubled.

1½ cups flour	⅓ cup vegetable oil
½ cup sugar	1 large egg
1½ teaspoons baking powder	2 tablespoons butter or
½ teaspoon salt	margarine
¼ teaspoon nutmeg	⅓ cup sugar
½ cup milk	1 teaspoon cinnamon

Sift first 5 ingredients into a bowl. Make a well in center. Beat milk, oil and egg together and add to dry ingredients, mixing with a fork just enough to moisten. Spoon into greased muffin tins, filling ⅔ full. Bake in a pre-heated 375° oven for 20 minutes. Mix sugar and cinnamon and dip tops of hot muffins in melted margarine or butter then in cinnamon-sugar mixture.

Yield: 1 dozen

For variation: Try putting ½ a teaspoon of different preserves on top of unbaked muffins. Make an indentation with a spoon and insert preserves. For coffees, use 3 kinds of preserves of different colors, such as pineapple, cherry and blueberry.

Super Pineapple Muffins

These are a delicious cake-like muffin. They could be iced with a butter icing and served as cupcakes.

1 stick margarine, softened	2 cups flour
1 cup sugar	3 teaspoonfuls baking powder
2 eggs	½ teaspoon salt
¼ teaspoon almond extract	1 (8 ounce) can crushed
¾ teaspoon vanilla	pineapple, undrained

Cream margarine and sugar until light and fluffy. Add eggs, one at a time, beating well after each addition. Add vanilla and almond flavoring. Sift flour, baking powder and salt. Add to creamed mixture alternately with pineapple, beginning and ending with flour. Mix just until combined. Fill greased muffin tins half full. Bake in a pre-heated 375° oven for 20 to 25 minutes.

Yield: 20 to 24 muffins

Grandma's Cruells

This recipe was given to me by Lucille Hollocher, a talented artist of the Hill Country. It was an old family recipe that she always made for Christmas. They seem like a lot of trouble but are delicious and addictive. I hope you will try them.

1	cup sugar less 2 tablespoons	¼	of a whole nutmeg, grated. Do not use ground nutmeg
½	cup shortening	½	cup milk
3	large eggs	4½ to 5 cups flour	
½	teaspoon salt		

Cream sugar and shortening, add eggs, one at a time, beating well after each addition. Add salt and nutmeg. Then add flour alternately with milk, beginning and ending with flour. Use just enough flour to make a dough similar to pie crust. If dough tears when you pick cruells up, it needs more flour.

Pinch off dough the size of a golf ball and roll it into a circle as you would a pie crust. With a pastry wheel or pizza cutter, cut dough into ½" strips , but leaving a ½" border around the edge. Pick up every other strip with your fingers and place it in 350° deep fat. Let brown on under side, then turn over with a slotted spoon. When under side is golden brown, remove with slotted spoon and drain on brown paper. When cool, place in plastic bag in a container about the size of a wastebasket and dust with sifted powdered sugar. Close bag with tie. This recipe can be doubled.

Yield: About 24

These are the most amazing breads. They will keep crisp indefinitely in just the plastic bag without being in a metal container and do not have to be refrigerated. When I make them in quantity, I place the bags in clean wastebaskets or new garbage cans.

Breakfast Puffs

⅓	cup shortening	¼	teaspoon nutmeg
½	cup sugar	½	cup milk
1	egg	⅓	cup butter, melted
1¼	cups flour	½	cup sugar
1½	teaspoons baking powder	1	teaspoon cinnamon
½	teaspoon salt		

Mix shortening and sugar thoroughly in mixer. Add egg and mix. Sift together the flour, baking powder, salt and nutmeg. Add to shortening mixture alternately with milk, beginning and ending with flour. Fill greased muffin tins ⅔ full of batter. Bake at 350° 20 to 25 minutes. Roll in melted butter and dip in mixture of sugar and cinnamon.

Yield: 12 to 16

Pancakes

These are very light pancakes and easy to mix up. This recipe can also be used for waffles. I have also made them with half whole wheat and half white flour. The whole wheat requires a little more milk.

3	cups flour	1	teaspoon salt
2	tablespoons sugar	2½	cups whole milk
2	tablespoons double-acting baking powder	½	cup vegetable oil
		3	large eggs

Combine milk, eggs and oil in a small bowl. Sift dry ingredients in large bowl. Make a well in dry ingredients and pour milk mixture in. With a fork, gradually pull dry ingredients into the middle of the bowl. Mix with the fork until moistened. Do not overmix. Batter will be slightly lumpy. Spoon onto griddle preheated to 350°. When bubbles appear on surface of pancake, turn over and cook until underside is a golden brown. Serve with warm pecan syrup, or top with Raleigh House Orange Butter.

Syrup:

1	cup maple flavored syrup	½	cup chopped pecans
1	stick butter or margarine		

Mix all ingredients in a small saucepan and simmer until butter is melted. Serve warm.

Yield: 12 to 14 pancakes

This recipe came from the manufacturer of the deep fryers I used at Raleigh House. They also made griddles and waffle makers.

Coconut Molasses Muffins

I served these at a luncheon at Raleigh House with an Hawaiian menu.

2	cups flour	½	cup shortening
¼	cup sugar	1	slightly beaten egg
½	teaspoon salt	⅔	cup milk
1	tablespoon baking powder	½	cup light molasses
½	teaspoon ground ginger	1	cup Angel Flake coconut

Sift flour, sugar, salt, baking powder and ginger into a mixing bowl. Cut in shortening until mixture resembles coarse crumbs. Stir together milk, egg and molasses. Add to dry ingredients and stir by hand just until dry ingredients are moistened. Fold in coconut. Fill greased muffin cups ⅔ full. Bake in a preheated 375° oven for 20 to 25 minutes or until done in center.

Yield: 16 muffins

I cut leftover muffins in half and spread them with cream cheese, for a tasty sandwich the next day.

Vincent's Prune Bread

This bread is unusually moist and delicious, healthful, too.

1	egg	½	cup honey
1	teaspoon vanilla	1½	cups flour
1	teaspoon soda	⅔	cup sugar
1½	cups chopped, pitted dried prunes	2	teaspoons baking powder
		½	cup salad oil
1	cup boiling water	1	cup chopped pecans

Beat egg in mixing bowl, add vanilla, soda and prunes. Mix well, then add boiling water gradually, stirring constantly. Cover and let stand 20 minutes. Add honey and oil, mix well. Sift flour, sugar and baking powder. Add with pecans to prune mixture. Stir well. Pour into a greased and floured large loaf pan. Bake at 325° for 1½ hours or until a toothpick inserted in center comes out clean. Remove from oven and let cool 10 minutes before turning out of pan.

Yield: 1 loaf

Flavor improves if eaten after 24 hours, but can be eaten fresh, if desired. Can be frozen, well-wrapped.

Mother's Custard Cornbread

This is a recipe from my childhood. My mother made it in a 9" iron skillet and took the skillet to the table to serve it so it was piping hot. There is a layer of custard in the center of the cornbread. It splits in two layers. Put butter in center.

2	tablespoons butter	1¼	teaspoon salt
1⅓	cups yellow cornmeal	1	cup milk
⅓	cup flour	2	eggs, unbeaten
1	teaspoon baking soda	1	cup buttermilk
4	tablespoons sugar	1	cup half and half

Start heating oven to 300°. Put butter in pan or skillet, heat in oven, then remove and set aside. Increase oven temperature to 400°. Sift flour, sugar, salt, soda, and cornmeal in medium-sized bowl. Stir in 1 cup milk and the eggs, then add buttermilk. Reheat skillet in oven about 2 minutes, then pour batter in. Place in oven and very gently pour half and half over entire cornmeal mixture. Do not stir. Bake on middle rack of oven for 30 to 35 minutes or until it tests done about 2 or 3 inches from center. Serve piping hot in wedges.

Yield: 9" × 9" pan

My Mother often served this with thick vegetable soup.

Banana Peanut Bread

I have always believed that bananas and peanuts have an affinity for each other. Hope you like this recipe.

3	large bananas, puréed (2 cups)	1	teaspoon vanilla
½	cup vegetable oil	2	cups flour
½	cup sugar	1	teaspoon baking soda
½	cup light brown sugar, packed	½	teaspoon baking powder
3	eggs	½	teaspoon salt
		1	cup chopped lightly salted peanuts

Pre-heat oven to 350°. Grease and flour two 7¾″ × 3⅝″ × 2¼in loaf pans. Set aside. Beat first 6 ingredients together. Sift flour, salt, soda, and baking powder together and stir into banana mixture. Add chopped peanuts. Spoon into prepared pans and bake about 60 minutes or until tester inserted in middle comes out clean. Cool 10 minutes before turning out of pan on wire rack.

Yield: 2 small loaves

My Mother often fixed a salad for lunch of bananas and ground salted peanuts. She peeled the bananas, cut them in half lengthwise, then cut halves in half crosswise, rolled them in mayonnaise, then in the peanuts and served them on torn lettuce.

Nut Apple Loaf

1	cup sugar	1	teaspoon soda
½	cup butter or margarine, 1 stick	1	teaspoon vanilla
2	eggs	½	teaspoon salt
3	tablespoons buttermilk	½	cup raisins
2	cups finely diced peeled apples	½	cup chopped pecans
2	cups flour	2	tablespoons butter, melted
1	teaspoon baking powder	¼	teaspoon ground cinnamon
		¼	cup brown sugar, packed

Cream shortening and sugar in mixer bowl. Add eggs and beat well. Stir, do not beat in mixer. Add the buttermilk and diced apple. Sift together the flour, baking powder, soda and salt. Stir into shortening mixture. Then stir in nuts, vanilla and raisins. Spoon into 2 greased and floured 7½″ × 3″ × 2″ loaf pans. Drizzle melted butter over loaves and sprinkle combined sugar and cinnamon on top. Bake in a preheated 350 degree oven about 40 minutes or until loaves test done in center.

Yield: 2 loaves

Mrs. Wahlborg's Coffee Cake

I have had this recipe over fifty years. It is economical to make, but very good. Mrs. Wahlborg also gave me the Swedish cookie recipe in this book. It is one of my family's favorites.

½	cup Crisco	½	teaspoon baking soda
1½	cups sugar	½	teaspoon salt
2	eggs	1	cup buttermilk
2¼	cups flour	1	teaspoon vanilla
½	teaspoon baking powder		

Cream Crisco and sugar very well in mixer about 5 minutes at high speed. This makes a finer grained cake. Add eggs, one at a time, beating after each addition. Sift flour, baking powder, baking soda and salt together. Add to creamed ingredients alternately with buttermilk, beginning and ending with dry ingredients. Add vanilla, mix well, then spoon into a greased and floured 9" × 13" × 2" pan. Sprinkle with topping.

Topping:

¾	cup brown sugar, packed	¾	cups chopped nuts of your
1	tablespoon cinnamon		choice
3	tablespoons flour		
3	tablespoons butter or margarine		

Mix together the sugar, cinnamon, and flour. Cut in the butter until mixture resembles coarse crumbs. Add nuts. Spread over unbaked cake. Bake in a pre-heated 350° oven for 35 or 40 minutes or until tester comes out clean when inserted in center. Serve warm or cold.

Yield: 12 to 15 servings

Be sure to sprinkle crumbs clear to edge of pan.

Helpful Hint: *You can ripen pears, avocados, peaches and nectarines by placing in a brown paper bag.*

Butter Thins

These are similar to bread sticks. Nice to serve with salads or soup. They reheat well and can be frozen.

1	stick butter, melted	3½	teaspoons baking powder
2¼	cups flour	½	teaspoon salt
¼	cup shortening	1	cup whole milk
1	tablespoon sugar		

Heat oven to 350°. Melt butter in a baking pan 13″×9″×2″. Remove from oven and increase temperature to 400°. Sift flour, sugar, baking powder and salt into mixing bowl. Add shortening and cut in until mixture resembles coarse meal. Add milk and stir slowly with a fork until dough just clings together. Turn on floured board and knead gently with finger tips about 10 times. Roll into a rectangle about 7″×11″. With floured knife or pastry cutter, cut dough in half lengthwise. Then cut into 16 fingers crosswise, making 32 fingers. Dip each finger into melted butter in pan, turn over and place in a row. Continue with rest of fingers, laying them close together in the pan. Bake 15 to 20 minutes or until golden brown. Serve hot.

Yield: 32 pieces

Slim Hush Puppies

These hush puppies still have calories, of course, but less than the traditional ones since they are baked, not fried.

1	cup yellow cornmeal	⅛	teaspoon red pepper
1	cup flour	½	cup finely minced onion
3	teaspoons double-acting baking powder	2	large eggs, beaten
½	teaspoon salt	⅔	cup milk
1	teaspoon sugar	4	tablespoons vegetable oil

Spray miniature muffin tins (1¼″ bottoms) with vegetable spray. Blend cornmeal, flour, baking powder, salt, sugar and red pepper in medium bowl. Stir in onion. Beat eggs, milk and oil in a small bowl, then add to cornmeal mixture, stirring with a fork until just blended. Spoon batter into prepared muffin tins filling ⅔ full. Preheat oven to 425°. Bake about 15 minutes or until light brown. Serve immediately.

Yield: About 3 dozen

Make plenty of these as they disappear fast.

Mrs. Drucker's Strudel

Mrs. Drucker was an Austrian lady in the Hill Country. She served this one afternoon for tea. The filling can also be made with fruit pie filling using half a can for each strudel.

2½ **cups flour**	4 **ounces sour cream**
2 **sticks margarine**	

Cut margarine into flour with pastry blender or tips of fingers. Add sour cream; mix, then make into a round, flat mound. Cut dough in half. Wrap each half well and place in refrigerator overnight. Next day, put cloth napkin on board and flour it; roll out each half of pastry to a rectangle about ⅛ of an inch thick. Divide cream cheese filling on the 2 strudel. Roll up and place, seam-side down, on a buttered baking sheet. Brush each strudel with egg wash, 1 egg mixed with 1 teaspoon water, being careful not to let any run down on pan.

Bake at 350° until brown, 25 to 35 minutes. Remove strudel from pan and place on wire rack to cool. Brush with melted butter. Let cool about 15 minutes, then sift powdered sugar over top. Cut in thick slices and serve warm.

Filling:

12 **ounces cream cheese, room temperature**	3 **egg yolks**
½ **cup sugar**	½ **cup white raisins**
	½ **teaspoon grated lemon rind**

Combine cream cheese, sugar and egg yolks; beat at medium speed in mixer until well blended and smooth. Stir in raisins and lemon rind. Divide mixture in half and spread on one side of dough. Roll up from that end using napkin, if needed. Do the same with the remaining half of dough. Proceed according to directions above.

Yield: 8 servings, 2 strudel

Mother's Nut Bread

My mother made this bread one Sunday night. We were almost out of bread and there were no stores open on Sunday in those days. I had forgotten to tell her that I had promised to bring sandwiches to school the next day. The teachers enjoyed my mistake.

3	cups flour	2	eggs, beaten
2	cups sugar	1½	cups milk
1	teaspoon salt	1	cup chopped nuts
3¾	teaspoons baking powder	¼	cup vegetable oil

Sift flour, sugar, salt and baking powder in a mixing bowl. Combine eggs, milk and oil in a bowl and add to flour mixture , blending thoroughly. Add nuts. Place in a greased and lightly floured loaf pan 9″ × 5″ × 3″. Bake 1 hour in a pre-heated 375° oven or until loaf tests done when a toothpick is inserted in center and comes out clean. Remove from oven and let cool 15 minutes before removing from pan to wire rack to cool completely. Flavor improves if eaten the second day.

Yield: 1 loaf

Praline Pecan Bread

This is an especially delicious bread and sweet enough to serve as a pound cake.

¾	cup chopped pecans	1½	teaspoons vanilla
½	cup Praline liqueur, divided	3	eggs
½	cup (1 stick) margarine or butter	¼	cup milk
1	cup firmly packed light brown sugar	2	cups flour
		3	teaspoons baking powder
		½	teaspoon cinnamon

Combine pecans and ¼ cup of the liqueur in a china or stainless steel bowl and let set overnight. Next day, cream butter or margarine. Gradually add sugar, beating about 5 minutes at high speed of mixer. Add vanilla and mix, then add eggs and milk, beat well. Combine flour, baking powder and cinnamon; add to creamed mixture, mixing well. Stir in pecan mixture. Pour batter into 2 greased and floured 7½″ × 3″ × 2″ loaf pans. Bake in a pre-heated 325° oven for 45 minutes or until a wooden pick inserted in middle comes out clean. Cool in pans 10 minutes. Remove from pans to wire rack. Drizzle remaining ¼ cup Praline liqueur over loaves. Let set about 30 minutes, then wrap in cheese-cloth or cloth towel, then in foil and place in refrigerator to season at least 3 days before serving.

Yield: 2 small loaves

Willie Mae's Biscuits

Willie Mae was an indispensible member of my son's household for over thirty years. Her biscuits are the best. Mixing properly is the key. I stood beside her while she made them in order to get every detail.

2	cups flour, soft wheat, if possible	½	teaspoon baking soda
1	teaspoon salt	⅓	cup shortening
3	teaspoons baking powder	1	cup buttermilk or more

Sift flour, salt, baking powder and baking soda into a bowl. Cut in shortening until only fine lumps remain. Make a well in the dry ingredients, add buttermilk and mix gently until moistened. Add more buttermilk, if needed to make a soft, not sticky dough. Knead gently with fingers several times. Roll about ¼ of an inch thick into a rectangle. Brush with melted margarine and fold in half to make two layers. Roll dough lightly with rolling pin to press layers together. Cut biscuits with a 2″ cutter. Place on a cookie sheet well-coated with melted margarine. Willie Mae dips one side of biscuit in the margarine on the pan, then turns it over and places it on the pan. Roll scraps of dough to make extra biscuits. Bake in a pre-heated 425° oven until lightly browned on bottom. Serve piping hot.

Yield: About 2 dozen

Pumpkin Nut Bread

1	cup butter or margarine, softened	1	teaspoon baking soda
3	cups sugar	1	teaspoon baking powder
3	eggs	1	teaspoon cloves
1	can solid pumpkin	1	teaspoon cinnamon
1	teaspoon vanilla	½	teaspoon nutmeg
3	cups flour	1	cup chopped pecans
1½	teaspoons salt	1	cup golden raisins

Cream butter and sugar; add eggs, one at a time beating after each addition. Add pumpkin and vanilla, mix to combine. Sift together the flour, salt, soda, baking powder and spices, blend with pumpkin mixture. Add nuts and raisins. Pour into a greased and lightly floured loaf pan 9″×5″×3″. Bake in a pre-heated 350° oven for 60 to 65 minutes or when tester placed in the middle comes out clean. Let cool about 15 minutes before removing from the pan.

Yield: 1 loaf

Biscuits

This is a recipe for biscuits made with self-rising flour.

2 cups unsifted self-rising flour	¾ cup milk
⅓ cup shortening	
¼ teaspoon salt, self-rising flour contains some salt, but a little extra was put in for flavor	

Measure flour by spooning it from the flour canister into a cup measure. When overflowing, level off top with the straight side of a table knife. Pour into medium-size mixing bowl, add salt. You may use the "wet" measure for the shortening, if you like. Fill a measuring cup ⅔ full of cold water, then add enough shortening to make water come to top of the cup. Drain off all the water and add to flour. Cut in shortening with 2 knives, a pastry blender or the tips of your fingers. Be careful not to let the heat of your hands warm the shortening if you use your fingers as biscuits will not be as flaky. Make a well in the flour and add milk all at once. Stir milk in with a fork just until it forms a soft dough that begins to leave the side of the bowl. Leave the dough as moist as you can work with for the best biscuits.

With well-floured hands, gather dough into a neat packet on a generously floured board. For biscuits, the best kneading is a gentler spread-finger pressing, which is called stroking. Press the dough with fingers, then fold it over ready for the next stroking. Stroke 10 to 15 times for light biscuits. With a rolling pin, roll dough to ½″ thickness if you like plump biscuits, ¼ to ⅜″ for crustier biscuits. With a floured biscuit cutter, press straight down into the dough. Do not twist the cutter. Gently lift the cut biscuits with a spatula onto an ungreased baking sheet. If you want soft sides, place biscuits close together. For crustier edges, space them 1″ or more apart. Bake in a pre-heated 450° oven for 8 to 12 minutes or longer as needed to brown lightly.

My mother used to break a piece of loaf sugar in half, dip it in orange juice and place it on the unbaked biscuit for a sweet topping.

Zucchini Cornbread

1	pound zucchini, washed in salt water, rinsed, grated	1	cup buttermilk
1½	teaspoon salt	1	egg, slightly beaten
1	cup flour	½	stick butter, melted and cooled
¾	cup cornmeal	½	cup grated sharp cheddar cheese
1	tablespoon baking powder		
½	teaspoon soda	2	tablespoons grated onion
1	teaspoon salt		Dash red pepper

Spread grated zucchini in colander, sprinkle with the 1½ teaspoons salt, toss, then let it drain for 30 minutes. Transfer zucchini to a towel and squeeze until dry. Mix the flour, cornmeal, baking powder, soda and salt in a large bowl. Combine the buttermilk, egg and butter and add to dry ingredients, stirring with a fork. Add the zucchini, cheese, onion and red pepper. Pour batter into a well greased 9″ cake pan. Bake at 400° for 30 to 40 minutes or until tester comes out clean.

Yield: 9″ cake pan

Potato Biscuits

This is a fluffy biscuit.

1	cup mashed potatoes	½	teaspoon salt
1½	cups all purpose flour	3	tablespoons shortening
4	teaspoons baking powder	⅓	cup milk

Peel and dice potatoes, cook in about 2 inches of water until tender. Drain very well then mash. Do not add any seasoning, milk or butter. Sift dry ingredients into a bowl, cut in shortening until mixture resembles coarse meal. Add potatoes, stirring lightly, add milk and stir with a fork until a soft dough is formed. Turn out on a floured board and knead lightly with fingers, not palm of hand, 10 to 12 times. This is called stroking and differs from kneading yeast doughs. Roll dough out ⅓ of an inch thick, cut with either a 2″ or 2½″ biscuit cutter. Place biscuits on lightly greased cookie sheet and bake in a pre-heated 400° oven for 15 minutes or until lightly browned.

Yield: 12 to 14 depending on size

Pineapple Rollups

2	cups flour	½	stick butter or margarine,
¼	cup sugar		softened
3	teaspoons baking powder	⅔	cup brown sugar, packed
1	teaspoon salt	1	cup pineapple tidbits,
⅛	teaspoon cloves		drained, and cut in 2
½	teaspoon cinnamon		pieces.
¼	cup shortening	½	cup chopped pecans
⅔	cup milk		

Sift together flour, sugar, baking powder, salt, cloves and cinnamon. Add shortening and cut into dry ingredients with a pastry blender or the tips of your fingers until the consistency of coarse crumbs. Stir in milk until dry ingredients are just moistened. Turn onto waxed paper and knead gently about 10 times.

Roll dough out on a floured board to a rectangle about 10" × 13". Spread with softened butter or margarine, then sprinkle with brown sugar, nuts and drained pineapple tidbits. Roll dough from long side, jellyroll fashion, then cut into 12 pieces. Place, cut-side down in a well greased 9" × 13" pan. Bake in a 375° oven for 25 to 30 minutes or until rolls are golden brown. Serve Warm.

Yield: 1 dozen

Pecan Muffins

This is quickly made in a food processor.

1½	cups flour	½	cup pecan halves
½	cup sugar	1	egg
2	teaspoons baking powder	½	cup milk
½	teaspoon cinnamon	¼	cup vegetable oil
½	teaspoon salt		

Position knife blade in food processor; add first 5 ingredients to processor. Pulse 2 or 3 times to combine ingredients. Add pecans, pulsing 2 or 3 times until chopped. Add remaining ingredients, pulse about 4 times or until ingredients are just mixed. Do not overmix. Fill greased muffin tins ⅔ full. Bake at 400° for 20 to 25 minutes.

Yield: 1 dozen

Golden Puffs

These are easy to make for breakfast or a snack, dipped in cinnamon and sugar or a thin glaze.

2	cups flour	¼	cup oil
¼	cup sugar	¾	cup milk
3	teaspoons baking powder	1	egg, beaten
1	teaspoon salt	½	teaspoon nutmeg or mace

Sift first 4 ingredients, then add rest of ingredients. Stir with a fork until dry ingredients disappear. Drop by teaspoonfuls into 375° deep fat. Turn once and fry to a golden brown. Dip in either of the following toppings.

Glaze:

1	cup powdered sugar, sifted after measuring	⅓	cup boiling water
		¼	teaspoon vanilla

Add boiling water gradually to sugar, add vanilla. Dip puffs into warm glaze.

Cinnamon-sugar:

½	cup sugar	2	teaspoons cinnamon

Mix, then dip warm puffs in mixture. You can increase this to your needs, just use the same proportions of cinnamon and sugar.

Yield: 40 to 45 puffs

These are good warm or cold. I happen to like them better warm.

Patti's Mexican Cornbread

This is a very good bread as it has sour cream in it.

½	cup flour	1	jalapeño pepper, chopped
1	teaspoon salt	1	cup sour cream
1	tablespoon baking powder	1	can creamed corn
1½	cup cornmeal	2	eggs, beaten
1	cup grated cheese	½	cup oil
½	cup finely chopped onion		

Mix first 7 ingredients in a large bowl, add sour cream, corn , eggs and oil. Mix well with a spoon. Pour into a greased 13"×9"×2" baking pan. Bake in a 350° oven about 30 minutes or until firm in the center. Serve piping hot.

Yield: 13"×9"×2" pan

Be sure to wear rubber gloves when chopping jalapeño pepper

Glazed Lemon Bread

This is a delicious, moist bread. Can be frozen. It could serve as a pound cake.

⅓	cup melted butter, do not substitute	1	teaspoon baking powder
1¼	cups sugar	½	teaspoon salt
2	eggs	½	cup milk
¼	teaspoon almond extract	1	tablespoon grated lemon peel
1½	cups flour	½	cup chopped nuts

Grease glass oven-proof loaf pan. Set aside. Beat sugar and butter in mixer until light and fluffy, beat in eggs, one at a time, mixing well after each addition. Add extract. Sift together dry ingredients and add at low speed of mixer alternately with milk; beginning and ending with flour. Blend just to mix. Do not overbeat. Fold in lemon peel and nuts. Turn into prepared pan and bake in a pre-heated 325° oven about 60 minutes or until loaf tests done in center. While bread bakes, mix glaze below.

Glaze:

3	tablespoons fresh squeezed lemon juice	¼	cup sugar

Mix and let stand while bread is baking, stirring every once in a while until sugar dissolves. As soon as loaf is removed from oven, spoon glaze by spoonfuls over the loaf. I usually spoon some over, let it sink in , then spoon over the rest. Let bread cool 10 minutes, then remove from pan; Cool on rack. Slices better the second day.

Yield: 1 loaf

Oatmeal Muffins

Raisins or chopped nuts may be added to batter, if desired.

¼	cup sugar	2	eggs, beaten
1½	cups flour	¾	cup milk
3	teaspoons baking powder	½	stick butter or margarine, melted
1	teaspoon salt		
1	cup quick oatmeal	¼	cup molasses

Sift sugar, flour, baking powder and salt into a medium-sized bowl,and add oats. Combine milk, eggs, melted butter and molasses. Add all at once to flour mixture, stirring with a fork or spoon, just until dry ingredients are combined. Do not overmix. Spoon into greased muffin pan and bake in a pre-heated 400° oven about 20 minutes or until browned. Remove from pan at once.

Yield: 1 dozen

Chocolate Bread

This is another delicious bread that could serve as a pound cake, particularly if dusted with powdered sugar.

1	cup water	1	cup sugar
2	(1 ounce) squares	1	egg
	unsweetened chocolate	1	teaspoon vanilla
1	cup chopped dates	2	cups flour, sifted before
½	cup chopped pecans		measuring
1	teaspoon soda	½	teaspoon salt
½	stick butter or margarine		

Bring 1 cup water to a boil. Reduce heat and add chocolate cut into pieces. Cook at very low heat until chocolate is melted. Stir in dates, nuts and soda. Remove from heat and set aside. Beat together the sugar and butter until light and fluffy, then beat in egg and vanilla until blended. Combine flour and salt, add to butter mixture alternately with flour, beginning and ending with flour. Beat well after each addition. Spoon batter into a greased bread pan 9¼" × 5½". Bake at 350 degrees for 55 minutes or until a toothpick inserted in center comes out clean. Cool in pan on wire rack. When completely cold, remove from pan, wrap in film and then in foil. Place in refrigerator a day or two before serving.

Yield: 1 large loaf

The flavor improves if left in the refrigerator a day or two, but it can be eaten the same day.

Heritage Gingerbread

This is made like a crumb cake, but with dark brown sugar instead of molasses. It is unusually moist and good.

1	pound dark brown sugar	1	teaspoon nutmeg
2	cups flour	1	teaspoon soda
1½	sticks margarine	2	eggs, beaten
½	teaspoon ginger	1	cup buttermilk
2	teaspoons cinnamon		

Cut sugar, margarine and flour together to make fine crumbs. Reserve 1 cup of the crumbs for topping. To rest of crumbs, add spices and soda. Mix well, add eggs, then lightly stir in buttermilk. Mix only until dry ingredients disappear. Pour into a 9" × 13" × 2" well-greased pan. Sprinkle reserved crumbs evenly on top. Bake in a pre-heated 350° oven for 35 minutes or until done when tested in center with wooden pick.

Yield: 12 to 15 servings

Monkey Bread

This is the most satisfactory bread to freeze that I know of. I always keep some in my deep freeze for emergencies. It makes a welcome gift to your hostess or to a shut-in or a neighbor.

1	cup milk, scalded	1	package dry yeast
1	tsp salt	½	cup very warm water, 110
⅔	cup sugar		to 115°
⅔	cup shortening	5½ to 6 cups flour, preferably	
2	eggs		hard wheat
⅔	cup potato flakes	2	sticks butter, melted, for
½	cup cold water		dipping

Combine scalded milk, shortening, sugar and salt in mixer bowl. Beat until shortening is melted. Let cool to lukewarm. In the meantime, combine potato flakes and cold water and let set until flakes are moistened. Sprinkle yeast over warm water to which 1 teaspoon of sugar has been added, let dissolve. Add potato flake mixture to milk, shortening mixture. Mix, then add eggs. Beat well, then add dissolved yeast, Mix, then add 2 cups flour, beat at high speed about 5 minutes, then add 3½ cups of flour, and beat until mixture begins to leave sides of the bowl. Feel of dough. If it is sticky, add remaining ½ cup flour, beat until dough is elastic. You can feel this with your fingers. Turn out of bowl on lightly floured board and knead about 5 times. Put 1 tablespoon oil in same bowl dough was mixed in, Turn dough into bowl and turn over so top is oiled. Cover with plastic, then a towel, and place in a draft-free place to rise more than double. A cupboard is good for this.

Lightly butter 4 8" or 8½" ring molds around the tube and sides. When dough has risen, place on lightly floured board and roll into a rectangle about 16" × 12" × ½" thick. Divide into 4 squares, 8" × 6". Cut each piece into 12 squares, about 2" square. 12 of these squares will fill 1 ring mold. Pull opposite corners of square to make a diamond-shape. Dip 6 of the pieces on both sides in the melted butter and place in bottom of ring mold repeat with the remaining 6 pieces, placing them alternately over the first layer, in other words the second layer should be placed over where the pieces of the first layer join. Repeat with remaining three ring molds. Cover rings and let rise until dough reaches top of the pan. Bake on the lower shelf of a 350° oven for about 25 minutes or until golden brown. Turn out on serving plate. Leave upside down so guests can pull off pieces. This bread really does not need extra butter, but I usually offer it. To freeze, I put rings in a pie plate, cover with film and then with foil. Reheat in a 250° oven, removing film but leaving foil on.

Yield: 4 rings

Flora's Rolls

This dough is similar to the dough for monkey bread. It may be used for a variety of sweet rolls or plain rolls.

⅔ cup sugar
⅔ cup shortening
1 egg
⅔ cup potato flakes
½ cup cold water

1 package dry yeast
1½ cups warm milk, divided
2 teaspoons salt
6 cups flour

Combine cold water and potato flakes in a small bowl. Let set until water is absorbed. Meanwhile, cream shortening and sugar, add egg and potatoes. Mix well. Dissolve the yeast in ½ cup of the warm milk to which a pinch of sugar has been added. Add dissolved yeast to first mixture. Mix salt and flour together and add to creamed mixture, in 2 sections, alternately with rest of warm milk. Remove from bowl and knead until dough no longer sticks to the board. Place in a lightly oiled bowl and let rise until more than doubled, about 2 hours. Make into rolls of your choice. Let rise again until double. Bake at 400° until lightly brown.

Yield: 4 to 5 dozen

Whole Wheat Raisin Bread

This is an unusually delicious wheat bread.

1 cup raisins
1 cup water
3 packages dry yeast
1 cup 115° water
2 tablespoons sugar
1 teaspoon salt

3 eggs
2 tablespoons soft butter or margarine
½ cup molasses
3 cups all purpose flour
2 cups whole wheat flour

Soak raisins in 1 cup water for 15 minutes or until plump. Drain and reserve. In mixer bowl, dissolve yeast in warm water to which the 2 tablespoons of sugar have been added. When foamy, add salt, eggs, butter or margarine and molasses. Beat well, then add the all purpose flour. Beat well, then add whole wheat flour. Beat until dough is elastic. Add raisins and beat well. Place dough on floured board and knead in about ½ to 1 cup more whole wheat flour until dough is not sticky. Place in lightly oiled bowl, cover, and let rise in a warm place until doubled. Turn out on lightly floured board. Divide in half and make into loaves. Place in greased regular-size loaf pans. Let rise again until well over tops of pans. Bake in a pre-heated 350° oven about 35 minutes or until loaves sound hollow when thumped.

Yield: 2 loaves

Raleigh House Orange Rolls

These rolls made Raleigh House famous. Patrons who had not had the opportunity to visit for several years, asked if we still served the orange rolls before they even sat down.

2	packages dry yeast	⅓	cup vegetable oil
7/8	cup hot water, 1 cup less 2 tablespoons	4	cups flour
		1	teaspoon salt
½	cup sugar	2	eggs

Put hot water in mixing bowl, add 2 teaspoons of the sugar, then sprinkle yeast over. Let stand until foamy, then add salt, sugar and oil. Beat well. Add eggs and 2 cups flour and beat on high for 5 minutes. Stop mixer and add rest of flour, beat until mixture starts to leave sides of bowl, about 10 minutes. In this way, the dough does not have to be kneaded. Cover and let rise in a warm place until more than doubled. Turn out on lightly floured board and roll into a rectangle about ⅓″ thick. Spread with soft margarine. Roll up in a tube-shape about 1½ to 2 inches thick, cut into 1″ slices with a floured pastry cutter or floured knife. Place on greased or parchment-lined cookie sheet about 2 inches apart. Let rise again until at least double. Bake at 375° about 20 minutes or until light brown. Serve hot with orange butter.

Note: If your mixer will not take the entire amount of flour, remove dough to a floured board and knead rest of flour in, continue kneading until dough is elastic.

Orange Butter:

1	pound box powdered sugar	¼	cup frozen orange juice, undiluted
1⅓	sticks margarine		

Mix margarine and sugar until creamy, add orange juice and beat until fluffy. This butter keeps well in the refrigerator and freezes well.

Yield: About 4 dozen

The orange butter is good spread on hot gingerbread and also on pancakes and waffles. It is my original recipe that I made in desperation. It was too time consuming to squeeze orange juice and grate the rind as most orange butter recipes directed.

Muenster Bread

This is delicious served as an appetizer

3½ teaspoons sugar	2 eggs
2 teaspoons salt	2 pounds Muenster cheese,
2 packages dry yeast	shredded
4 cups all purpose flour	3 tablespoon sliced blanched
½ cup butter	almonds
1 cup whole milk	

In mixer bowl, combine sugar, salt, yeast and 1 cup flour. In small saucepan, over low heat, heat milk and butter until very hot, 120 to 130 °. Butter does not need to melt completely. Gradually beat liquid into dry ingredients at low speed, just until mixed. Increase speed to medium, beat 2 minutes, occasionally scraping sides and bottom of bowl with rubber spatula. Add another cup of flour, beat 2 minutes, occasionally scraping sides of bowl with spatula. Continue beating for 2 more minutes,then with a spoon, stir in 2 more cups of flour to make a soft, not sticky dough. Turn out on a floured board and knead about 10 minutes, adding more flour if need be while kneading. Knead until soft and elastic. Place in a lightly oiled bowl,cover and let rise until double.

Reserve 1 egg white, combine the egg yolk and the whole egg in a large bowl, add cheese and mix thoroughly. When dough has risen, roll on a lightly floured board, into a rectangle 18″×8″. Place it on a greased cookie sheet. Make a cylinder of the cheese and place it in the center of the rectangle of dough. Fold over sides of dough overlapping 1″ to 1½″. Pinch to seal and pinch to seal ends. Cover with a towel; let rest in a warm place for 30 minutes.

Preheat oven to 375°. Brush loaf with slightly beaten egg white, garnish top with almonds. Bake 1 hour until golden and bread sounds hollow when lightly tapped with fingers. Remove from sheet immediately on removing from oven. Let stand about 15 minutes before cutting. Note: Bread may be frozen. To reheat, wrap in foil and place in a 350° oven until bread is warm and cheese melted.

Yield: 16 snack, 8 dinner servings

Bohemian Coffee Cake

This is one of my favorite coffee cakes. It has a wonderful rich flavor due to the cream in the ingredients.

3	cups flour	3	egg yolks
½	teaspoon mace	1	cup heavy cream
1	teaspoon salt	¼	cup milk, heated to fairly
1	stick butter, do not		hot (115°)
	substitute	1	package dry yeast
⅓	cup sugar		

Put flour in mixing bowl with salt and mace. Cut in butter until coarse crumbs. Beat egg yolks with sugar and add to butter-flour mixture. Then add cream, Mix well. Dissolve yeast in warm milk and add to other ingredients and mix well at high speed, about 5 minutes. Let stand in refrigerator overnight, Next morning, roll into rectangle about 8″ × 12″.Spread with softened or melted margarine, then with one of the fillings given below. Roll up from long side and pinch edges to seal. Place in well greased and floured bundt pan; cut-side down. Press ends together to seal. Let rise for 2 hours or until more than doubled in bulk. Bake in a pre-heated 350° oven for 30 minutes or until golden brown. Let cool 10 minutes, then turn out on serving plate. Glaze with 1 cup sifted powdered sugar mixed with 1 to 2 tablespoons water and ½ teaspoon vanilla.

Filling:

¾	cup blanched almonds, toasted and chopped	½	cup brown sugar, packed
3	ounces semi-sweet chocolate		

Grate or finely chop chocolate. Mix with other ingredients and sprinkle on half of coffee cake dough, then roll up as directed.

Filling #2:

¾	cup granulated sugar	¾	cup finely chopped pecans
2	teaspoons cinnamon		

Mix all ingredients together and spread over dough.

Yield: 1 cake, about 12 servings

Sally Lunn

This is my mother's recipe. It is a very light bread and does not have to be kneaded. The soft dough is placed in a greased tube pan. Serve warm cut into wedges. Leftovers make delicious toast.

3¾ to 4 cups flour		1	cup milk
¼	cup sugar	¼	cup water
1	envelope dry yeast	½	cup butter, cut into chunks
1	teaspoon salt	3	eggs, room temperature

In large mixer bowl, mix well 1 cup flour, sugar, yeast and salt, set aside. Heat milk, water and butter over low heat until liquids are very warm (120 to 130 °; butter need not melt. Gradually beat into flour mixture. Beat at medium speed 2 minutes, scraping bowl occasionally. Stir in enough remaining flour to make a stiff batter; cover and let rise in a warm, draft-free place about an hour or until doubled. Stir down; spoon into a well-greased and floured 9″ tube pan.

Cover and let rise in draft-free place 45 minutes or until doubled. Bake in a preheated 400° oven 30 minutes or until top is golden. Turn out on wire rack. Serve warm, cut in wedges.

Yield: 12 servings

Never Fail Rolls

These are the easiest rolls you will ever make. They are good plain but also make delicious cinnamon rolls or sweet rolls of your choice.

½	cup sugar	1	cup warm water
½	cup shortening	3¾	cups flour
3	eggs, unbeaten	¾	teaspoon salt
1	package of dry yeast		

Cream together sugar and shortening in mixer bowl, add eggs and beat well. Dissolve yeast in warm water. Sift flour with salt and add alternately with the yeast mixture to the creamed mixture beginning and ending with flour. Beat about 5 minutes. Put in refrigerator overnight. Next day, take out amount of dough wanted. Place on floured board and knead a few times. Make into rolls of your choice.Let rise until double in size. Bake in 425° oven until brown, about 10 minutes.

Note: This is a soft dough so additional flour will be incorporated in the kneading, but do not add very much — just enough so you can handle it. It should still be soft.

Yield: About 4 dozen

This, too, is a very old recipe. The dry yeast is substituted for the cake yeast.

Swedish Tea Ring

Pretty for the holidays

1	cup warm water, 105 to 115°	3	large eggs, room temperature
2	packages dry yeast	1	teaspoon salt
½	cup instant nonfat dry milk	4½	cups flour
½	cup sugar		
½	cup butter or margarine, melted		

In a large mixer bowl, sprinkle yeast over warm water, let dissolve. With spoon, stir in dry milk, sugar, butter, eggs and salt until well blended. Add 2 cups flour; beat in mixer 2 minutes, add remaining flour (2½ cups) and beat until elastic, about 5 minutes. Place in a lightly oiled bowl, cover with a cloth and let rise until more then doubled. Refrigerate at least 2 hours or dough may be covered tightly with wrap and placed in refrigerator overnight. It will have it's first rising in the refrigerator.

To form, turn out dough on lightly floured board, roll out to a 20″ square. Brush with ¼ cup melted butter or margarine, then spread filling evenly over the dough.

Filling:

½	cup sugar	½	cup chopped nuts
1	tablespoon cinnamon		

Mix in small bowl

To shape ring, roll dough up tightly, jelly roll fashion, keeping ends as even as possible; pinch seam to seal. Arrange roll, seam-side down, in a circle on a lightly greased cookie sheet, dampen ends with water; pinch to seal. With a sharp knife or scissors, and cutting all the way through the dough, make cuts ½″ apart all around ring within ½″ of center. Turn each piece slightly to right so cinnamon swirl is exposed, fanning out pieces as you do so. Let rise, covered with a slightly damp tea towel, in a warm, draft-free place, until double in bulk, about an hour. Heat oven to 375° and bake 30 to 40 minutes until wooden pick inserted in center comes out clean; cover with foil after 30 minutes to avoid overbrowning, if additional cooking time is needed. Remove from cookie sheet to wire rack to cool. Brush with following glaze and garnish with pecans and cherries.

Continued on next page

Glaze:

¼ cup water

3 cups powdered sugar, sifted
after measuring

½ teaspoon vanilla

Mix all ingredients together. Mixture will be stiff. Spread over ring and garnish with ½ cup pecan halves and a 4 ounce container of candied cherries, each cut into ⅛'s.

Yield: 1 ring

Cinnamon Twists

I make these with the Raleigh House roll dough.

1 recipe of Raleigh House roll
dough

Soft butter

1 cup light brown sugar,
packed

4 teaspoons cinnamon

Roll dough into a rectangle 18″ × 12″ on a lightly floured board. Cut dough lengthwise into 2 6″ strips. Brush dough with soft butter, then sprinkle half of each strip with the brown sugar mixed with the cinnamon. Fold other half over. press down, then cut crosswise in 1″ strips. Pick up strips and holding by both ends twist in opposite directions. Place on well-greased cookie sheet about 2 inches apart. Press ends firmly down on sheet. Place in a warm draft-free place until doubled in size. Bake in a pre-heated 375° oven for 12 – 15 minutes or until brown. Remove from oven and spread with glaze. Sprinkle with chopped nuts.

Glaze:

1 cup powdered sugar, sifted

1 to 2 tablespoons water, milk
or cream, or enough to
make a thin glaze

½ teaspoon vanilla

Mix all ingredients in a small bowl until smooth.

Yield: About 4 dozen

Rich Sweet Dough

This dough can be used for sweet rolls or fancy breads as well as kolachy.

1	package dry yeast	½	teaspoon salt
¼	cup 115° water	⅓	cup sour cream
2	eggs	⅓	cup butter, melted
½	cup sugar	3	cups flour

Sprinkle yeast on warm water to which ½ teaspoon sugar has been added. This helps the yeast to foam up. In a large mixer bowl, combine eggs, sugar, salt, sour cream, butter, dissolved yeast, and 1½ cups flour. Beat at high speed for 3 minutes. Beat in remaining 1½ cups flour until smooth, about 5 minutes. Turn out on lightly floured board and knead until elastic. Shape dough into a ball and place back into the mixer bowl with 1 tablespoon oil in bottom. Turn over dough to oil top. Cover and let rise in a warm place until doubled in bulk, about 2 hours. Punch dough down and place on lightly floured board.

For kolachy, shape dough into 2″ balls, place on greased cookie sheet about 2″ apart and let rise until double. Then make an indentation in the center of each ball and fill with any of the following fillings. Bake at 375° for 15 or 20 minutes. Dust with powdered sugar.

Prune Filling:

30	prunes, pits removed	½	teaspoon cinnamon
4	tablespoons sugar	2	tablespoons melted butter

In a bowl, cover prunes with water and let soak for an hour, then drain and mash with a fork. Add the sugar, cinnamon and melted butter. Mix well

Poppyseed Filling:

½	pound poppyseed	½	cup chopped nuts, optional
¾	cup milk	3	tablespoons honey
½	cup sugar		

Blend poppyseed in a blender. Combine in a saucepan with milk and sugar. Stir constantly over medium heat until mixture thickens.Remove from heat and stir in honey. Cool. Add nuts, if you desire.

Yield: about 3 dozen

Irene's Nut-Filled Brioche

Brioche is a rich, fine-grained bread. One of my favorites.

½	cup warm water, 105 to 115°	1	cup butter, softened
1	package dry yeast	6	eggs
¼	cup sugar	4½	cups all-purpose flour, sifted before measuring
1	teaspoon salt	¼	cup melted butter
1	teaspoon grated lemon peel		

Sprinkle yeast over warm water in mixer bowl; add ½ teaspoon sugar. This will make yeast foam up faster. When yeast foams up, add sugar, salt, lemon peel, the butter, eggs and 3 cups flour; beat at medium speed for 4 minutes. Add remaining flour; beat at medium speed about 5 minutes or until smooth. Cover bowl with plastic wrap and a towel and refrigerate overnight. Next day, make filling below. Remove dough from refrigerator, turn out on a lightly floured board. Dough will be soft. Cut dough in half and place one half back in refrigerator. Roll dough in a rectangle 14"×9". Brush with 1 tablespoon melted butter. Spread with half the filling, leaving a ½ inch border. From each end, roll toward the center like a jellyroll; in other words, you will have a double jellyroll. Turn loaf over and place in greased loaf pan, 9"×5"×3", smooth-side up. Brush top with melted butter. Make second loaf the same way. Let rise until double. Preheat oven to 350°. Bake loaves for 35 minutes or until golden brown. Remove from pans to a wire rack to cool. Brush with melted butter before serving, sprinkle with powdered sugar.

Filling:

3	tablespoons butter, softened	2	tablespoons milk
⅔	cup light brown sugar, packed	½	teaspoon vanilla
2	egg yolks	2	cups ground unblanched almonds

In medium bowl, mix butter, sugar and egg yolks, then stir in milk and blend in nuts and vanilla.

Yield: 2 loaves

Sohme's Easter Bread

This is the recipe of a very dear neighbor of mine who was born in the Holy Land. Easter Bread was only baked there at Easter. It has a heavenly smell while baking due to the mixture of spices. I do hope you will try it.

4	cups flour	¼	level teaspoon mahleb seed, ground
¾	cup sugar plus 1 tablespoon	1	teaspoon plus ⅛ teaspoon black seed, ground
1	package dry yeast		
⅔	cup water		
1	scant teaspoon salt	1	egg beaten with 1 tablespoon water for egg wash
2	eggs		
7	tablespoons shortening, melted and cooled		Sesame seeds
1½	rounded teaspoons anise, ground		

Grind parched seeds separately. I use a coffee grinder.

Heat water a little hotter than lukewarm and put in mixing bowl with 1 teaspoon sugar. Sprinkle yeast over and let stand until foamy. Add sugar, salt and melted shortening. Add eggs and beat well. Then mix the ground spices with 2 cups of the flour and add to yeast mixture. Beat at high speed for 5 minutes. Add rest of flour and beat until elastic. If dough seems a little soft, add ½ to 1 more cup flour and beat again for a few minutes. Let rise until more than double. This will take quite a while as this dough does not rise as quickly as other doughs. Roll dough on floured board about ⅓ third of an inch thick to a square of about 12". Cut into ⅓ inch strips which will be 12" long. Cut ⅓ off each strip and place it in the center of the remaining strip. Press down well, then braid the 3 strips. Turn under the ends and place about 2" apart, on well greased cookie sheet or one lined with parchment. Brush with egg wash, being careful not to let any run onto pan, and sprinkle with sesame seeds. Let rise again until double. Bake in a pre-heated 375° oven until lightly brown. Recipe can be doubled. These freeze well.

Yield: 2 to 2½ dozen

The seeds can be obtained at Antone's imported foods in Houston. They have to be picked over carefully and checked for foreign particles. Then place them on a cookie sheet and parch them in a 300° oven. Do not combine the seeds. Grind each separately.

Quick Rising Pineapple Rolls

1	package dry yeast	¼	cup sugar
¼	cup water 105 to 115°	1	teaspoon salt
¾	cup lukewarm milk	1	egg, beaten
¼	cup shortening	3½	cups hard wheat flour

Dissolve yeast in water in mixer bowl. Add shortening, sugar, egg, milk and salt. Mix, then add 2 cups of the flour and beat well. Add rest of flour and beat until dough is elastic. Let rise in a warm place covered with plastic and a towel, until doubled in bulk. In cold weather, I usually put the dough in a cupboard to rise. When risen, remove from bowl to a well-floured board. Roll into a 10″×20″ rectangle. Spread cooled pineapple filling over within ½″ of edge. Roll, jellyroll fashion from long side. Cut into 1″ slices and place, cut-side down, on a greased cookie sheet with 1″ sides. Bake in a 425° oven for 12 to 15 minutes. You may glaze with 1 cup powdered sugar mixed with 2 to 3 tablespoons milk and ¼ teaspoon almond flavoring.

Pineapple filling:

8	ounce can crushed pineapple, drained but save juice	2	tablespoons flour
¼	cup brown sugar, packed	1	tablespoon butter or margarine
		¼	teaspoon almond flavoring

Stir pineapple juice into the sugar and flour. Bring to a boil, lower heat and cook, stirring, until thickened. Add pineapple and cook 1 minute more. Remove from heat and stir in butter and flavoring. Cool thoroughly, then spread on dough.

Yield: 18 rolls

Melanie's Brioche

This is a bread fit for an elegant dinner. Leftovers are wonderful toasted.

1	package dry yeast	1	cup soft butter
½	cup warm water, 105 to 115°	6	eggs
		4½	cups flour
¼	cup sugar	1	egg yolk
1	teaspoon salt	1	cup whole milk
1	teaspoon grated lemon peel		

Sprinkle yeast over water in large mixer bowl; stir until dissolved. Add milk, sugar, salt, lemon peel, butter, eggs and 3 cups flour. Mix at moderate speed until ingredients are blended. Continue to beat at medium speed for 4 minutes. Add the remaining flour; when blended in, reduce mixer speed to low and beat until smooth, about 2 minutes. Cover with a piece of plastic, then with a damp towel. Let rise until double in bulk. Refrigerate dough, tightly covered, overnight.

Next day, grease 2 8″ brioche pans. With a rubber scraper, stir down dough and turn out on lightly floured board. Coat hands with flour and shape dough into a rectangle. With floured knife, cut dough in half. Then cut off ¼ of dough from each piece. On the floured board and with lightly floured hands, shape the large pieces of dough into smooth balls, gently kneading them and rolling them with the palms of the hands. Place each in prepared pan. With your first 2 or 3 fingers, make a hole about 2″ deep in the center of each large ball. With lightly floured hands, roll the remaining two pieces of dough into balls and then into a teardrop shape. Insert pointed end into holes in the large balls. These form the "hats" when they are baked. Cover with a towel and let rise in a warm place, until double in bulk, about 1 hour. Combine 1 egg yolk with 1 tablespoon water and brush on brioches, being careful not to glaze the area where the "hat" joins the body as this could prevent the "hat" from rising.

Bake in a pre-heated 375° oven for 20 minutes, cover tightly with a piece of foil and continue baking an additional 40 minutes. Serve hot or cold.

Yield: 2 Brioche

Note: This versatile bread is marvelous at brunch or lunch. Make individual brioche. Simply remove the "hat" and spoon in any entree, scrambled eggs, ham and mushrooms, chicken in a wine sauce, or filling of your choice.

One Hour Cinnamon Rolls

This dough may be used for other rolls, too. Rolls are best eaten warm. It is a great way to have sweet rolls for breakfast.

½ cup milk, heated to lukewarm	2 tablespoons soft shortening
1 teaspoon salt	2 to 2¼ cups flour
1 tablespoon sugar	Soft margarine
1 envelope dry yeast	¼ cup sugar
1 egg, beaten	1 teaspoon ground cinnamon

Mix first 4 ingredients in mixing bowl. Let yeast dissolve, then mix in egg and soft shortening. Add 2 cups flour and beat at high speed until dough "strings." If dough seems too soft, add the remaining ¼ cup flour. Turn out on floured board and knead until dough no longer sticks to the board.

Roll into a 7″×12″ rectangle, spread with softened margarine and sprinkle combined sugar and cinnamon over. Roll up from long side, pressing edge onto roll. Cut into 12 1″ slices. Lay, cut-side down, in a well-greased 13″×9″ pan. Let rise in a warm, draft-free place about 35 to 40 minutes or until double in bulk. Bake at 350° for about 25 to 30 minutes or until golden brown. Ice with following glaze while hot and serve.

Glaze:

1 cup powdered sugar	½ teaspoon vanilla
1 to 2 tablespoons water or milk	

Sift powdered sugar in a small bowl, add enough milk or water to make a spreading consistency. Add vanilla. Glaze can be quite stiff as warm rolls will melt it.

Yield: 12 rolls

Whole Wheat Bread

This recipe is made with all whole wheat flour and is delicious.

⅓ cup honey	1 cup warm water (110-115°)
¼ cup oil	2 envelopes dry yeast
2 teaspoons salt	1 cup milk, scalded and
2 eggs, beaten	cooled
5½ to 6 cups whole wheat flour	

Dissolve yeast in warm water in large mixer bowl. Add milk, honey, oil, salt and eggs, stir in 2 cups of the whole wheat flour. Beat 3 or 4 minutes in mixer. Cover bowl and allow sponge to rise until doubled, about 45 minutes. Mix in remaining flour, reserving ½ cup for kneading. Turn out on floured board and knead until elastic. Place 2 tablespoons oil in mixer bowl and replace dough, turning from bottom to top so top is oiled. Cover and let rise until doubled.

Punch down and turn out on lightly floured board and make into 2 loaves. Place in well greased large loaf pans. Cover and let rise until doubled. Bake at 375° about 40 minutes, or until loaf sounds hollow when thumped on the bottom. Remove from pans and cool on wire rack.

Yield: 2 large loaves

Potato Rolls

This dough can also be made into cinnamon rolls. Bake them in 2 13″ × 9″ × 2″ baking pans and double the recipe for cinnamon-sugar mixture and glaze in One Hour Sweet Dough recipe.

⅔ cup sugar	1 package dry yeast
⅔ cup shortening	1½ cups warm milk
1 egg	2 teaspoons salt
⅔ cup dehydrated potato flakes, do not use granules	6 cups all purpose flour or about 5½ cups hard wheat flour
½ cup cold water	

Combine potato flakes and cold water in small bowl and set aside. Cream shortening and sugar in large mixing bowl, then add egg and potato mixture. Dissolve yeast in warm milk and add to first mixture. Add salt and 3 cups flour. Beat at high speed for 2 minutes. Add rest of flour or enough to make a soft, but not sticky, dough. Beat until dough starts to leave sides of the bowl. Cover and let rise until more than double, 2 hours or more.

Make into rolls and let rise again until double. Bake at 400° about 20 to 25 minutes or until golden brown.

Yield: 2 dozen rolls

Cheese Bread

We were served this cheese bread at a wine tasting in the Sonoma Valley several years ago. It is delicious for any time.

7 to 7½ cups flour	**3 cups grated sharp cheddar**
⅓ cup sugar	**cheese**
1 tablespoon salt	**(¾ pound)**
2 packages Fleischmann's dry	**1 egg white**
yeast	**1 tablespoon water**
2 cups water	**Sesame seed (optional)**
⅔ cup milk	

Mix 2½ cups flour, sugar, salt and undissolved yeast. Heat water and milk until very warm (120° – 130°). Add to dry ingredients; beat 2 minutes at medium speed in mixer. Add cheese and ½ cup flour. Beat at high speed 2 minutes. Add 3 more cups of flour and beat about 5 minutes. If your mixer is powerful enough to mix in the remaining 1 to 1½ cups remaining flour, add it and beat until dough is elastic. If not, mix in rest of flour by hand and knead on lightly floured board until elastic. Add 2 tablespoons oil to mixing bowl and return dough to bowl turning dough so top is oiled. Cover and let rise, free from draft, until doubled in bulk.

Punch dough down and turn out on a floured board. Cover, and let rest 15 minutes. Divide into 6 equal pieces. Roll each into a 16" long rope. Braid 3 ropes together, fold ends under and place in a greased 9"×5"×3" loaf pan. Repeat with other 3 ropes. Cover and let rise about 1 hour or until doubled.

Mix egg white and water and brush on loaves. Sprinkle with sesame seed. Bake at 375° for 40 to 45 minutes or until loaves sound hollow when thumped on bottom. If loaves start browning too much during baking, cover loosely with foil halfway through baking. Cool on wire racks.

Yield: 2 loaves

Carrot Bread

2 cups flour	1 cup salad oil
1 teaspoon baking soda	1 cup grated carrots
1 teaspoon salt	1 cup drained canned crushed
1½ teaspoons cinnamon	pineapple, unsweetened
3 eggs	2 teaspoons vanilla
1 cup sugar	

Sift flour, soda, salt and cinnamon onto a piece of waxed paper. In mixer bowl, beat eggs and the sugar until light and fluffy. Add the oil, a little at a time, then the carrots, drained pineapple, vanilla and flour mixture. Stir the batter with a spoon or fork just until the flour is combined.

Grease and flour a loaf pan, 9″×5″×3″. Spoon batter in and bake in a preheated 325° oven about 1 hour and 20 minutes, or until bread pulls away from sides of pan. Cool 10 minutes, then turn bread out on a rack to cool.

Yield: 1 loaf

Types of Flour

It was not until I entered the restaurant business that I learned about the different types of flour. I had three bins for the 3 flours I used, hard wheat for my rolls, all-purpose for piecrust and self-rising flour for my muffins and biscuits.

There are different types of flour for different breads. Hard wheat flour is desirable for yeast breads, quick breads (those raised with baking powder or baking soda) get their characteristic lightness from all-purpose flour which contains more soft wheat than hard wheat in it's blend. So the flour that makes the best bread does not necessarily make the best biscuits.

Then there is self-rising flour, generally a blend of all or predominantly soft wheat thoroughly mixed with leavening and salt. Self-rising flour produced in the south where quick bread, such as biscuits, are most popular, is more likely to be entirely soft wheat or a higher proportion of soft wheat than all-purpose flour. Learn to read the labels on the flour you buy.

You may substitute soft wheat flour for the self-rising, if you wish, in recipes. You will have to add a leavening agent and salt to the plain soft wheat.

Cakes

Sabra Chocolate Almond Torte

Sabra is the liqueur of Israel with the flavor of Jaffa oranges and a hint of chocolate.
This is a delicious fine-textured cake.

½	cup butter	2	teaspoon baking powder
1½	cups sugar	½	teaspoon salt
1	teaspoon vanilla	½	cup water
2	(1 ounce) squares	¼	cup cold strong coffee
	unsweetened chocolate	¼	cup Sabra
2	eggs	½	cup chopped toasted
1¾	cups flour		almonds

Grease and flour two 9″ cake pans. Cream together butter, sugar and vanilla until light and fluffy. Beat in melted chocolate and the eggs. Sift together the flour, baking powder and salt. Add alternately with the mixture of water, coffee and Sabra, beginning and ending with flour. Fold in the chopped almonds. Spread in pans, bake in a pre-heated 350° oven about 35 minutes, or until cake tests done. Fill and frost with the following icing.

Icing:

3	(1 ounce) squares	1	teaspoon grated orange rind
	unsweetened chocolate	¼	cup butter, softened
½	cup Sabra	1	pound powdered sugar

In heavy saucepan, melt chocolate with Sabra. Stir in grated orange rind. Beat in powdered sugar and softened butter. Spread between layers and on top of cake.

Yield: 10 to 12 servings

Helpful Hint: *Round pans and square pans may be labelled as the same size (i.e. 8″ pans) but a round pan holds one-quarter less food than a square pan of the "same size."*

Bourbon or Amaretto Pound Cake

I served this for a tea baked in a 15" ring mold. It cut into 40 slices and fit on the smaller sized plate along with sandwiches etc. It also makes an attractive presentation on a large silver tray.

1	cup golden raisins	2¼	cups flour
1	cup chopped toasted pecans (if you use the bourbon) or almonds, if you use Amaretto	½	teaspoon salt
		¼	teaspoon baking soda
		1	(8 ounce) carton of sour cream
¼	cup flour	3	tablespoons bourbon or 4 tablespoons Amaretto
1	cup butter, softened		
3	cups sugar	1	teaspoon vanilla
6	eggs		

Dredge raisins and nuts in the ¼ cup flour. Set aside. Cream butter, then gradually add sugar, beating until light and fluffy. Add eggs, one at a time, beating well after each addition. Sift flour, salt and soda together and add to creamed mixture alternately with sour cream, beginning and ending with flour. Mix just until blended after each addition. Stir in raisin and pecan mixture and flavorings. Pour batter into a greased and floured bundt or tube pan or into the aforementioned ring mold. Bake at 325° for 1 hour and 30 minutes or until pick inserted in center comes out clean. Ring mold will be done in about an hour, but test it. Turn out of pan after cooling for 15 minutes. When cake is completely cold, gradually spread glaze over, letting it sink into cake before adding more.

Glaze:

2	cups powdered sugar, sift before measuring	2	tablespoons milk
3	tablespoons bourbon or Amaretto		

Mix all ingredients in a bowl until smooth.

Yield: 1 cake

Once this recipe was enough to fill the 15" ring mold.

Dora's Oatmeal Cake

This is delicious cake with coconut, pecan icing. It freezes well.

1 cup Quick oats	2 eggs, well beaten
1½ cups boiling water	1½ cups flour
1 stick butter or margarine	1 teaspoon soda
1 cup brown sugar, packed	1 teaspoon cinnamon
1 cup granulated sugar	½ teaspoon salt

Combine the oats and boiling water. Set aside. Cream butter and sugars until light and fluffy, add eggs and mix well. Add oatmeal mixture, mix well, then mix in dry ingredients gently until just blended with a spoon. Do not mix in a mixer. This is very important for a light cake. Pour into 13″ × 9″ × 2″ cake pan that has been greased and floured. Bake in a 350° oven for 30 to 40 minutes or until it tests done in center. Cool and ice either in pan or turned out on platter.

Icing:

½ cup brown sugar, packed	1 cup chopped pecans
⅔ stick butter or margarine	1 cup coconut
¼ cup evaporated milk	

Melt butter in saucepan, then add sugar and milk. Cook over low heat, stirring, until sugar is dissolved. Remove from heat and stir in nuts and coconut. Ice cake.

Yield: 12 servings

Apple Coconut Pound Cake

2 cups sugar	1 teaspoon salt
1½ cups oil	1½ teaspoons vanilla
3 large eggs	3 cups diced peeled apples
3 cups flour	¾ cup flaked coconut
1 teaspoon soda	1 cup chopped nuts

Mix sugar and oil with a spoon, add eggs and beat well with a spoon. Sift flour, soda and salt together and add to oil mixture. Stir in vanilla, apples, coconut and nuts and mix well. Spoon batter into a greased and floured tube pan and bake at 350° for 1 hour and 20 minutes. Let set for 10 minutes before turning out of pan. This freezes well. Does not need any icing.

Yield: 1 cake

Gladys' Swedish Almond Cake

This is a delicious rich cake

2 tablespoons ground almonds	1½ teaspoon double-action baking powder
2 large eggs, beaten until foamy	¼ teaspoon salt
1 cup sugar	¼ cup half and half
1 teaspoon almond extract	1 stick butter, melted and cooled
1 cup flour	

Butter a 10″ pie plate and sprinkle the almonds on the bottom. Set Aside.

Add sugar to eggs a little at a time and beat until mixture is light and lemon-colored, then beat in the almond extract. Sift the flour, baking powder and the salt together and fold into egg mixture alternately with the cream, then stir in the melted butter. Pour the batter into prepared pie plate and bake at 325° for 30 minutes or until a cake tester inserted in middle comes out clean. Remove from oven and set aside.

Topping:

1 tablespoon flour	¾ stick butter (6 tablespoons)
2 teaspoons milk	3 tablespoons honey
¼ teaspoon ground allspice	
½ cup sliced blanched almonds	

Mix the flour, milk and allspice in a small bowl. In a small saucepan, combine the almonds,butter,the honey and the flour mixture. Cook over moderate heat until mixture bubbles. Spoon mixture over cake and bake at 375° for 7 to 10 minutes longer or until bubbly and lightly browned.

Transfer cake to a rack and let cool for 30 minutes.

Garnish:

1 cup heavy cream	2 teaspoons dark rum
2 tablespoons powdered sugar	¼ teaspoon allspice

Beat the whipping cream until it holds soft peaks, Fold in the rest of ingredients and serve with cake.

Yield: 6 to 8 servings

Italian Angel Cake

This is similar to an Italian cream cake only made with a mix and served from a rectangular cake pan.

1	(18½ ounce) package white cake mix	½	teaspoon baking soda dissolved in buttermilk
3	eggs separated	1	teaspoon vanilla
1	stick margarine, softened	1	cup flaked coconut
1	cup buttermilk	¾	cup chopped pecans

Grease and flour a 13″ × 9″ × 2″ cake pan, or 3 (9″) cake pans. Combine cake mix, egg yolks, margarine, buttermilk-soda mixture, vanilla and coconut in bowl of electric mixer. Beat until well blended, then fold in pecans. Beat egg whites until stiff but not dry and fold into cake mixture. Pour into prepared pan or pans, and bake at 350° 25 to 30 minutes or until cake tests done when toothpick is inserted in the center. Frost with cream cheese frosting when cool.

Frosting:

1	pound powdered sugar	1	teaspoon vanilla
1	stick margarine, softened		
8	ounces cream cheese, room temperature		

Mix all ingredients together until smooth and frost cake.

Yield: 12 servings

This can be made in 3 (9″) cake pans and served as a layer cake, if desired.

Meredith's Pear Spice Cake

This freezes very well. It is delicious and moist. It is my granddaughter's recipe.

4	cups chopped fresh pears	½	teaspoon cinnamon
2	cups sugar	2	teaspoons baking soda
1	cup chopped pecans	2	eggs
3	cups flour	1	cup oil
½	teaspoon salt	1	teaspoon vanilla
½	teaspoon nutmeg		

Combine pears, sugar, and pecans in a bowl and let stand for 1 hour or more in the refrigerator. I have even left it overnight. Sift dry ingredients into a large bowl, add pear mixture and beat well with a spoon, not in a mixer. Add eggs, oil and vanilla and beat with a spoon until combined. Spray a bundt pan with vegetable spray, then dust with flour. Pour batter in and bake at 350° for 1 hour and 15 minutes. Let cool in pan for 10 minutes, then turn out on a plate and enjoy.

Yield: 16 to 20 servings

Cranberry Cake

This recipe makes one 10" round cake pan.

2	cups flour	1	egg, beaten
1½	cups sugar	1	cup milk
½	teaspoon salt	½	teaspoon almond extract
2	teaspoons baking powder	3	cups cranberries, washed
4	tablespoons butter, cut into bits		and cut in half

Sift flour, sugar, baking powder and salt into a bowl, cut in butter until mixture resembles coarse meal. Add egg, milk, cranberries and almond extract. Stir well with a spoon. Pour into a 10" round cake pan lined with a buttered, floured round of waxed paper. Bake at 350° on middle shelf of oven for 40 to 45 minutes or until batter pulls away from sides of pan and cake tests done in center. Cool cake in the pan on a wire rack for 10 minutes, then turn out onto the rack. Remove waxed paper. Serve cake, cut in wedges, with butterscotch sauce.

Butterscotch Sauce:

½	cup brown sugar, packed	½	cup whipping cream
½	cup sugar	2	tablespoons butter

In a heavy saucepan, combine all ingredients. Bring mixture to a boil over moderate-low heat, stirring constantly. Boil it, stirring constantly, until sugar is dissolved. Serve warm on cake.

Yield: 6 to 8 servings

Helpful Hint: Large Grade A eggs weigh approximately two ounces, including their shells. As a rule, five large eggs equal about one cup. Unless specified, most recipes are designed for large Grade A eggs.

Sour Cream Cake with Chocolate Coffee Filling

This filling can be used for coffee cakes as well.

3	cups flour	2	cups sugar
1	teaspoon baking powder	3	eggs
1	teaspoon baking soda	1	cup sour cream
½	teaspoon salt	1	teaspoon vanilla
2	sticks butter, room temperature	½	teaspoon almond extract

Beat butter and sugar in mixer until light and fluffy. Add eggs, one at a time, beating after each addition. Sift baking powder, soda and salt with the flour and add alternately with the sour cream, beginning and ending with flour mixture. Add extracts, mix, then pour ⅓ of the batter into a greased and floured bundt pan. Sprinkle with ½ the filling mixture. Cover with ½ of the remaining batter, sprinkle the rest of the filling over. Cover with remaining cake batter. Bake in a 350° oven for about 1 hour and 20 minutes or until cake tests done in center. Cool for 15 minutes before turning out on serving plate. Drizzle with coffee glaze when cool.

Filling:

1	cup semi-sweet chocolate morsels (6 ounces)	2	tablespoons freeze dried coffee
½	cup firmly packed brown sugar		

Combine ingredients in small bowl and use as above.

Glaze 2:

2	teaspoons Taster's Choice Freeze Dried Coffee	1¾	cup powdered sugar, sift before measuring
3	tablespoons boiling water		

Dissolve coffee in boiling water. Add to powdered sugar and mix until smooth. Spoon over cake letting glaze dribble down sides.

Yield: 12 to 16 servings

Mabel's Cherry Cake

This is a delicious substitute for those who do not like fruit cake.

4 large eggs	1 pound pecans, broken up
1 cup sugar	4 slices candied pineapple, cut into thin slices
1 cup flour	½ pound candied red cherries, cut into ¼ths
1 teaspoon baking powder	
1 teaspoon vanilla	
¼ teaspoon salt	
1 pound dates, cut into pieces with scissors	

Beat eggs, add sugar, mix well; add vanilla, then flour, baking powder, and salt which have been sifted together. Mix well, then add fruits and nuts. Combine to distribute through batter. Line the bottom of a tube pan with 2 thicknesses of waxed paper, then grease and flour sides of pan and waxed paper lining. Pour in batter and bake at 275° about 2 hours or until tester comes out clean when inserted in middle.

For petite cakes, bake only about 20 to 25 minutes in a 300° oven, or until done in center.

Yield: 1 cake or about 3 dozen small

I make this in petite muffin pans lined with foil liners. Green and red ones are nice for Christmas if you can find them. I top each small cake with a half or quarter of green or red candied cherries. Pretty on buffet or tea table.

Homestead Sauce

I had to cut down this recipe as we used it in a much larger quantity at church dinners, hence the peculiar measurements. It is good served over gingerbread, cakes and puddings.

1 egg	⅔ teaspoon vanilla
3 tablespoons sugar	½ cup plus 2 tablespoons whipping cream
Dash salt	
½ stick butter or margarine, melted	

Beat egg and salt until light and fluffy, gradually add sugar and beat until thick. Gradually add vanilla and melted butter or margarine, then beat at high speed until well combined. Beat whipping cream to stiff peaks and add about ½ to the egg yolk mixture, then fold in the rest of the cream. Serve over gingerbread, chocolate cake or whatever you wish.

Yield: A little over 2 cups

German Fruit Cake

This is another cake good for Christmas, Thanksgiving or any occasion. It freezes well.

¾	cup butter or margarine	¾	teaspoon soda
2	cups sugar	1	cup buttermilk
4	eggs	⅔	cup cherry preserves
3	cups flour	⅔	cup pineapple preserves
½	teaspoon allspice	⅔	cup peach preserves
½	teaspoon nutmeg	1	cup chopped nuts
½	teaspoon cinnamon	1	teaspoon vanilla

Cream butter, sugar and eggs together until light. Sift dry ingredients and add them alternately with buttermilk, add vanilla, then fold in preserves and nuts, mixing just enough to combine. Pour into a well greased and floured Bundt pan. Bake at 325° for 1½ hours. Cool 15 minutes before removing from pan. This cake does not need icing. You can dust with powdered sugar, if you like, or dribble the following sour cream glaze over slightly warm cake.

Glaze:

½ pound powdered sugar	1 teaspoon vanilla
About 2 tablespoons sour cream	Dash salt

Mix all ingredients together, adding more sour cream, if necessary to make a glaze that will slowly run down sides, but not off cake.

Yield: 1 Bundt cake

You may use any combination of preserves you wish, if some of those mentioned are unobtainable or too expensive.

Helpful Hint: *To powder sugar: When you run out of powdered sugar, blend 1 cup granulated sugar and 1 tablespoon cornstarch in blender on medium-high for 2 minutes.*

Anna Yankey's Almond Cake

This cake was nearly always served for birthdays in the Yankey family. It is one of my favorites, too.

8	ounces unblanched whole almonds	¼	teaspoon salt
8	eggs, separated	2	cups heavy cream, whipped with powdered sugar
1	cup sugar, divided	1	cup blanched, slivered almonds
1	teaspoon almond flavoring		
1	teaspoon baking powder		

Grind almonds to a fine meal in blender or food processor and mix with baking powder and salt. Beat egg yolks until lemon colored, add ½ cup sugar and beat until creamy, Add almond flavoring. In a separate bowl, beat egg whites until soft peaks form, then gradually add the remaining ½ cup sugar, by tablespoonfuls, and beat until egg whites are stiff but not dry. Carefully fold them into egg mixture, Then add ground almond mixture, gradually, and fold in. Place in ungreased tube pan and knock on table twice to remove air holes. Bake at 325° for 45 to 60 minutes or until no indentation is left when finger is gently pressed in the middle. Invert over funnel or bottle to cool completely. Ice with whipped cream just before serving and stud with blanched, slivered almonds. Enjoy!

Yield: 8 to 10 servings

Willie Mae's Buttermilk Pound Cake

Willie Mae was with my son's family for over 30 years. She is also a very dear friend of mine. We love to exchange recipes. She is the one who taught me the secret of a good pound cake — beating the butter, sugar and eggs until cream-colored and fluffy.

3	cups sugar	1	teaspoon salt
2	sticks butter, do not substitute	1	cup buttermilk
5	eggs	¼	teaspoon soda
3	cups flour	1	tablespoon warm water
		2	teaspoons vanilla

Cream butter and sugar until light in color and fluffy. Add eggs, one at a time, beating well after each addition until mixture is, again, light and fluffy. Add salt to flour and mix with creamed mixture, alternately, with buttermilk, beginning and ending with flour. Mix in vanilla and soda dissolved in the tablespoon water. Pour into a well greased and floured bundt pan and bake at 300° for 1 hour and 20 minutes or until pick inserted in center comes out clean. Let cool 10 minutes before removing from pan. This cake needs no icing as it has a macaroon-like crust.

Yield: 12 to 16 servings

Chocolate Cake with Kahlua

3 eggs, separated	½ cup cocoa
¾ cup sugar	1½ teaspoons baking soda
½ cup shortening	½ teaspoon salt
1 cup brown sugar, packed	¾ cup strong coffee
2¼ cups flour	¾ cup Kahlua

Grease and flour 2 9″ cake pans. Beat egg whites to soft peaks, then gradually add the ¾ cup sugar, by tablespoonfuls; beating until stiff, but not dry, peaks form. Set aside. Cream shortening and brown sugar until fluffy, add egg yolks, one at a time, beating well after each addition. Mix coffee and Kahlua together. Sift flour, salt, soda and cocoa together and add, alternately, with coffee Kahlua mixture beginning and ending with flour. Gently fold beaten egg whites into batter. Pour into prepared pans and bake in a 350° oven for 30 to 35 minutes or until cake tests done in middle. Cool 10 minutes, turn out on wire rack. Frost layers, top and sides with Kahlua frosting.

Kahlua Frosting:

6 tablespoons butter	3 tablespoons Kahlua
1 pound powdered sugar	2 to 3 tablespoons hot coffee
5 tablespoons cocoa	Dash salt

Cream butter, add sugar, cocoa and salt. Beat together while adding Kahlua, then add 2 to 3 tablespoons hot coffee to make of frosting consistency.

Yield: 8 to 10 servings

Helpful Hint: *Never beat egg whites until ready to use or they will deflate. You may add one teaspoon cream of tartar to every one cup of egg whites for volume.*

Kate's Sponge Cake

6	large eggs, separated	1	teaspoon cream of tartar
1⅓	cups sifted cake flour, sift before measuring	¼	cup water
		1	teaspoon vanilla
½	teaspoon baking powder	½	teaspoon almond extract
½	teaspoon salt		
1½	cups granulated sugar, divided		

An hour before baking, separate eggs in two different bowls. Set aside, covering yolks tightly. Sift flour, baking powder, salt and 1 cup of the sugar in small bowl. Combine egg whites and cream of tartar in mixer bowl, beat at high speed until soft peaks form, then beat in the remaining ½ cup sugar a tablespoon at a time, beat until stiff but not dry, peaks form. Combine yolks of eggs, water and extracts. With a spoon, stir into sifted flour mixture; beat with a spoon ½ a minute just to blend. Then with a spoon or spatula, fold yolk mixture into beaten whites until blended. Turn batter into ungreased 10″ × 4″ tube pan; cut gently with a knife through batter to remove air bubbles. Bake about 35 minutes at 375°.

Cool cake inverted over funnel or bottle until completely cool, about an hour. Remove from pan by inserting a slender spatula between cake and side of pan until tip touches bottom. Then press gently on sides of pan cutting away clinging cake. Pull spatula out and repeat around tube of pan. Then invert cake on cake rack and lift off pan.

Yield: 1 10″ cake

Helpful Hint: *For the greatest volume when beating egg whites, use eggs that are at least twenty-four hours old and at room temperature. When I was at the Cordon Bleu in Paris, the chef always rubbed a little vinegar and salt in the copper mixing bowl, then wiped the bowl with a towel, before whipping egg whites. Any grease or oil remaining after washing the bowl could prevent the egg whites from gaining in volume. If a little yolk gets into the white, use the egg shell to remove it. The shell will also remove any small piece of shell in the white.*

Venetian Coffee Cake

This is my version of a favorite dessert of mine that was served at the Snack Shop in Houston many years ago. Belying it's name, they served very fine gourmet dinners and lunches. This dessert can be made many weeks ahead of time and frozen, well wrapped.

1	large chiffon or sponge cake	5	teaspoons instant coffee
1	pound butter	8	eggs, separated
4	cups powdered sugar, divided	2	cups toasted pecans, chopped

Cream butter, 3 cups powdered sugar, instant coffee and egg yolks until fluffy, add pecans. Beat egg whites until soft peaks form, then add the remaining 1 cup sugar gradually, beating until stiff, not dry, peaks form. Add about a third of the whites to creamed mixture to lighten mixture, then gently fold in rest of whites.

Slice cake into 6 layers horizontally, laying one slice down on each of two cake plates. Spread filling about a ¼ inch thick, barely covering cake. Add another layer on top of each, Spread again with the filling. Place last of cake layers on top and use rest of filling to ice top and sides. Place in freezer. As soon as cakes are frozen, cover with several layers of film or place in a large metal box lined with film. Use as you wish. This cake is very rich so small wedges suffice. Remove from freezer about 20 minutes before serving.

Yield: 2 cakes, 16 – 18 servings

Helpful Hint: *To test for freshness, submerge raw eggs in a bowl of water — if they sink, they are fresh; if they float, they are old.*

Chocolate Meringue Cake

2	cups flour	1	ounce unsweetened
1	tablespoon baking powder		chocolate, grated
¼	teaspoon salt	1	stick margarine, room
4	large eggs, separated		temperature
2	cups sugar, divided	1	teaspoon vanilla
1	cup finely chopped pecans	¾	cup milk

Sift together flour, baking powder and salt. In mixer bowl, beat whites of eggs until soft peaks form, beat in 1 cup of the sugar gradually by tablespoonfuls until whites form stiff, but not dry peaks. Fold in nuts and grated chocolate. Grease a 9 or 10″ tube pan and line bottom with waxed paper. Spread meringue mixture on bottom and ¾ up the sides of the pan as if lining it. Be sure there is a thick layer on the bottom.

In mixer bowl, cream remaining 1 cup of sugar and the margarine until light and fluffy. Beat in egg yolks and vanilla until well blended. Stir in flour mixture alternately with the milk until well blended. Pour cake mixture in pan making sure that it is surrounded by meringue on all sides and lower than top of meringue, Bake in a pre-heated oven at 375° for 65 to 75 minutes or until toothpick inserted in the center comes out clean. Do not invert pan. Cool on rack 25 minutes or until sides can be loosened easily with a spatula. Turn out on a serving plate. Peel off waxed paper; cool completely.

Yield: 1 (9″ or 10″) tube pan

Lemon-Filled Angel Food.

1	large angel food cake, homemade or store bought	1	tablespoon grated lemon peel
1	(3⅜ ounce) package lemon pie filling	2½	cups whipping cream, divided
2	tablespoons fresh lemon juice		

Bake angel food cake the day before or buy one. Cut into 5 layers with a serrated knife. Prepare pie filling using only 2 cups water. Remove from heat and add lemon juice and grated rind. Refrigerate, covered, at least an hour. Whip 1 cup of the whipping cream and fold into cooled filling. Divide between layers of cake leaving top uncovered. Whip rest of cream and ice the cake with it. Refrigerate until served.

Yield: 8 servings

Quick-Mix Cake

This is an easy bake-in-pan cake for a quick snack. Unfrosted, it is perfect for a cake and fresh fruit dessert with a scoop of ice cream.

1¼	cups all purpose flour	¾	cup milk
1	cup sugar	⅔	stick margarine, softened
1½	teaspoons baking powder	1	egg
¼	teaspoon salt	1	teaspoon vanilla

Preheat oven to 350°. Grease a 9″×9″×2″ cake pan, or, if you want to turn cake out of the pan, line bottom with waxed paper. Measure flour, sugar, baking powder, salt, milk and margarine in mixer bowl. Add egg and vanilla. Beat ½ minute at slow speed. Time it, then 3 minutes at high speed, scraping bowl occasionally.

Turn into prepared pan. Bake at 350° about 35 minutes or until top springs back when lightly pressed with finger. If pan has been lined with waxed paper, turn out on plate and peel off waxed paper. If not, serve from pan.

Yield: 9″ cake

I sometimes grate 3 or 4 ounces of semi-sweet or sweet chocolate and sprinkle it over the unbaked dough and then top with ½ cup chopped nuts. You have a delicious pre-iced cake when it comes out of the oven. Can be used on Picnic Chocolate Cake.

Mace Pound Cake

This recipe was given to me by the organist at St. Luke's Methodist church in Houston. He was an excellent cook.

3	cups flour	½	teaspoon salt
3	cups sugar	¼	teaspoon baking soda
1	cup Crisco	1	teaspoon vanilla
1	cup buttermilk	1½	teaspoons mace
5	eggs		

Cream shortening and sugar, until fluffy, add eggs, one at a time, beating well after each addition. This is very important for a fine-grained cake. Sift flour, salt and soda together and add alternately with the buttermilk to creamed mixture, beginning and ending with flour. Add vanilla and mace. Bake in a greased and floured bundt pan in a 350° oven for 1 hour and 20 minutes or until done in center when a wooden pick is inserted.

Yield: 12 to 16 servings

Chocolate Creme Cake

This is a variation on sour cream cake.

Creme Fraiche:
1   cup whipping cream   1   tablespoon buttermilk

Mix cream and buttermilk in a jar with a tight lid. Shake 2 minutes until well combined. Let stand at room temperature about 8 hours. Store in refrigerator. Will keep 4 to 6 weeks.

Cake:
4 large eggs	¾ cup creme fraiche
1 cup flour, sifted after measuring	¼ teaspoon salt
	½ teaspoon pure vanilla
¾ cups sugar	
4 ounces semi-sweet chocolate, grated	

Beat eggs and sugar until light and fluffy, about 5 minutes. Fold in flour, salt, chocolate, creme fraiche and vanilla. Pour batter into a buttered and floured 9″ cake pan. Bake at 325° for 40 minutes. Cool completely on rack before frosting. Remove from pan.

Chocolate Glaze:
4 ounces semi-sweet chocolate, broken into pieces	⅓ stick margarine
	2 tablespoons strong coffee
	½ teaspoon vegetable oil

Melt butter, chocolate and coffee in top of double boiler. Remove pan from heat and beat in oil. Spread while hot over cake.

Yield: 1 (9″) layer

Helpful Hint: *To decrease a recipe and use a fraction of an egg, beat a large Grade A egg slightly and measure; 1½ tablespoons equals half an egg, 1 tablespoon equals a third.*

German Chocolate Pound Cake

This recipe also came from Bob Bennett

2	cups sugar	3	cups flour
1	cup margarine	½	teaspoonful baking soda
4	eggs	½	teaspoon salt
2	teaspoons vanilla	4	ounce package German
1	cup buttermilk		sweet chocolate, melted

Cream sugar and margarine until light and fluffy. Add eggs, one at a time, beating after each addition. Add vanilla and melted chocolate. Sift flour and salt. Dissolve soda in buttermilk and add, alternately with flour, beginning and ending with flour. Blend well. Pour into a greased and floured bundt pan. Bake at 300° about 1½ hours or until a pick inserted in center comes out clean. Cool, then dust with sifted powdered sugar, if desired.

Yield: 1 Bundt Cake

Honey Glazed Pound Cake

1	tablespoon vinegar	1	teaspoon vanilla
Milk, enough to fill a cup when		2	cups flour
	combined with vinegar	1	teaspoon baking powder
1	cup vegetable oil	½	teaspoon baking soda
1½	cups sugar	¼	teaspoon ground cloves
3	eggs	½	cup chopped pecans

Mix oil and sugar in mixer bowl, add eggs and vanilla. Beat 2 minutes at high speed. Sift together flour, baking powder, soda and cloves. Add alternately with vinegar milk mixture to egg mixture, beginning and ending with the flour. Beat 2 minutes more. Stir in pecans. Pour into a greased and floured bundt pan and bake at 350° for about 40 minutes or until pick inserted in center comes out clean. Let stand 10 minutes, then remove from pan. Prick holes in hot cake and drizzle with Honey Syrup.

Honey Syrup:

¼	cup honey	1	tablespoon lemon juice
1	tablespoon water		

Mix all ingredients and bring to a boil for 2 minutes. Pour over cake while hot.

Yield: 1 Bundt pan

Fabulous Pecan Torte

6   eggs, separated
1½   cups sugar, divided
2   tablespoons flour
2   teaspoons baking powder
¼   teaspoon salt

3   cups very finely chopped
     pecans
Whipped Cream Filling
Pecan halves or strawberries or
     semi-sweet chocolate

Beat egg yolks and add 1 cup of the sugar gradually. Beat until light lemon-colored. Mix together the flour, baking powder and salt, then stir in pecans. Beat egg whites until soft peaks form, then gradually add the remaining ½ cup of sugar by tablespoonfuls, beating well after each addition. Carefully fold in the egg yolk mixture, then the nut mixture. Divide into 2 round 9″ cake pans lined with greased waxed paper. Bake at 350° for 25 to 30 minutes or until no imprint remains when finger is pressed gently in the center. Cool, remove from pans, then spread the whipped cream filling between the layers and over top and sides. Garnish with grated semi-sweet chocolate or fresh fruit.

Whipped Cream Filling:

½   tablespoon unflavored
     gelatin
1   tablespoon milk

1   cup heavy cream
¼   cup powdered sugar
1   teaspoon vanilla

Soften gelatin in the milk and dissolve over hot water. Whip cream until stiff and beat in powdered sugar, the cooled gelatin and vanilla.

Yield: 16 servings

Helpful Hint: *You can keep unbroken egg yolks in the refrigerator for several days covered with milk or water. To freeze egg yolks, "stabilize" them by adding two teaspoons salt for each pint of egg yolks for use in unsweetened foods, or 2 tablespoons sugar for each pint for use in desserts. Before beating, always bring eggs to room temperature for best volume.*

Mother's Sunshine Cake

We loved this, split and filled with a custard filling, then dusted with powdered sugar.

5	eggs, separated	1	cup flour
1	teaspoon vanilla	¼	teaspoon cream of tartar
1	cup sugar, divided	¼	teaspoon salt

Beat egg yolks and vanilla in mixer until light and fluffy, add ¾ cup of the sugar, 1 tablespoon at a time, and beat until mixture forms a ribbon when lifted. In another bowl, beat the egg whites until foamy, add the ¼ teaspoon cream of tartar and the salt and beat until soft peaks form. Gradually add the remaining ¼ cup of sugar by tablespoonfuls and beat until stiff, but not dry, peaks form. Fold the meringue into the yolk mixture alternately with the flour. Pour into a buttered and floured 9″ springform pan. Bake on middle shelf of a 350° oven for 35 or 40 minutes or until cake tester inserted in the center comes out clean. Cool on rack for 10 minutes, then remove sides of pan and cool completely.

Yield: 8 servings

You can also make a Washington Cream Pie with this recipe by splitting the cake, filling it with custard filling and icing it with an uncooked chocolate frosting.

Coconut Cake

½	cup egg whites	¼	cup oil
1	cup cake flour, sifted before measuring	3	egg yolks
⅔	cup sugar	1	teaspoon coconut extract
1¼	teaspoons baking powder	1	teaspoon vanilla
½	teaspoon salt	¼	teaspoon cream of tartar
		½	cup coconut

Let egg whites come to room temperature or set mixing bowl in warm water for a few minutes. Sift flour, sugar, baking powder and salt into a large bowl, Make a well in center and add in the order given: oil, egg yolks, ⅓ cup water and coconut and vanilla extracts. Beat until smooth. Beat egg whites with cream of tartar until very stiff. Do not underbeat. Fold egg yolk mixture into egg whites along with coconut just until blended. Pour into an ungreased loaf pan or half-sized tube pan. Bake at 350° about 50 minutes or less or until tester inserted in center comes out clean. Invert cake by setting ends or sides on two shallow pans. Let cool 1 hour. Remove from pan and dust with powdered sugar or slice and serve with whipped cream.

Yield: 12 servings

Picnic Chocolate Cake

This cake is served from the pan it is baked in so is easy to take to a picnic. It tastes rich and moist even though it has no eggs or milk in it. In addition, it is mixed in the pan it is cooked in. No dishes to wash.

1½	cups flour	1	teaspoon vanilla
1	cup sugar	1	tablespoon vinegar
3	tablespoons cocoa	⅓	cup oil
½	teaspoon salt	1	cup cold water
1	teaspoon soda		

Sift dry ingredients on a square of waxed paper, then sift dry ingredients again into an ungreased 9″ square cake pan. Be sure that cocoa is well mixed in. Make 3 holes in dry ingredients. Put the vanilla in one, the vinegar in another and the oil in the third. Pour the cold water over all and mix with a fork until the dry ingredients disappear. Bake at 350° about 25 minutes or until a toothpick inserted in the center comes out clean.

Cool and serve from the pan with chocolate sauce, ice cream, whipped cream or with an uncooked icing on top.

As in another cake recipe in this book, I have also topped this cake before it is baked with 3 ounces of grated semi-sweet chocolate and ½ cup chopped pecans, and had a cake ready to eat as soon as it came out of the oven.

Yield: 6 servings

This recipe can be doubled to fill a 13″ × 9″ rectangular cake pan. Just allow a little more baking time.

Bourbon Pecan Cake

This is a very rich cake. It is made in a bundt cake pan, but is so rich, the servings should be small.

2	sticks unsalted butter	1	teaspoon salt
2	cups sugar	1	cup bourbon
6	eggs, separated	4	cups coarsely broken pecans
3	cups flour		
4	teaspoons baking powder	3	cups white raisins
2	teaspoons freshly grated nutmeg	½	cup flour

Heat oven to 325°. Grease and flour a bundt or tube cake pan shaking out the excess flour. Cream sugar and butter in mixer until light, add the 6 egg yolks, one at a time, mixing after each addition. Sift dry ingredients together. Combine the nuts and raisins with the ½ cup flour. Add sifted dry ingredients, alternately with the bourbon to creamed mixture, beginning and ending with flour; beating until just combined. Stir raisin, nut mixture into batter. Beat egg whites in another bowl until stiff but not dry. Gently fold ½ the whites into batter, then add the rest of the beaten whites, gently folding in. Spoon batter into prepared pan. Bake about 1¼ hours or until a tester inserted in the middle, comes out clean. Cool in pan 15 minutes, then turn out on rack to cool completely. Wrap in a sherry soaked cheesecloth and then in plastic and let ripen at least a week. Will freeze, if desired.

Yield: 16 to 20 servings.

Eastman Cake

This was Grandmother Eastman's recipe.

1½	cups unsweetened applesauce	2	cups flour, sift before measuring
1½	teaspoons soda	2	tablespoons cocoa
1	cup chopped pitted dates	½	teaspoon salt
1	cup chopped nuts, Grandmother used walnuts	½	teaspoon cinnamon
		½	teaspoon cloves
½	cup shortening	½	teaspoon nutmeg
1⅓	cups sugar	1	teaspoon vanilla
2	eggs	½	cup raisins

Grease bottom of a 10″ tube pan, line bottom with waxed paper. Grease and flour lining and pan. Combine applesauce and soda; set aside. Combine raisins, dates and nuts; set aside. Cream shortening, then gradually add sugar. Beat until light and fluffy; add eggs, one at a time, beating well after each addition. Sift dry ingredients onto waxed paper; add ½ cup to fruit mixture, toss to mix. Gradually add remainder of flour mixture to creamed shortening and sugar in mixer bowl. Mix well. Add applesauce mixture and raisin mixture, then vanilla. Mix at slow speed just until dry ingredients disappear. Spoon batter into prepared pan. Bake at 325° for about 1 hour or until pick inserted in center comes out clean. Cool in pan 15 minutes before turning out. Dust with sifted powdered sugar.

Yield: 12 to 16 servings

Helpful Hint: *Poaching peeled whole fruit in a syrup is successful with fruits such as peaches, nectarines and pears, to name a few. To prepare a basic syrup, add 6 tablespoons of sugar for every cup of liquid. Before poaching, pour enough water over the fruit to cover and then drain it into a measuring cup to determine how much liquid and sugar you will need. You may combine liqueur or spices with the water to add flavor to the syrup. Place the fruit in a deep pot, pour syrup over and bring to a simmer. Do not boil. A firm, ripe peach should take no more than 10 or 12 minutes to cook. Hard Anjou pears may take up to 45 minutes.*

Super Pineapple Cake

1	(8 ounce) can crushed pineapple canned in its own juice	2	cups cake flour, or 2 cups flour less 4 tablespoons
6	eggs, separated	1	tablespoon baking powder
½	teaspoon cream of tartar	½	teaspoon salt
1	cup sugar, divided	¼	teaspoon almond extract

Drain pineapple, add water to pineapple juice to make ¾ cup. Set aside. Beat egg whites and cream of tartar until soft peaks form. Then, beating at high speed, add ½ cup sugar 2 tablespoons at a time, beating well after each addition. Continue beating until stiff, but not dry, peaks form when beater is lifted. Preheat oven to 350°. Beat egg yolks with flour, baking powder, salt, almond flavoring, pineapple juice with water and ½ cup sugar. Beat until light and fluffy, about 3 minutes. Gently fold in beaten whites and drained pineapple until just blended. Pour into ungreased tube pan. Bake for 60 to 65 minutes. Invert pan on a funnel or bottle and let cool completely. Remove to cake plate and drizzle following glaze over cake.

Glaze:

1	cup powdered sugar	½	teaspoon almond extract
2	tablespoons milk		

Mix all ingredients until smooth. Slowly drizzle over cake, letting fall down over sides.

Yield: 12 servings

Fresh Apple Nut Cake

2	cups tart apples, chopped	1	teaspoon baking soda
1	cup sugar	1	teaspoon salt
1	cup vegetable oil	1	teaspoon cinnamon
1	egg	1	cup chopped pecans
1½	cups flour	1	teaspoon vanilla

Mix apples and sugar in large bowl and let stand at least ½ hour. Mix well, then add in order the oil, egg, flour,soda,salt and cinnamon. Beat well with a spoon, then fold in the nuts and vanilla. Pour batter into a well greased and floured bundt pan. Bake at 325° for 45 minutes to an hour or until cake tests done in the center.

Yield: 12 servings

Mother's Angel Food Cake

Mother had plenty of practice making her delicious angel food cakes. Years ago, egg yolks were considered good for you but whites were not as they contained albumen. My father had 2 eggs yolks in a milk shake every morning. The whites went into cakes.

1¼ cups egg whites	1¼ teaspoons cream of tartar
1 cup plus 2 tablespoons cake flour, sift before measuring	¼ teaspoon almond extract
½ cup granulated sugar	1 teaspoon vanilla
¼ teaspoon salt	1 cup sifted granulated sugar, sift after measuring

An hour before baking, set out the egg whites so they will be at room temperature before beating. Heat oven to 375°. Sift flour with ½ cup sugar 4 times. Beat egg whites at high speed in mixer bowl with extracts, salt and cream of tartar until stiff enough to hold soft peaks. With mixer still at high speed, beat 1 cup of sugar, ¼ cup at a time. sprinkling over egg whites. Beat until sugar is just blended. Stop mixer. Sift flour mixture in fourths over beaten egg whites, folding each addition in with 15 complete fold-over strokes of a rubber spatula or spoon, turning bowl often. After flour is folded in, give batter 10 or 15 extra strokes.

Gently push batter into an ungreased 10″×4″ deep tube pan. Take a knife and pass it through batter to bring any air holes to surface. Bake in a pre-heated 375° oven for 30 to 35 minutes, or until cake tester inserted in middle comes out clean. Invert on funnel or bottle until completely cool. Cut with a serrated knife in wedges. Serve with fresh fruit and whipped cream.

Yield: 12 servings

Sometimes, my mother varied the cakes by adding finely chopped, candied cherries and nuts to the batter as we got tired of the plain cakes. They were delicious served with whipped cream. This recipe has more sugar than most recipes have.

Chocolate Mousse Cake

This is a cake to be served at the table on your prettiest crystal plate or silver tray. I sometimes serve it with the accompaniment of sliced strawberries.

7	ounces unsweetened chocolate or 5 ounces unsweetened chocolate and 2 ounces semi-sweet chocolate	½	cup plus 2 tablespoons sugar, divided
7	tablespoons butter, do not substitute	5	eggs, separated
		1½	teaspoon vanilla
		1	tablespoon Amaretto, optional

Heat oven to 250°. Heat chocolate and butter in top of double boiler over simmering water, stirring, until melted. Add ¼ cup of the sugar and stir until sugar is almost dissolved. Beat egg yolks in a bowl, then add a little of the chocolate, beating constantly until well combined; continue adding chocolate until chocolate and yolks are well combined, then return chocolate mixture to double boiler and cook, stirring, until slightly thickened. Remove from bottom of double boiler.

Beat egg whites until soft peaks form, then add the remaining sugar by tablespoons, beating until stiff but not dry peaks form.

Stir vanilla and Amaretto into chocolate mixture, mixing well. With a rubber scraper. scrape chocolate mixture on top of egg whites. Fold egg whites carefully into the chocolate. Spoon mixture into a buttered and floured 9" springform pan. Bake about 1¾ hours. Let cool to room temperature, then chill. Place on a serving plate and either dust with powdered sugar or spread chocolate mousse over top and sides. Garnish with ¾ cup sliced, toasted almonds before serving.

Chocolate Mousse:

4	ounces semi-sweet chocolate	⅛	teaspoon salt
3	tablespoons Amaretto or water	⅛	teaspoon cream of tartar
4	eggs, separated	2	tablespoons sugar
		½	cup heavy cream, whipped
		¾	cups toasted sliced almonds

Melt chocolate and Amaretto or water in heavy saucepan over very low heat, stirring, until chocolate is melted. Beat egg yolks until thick and add to chocolate mixture gradually, stirring constantly.

Beat the egg whites with the salt and cream of tartar and sugar until stiff, but not dry peaks form. Whip cream and fold into egg whites, then fold in chocolate mixture. Spoon over cake and refrigerate until serving. Add toasted sliced almonds on top just before serving.

Yield: 8 to 10 servings

Vivian's Sherry Wine Pound Cake

This recipe came from my neighbor. It is a delicious, exceptionally fine-grained cake.

6	eggs	1	cup sherry wine
3	sticks margarine	1	teaspoon vanilla
3	cups sugar	1	teaspoon almond extract
3½	cups flour	1	teaspoon nutmeg or mace

Cream margarine and sugar at high speed until light and fluffy. Add eggs, one at a time, beating at medium speed. Add nutmeg or mace to flour and flavorings to sherry. At lowest speed, add flour to creamed mixture alternately with sherry, beginning and ending with flour. This will be a fairly thick batter. Bake in a well greased and floured teflon lined bundt pan plus a small loaf pan. Batter is too much for bundt pan. A 10″ tube pan will hold all the batter and can be used, if you prefer. Put in cold oven, then turn to 250°.It must rise slowly and at the edges first. Bake at 250° for 20 minutes, then 20 minutes at 275°, then 20 minutes at 300°. Bake until toothpick inserted in center comes out clean. Cool 10 minutes before removing from pan to cool completely.

Yield: 12 to 14 slices

Mrs. Drucker's Pound Cake

The ingredients in this cake are quite different from most pound cakes. It is easy to make, if you have a good kitchen scale. The butter is simple to measure without a scale as 2 tablespoons make 1 ounce and sticks are marked in tablespoons.

4	large eggs	**Butter**
Sugar		1 teaspoon pure vanilla
Cornstarch		

Weigh eggs in their shells, then weigh an equal amount of sugar, cornstarch and butter. Cream sugar, butter and cornstarch together well, add eggs and vanilla and beat at slow speed just until blended. Place in a greased and floured 8½″ × 4½″ × 3″ loaf pan or 8 inch tube pan. Bake at 325° for 1 hour or when done in center when tested with a wooden pick. Let set 10 minutes before removing from pan. Dust with sifted powdered sugar,if you like.

Yield: 6 to 8 servings

This is an exceptionally fine grained cake. The ingredients are correct. The cornstarch takes the place of the flour.

Cream Topping

This topping will not weep and can be used to garnish desserts or ice cakes ahead of serving.

1 teaspoon unflavored gelatin	½ cup powdered sugar, sifted
2 tablespoons cold water	2 teaspoons vanilla
2 cups whipping cream	

Remove 2 tablespoons of whipping cream to a small bowl and let come to room temperature

Sprinkle gelatin over cold water in heat-proof cup. Put cup in a pan of hot water and heat until gelatin is dissolved. Put remaining cream in chilled bowl; add sugar and vanilla and beat until cream barely begins to thicken. Stir the reserved 2 tablespoons cream into the dissolved gelatin and beat into the bowl of cream. Beat until mixture holds its shape and use as you wish.

Yield: about 4 cups

Lemon-Glazed Cake

This is another make-in-the pan cake.

1½ cups flour	⅓ cup vegetable oil
1 cup sugar	2 teaspoons grated lemon
1½ teaspoons baking powder	rind
¼ teaspoon salt	½ cup milk
2 eggs	

Sift dry ingredients onto a square of waxed paper, then sift again into an ungreased 9″ square cake pan. Make 2 holes; put grated lemon peel in one and the oil and eggs in the other. Mix oil and eggs together, slightly, with a fork. Pour milk over and mix with a fork until dry ingredients disappear. Bake at 350° about 25 minutes or until cake tests done in center. Remove from oven and pour lemon glaze over. Serve cake from the pan.

Lemon Glaze:

3 tablespoons lemon juice	½ cup sugar

Combine ingredients in small bowl and stir until sugar is dissolved.

Yield: 9″ cake

Banana Cake

You notice this recipe uses part cornstarch. A friend of mine who is a registered dietician, explained that the addition of cornstarch to the flour is equivalent to cake flour.

1¼	cups flour	1	cup mashed ripe bananas
⅔	cup sugar	⅓	cup oil
¼	cup cornstarch	1	egg, slightly beaten
1	teaspoon baking powder	1	tablespoon lemon juice
½	teaspoon salt	1	teaspoon vanilla

Sift dry ingredients onto waxed paper, then sift again into an ungreased 9" cake pan. Make 3 holes and put lemon juice in one, oil and egg in another and vanilla in the third. Add mashed banana and mix with a fork until dry ingredients are moistened. Be sure to get in the corners. Bake in a pre-heated 350° oven for 30 or 35 minutes or until cake tests done in middle. Ice with lemon uncooked powdered sugar icing or icing of your choice.

Lemon Frosting:

⅓	cup margarine, softened	1	tablespoon lemon juice
1½	cups powdered sugar, sifted		

Cream margarine and sugar well, then blend in lemon juice.

Yield: 9" Cake

If you do not have cake flour for a recipe, you can use this same formula, or use the same measurement of all-purpose flour the recipe calls for less 2 tablespoons per cup.

Cynthia's 7 Up Pound Cake

3	sticks butter	3	cups flour
3	cups sugar	2	teaspoonfuls lemon extract
5	eggs	¾	cup 7 Up

Cream butter and sugar until light and fluffy. Add eggs, one at a time, beating well after each addition. Add flour, alternately with lemon extract mixed with 7 up, beginning and ending with flour. Pour into a greased and floured bundt pan. Bake at 325° for 1 hour or 1¼ hours or until pick inserted in middle comes out clean. Let cool in pan for 10 minutes before removing to serving plate.

Yield: 12 to 16 servings

Quick Spice Cake

A mix-in-the-pan cake

1¼	cups flour	¾	teaspoon all spice
1	cup brown sugar, packed well	½	teaspoon salt
		⅓	cup oil
¼	cup cornstarch	1	egg, slightly beaten
1	teaspoon cinnamon	1	tablespoon vinegar
1	teaspoon baking powder	1	cup cold water

Sift dry ingredients onto waxed paper, then sift into an ungreased 9" square or round cake pan. Make 2 holes, put vinegar in one and oil and egg in another. Pour water over all and mix with a fork until dry ingredients disappear. Bake in a pre-heated 350° oven for about 30 minutes or until cake tests done when wooden pick is inserted in the center.Cool, then ice with brown sugar icing, or serve as a pudding with a sauce.

Brown Sugar Icing:

½	stick margarine	1	cup powdered sugar
½	cup brown sugar, packed well	½	teaspoon vanilla
2	tablespoons milk	Dash salt	

Melt margarine in a small heavy saucepan, add brown sugar and stir over low heat until sugar is dissolved. Add milk and heat. Remove from heat and then add powdered sugar, salt and vanilla. Beat until smooth and thick enough to spread.

Yield: 9" cake

Chocolate Angel Food

This makes just one 8" layer, just right for 6 servings. As with most angel food cakes, it is low in calories, without the topping, of course. It is made with the less fattening cocoa, instead of chocolate.

½   cup cocoa
⅓   cup water
½   teaspoon vanilla
4   egg whites, large eggs
Few grains salt

⅓   cup sugar
¼   cup all purpose flour
2   teaspoons baking powder
½   cup finely chopped pecans
Chantilly Cream topping

Heat oven to 350°. Cook cocoa and water in a small saucepan over low heat, about 1 minute, stirring constantly, until mixture is thick and has just begun to boil. Remove from heat and stir in vanilla. Beat egg whites and salt in large mixer bowl until soft peaks form when beater is lifted. Add sugar, 1 tablespoon at a time, beating well after each addition. Beat until stiff peaks will hold when beater is lifted. Quickly add cocoa mixture and beat until just blended. Remove bowl from mixer and sift combined baking powder and flour over egg white mixture, ¼ at a time, folding in after each addition, along with the chopped pecans. Scrape batter into an ungreased 8" layer cake pan. Bake 20 to 25 minutes, until cake begins to pull away from the sides of the pan. Remove from oven and place upside down on a wire rack. Cool for 20 minutes, then run a knife around the edges and turn out on wire rack to cool completely. To serve: Pipe Chantilly Cream around edge or serve separately.

Chantilly Cream:
White of 1 large egg
2   teaspoons sugar

½   cup heavy cream

Beat egg white in electric mixer at high speed until soft peaks form, add sugar, 1 teaspoon at a time, beating well after each addition. Beat to stiff peaks. In another bowl, beat cream until soft peaks form. Gently fold beaten egg white into cream with a spatula.

Yield: 6 servings

Caramel Torte

⅔	cup butter or oleo (1⅓ stick)	1½	cups flour
2	tablespoons half and half	2	teaspoons baking powder
¼	teaspoon almond flavoring	4	eggs, room temperature
		1	cup sugar

In small saucepan over low heat, melt butter. Remove from heat and add half and half and extract;set aside. In large mixer bowl, beat eggs slightly. Add sugar gradually and beat until mixture is lemon-colored and fluffy, about 15 minutes. Sift flour with baking powder and add alternately with butter mixture to egg mixture. Mix until well blended. Turn into a greased 9" springform pan. Bake at 375° about 40 minutes or until top is firm and golden. Carefully spoon almond topping evenly over top. Bake 8 to 10 minutes more or until topping is bubbly and golden. Cool on wire rack 5 minutes. Run knife around edge of pan to loosen. Remove sides of pan. Serve warm or cold. Slice with a sharp knife.

Caramel Almond Topping:

¼	cup butter or margarine	1	tablespoon flour
1	tablespoon half and half	¾	cup blanched, sliced almonds
⅓	cup brown sugar, packed		

Melt butter in heavy pan, add half and half and brown sugar. Add flour and stir until smooth. Bring just to a boil, add almonds. Pour over cake while hot.

Yield: 12 servings

Brownie Cake Squares

This is a rich cake. Can be eaten as is or served as a dessert with the addition of ice cream. A recipe children could make.

1	(4 serving size) package chocolate pudding	1	(6 ounce) package semi-sweet chocolate morsels
1	(18.5 ounce) package chocolate cake mix	1	cup chopped pecans

Prepare pudding according to directions on package. Cool, stirring occasionally. Add dry chocolate cake mix and blend well. Pour into a buttered 13"×9"×2" cake pan. Sprinkle with chocolate morsels and nuts. Bake at 350° about 20 to 25 minutes or until toothpick inserted in center comes out dry but still moist. Cool completely before cutting into squares.

Yield: 12 to 15 bars.

Sunshine Nut Cake

A larger variation of my mother's Sunshine Cake

7	tablespoons flour	7	egg whites	
7	tablespoons ground pecans	½	teaspoon cream of tartar	
¼	teaspoon cinnamon		Pinch salt	
7	egg yolks	¼	cup sugar	
1	teaspoon grated lemon rind		Whipped cream or ice cream.	
3	tablespoons sugar			

Combine flour, cinnamon and ground pecans in a small bowl. In mixer bowl, beat the egg yolks with the lemon rind and 3 tablespoons sugar until mixture forms a ribbon when beater is lifted. In another mixer bowl, beat egg whites with the cream of tartar and salt until they hold soft peaks, then beat in the ¼ cup sugar, 2 tablespoons at a time. and beat until meringue is stiff and shiny. Fold the egg yolk mixture into the beaten egg whites, then fold in the nut mixture gently.

Pour the batter into a buttered and floured 9″ springform pan and bake in a 325° oven for 1 hour or until it is brown and pulls away from sides of the pan. Remove sides of pan and transfer to a wire rack. Let cool before slicing. Serve with ice cream or whipped cream or with a dusting of sifted powdered sugar.

Yield: 10 servings

Cocoa Chiffon Cake

This is one of my family's favorite birthday cakes.

¾	cup boiling water	½	cup oil	
½	cup cocoa	7	unbeaten egg yolks	
1¾	cups flour	1	teaspoon vanilla	
1¾	cups sugar	7	egg whites	
3	teaspoons baking powder	½	teaspoon cream of tartar	
1	teaspoon salt	1½	cups chopped pecans	

Mix the boiling water and the cocoa and let cool. Sift the dry ingredients together in a large bowl. Make a well in the center and add in this order: the oil, egg yolks and the vanilla. Add cocoa mixture. Beat with a spoon until smooth.

Beat egg whites and cream of tartar until very stiff, do not underbeat. Fold about ¼ of the egg whites into yolk mixture. Mix well, then fold in the rest of the whites and the chopped pecans just until blended. Pour into an ungreased 10″×4″ deep tube pan. Bake at 325° about 55 minutes or until top springs back when lightly touched. Invert pan over funnel or bottle until entirely cool. Ice with chocolate or white icing or icing of your choice.

Yield: 12 to 16 servings

Patti's Hot Cocoa Cake

This is an exceptionally good cake with a delicious icing.

1	stick margarine	½	cup buttermilk
1	cup water	2	eggs, beaten
½	cup Crisco	1	teaspoon vanilla
4	tablespoons cocoa	¼	teaspoon salt
2	cups sugar	1	teaspoon soda
2	cups flour		

Place first 4 ingredients in a saucepan, cook over medium heat, stirring, until shortening is melted. Pour into a mixing bowl and add sugar, flour, salt and soda that has been sifted together. Mix well, then add buttermilk, eggs, and vanilla. Mix well, then pour into a greased 13"×9"×2" pan. Bake at 400° for 25 minutes. Spread topping over as soon as cake comes out of the oven. Cool before serving.

Topping:

1	stick margarine	1	pound powdered sugar
4	tablespoons cocoa	1	teaspoon vanilla
6	tablespoons milk	1	cup chopped nuts

Cook over medium heat in a saucepan just until margarine is melted. Mixture should be hot but should not boil. Add to powdered sugar in a large bowl, mix and add vanilla and nuts.

Yield: 12 to 15 servings

Agnes' Poppyseed cake

This same friend is responsible for the Butter Drop recipe in this book, another very good recipe.

1	box Duncan Hines Butter Cake Mix	¼	cup poppyseeds
½	cup sugar	4	eggs
¾	cup Wesson oil	1	cup sour cream

Mix dry ingredients, then add oil and eggs, one at a time, beating after each addition. Fold in sour cream and poppyseeds. Pour into a greased and floured Bundt pan and sprinkle with sugar. Bake at 350° for 45 to 50 minutes or until cake tests done, when a pick is inserted in the middle. This cake can also be baked in 2 8"×3" loaf pans. The baking time will be a little shorter.

Yield: 12 servings

Queen Elizabeth Cake

1	cup boiling water	1	teaspoon vanilla
1	cup chopped dates	1½	cups flour, sifted before
1	teaspoon soda		measuring
1	cup sugar	1	teaspoon baking powder
¼	cup butter	½	teaspoon salt
1	egg, beaten	½	cup nuts, chopped

Pour the boiling water over the dates and soda and let stand until the rest of ingredients are mixed. Cream butter and sugar in mixer, then add egg and vanilla and mix. Sift dry ingredients and add them alternately with the date mixture, beginning and ending with flour. Add nuts. Pour into a greased 13"×9"×2" baking pan. Bake for 35 minutes in a 350° oven.

Icing:

10	tablespoons brown sugar, packed well	4	tablespoons butter
		¾	cup chopped nuts
10	tablespoons cream or evaporated milk	¾	cup flaked coconut

Mix first 3 ingredients in a heavy saucepan. Cook, stirring, over medium heat until sugar dissolves, and mixture thickens slightly. Pour over cake and sprinkle with the nuts and coconut.

Yield: 12 to 15 servings

Date and Nut Cake

This cake needs to season for at least a week. It can be stored for several weeks in refrigerator, well wrapped in film, then foil. It also freezes well.

1	cup butter	2	teaspoons baking powder
2¼	cups sugar	4	cups pecans, chopped
6	eggs, separated	1	pound pitted dates, chopped
4½	cups cake flour, sifted before measuring	1	teaspoon nutmeg
		¾	cup sherry

Cream butter and sugar until light and fluffy, add egg yolks and beat well. Sift flour and baking powder, add to butter mixture. Stir in dates and pecans, then add sherry and nutmeg.

Beat egg whites until stiff and fold into batter. Grease and flour a large tube pan. Pour batter in and bake in a 275° oven about 1½ hours or until cake tests done in middle. Remove from pan, wrap in film, then in foil and refrigerate.

Yield: 12 to 16 slices

Pie Filling Sauces

This is an easy way to fill or sauce a plain cake.

Cherry Pie Filling:
1   can cherry pie filling
1   tablespoon Amaretto or ¾ teaspoon almond extract

Pineapple Pie Filling:
1   can pineapple pie filling
1   tablespoon Kirsch

Peach Pie Filling:
1   can peach pie filling
1   tablespoon Amaretto
½   cup slivered blanched almonds

Strawberry Pie Filling:
1   can strawberry pie filling
1   tablespoon Chambord liqueur

Mix gently with rubber spatula to avoid breaking up fruit. Add more liqueur to your taste, if you desire.

Undiluted frozen orange juice makes an easy glaze for gingerbread, or cakes. Just spread the thawed orange juice over bread or cake, as you would any glaze.

Harvest Cake

This is another delicious substitute for a fruit cake. It has to age for at least two weeks as there is brandy in it.

1	cup butter	1	teaspoon all spice
2	cups sugar	¼	teaspoon salt
2	teaspoons soda	3	cups flour
2	cups unsweetened, juicy stewed dried apples	2	cups pecans, chopped. More can be added, if desired
2	teaspoons cinnamon	2	cups dark raisins
1	teaspoon ground cloves	⅓	cup good brandy

Soak brandy and raisins overnight in a bowl. Cut dried apple slices into fourths, barely cover them with water in a saucepan and let soak overnight. Next day, bring to a boil and simmer, covered, until tender. Apples should still be juicy with about 3 tablespoons of juice remaining. Cool.

Cream butter and sugar until light and fluffy. Mix apples and soda and add. Sift spices, salt and flour and add. Then add raisin-brandy mixture and nuts and mix well. Bake in a buttered and floured Bundt pan at 325° for about 1 hour and 30 minutes or until done when tested in center. Let cool about 10 minutes, then remove from pan and let cool completely. Wrap well in film, then in foil and either place in refrigerator or freezer until needed.

Yield: 12 to 16 servings

Penuche Icing

This amount will also ice a 2 layer cake.

⅔ cup margarine (1⅓ stick)	⅛ teaspoon salt
1⅓ cups brown sugar, firmly packed	1 teaspoon vanilla
⅔ cup milk	1 pound powdered sugar

Melt margarine in heavy saucepan, add brown sugar and salt. Cook over low heat, stirring constantly, until sugar is melted. Slowly add milk, bring to a boil and boil 2 minutes. Remove from the heat and add vanilla. Sift powdered sugar into a large bowl, then pour hot brown sugar mixture over, beating until well combined. Ice cake. If icing thickens too much, add a little more milk.

Yield: For 9″ × 13″ cake

Chocolate Cream Icing

This is a staple recipe of mine. A vanilla cream icing can be made by eliminating the cocoa and adding ¼ teaspoon almond flavoring.

1 pound powdered sugar	¼ teaspoon salt
5 tablespoons cocoa	¼ cup milk, about
¾ stick margarine, softened	1 teaspoon vanilla

In mixer bowl combine powdered sugar and cocoa. Mix well, add salt, softened margarine, vanilla and milk. Beat until creamy and light. Add more milk, if needed, to make of icing consistency. Try a little on your cake to see if it spreads easily without running off cake.

Yield: 2 layer or 9″ × 13″ cake

This same recipe can be made substituting sour cream for the milk. However, add sour cream gradually as it does not seem enough at the first, but thins after beating. The sour cream makes a richer icing.

Cloud Sponge Cake

This cake can be used as is dusted with powdered sugar or to make Washington Cream Pie or layered with a variety of cake fillings of your choice.

1⅓ cups cake flour, stirred and lightly spooned into measuring cup. When heaping, level off with straight edged knife.
½ teaspoon baking powder
¼ teaspoon salt

5 eggs, room temperature, separated
½ cup ice water
1½ cups sugar
½ teaspoon almond extract
¾ teaspoon cream of tartar

Stir together the flour, baking powder and salt; set aside. in mixer bowl, beat egg yolks at high speed until thick and lemon-colored. Gradually beat in water until pale and foamy. Gradually beat in sugar until completely dissolved, 8 to 10 minutes. Add extract. Fold flour mixture in 3 additions into yolk mixture; set aside.

Beat egg whites in mixer to foamy, add cream of tartar and beat until stiff, but not dry, peaks form. Gently fold into yolk mixture with rubber spatula or wooden spoon. Pour into an ungreased 10″ tube pan. Bake at 325° until cake springs back when lightly touched, about 1 hour. Invert pan to cool.

For layers, grease bottom only of 3 9″ layer cake pans and line bottoms with waxed paper. Divide batter evenly between pans and bake at 350° until cake springs back when touched lightly. Cool in pans on wire racks, turn out and remove waxed paper.

Yield: 1 tube pan or 3 layers

If you are going to use lemon filling, use lemon flavoring in your cake, almond icing or filling, use almond extract etc.

Sponge Sheet Cake

This sheet cake can be used for jelly rolls or custard rolls or for ice cream rolls.

¾   cup cake flour, stirred and lightly spooned into measuring cup When heaping, level off with a straight-edged knife.
¾   teaspoon baking powder
⅛   teaspoon salt

3   eggs, room temperature, separated
⅓   cup ice water
¾   cup sugar
⅜   teaspoon almond extract
½   teaspoon cream of tartar

Grease 15″×10″×1″ jelly roll pan. Line with waxed paper, then grease paper; set aside.

Stir together the flour, baking powder and salt; set aside. Beat egg yolks in mixer until thick and lemon-colored. Gradually beat in water until pale and foamy. Gradually add sugar and beat until sugar is completely dissolved, about 10 minutes. Add extract. Fold flour mixture into egg yolk mixture in 2 additions.

Beat egg whites in mixer until foamy, add cream of tartar and beat until stiff peaks form when beater is lifted. Gently fold beaten whites into batter with a rubber spatula or wooden spoon. Spread evenly in the prepared pan. Bake at 375° until cake springs back when lightly pressed. Loosen edges with a table knife and turn out on a large rack to cool.

If using for a rolled cake, turn out on a towel with sifted powdered sugar on it . Roll warm cake up with towel, from long side and let cool. Unroll and spread filling or ice cream on it and reroll. Place seam-side down on serving tray and refrigerate, covered. If filled with ice cream, place in freezer.

Yield: 15″×10″×1″ pan

Peanut Butter Cake

Recipe calls for chunky peanut butter, however, I make it with the smooth peanut butter as some of my great-grandchildren do not like nuts. When I make it for myself, I use the chunky peanut butter. Either one is good.

2 cups flour	1½ teaspoons vanilla
3 teaspoons baking powder	3 eggs
¾ teaspoon salt	1 cup milk
1 cup chunky or smooth peanut butter	Fine dry bread crumbs (optional)
¼ cup shortening	About ⅓ cup roasted salted peanuts
1½ cups dark brown sugar, packed	

Sift together the flour, baking powder and salt. Set aside. In large mixing bowl, cream peanut butter and shortening. Beat in sugar, then add eggs and vanilla and beat until light and fluffy. At low speed mix in flour and milk alternately, beginning and ending with flour. Pour into a greased and floured bundt pan heavily coated with bread crumbs. Bake in a preheated 350° oven for 40 to 45 minutes or until a toothpick inserted in the center comes out clean, Let cool 10 minutes, then turn out on serving plate and pour chocolate glaze over and decorate with the salted peanuts.

Chocolate Glaze:

½ cup semi-sweet chocolate morsels	2 to 3 tablespoons hot water

Place chocolate morsels in heavy saucepan with 2 tablespoons hot water. Place over very low heat and stir until chocolate is melted. If mixture is too thick, add the other tablespoon water. Dribble over cake. Garnish with peanuts, if desired.

Yield: 1 Bundt pan

This can also be baked in a 13″ × 9″ cake pan, glazed and cut into squares.

Butter and Sauce Cake

2   cups butter (1 pound) room
    temperature
2   cups firmly packed light
    brown sugar, remove ⅓ cup
    very firmly packed sugar
    from 1 pound, which leaves
    2 cups. Wrap the ⅓ cup
    and label for future needs.

6   eggs, separated
4   cups flour
2   teaspoons baking powder
¼   teaspoon salt
⅔   cup milk
2   cups chopped pecans

Preheat oven to 325°. Butter bottom of 10″ tube pan. Line bottom with waxed paper. Beat sugar and butter until light and creamy. Add yolks, 2 at a time, beating well after each addition. Mix in flour, baking powder and salt. Gradually blend in milk. Add pecans. Beat egg whites until stiff, but not dry, peaks form. Fold ¼ of whites into batter to lighten, then gently, but thoroughly fold in remaining whites. Pour batter into prepared pan, smoothing top with spatula. Bake until top starts to crack and is no longer moist, about 1½ hours. Invert cake onto rack and cool completely in pan.

Caramel Sauce:
1   cup firmly packed light
    brown sugar
1   stick butter

½   cup whipping cream or half
    and half

Combine sugar, butter and cream in heavy-bottomed small saucepan. Cook over low heat, stirring constantly, until sugar is dissolved. Remove from heat and whisk 1 minute. Store in refrigerator in a jar with a tight-fitting lid until ready to serve. To serve: Cut cake into wedges. spoon some of the sauce over. Pass remaining sauce separately.

Yield: 10 to 12 servings

Vanilla Chiffon Cake

This is the cake I use most often for the Venetian Coffee Cake. It is a versatile cake, delicious with strawberries and whipped cream or served with Grand Marnier or Amaretto sauce or sauce of your own choice.

2	cups flour	7	large eggs, separated
1½	cups sugar	¾	cup cold water
3	teaspoons baking powder	1	teaspoon vanilla
1	teaspoon salt	½	teaspoon almond flavoring
½	cup salad oil	½	teaspoon cream of tartar

Sift the flour, sugar, baking powder and salt into a very large mixing bowl. Make a well and add, in this order; the oil, egg yolks, cold water and extracts. Beat with a spoon until smooth. Beat egg whites until frothy, add cream of tartar; then beat until very, very stiff, do not underbeat. Pour egg yolk mixture over whites, folding in gently with a rubber spatula, until just blended. Pour into an ungreased 10" tube pan. Bake at 325° about 1 hour and 20 minutes or until no imprint remains when touched lightly in center with your finger. Invert over funnel or bottle until completely cold, about an hour. This can be baked in a large loaf pan, about 16" × 4¼". Bake at 325° for 50 to 55 minutes, or until it tests done in center.

Yield: 12 servings

Chocolate Loaf Cake

If you do not have cake flour on hand, use all purpose flour less 2 tablespoons per cup.

1	cup shortening	1	teaspoon soda
2	cups sugar	1	cup buttermilk
5	eggs, well beaten	2½	cups sifted cake flour, sifted
3	(1 ounce) squares		before measuring
	unsweetened chocolate,	½	teaspoon salt
	melted and cooled	2	teaspoons vanilla
1	cup chopped pecans		

Cream shortening and sugar until light and fluffy, add eggs and mix well. Stir in the chocolate and nuts. Dissolve soda in buttermilk; add alternately with flour, sifted with salt, to creamed mixture; beating well after each addition. Add vanilla; mix, then pour into 2 greased and floured 9" × 5" × 3" loaf pans. Bake at 325° for 1 hour. Let cool in pans for 10 minutes, then turn out of pans onto wire rack to cool completely

Yield: 2 cakes

This cuts better the next day to baking.

Date Nut Cake

1	cup sugar	¼	teaspoon salt
¾	cup (1½ sticks) butter	1	cup chopped nuts
3	eggs	1	cup flaked coconut
1	cup sour milk or buttermilk	1½	cup chopped dates
2½	cups flour		Grated rind of 1 orange
1½	teaspoons baking soda	1	teaspoon vanilla

Cream sugar and butter until fluffy; add eggs, one at a time, beating well after each addition. Sift flour with baking soda and salt. Add alternately with buttermilk or sour milk. Mix well, then add nuts, coconut, dates, orange rind and vanilla. Place in two greased and floured 8″ × 4″ loaf pans. Bake about 45 minutes to 1 hour in a 350° oven or until cake tests done in center. While warm and still in pan, spread syrup over cakes.

Syrup:
Grated rind of 1 orange   1   cup sugar
Juice of 1 orange

Combine all ingredients in small bowl after you put cake in oven. Stir occasionally until sugar is dissolved. Pour over hot cake. Let cool in pan for 30 minutes, then turn out on plates.

Yield: 2 loaf pans

Crumb Cake

I have had this recipe over 50 years. I have used it as a coffee cake, a cookie, cut into small squares, and as a dessert with whipped cream or ice cream, or just as it is, a cake.

2¼	cups flour	1	stick margarine
1	teaspoon cinnamon	1	teaspoon vanilla
2	cups brown sugar, well packed (1 pound less ⅓ cup firmly packed)	½	teaspoon soda
		1	egg
		⅔	cup buttermilk

Make crumbs of the flour, cinnamon, sugar and margarine. Set aside ⅔ cup. To the rest of the crumbs, add buttermilk, soda, vanilla and egg. Mix with a spoon until combined, then put in a greased 13″ × 9″ × 2″ rectangular pan. Sprinkle reserved crumbs on top. Bake at 350° for 30 to 35 minutes or until wooden pick inserted in center comes out clean, but moist. Do not overbake.

Yield: 12 to 15 servings

This cake freezes well.

Chocolate Glazed Pound Cake

1 cup butter	½ teaspoon salt
½ cup shortening	½ cup cocoa
3 cups sugar	1 cup milk
5 eggs	¼ cup Amaretto
3 cups flour	1 teaspoon vanilla
1 teaspoon baking powder	

Cream butter and shortening, gradually add sugar and beat until light and fluffy. Add eggs, one at a time, beating well after each addition. Sift flour, baking powder, salt and cocoa and add to creamed mixture alternately with milk, beginning and ending with flour. Stir in Amaretto and vanilla. Pour batter into a greased and floured Bundt or 10" tube pan. Bake at 350° for 1 hour and 15 minutes or until a wooden pick inserted in center comes out clean. Cool in pan for 10 to 15 minutes, then invert onto a serving plate. Spoon chocolate glaze over.

Glaze:

1 pound powdered sugar, sifted	½ stick margarine, softened
4 tablespoons cocoa	3 to 4 tablespoons Amaretto
	Chopped pecans

Combine sugar and cocoa, add remaining ingredients and beat until smooth. Spoon over warm cake letting some drizzle down the sides. Sprinkle pecans over. If glaze is too thick to drizzle down the sides, add a little milk.

Yield: 12 to 20 slices

Almond Caramel Topped Cake

Topping:

1 stick butter or margarine	⅔ cup coconut
¾ cup plus 1 tablespoon brown sugar, packed	1 teaspoon vanilla
⅓ cup half and half	⅛ teaspoon salt
⅔ cup sliced blanched almonds	1 box yellow cake mix or 13"×9" homemade cake

Mix butter, sugar, cream, almonds, coconut, vanilla and salt in bowl. Mix cake according to package directions. Bake in a greased 9"×13" rectangular cake pan. When cake is done, remove from oven and sprinkle crumbs evenly over hot cake. Return to oven and bake at 350° 10 or 15 minutes or until topping is golden brown and bubbly. Serve from the pan warm or cold.

Yield: Topping for 9"×13"

Cookies

Johnson Grandchildren on Family Fire Truck
(Mrs. Johnson's Great-Grandchildren)

From left to right:

In front of the Fire Truck
Katie Wooldridge, Mindy Wooldridge, Lacy Johnson holding John Wooldridge, and Carter Johnson

Seated in the Fire Truck
Bin Johnson, Eastman Landry holding Elyse Landry, Ayla Landry, Kyle Landry, Alice Colvin, and Richard Colvin holding Elizabeth Adkins

Sohme's S Cakes

The Hovis family were neighbors and dear friends. Mrs. Hovis and her husband were born in the Holy Land. This is an Armenian recipe.

1	pound butter, softened. Mrs Hovis melted it, then cooled it	4	cups sugar
		5	cups flour

Combine butter and sugar and beat in mixer until sugar is dissolved. Add flour and beat again until well combined. Place in refrigerator until dough is easy to handle. With hands, remove 2 rounding teaspoons of dough and roll into a tube about 2½″ long. Place on ungreased cookie sheet and form into an S. Continue with rest of dough. Bake at 300° until lightly brown around edges and on the bottom. The cakes will not be brown on top. Allow to cool slightly before removing from pan. Store in a tightly covered container in the refrigerator or freezer.

Yield: about 6½ dozen

Mrs. Hovis creamed the sugar and butter by hand until the sugar was melted, a time-consuming process. I make these in an electric mixer, mixing at high speed at least 10 minutes or until sugar is dissolved.

Molasses Spice Cookies

½	cup shortening	1	teaspoon baking powder
¼	cup sugar	½	teaspoon salt
1	egg	½	teaspoon ground cloves
½	cup molasses	½	teaspoon cinnamon
1	cup grated carrots	½	teaspoon ginger
1	teaspoon grated orange rind (optional)	½	teaspoon baking soda
		½	cup buttermilk
2	cups flour		

Cream shortening in mixer with sugar, add egg and beat well. Add molasses, carrots and orange rind. Mix thoroughly. Sift remaining dry ingredients and add to creamed mixture alternately with the buttermilk, beginning and ending with the flour mixture. Drop by teaspoonfuls onto greased cookie sheet. Bake in a 350° oven about 15 minutes or until light brown and firm to the touch.

Yield: 3 dozen

Chocolate Squares

These can be served as a dessert or as a cookie.

Crust:

1¼ cups flour
⅓ cup sugar
½ cup (1 stick) margarine, softened

¼ cup finely chopped or grated semi-sweet chocolate

In mixer bowl, stir together flour and sugar, add margarine and beat at low speed, scraping sides of bowl often, until mixture resembles small peas. Stir in chopped chocolate. Press evenly into sides and bottom of 9″ square baking pan. Be sure to press well into sides of pan and corners. If crust is too thick there, it will be too firm to cut easily. Cool.

Filling:

1 (4½ ounce) package instant chocolate pudding
1 cup milk
1 cup sour cream

3 tablespoons powdered sugar
3 tablespoons finely chopped semi-sweet chocolate

Mix pudding with milk. When it starts to thicken, fold in sour cream, powdered sugar and chocolate. Pour into cooled crust and refrigerate until firm. Cut into squares and serve.

Yield: 8 to 9 servings

Chocolate Peanut Butter Cookies

1 cup shortening
½ teaspoon salt
1 cup granulated sugar
½ cup light brown sugar, packed
1 teaspoon vanilla

2 eggs
2 cups unsifted flour
1 teaspoon baking soda
1 cup peanut butter chips
1 cup semi-sweet chocolate chips

Cream shortening, salt, sugar, brown sugar and vanilla until light and fluffy. Add eggs and beat well. Combine flour and baking soda and blend into creamed mixture. Stir in peanut butter chips and chocolate chips. Drop by rounded teaspoonfuls onto ungreased cookie sheet. Bake at 350° for 10 to 12 minutes or until lightly browned. Cool slightly before removing from pan.

Yield: About 5 dozen

Old Fashioned Tea Cakes

This is another memory from my childhood. A next door neighbor, who was Scottish, always had tea in the afternoon and served these tea cakes along with shortbread. I loved it when she saw me out playing and asked me in for tea.

1 cup butter, softened. Do not substitute	1 teaspoon baking soda
2¼ cups sugar	½ teaspoon freshly grated nutmeg
4 eggs	¼ cup buttermilk
4½ cups flour	2 teaspoons vanilla
1 teaspoon baking powder	

In mixer bowl, cream butter and sugar until lemon-colored and fluffy. Add eggs, one at a time, beating after each addition. Sift dry ingredients and add with buttermilk and vanilla. Drop by dessert spoonfuls onto well greased cookie sheet. Bake at 350° until golden brown. Cool and place in tightly covered container.

Yield: about 2 dozen

These are best served within 2 days.

Aunt Matilda's Sugar Cookies

2½ cups sifted flour	1 cup margarine or butter
1 teaspoon baking soda	1 teaspoon vanilla
1 teaspoon cream of tartar	2 cups sugar
½ teaspoon salt	3 egg yolks

Sift first 4 ingredients together; set aside. Cream butter and vanilla until butter softens. Add sugar gradually, beating until fluffy. Add egg yolks, one at a time, beating well after each addition. Add dry ingredients, in fourths, to creamed mixture, beating just until blended. Form dough into balls about 1" in diameter. Roll in additional sugar. Place about 2" apart on lightly greased cookie sheet. Bake at 350° about 10 minutes or until golden.

Yield: About 10 dozen

Ginger Sugar Crisps

These are easy to make and they have small cracks on top when baked just like gingersnaps. They get crisp when cool.

¾	cup shortening	2	cups flour
1	cup sugar	½	teaspoon cloves
¼	cup molasses	½	teaspoon ginger
1	egg	1	teaspoon cinnamon
2	teaspoons baking soda	½	teaspoon salt

In large saucepan, melt shortening over low heat. Remove and let cool, then add sugar, molasses and egg; beat well. Sift remaining ingredients together and add to first mixture. Mix well and chill at least 2 hours. Form into 1″ balls and roll in additional sugar. Place about 2″ apart on lightly greased cookie sheet. Bake at 350° for 8 to 10 minutes. Cookies will still be soft. Let cool slightly, then remove from pan and keep in a tightly covered container.

Yield: 4½ dozen

Ruth's Dream Bars

Crust:

½	cup butter	1	cup flour
½	cup brown sugar, packed		

Mix all ingredients together to make crumbly mass like pie crust. Press into 9″ square cake pan.Bake at 350° until lightly browned. Cool.

Topping:

1	cup brown sugar, firmly packed	½	teaspoon baking powder
		¼	teaspoon salt
2	eggs, beaten	1	cup fine coconut
1	teaspoon vanilla	½	cup nuts, chopped
2	tablespoons flour		

Mix all ingredients together and pour over baked crust; bake at 350° until browned, about 20 to 25 minutes. Cool and cut into bars. Sprinkle with sifted powdered sugar.

Yield: 24 to 32 bars

Coconut Oat Bars

Crust:

⅓	cup butter or margarine	½	teaspoon baking soda
⅓	cup brown sugar, packed	½	teaspoon salt
¾	cup flour	¾	cup quick cooking oats

Cream butter and brown sugar in mixing bowl until light and fluffy. Sift together flour, baking soda and salt. Add to creamed mixture along with oats. Press into bottom of greased 8" cake pan.

Topping:

2	eggs, beaten	1	tablespoon lemon juice
¾	cup brown sugar, packed	¾	cup flaked coconut
1	tablespoon flour	½	cup chopped nuts

Beat eggs in a bowl, add rest of ingredients. Mix well and spread over crust, bake at 350° for 25 to 30 minutes or until brown on top. Cool in pan on rack. Cut into 1" × 1½" bars.

Yield: 20 bars

Swedish Cookies

This is another of Mrs. Wahlborg's recipes and one of my family's favorites. The butter and almond flavoring make them special. They are thin and crisp. I make them at Christmas.

1	cup butter, do not substitute	1	teaspoon almond flavoring
1	cup sugar	2½ to 3 cups flour
1	egg	

Mix sugar and butter and almond flavoring. Beat well, then add egg and 2½ cups all purpose flour. Beat well in mixer. You should have a fairly stiff dough, one that will hold it's shape when put through the cookie press. You may need the additional flour. Bake on lightly greased cookie sheets in a 325° oven until light brown. Another way to form the dough is to make small rings from the narrow fluted knife of a cookie press and, especially for Christmas, dust them with red sugar.

I had a Swedish cookie press with a handle at one end that turned, much easier than the heavy ones you have to squeeze. I used a "ribbon" knife which extruded the dough in a ribbon 1" wide, which I cut into 2" lengths on the pan before they cooled.

Diane's Brownies

2 eggs. slightly beaten	1½ (1 ounce) squares
1 cup sugar	unsweetened chocolate,
½ cup flour	broken up
¼ teaspoon salt	½ cup chopped pecans
½ cup melted butter	1 teaspoon vanilla

Place butter in heavy saucepan, add chocolate and place over very low heat until melted. Beat eggs in mixer bowl, then add rest of ingredients including melted chocolate. Mix well. Pour into a 9″ square cake pan and bake at 325° until barely firm in center. Do not over bake. Cool and cut into squares.

Yield: 9″ square cake pan

Honey Bars

These are a granola-type bar, a good and healthful snack.

¼ cup butter or margarine	¼ cup honey
¼ firmly packed light brown	½ teaspoon vanilla extract
sugar	2 cups quick cooking oats

Melt butter in saucepan, then add rest of ingredients; stir until blended. Press into a well buttered 8″ cake pan. Bake at 400° for 15 minutes or until brown on the edges. Let cool about 10 minutes, then cut into bars while still warm. Let remain in pan until cold.

Yield: 15 1″ × 1¾″ bars

Chewy Coconut Macaroons

These are deliciously moist and chewy

1 stick butter or margarine,	1 cup molasses
room temperature	2⅔ cups moist coconut
½ cup brown sugar, packed	2 cups flour

Cream butter and brown sugar until light and fluffy. Stir in molasses, coconut and flour. Put batter in refrigerator over night. Drop by teaspoonfuls on well-greased cookie sheets. Bake at 350° about 20 minutes or until they hold together when touched. Let macaroons cool partly before removing from pan. Dip in powdered sugar when cold.

Yield: About 4 dozen

Polly's Chocolate Snowballs

1¼ cups butter or margarine
⅔ cup sugar
1 teaspoon vanilla
2 cups flour

⅛ teaspoon salt
½ cup cocoa
2 cups finely chopped pecans
Powdered sugar

Cream butter and sugar until light and fluffy. Add vanilla, then sift together the flour, cocoa and salt. Add chopped nuts, and add to creamed mixture. Mix well. Chill in refrigerator several hours. Then form into balls about the size of marbles. Place on an ungreased cookie sheet and bake at 350° for 20 minutes. Roll in sifted powdered sugar. Store in refrigerator.

Yield: 6 dozen

Cookie or Candy

1½ squares unsweetened chocolate
2 tablespoons shortening
1 teaspoon vanilla

1 cup sugar
2 eggs, well beaten
½ cup flour
1 cup raisins, chopped

Melt chocolate and shortening in heavy saucepan, add vanilla and sugar, cream well. Add eggs, flour and raisins, beat well. Pour into a shallow greased 8″×8″ pan. Bake at 350° for about 30 minutes or until just done in center. Cool and cut into squares.

Yield: 16 2″ bars

Diane's Sand Tarts

2 sticks margarine, softened
½ cup sugar
2 cups flour

½ cup pecans, finely chopped
1 teaspoon vanilla

Cream margarine and sugar. Add flour, nuts and vanilla. Mix well. Pinch off balls of dough about 1½″ in diameter. Form either into balls or crescent shape. Bake on ungreased cookie sheets in a 300° oven until lightly brown on bottom, about 15 to 20 minutes. Roll in sifted powdered sugar.

Yield: About 60 small tarts

Butter Drops

These are the most delicate and delicious cookies you will ever taste. They are light as air and habit forming. I raved over them so much when I first tasted them that my hostess insisted on giving me the rest of the batch.

1 cup butter	1 teaspoon vanilla
½ cup powdered sugar	
1¾ cups flour lightly measured and leveled off	

Place all ingredients in bowl of mixer, beat at high speed for 10 minutes. This is the secret of their lightness. Drop by well-rounded teaspoonfuls onto lightly greased cookie sheet. Bake at 300° until lightly brown on bottom, about 20 minutes. Top will not be brown. Time depends on how large the "drops" are. Remove from pan carefully with a metal spatula. Cool, then store in a tightly covered container in refrigerator.

Yield: About 65 drops

Do not substitute for the butter.

Chocolate Date Brownies

2 (1 ounce) squares unsweetened baking chocolate	½ teaspoon baking powder
	¼ teaspoon salt
	½ cup toasted pecans, chopped
⅓ cup margarine (⅔ stick)	
2 eggs, beaten	½ cup chopped dates
1 cup sugar	1 teaspoon vanilla
¾ cup flour	

Combine margarine and chocolate in top of double boiler; place over boiling water. Immediately reduce heat to low; cook until chocolate is melted. Remove from hot water and cool.

Combine eggs and sugar; beat well, then add chocolate mixture. Combine flour, baking powder and salt and stir into batter. Reserve 2 tablespoons of the toasted pecans. Add the rest along with the dates and vanilla to batter. Spoon batter into a greased and floured 8″ square pan; sprinkle with the 2 tablespoons toasted pecans. Bake at 350° for 20 to 25 minutes or until a wooden pick inserted in the center comes out clean but not dry. Cool and cut into squares.

Yield: 16 squares

Kathryn's Chocolate Candy Ring

This is pretty on a buffet table with the center filled with green grapes.

6   ounces semi-sweet
    chocolate morsels
6   ounces butterscotch morsels
1   can sweetened Eagle Brand
    milk

1   cup chopped pecans
½   teaspoon vanilla
1   cup pecan halves

Melt milk, chocolate and butterscotch morsels over hot, not boiling water. Remove from heat and add nuts and vanilla, blend well. Chill until thickened. Line a round cake pan with heavy duty foil. Place pecan halves in a circle on the bottom. Pour thickened chocolate, butterscotch mixture carefully in the pan making a ring. Chill overnight in the refrigerator. To serve, place ring with nut-side up on a pretty serving plate and fill center with green grapes. Have a small, sharp knife near so guests can cut their own portions.

Fudge Bars or Pie

Mary was the best cook I ever had. This is her recipe. She lived on the place and had a natural talent for baking as well as seasoning foods.

½   cup butter, do not substitute
4   eggs, beaten
½   teaspoon salt
2   teaspoons vanilla
2   cups sugar

4   (1 ounce) squares
    unsweetened chocolate,
    melted
⅔   cup flour
1   cup chopped nuts

Cream butter and sugar, add beaten eggs, then melted chocolate. Stir in flour and salt, nuts and vanilla. Mix well. Spread mixture ½" thick in a buttered 9" × 13" baking pan; or in two buttered 9" pie tins, if making pies. Bake at 300° for 20 minutes or until barely done in center when toothpick in inserted. Pies should be baked for 20 minutes also. They can be left in the pans until served cut into wedges with a sharp, thin knife. As in previous directions, cut bars while still lukewarm with thin sharp knife. Remove from pan carefully. Dust with sifted powdered sugar, if desired.

Yield: 24 squares or 2 9" pies

These bars must be cut with a very sharp knife while still lukewarm as they are very delicate. Handle carefully.

Chocolate Coconut Macaroons

1	(4 ounce) package German Sweet chocolate, cut into bits	½	cup sugar
		¼	teaspoon vanilla
		7	ounces flaked coconut
2	egg whites, room temperature		

Place chocolate in top of a double boiler; bring water to a boil. Reduce heat to a simmer and cook until chocolate melts, stirring occasionally. Remove from heat and cool. Beat egg whites at high speed for 1 minute, gradually add sugar, 1 tablespoon at a time, beating until stiff but not dry peaks form. Add melted chocolate and vanilla; blend well. Stir in coconut. Drop by teaspoonfuls onto cookie sheets lined with brown paper. Bake at 350° for 12 to 15 minutes. Transfer cookies, leaving them on the brown paper, to cooling rack to cool. Carefully remove from paper. Store in covered container.

Yield: 4½ dozen

Peanut Butter Oat Cookies

I make these for my great grandchildren. Their mothers do not object as they are nutritious as well as good.

1	cup shortening	2	cups flour
1	cup brown sugar, packed well	¼	teaspoon soda
¾	cup sugar	2	teaspoons salt
2	eggs	1	cup quick oats
1	cup creamy peanut butter	1	teaspoon vanilla

Beat shortening and sugars together until creamy, add eggs, vanilla, and peanut butter and beat well. Combine flour, soda and salt. Add to creamed mixture, mixing well. Stir in oats. Shape dough to form 1" balls. Place on ungreased cookie sheets. With tines of a fork, make crisscrosses on each. Dip fork in flour if dough sticks to it. Bake at 350° about 8 to 10 minutes.

Yield: 6 dozen

Chocolate Chews

These are almost like caramels and so easy to make.

2	cups graham cracker crumbs	6	ounce package semi-sweet chocolate chips
1	cup sweetened condensed milk	½	cup chopped nuts

Mix all ingredients and spread in an 8″×8″ cake pan lined with waxed paper. Bake in a 350° oven for 30 minutes. Cut while warm.

Yield: 24 small chews

Chinese Crunch Balls

Serve as a dessert after a meal of Chinese food.

⅓	cup butter, do not substitute	1	(3 ounce) can Chow Mein noodles
1	cup brown sugar, packed		
4	tablespoons toasted unblanched almonds, chopped		

Melt butter in skillet, stir in sugar and cook over low heat until sugar is dissolved and bubbling. Add noodles and almonds. Mix lightly until noodles are well coated with butter mixture. Turn out on a buttered cookie sheet and pull noodles apart in bite-sized pieces. Keep in a tightly covered container.

Pecan Dainties

1	egg, beaten	5	tablespoons flour
1	cup sugar	½	teaspoon vanilla
1	cup pecans, grated		

Beat egg well, gradually add sugar and beat until light in color. Add nuts and vanilla, stir well, then add flour, gradually, scraping sides and bottom of bowl to be sure sugar mixture is well mixed in. Drop by teaspoonfuls onto greased cookie sheet, about 1½″ apart as they will spread. Bake at 350° about 10 minutes or until light brown on edges and light brown on bottom. Top will be just turning brown. Remove from pan immediately. Keep in a tightly covered container.

Yield: About 2½ dozen

Caramel Coconut Squares

1 stick margarine, softened	1 cup flour
½ cup powdered sugar	

Cream margarine and sugar until fluffy, add flour and mix well. Pat into an ungreased 9″×9″ ungreased cake pan, Bake at 350° for 12 to 15 minutes. Set aside.

Topping:

1 (14 ounce) can condensed milk	1 (3½ ounce) can flaked coconut (1⅓ cups)
1 (6 ounce) package butterscotch morsels	1 teaspoon vanilla

Combine milk, butterscotch morsels, coconut and vanilla; spread over baked layer. Bake at 350° until golden brown around the edges, 25 to 30 minutes. Cookie will not appear set, do not overcook. Cool and cut into squares.

Yield: 36 squares

Sinfully Rich Chocolate Chip Cookies

These are best served slightly warm, but delicious at any time. The nuts are optional.

1 cup butter, softened	1 teaspoon baking soda
¾ cup granulated sugar	½ teaspoon salt
¾ cup brown sugar, packed	2½ cups flour
2 teaspoons vanilla	24 ounces milk chocolate chips
1 tablespoon Tia Maria	1 cup walnut halves
1 tablespoon Frangelico	½ cup pecan halves
2 eggs	½ cup macadamia nuts

Cream butter, sugar, vanilla, Tia Maria and Frangelico until light and fluffy, add eggs and beat well. Sift flour, baking soda and salt; gradually beat into creamed mixture. Stir in chocolate chips and nuts. Mix well. Refrigerate, covered, overnight. Drop by teaspoonfuls onto ungreased cookie sheet. Bake in pre-heated 325° oven for about 10 to 13 minutes or until golden brown. Cool slightly and serve immediately while guests can still smell the delicious aroma.

Yield: 3 to 4 dozen

Polly's Pecan Macaroons

3 egg whites, beaten stiff but not dry
3 cups pecans, ground fine

2 cups brown sugar, packed
½ teaspoon cinnamon

Beat egg whites in a medium bowl, mix rest of ingredients and fold into egg whites. Shape into small balls with the hands. Place on a well greased cookie sheet. Bake in a slow oven, 300°, about 20 minutes or until slightly brown. Remove from oven and roll in sifted powdered sugar.

Yield: About 24

Easy Pecan Bars

This recipe was given to me many years ago by an artist from Fredericksburg, who was painting a picture of my son's log cabin next door to Raleigh House.

4 eggs
1 pound light brown sugar
2 teaspoons vanilla
1 or 2 cups chopped nuts

2 cups Bisquick or use 2 cups flour mixed with 1 teaspoon baking powder and ½ teaspoon salt

Beat the eggs, brown sugar and vanilla together. Add Bisquick and mix well, then add 1 or 2 cups nuts. Pour into 13″×9″×3″ well greased cake pan. Bake in a pre-heated 300° oven about 30 minutes or until barely done in center. Do not overbake as they will lose their chewiness.

Yield: 12 to 15

Mrs. Giraud's Fruit Cookies

These should be made about two weeks in advance of Christmas to season properly. They resemble fruit cake as they are full of fruit and nuts. Delicious!

½	cup butter, do not substitute	1½	pounds pecans, broken up
1	cup brown sugar, packed	4	eggs, beaten
3	cups flour	1	scant teaspoon soda
½	pound candied green pineapple, cut up	6	tablespoons brandy
½	pound candied cherries, cut up	1	teaspoon allspice
1	pound raisins	1	teaspoon cinnamon
		1	teaspoon nutmeg

Cream butter and brown sugar, add eggs. Sift flour, baking soda and spices. Add to creamed mixture. Add brandy, nuts and candied fruit. Mix well, then drop by spoonfuls onto well greased cookie sheet. Bake at 350° just until brown on bottom. When cool, place in metal can lined with film and cover with a cloth soaked in sherry.

These cookies will keep for months.

Mae's Zeppole

This delicious recipe was given to me by a friend in Florida.

1	cup Ricotta cheese — regular, beaten until very creamy	1	teaspoon rum, brandy or vanilla, whichever you prefer
1	cup Swansdown cake flour	2	tablespoons granulated sugar
2	eggs, slightly beaten		Powdered sugar
4	teaspoons baking powder		
	Dash salt		

Cream Ricotta cheese in mixture, add beaten eggs and sugar. Continue beating until well blended. Sift flour, baking powder and salt together and add to Ricotta mixture. Mix thoroughly and add rum. Mix. Allow batter to stand, covered, at room temperature, about a ½ hour. Drop by heaping teaspoonsful into 375° deep vegetable oil. Do not overcrowd the oil with batter. Dropped batter will take the shape of a ball and will roll over in the oil, cooking uniformly. Lift out zeppole with tongs when golden brown. Drain on brown paper or paper towels. Dust with powdered sugar. Serve warm.

Yield: 30 to 35 zeppole

Graham Cracker Bars

This is a recipe from the Memorial Hospital in Houston.

30	graham crackers	1	cup graham cracker crumbs
1	cup brown sugar, packed	2	cups powdered sugar
½	cup butter	5	tablespoons melted butter
½	cup milk	3	tablespoons half and half
1	cup flaked coconut	½	teaspoon vanilla

Grease a 13″×9″×2″ pan. Arrange 15 graham crackers on the bottom. In saucepan, combine sugar, butter, milk, coconut and graham cracker crumbs. Bring to a boil, lower heat and cook about 10 minutes, stirring constantly. This will burn very easily so watch carefully. Spread evenly over crackers, then top with remaining crackers. Beat powdered sugar, melted butter, half and half and vanilla until smooth. Spread over top layer of crackers. Cover with waxed paper or film and let stand overnight in refrigerator. Cut into 1″×3″ bars.

Yield: 39 Bars

Chocolate Pecan Graham Bars

22	graham cracker bars	½	cup sugar
1	cup chocolate morsels (6 ounces)	1	teaspoon vanilla
2	sticks butter or margarine	1	cup chopped pecans or slivered almonds

Melt butter in saucepan, add sugar and cook for 2 minutes. Remove from heat and add chocolate morsels and the vanilla. Stir until chocolate is melted. Line cookie sheet with foil. Lay graham crackers on foil. Pour chocolate mixture over and sprinkle with pecans or almonds. Bake at 350° for 8 minutes. Cut into fingers.

Yield: 44 fingers

Ann's Toffee Bars

1½	cups sugar	1	cup slivered almonds
2	sticks butter	15	graham crackers

Melt butter in saucepan, add sugar and cook for 5 minutes. Pour over crackers on a foil-lined cookie sheet sprinkle slivered almonds over and bake at 350° for 8 minutes. Cool and cut into fingers.

Yield: 44 fingers

Vienna Tarts

I first ate these at a friend's house over 50 years ago.

1 cup flour	4½ ounces cream cheese, room
¼ teaspoon salt	temperature
1 stick butter, do not	Fruit jam of your choice
substitute	

Sift flour and salt together, then cut in butter and cream cheese. When blended, wrap dough in foil and refrigerate for at least 12 hours. Roll ⅛" thick, adding as little flour to the board as possible. Cut into about 2" or 2½" squares. Dot with jam and pinch opposite corners together. Place on ungreased cookie sheet and bake at 325° until light brown.

This pastry can be cut into rounds and sprinkled with sesame seeds to be served as a snack or appetizer, or rolled and cut into rounds to fit muffin tins or individual tart pans. Bake and fill with filling of your choice.

Grandmother's Shortbread

1 stick butter, do not	1 cup flour, less 2
substitute	tablespoonsful
⅓ cup light brown sugar,	¼ teaspoon cinnamon
packed	⅔ cup quick oats

Cream butter and sugar in mixer until light and fluffy. Sift flour, and cinnamon and add to oats in a bowl, then add to creamed mixture, mix just until combined. Press into ungreased pie tin or 9" square cake pan. Bake at 350° for 40 minutes. Mark in wedges for the pie tin, in squares for cake pan. When cool, break into portions.

Yield: 8 to 10 wedges or squares

Oatmeal Fudge Cookies

2 cups sugar	1 stick butter or margarine
½ cup milk	3 cups Quick oats
½ cup cocoa	2 teaspoons vanilla

Mix sugar, milk, cocoa and butter in a saucepan and boil, stirring constantly, 2 minutes or until 230°F on candy thermometer. Remove from fire and stir in oats, add vanilla. Mix well and drop by spoonfuls on waxed paper. These do not have to be baked. Refrigerate in covered container.

Yield: About 3 dozen

Mother's Shortbread

Be sure to use butter to make this.

1 cup butter, softened, do not substitute

½ cup superfine sugar, if you do not have superfine sugar, put granulated sugar in blender and blend until fine. Measure after you have blended it.

2½ cups flour

In mixer, beat butter and sugar at high speed until light and fluffy and sugar is dissolved. Reduce speed to medium and add flour in 3 additions, beating after each addition until mixture is smooth. Chill for 1 hour.

On a lightly floured board, roll dough into a rectangle approximately 8" × 6" and ⅓" thick. Cut into 12 2" squares with a knife dipped in flour. Cut squares diagonally into triangles. Prick with tines of a fork and place on ungreased cookie sheets at least 1" apart. Bake at 350° about 15 minutes or until lightly brown on edges. Cool, then store in tightly covered container. Recipe can be doubled.

Yield: 24 triangles

Almond Shortbread

These are delicious served on a dessert plate with fresh fruit and garnished with whipped cream and sliced toasted almonds.

1 stick unsalted butter

¼ cup sugar

½ teaspoon vanilla

¼ teaspoon almond extract

¼ teaspoon salt

1 cup plus 3 tablespoons flour

⅓ cup blanched, toasted almonds, finely chopped

Cream butter and sugar in mixer, add vanilla, almond extract and salt and beat until mixture is light and fluffy. Beat in flour, then add the almonds, Mix again. Roll the dough on a floured piece of waxed paper into a 9" round. Transfer it on the paper to a baking sheet. Dip a sharp knife in flour and press it ¹⁄₁₆" deep into dough to mark 8 wedges. Sprinkle with 1 to 2 tablespoons sugar and bake at 375° for 15 to 20 minutes, or until it is light brown on the edges and light brown on bottom. Finish cutting into wedges with a sharp knife while still warm.

Yield: 8 t0 10 wedges

Ladyfingers

½   cup flour, sifted before   ⅛   teaspoon salt
      measuring   3   eggs, separated
⅔   cup powdered sugar, sifted ½   teaspoon pure vanilla
      after measuring

Sift the flour, ⅓ cup of the sugar and the salt together 3 times. Beat egg whites until soft peaks form, then beat in remaining sugar. Beat the egg yolks and vanilla until thick and lemon-colored. Sift the flour mixture, ⅓ at a time, over the eggs and fold in with a spatula. Then fold in beaten egg whites. Line ungreased baking sheets with brown paper or parchment. Press the batter through a pastry tube without a tip in it onto the paper or shape batter with a spoon into strips about 4″ × ¾″. Bake in a 350° oven 12 to 15 minutes or until golden brown. Remove from pan and cool on wire rack.

Great Grandchildren's Brownie Mix

I make this mix for my great grandchildren who like to cook. They can mix it by themselves, which they like.

4   cups all purpose flour   8   cups sugar
1   tablespoon plus 2 teaspoons 2½   cups cocoa
      baking powder   2   cups shortening
1   tablespoons salt

Combine first 5 ingredients and mix well. Cut in shortening with a pastry blender or tips of fingers as you would for pie crust, until mixture resembles coarse meal. Place in an air-tight container and store in refrigerator.

For brownies:
3   cups brownie mix   1½   teaspoons vanilla
3   eggs, beaten   ½   cup chopped nuts (optional)

Combine all ingredients. Stir until well mixed. Spoon into a greased and floured 8″ pan. Bake at 350° for 30 to 35 minutes. Do not overbake. Cool and cut into 16 squares.

Yield: 16 cups

Mix keeps in refrigerator for up to six weeks.

Crunchy Chocolate Cookies

1¼ cups flour
½   teaspoon soda
¼   teaspoon salt
1   stick margarine, softened,
    (½ cup)
1   cup sugar

1   egg
1   teaspoon vanilla
2   cups Rice Krispies
6   ounce package (1 cup) semi-
    sweet chocolate morsels

Sift together flour, soda and salt. Set aside. Place margarine and sugar in mixing bowl; beat until well blended and smooth, add egg and vanilla; beat well. Sift dry ingredients, add to creamed mixture and mix until combined. Fold in Rice Krispies and chocolate morsels. Drop by level tablespoonfuls onto lightly greased cookie sheets. Bake at 350° about 12 minutes or until lightly browned. Remove immediately. Store in covered container.

Yield: 3½ dozen

Mrs Wahlborg's Coconut Cookies

I knew Mrs. Wahlborg when I was a new bride. She taught me many things about cooking.

2   cups coconut
2   cups quick oatmeal
½   cup butter and
½   cup Crisco or
1   cup Crisco
1   cup sugar
1   cup brown sugar, packed

2   eggs
2   cups flour
2   teaspoons soda
½   teaspoon salt
1   teaspoon baking powder
1   teaspoon vanilla

Cream butter and Crisco or all Crisco with both sugars until light and fluffy, add eggs and mix well. Sift dry ingredients, add and mix well, then mix in oatmeal, vanilla and coconut. Make dough into balls the size of a large marble. Place them on a greased cookie sheet about 2″ apart as they will spread while cooking. Bake at 350° about 15 minutes.

Yield: about 5 dozen

Coconut Belles

I have used this recipe as a dessert by cutting in larger pieces and serving with whipped cream or ice cream. I have had this recipe well over 50 years.

⅓	cup Crisco	1	teaspoon lemon juice
1	cup sugar	1½	cups flour
2	eggs (reserve 1 white for meringue topping)	1	teaspoon baking powder
		½	teaspoon salt
1	teaspoon vanilla	2	tablespoons milk

Cream Crisco and sugar, add eggs then add sifted dry ingredients. Add lemon juice, vanilla and milk, mix well. Pour into greased 8″ × 10″ pan. Top with Meringue topping and bake at 350° about 25 minutes or when a toothpick inserted in center comes out clean.

Meringue Topping:

1	egg white, beaten until stiff, not dry peaks form.	½	teaspoon milk
1	cup brown sugar, packed	⅔	cup flaked coconut

Mix all ingredients together gently and spread over unbaked cake layer. Cut into squares when cool.

Yield: 12 to 15 squares

Trinity Squares

This was given to me by one of my waitresses at Raleigh House, who loved to cook. It can also be used as a dessert by cutting into bigger portions and serving with ice cream.

½	cup butter or margarine	2	cups all purpose flour
2	cups brown sugar, packed	½	teaspoon soda
2	eggs	2	teaspoons baking powder
1	cup prepared mincemeat	1	teaspoon vanilla

Melt butter or margarine, add sugar, mix well. Then add eggs and vanilla, mix again. Then stir in mincemeat. Sift dry ingredients and add. Place in a greased 9″ × 13″ pan. Bake at 350° for 35 or 40 minutes or until done in center. Dust with powdered sugar and cut into squares.

Yield: 12 to 15 squares

Susan's Fudge Muffins

This is also a recipe from the waitress at Raleigh House. They are delicious and "fudgy" if not overcooked.

1	stick butter, do not substitute	¾	cup flour
1	(1 ounce) square unsweetened chocolate	2	eggs
		1	teaspoon vanilla
1	cup sugar	½	cup chopped nuts

Melt butter and chocolate in 200° oven or in heavy saucepan. Add sugar and mix well, then add eggs, flour and vanilla and mix well again. Stir in pecans. Spoon into muffin tins either buttered or sprayed with vegetable spray. Bake in a 350° oven 15 minutes for the small muffins, 25 to 30 minutes for the large or until a toothpick inserted in the center comes out clean but not dry.

Yield: 1 dozen large, 3 dozen small

The small muffins, baked in petite muffin pans are more suitable for parties, the large for the family to eat.

Skillet Cookies

I begged this recipe from a member of the Theta sorority. They freeze well, covered tightly, but will keep in the refrigerator for weeks.

1	stick butter, do not substitute	1½ cups finely chopped dates
1	cup brown sugar, packed	3 cups Rice Krispies
1	egg, beaten	Flaked coconut

Place butter and sugar in electric skillet. Cook at medium heat until butter and sugar are melted. Add a little of the hot mixture to the beaten egg, then add to skillet, mixing well. Add dates and cook at medium low heat for 5 minutes, stirring constantly. Turn off heat and fold in Rice Krispies. Roll into 1" balls between palms of the hands, then drop into the coconut and coat well. Set on waxed paper until cool.

Yield: About 5 dozen 1" balls.

Bourbon Bars

1	cup butter	2	cups flour plus 2
1	pound brown sugar		tablespoons
2	eggs, well beaten	1	teaspoon baking powder
⅔	cup bourbon	2	cups chopped pecans
1	teaspoon vanilla		

In heavy saucepan over low heat, melt butter, add brown sugar, Blend well and set aside. When cool, stir in eggs, bourbon and vanilla. Sift flour and baking powder together and stir into mixture. Add nuts and mix well. Divide between 2 greased and floured 7″×11″ pans. Bake at 350° 20 to 30 minutes or until barely done (when a toothpick is inserted in center and it comes out clean but moist). When cool, spread with a thin coating of butter icing. Cut into bars when icing has set.

Butter Icing:

3	cups powdered sugar	About 3 tablespoons cream
⅔	stick margarine or butter, softened	2 teaspoons bourbon

Blend all ingredients together. Add more cream, if necessary, until icing is of spreading consistency.

Yield: 24 bars

Brickle Blondies

This is delicious and moist, if not overbaked. Can be cut into larger portions and used as a dessert with whipped cream or ice cream.

1½	cups flour	½	cup brown sugar, packed
2	teaspoons baking powder	2	eggs
½	teaspoon salt	1	teaspoon vanilla
1	stick butter or margarine	1	bag of Bits of Brickle
1	cup sugar		

Sift dry ingredients. Cream butter and both sugars until light and fluffy. Add eggs and vanilla, beat well. Add dry ingredients, mix, then stir in Brickle. Put in a greased 13″×9″×2″ pan. Bake at 350° about 30 minutes or when toothpick inserted in center comes out clean but not dry. Cool and cut into squares.

Yield: 12 to 15

Marguerites

This is another of my Mother's recipes. Easy to make and delicious.

2	egg whites, room temperature	¼	teaspoon vanilla
¾	cup sugar	¼	teaspoon almond flavoring
¼	teaspoon salt	1	cup chopped pecans

Beat egg whites with salt until foamy, add sugar gradually by tablespoonfuls, beating well after each addition. Beat until stiff but not dry. Add flavorings and pecans. Drop by rounded teaspoonfuls onto saltine crackers, flattening slightly so most of saltine is covered. Bake at 300° 8 to 10 minutes or until meringue is lightly browned. Do not try to make these on a rainy day.

For chocolate marguerites, fold in 1 (1 ounce) square of unsweetened chocolate, melted,into finished meringue.

Yield: 3 dozen

Do not overbake as meringue needs to be soft, not crisp. This is one of many recipes using egg whites, so remember to freeze any whites left over from other recipes. Put in freezer-proof jars. Thaw and use as you would fresh ones.

Moist Almond Macaroons

¼	pound blanched whole almonds	¼	teaspoon almond extract
⅓	cup sliced blanched almonds, optional	¼	teaspoon salt
½	cup sugar	2	large egg whites, room temperature

Finely grind the whole almonds, sugar, almond extract and salt in a food processor with a metal blade. Place into medium-size bowl. Beat egg whites until they just make soft peaks. Fold ¼ into almond mixture to lighten, then gently but thoroughly, fold in the rest. Line a cookie sheet with parchment paper, lightly buttered. Drop by teaspoonfuls 2 inches apart and sprinkle with sliced almonds, if you like. Bake in a 300° oven on the middle shelf, for 15 to 20 minutes or until lightly brown around edges. Let them cool, then peel off parchment and keep in tightly covered container.

Yield: About 40

Caramel Meringue Bars

1½	cups sifted flour	2	eggs, separated
1	teaspoon baking powder	½	cup brown sugar, packed
½	teaspoon salt	1	teaspoon vanilla
¼	cup shortening	¾	cup chopped nuts

Combine flour, baking powder and salt, cut in shortening until mixture resembles coarse meal. Add egg yolks and mix until crumbly and thoroughly combined. Press in bottom of a 7" x 11" baking pan.

Beat egg whites until soft peaks form, add brown sugar by tablespoonfuls, beating well after each addition. Beat whites to stiff peaks. Fold in nuts and vanilla. Spread on top of crumb mixture. Bake at 325° about 25 to 30 minutes or until lightly browned.

Yield: 30 Bars

Amaretto Macaroons

¾	cup almonds, blanched and skinned	2	egg whites
		2	tablespoons powdered sugar
1¼	cups sugar	1	teaspoonful almond extract

Dry almonds in 325° oven for about 5 minutes. Remove and grind in food processor with sugar until it makes a paste. Add unbeaten egg whites a little at a time. Add almond extract. Batter will be like a soft dough. Drop by teaspoonfuls, 2" apart, onto parchment or foil-lined cookie sheet. Bake on the middle shelf of a 300° oven for 15 or 30 minutes or until golden brown on the edges. Let them cool on the parchment, then peel off and store in a covered container.

Yield: About 30 macaroons

Pecan Macaroons

My Mother used to make these. We liked the taste of brown sugar.

¾	cup brown sugar, packed	2	cups pecan halves
1	egg white		

Beat egg white until foamy, add sugar gradually, beating mixture until stiff. Fold in pecans, mixing well. Drop by tablespoons, 2" apart, onto cookie sheet lined with foil. Bake 30 minutes in a 275° oven. Let cool before removing from foil.

Confections

Butterscotch Bars

⅔ cup light corn syrup
¼ teaspoon salt
3 tablespoons butter
1 cup butterscotch flavored
   morsels

6 cups bite-size shredded rice
   cereal
1 cup raisins or nuts

In a large microwave-safe bowl, combine corn syrup, butter and salt. Microwave on high for 2 to 3 minutes or until mixture boils. Add butterscotch morsels and stir until mixture is smooth. Stir in cereal and raisins or nuts and press into a foil-lined 13″ × 9″ pan. Chill until firm, then cut into 2″ × 1″ bars. Store in air-tight container.

Yield: 4½ dozen

Patti's Pralines

2 cups sugar
1 cup milk
½ teaspoon vanilla

8 large marshmallows
2 tablespoons margarine
2 or 3 cups pecans

Combine sugar, milk and marshmallows in a heavy 4 quart pan. Cook over medium heat, stirring constantly, to 230° on candy thermometer (soft ball stage). Remove from heat and stir in vanilla and margarine. Beat until creamy, then add pecans and beat until thickened. Drop on waxed paper by spoonfuls. Store in covered container.

Creamy Pralines

2 cups granulated sugar
1 cup brown sugar, packed
½ cup sweetened condensed
   milk
½ stick butter

¼ teaspoon salt
1 teaspoon vanilla
3 cups coarsely broken
   pecans

Combine ingredients in heavy saucepan and bring to a boil over medium heat. Add 3 cups broken pecans and continue boiling until soft ball stage (230°). Remove from heat, add vanilla and stir just enough to give a creamy look. Spoon onto buttered baking sheets. Cool and store in covered container.

Yield: 6 dozen small pralines

Selma's Buttermilk Pralines

3	cups white sugar	1	teaspoon vanilla
1	teaspoon baking soda	½	teaspoon salt
1	cup buttermilk	½	stick butter
3	cups pecans		

Cook sugar, soda and buttermilk to soft ball stage, (230°). Remove from heat, add pecans, vanilla, salt and butter. Beat until creamy and spoon onto waxed paper.

Yield: About 30 pralines

Patti's Peanut Brittle

1½	cups sugar	1½	cups raw peanuts
¼	cup water	1½	teaspoons baking soda
¾	cups white corn syrup		

In a very large saucepan, mix sugar, water and syrup. add peanuts and bring to a boil. Cook until peanuts begin to pop or until syrup begins to brown. Remove from heat and vigorously stir in soda until well mixed. Pour onto a foil-lined cookie sheet. quickly spread as thin as possible, but do not stir after poured. Break into pieces when cool. Be sure to make this in a very large pan as brittle will foam up and boil over the sides of a too small pan.

Polly's Two Ingredient Fudge

There are 3 variations: Turn fudge into pan, cut in squares and press a toasted almond in each square: Shape fudge into balls and roll in chopped salted peanuts or coconut: Shape into balls and press whole pecan or walnut onto each ball.

12	ounces semi-sweet chocolate morsels	¾	cup sweetened condensed milk

Melt chocolate over hot, not boiling, water in top of a double boiler. Remove from heat and stir in milk. Mix until well blended. Turn in buttered pan and cut or shape in desired form. Allow to stand several hours.

This is the easiest fudge recipe I know of. Recipe may be doubled, if you want a thicker fudge.

Pulled Molasses Taffy

Taffy pulls were very popular in my day and great entertainment for an afternoon or evening party. I had them for my children, but they seem to have declined in popularity. It is still fascinating to see this taffy change to a light, golden color.

2 cups light molasses	½ teaspoon baking soda
2 teaspoons cider vinegar	Plenty of extra butter for
1½ teaspoons butter	rubbing on hands when
⅛ teaspoon salt	pulling

In 3 quart saucepan, mix molasses and vinegar. Cook gently to 260° on a candy thermometer or until a little dropped into ice water becomes brittle. Remove from heat and add butter, salt and baking soda. Stir until foaming stops. Pour into well-buttered small pans (we used pie tins, as many as we had small children who wanted to pull).

As taffy cools, grease your fingers and pull away from sides of the pan into the center. As soon as it has cooled enough to handle, butter your hands and gather up taffy and pull into a rope, then fold over and keep pulling until a light golden color and taffy is getting firm. Spread into a rope onto a table or cookie sheet and cut with scissors into 1 or 1½" pieces. Wrap each piece in waxed paper.

Caramel Taffy

Vanilla or peppermint taffy can be made by substituting granulated sugar for the brown sugar and vanilla extract or peppermint extract or peppermint oil for the flavoring.

2 cups light brown sugar, packed	2 tablespoons butter
1 cup white corn syrup	1 teaspoon vanilla

Put all ingredients except vanilla into a large saucepan. Cook, stirring, until sugar is dissolved. Then cook to 270° on candy thermometer. Add vanilla. Pour into buttered pans and proceed according to directions for Molasses Taffy.

English Toffee

½ cup chopped toasted
almonds
1 cup butter, do not substitute
1 cup sugar
3 tablespoons water

1 tablespoon light corn syrup
¾ cup semi-sweet chocolate
morsels
½ cup chopped toasted
almonds

Line 13″×9″×2″ pan with foil letting it extend over edge of pan. Sprinkle ½ cup nuts over bottom. Butter sides of a heavy 2 quart saucepan. Melt butter in it over low heat, stir in sugar, 3 tablespoons water and corn syrup. Cook over medium heat to boiling, stirring constantly with a wooden spoon - about 4 minutes- until sugar is dissolved. Clip thermometer to side of pan and continue to cook until thermometer reaches 290°. Pour mixture over nuts in prepared pan. Let stand until surface is firm, then spread chocolate on top and sprinkle with remaining nuts, pressing into chocolate. Cool and break into pieces.

Vanilla Fudge

This recipe came from an old friend. It is a cream-color vanilla fudge, a change from the usual chocolate. Let ripen one day before eating.

2 cups sugar
1 cup heavy cream

⅛ teaspoon salt
1 teaspoon pure vanilla

Butter an 8″ square pan, set aside. In a 3 quart heavy saucepan, combine the sugar, cream and salt. Bring to a boil, stirring, over medium heat. Cover and boil 2 or 3 minutes. Uncover and wash down the sides with a pastry brush dipped in cold water. Continue to boil without stirring, over medium heat until mixture reaches 234° on a candy thermometer (soft ball stage). Remove from heat; cool without stirring, to 110° (lukewarm). Stir in vanilla and beat until creamy. Spread in pan and cover with a damp towel or paper towel for 30 minutes. This will keep it creamy. Uncover; let set until firm, then cut into 25 squares.

Yield: 25 Squares

Peanut Butter Fudge

2 cups sugar	⅛ teaspoon salt
¾ cup milk or ¾ cup cream	¼ cup creamy peanut butter
2 tablespoons white corn syrup	1 teaspoon vanilla

Butter an 8″ square pan. In 3 quart heavy saucepan, mix well the sugar,milk, corn syrup and salt. Bring to a boil over medium heat, stirring, boil for 3 minutes, then wash down sides with a pastry brush dipped in cold water. Continue boiling, stirring once in a while until thermometer reaches 234° (soft ball stage). Cool to lukewarm, add peanut butter and vanilla and stir until creamy and thickened. Pour into pan. When firm, cut into squares.

Yield: 25 squares

Sherry Walnuts or Pecans

1½ cups sugar	3 cups walnut or pecan halves
½ cup sherry	½ teaspoon cinnamon
Pinch salt	

Lightly butter cookie sheet. In 3 quart heavy saucepan over low heat, stir sugar, sherry and salt until sugar dissolves. Bring to a boil; cover; and boil 3 minutes. Wash down sides with a pastry brush dipped in cold water. Cook, stirring occasionally, until mixture reaches 236° on candy thermometer, (soft ball stage). Remove from heat and add walnuts or pecans and cinnamon. Stir rapidly until mixture looks cloudy. Turn out on the cookie sheet. Separate nuts with 2 forks and let cool.

Yield: 4 cups

Orange Sugared Pecans

1 cup sugar	3 tablespoons frozen orange juice, undiluted
2 cups pecan halves	

Cook orange juice and sugar over low heat in a heavy saucepan, stirring, until sugar dissolves. Cook over low heat to 240°, (soft ball stage). Remove from heat and add pecans. Stir until mixture begins to thicken, then drop with a teaspoon onto a sheet of waxed paper. Allow to cool, keep in a covered container.

Spiced Pecans

½ cup sugar	2 tablespoons water
½ teaspoon salt	1 cup whole nuts of your
1 teaspoon cinnamon	choice
¼ teaspoon each nutmeg and cloves	

Mix all ingredients together except nuts, cook to 235° or soft ball stage. Add the nuts and remove from heat. Beat until mixture thickens. Either pour into a buttered 8″ square pan or drop by spoonfuls onto waxed paper.

Minted Walnuts or Pecans

1 cup granulated sugar	Few drops peppermint extract
⅓ cup water	or peppermint oil, (if you
⅛ teaspoon salt	are using the oil, 1 or 2
4 large marshmallows	drops should be enough, it
	is very strong)
	2½ cups nuts

Combine sugar, water and salt in a heavy saucepan. Cook to 236° or soft ball stage. Remove from heat and add marshmallows, stirring until they are melted. Add flavoring and nuts. Beat until mixture becomes creamy. Turn out on waxed paper and separate nuts with 2 forks.

Yield: 1 pound

Molasses Popcorn Balls

When we were children, my mother made these using puffed rice or puffed wheat instead of popcorn — a clever way to get us to eat more cereal. They were very good, too.

6 cups popcorn, puffed rice or puffed wheat	½ cup white corn syrup
½ cup light molasses	1½ teaspoon vinegar
	1½ tablespoons butter

Combine molasses, corn syrup and vinegar in a 2 quart saucepan. Cook, stirring occasionally, to 240° on a candy thermometer. Continue cooking, stirring constantly, until thermometer registers 270°. Remove from heat and add the butter. Stir just enough to mix. Pour over popcorn in a very large bowl or pan and toss with a fork until coated. Quickly, with lightly buttered hands, shape into 2½″ balls. Place on waxed paper to cool, then enjoy.

Candied Orange Peel

My mother always made this for Christmas. When I was growing up, oranges were very scarce in Pennsylvania so were a delicacy. There was always one in the toe of our stocking Christmas morning.

4	navel oranges	1	cup water
2½	cups sugar, reserving ½ cup for dipping	¼	cup light corn syrup

Remove orange peel in about ⅓" wide strips with a sharp knife, leaving some of the white on the orange. Cut into 3" lengths. Put in a large, heavy saucepan and cover with cold water. Bring to a boil and boil 3 minutes. Drain, and repeat the procedure 3 times in all, discarding the water each time and replacing it with fresh. Drain peel after last boiling and set it aside in a bowl. Rinse out the saucepan and combine 2 cups of the sugar, water and syrup in it. Place over medium heat and cook, stirring, until sugar dissolves. Add orange peel, turn heat to simmer and cook gently, until peel is translucent, about 30 minutes. Cool in syrup about 45 minutes, then lift out each strip with a fork, draining over edge of pan, and roll in the reserved ½ cup sugar. Place on waxed paper to firm up.

Homemade Almond Paste

8	ounces blanched whole almonds	1	egg white
		1	teaspoon almond extract
1½	cups powdered sugar	¼	teaspoon salt

Grind almonds a part at a time, in a blender or food processor until fine meal. Combine the almonds, sugar, egg white, salt and extract and work into a stiff paste. Store until needed in a jar or plastic bag. Keep refrigerated.

Yield: 1⅓ cups

Creamy Fudge

1	cup semi-sweet chocolate morsels	½	teaspoon vanilla
		1	cup chopped nuts
⅔	cup condensed milk		

Melt chocolate morsels over warm water, stir until smooth. Add the sweetened condensed milk and cook 10 minutes, stirring frequently. Remove from heat, add the vanilla and chopped nuts. Pour into a well-buttered shallow pan. Cool. When firm cut into squares.

Yield: 2 dozen 1½" squares

Vivian's Puppy Chow

This is addictive. It is a favorite of my whole family, particularly the great grandchildren. It can be made with the butterscotch morsels, instead of the chocolate, if you wish.

12	ounce package semi-sweet chocolate morsels	¾	cup smooth peanut butter
2	sticks margarine		Large box Rice Chex
		1	pound powdered sugar

Melt morsels and margarine in heavy skillet over low heat, stirring constantly. Add peanut butter and cook, stirring constantly, until peanut butter is well mixed in. Place Rice Chex in large dishpan or roaster and pour chocolate mixture over slowly, stirring gently, with a wooden spoon until Chex are well coated. Let set for 2 hours, Place part of the sugar in a paper or plastic bag and add part of the Rice Chex. Shake until coated with the sugar. Repeat until all are coated. Spread out on cookie sheets until dry. This amount will fill 2 cookie sheets. Place in a covered container.

Yield: About 8 or 9 cups

Caramel Popcorn Balls

¾	cup light brown sugar, firmly packed	⅛	teaspoon salt
½	cup light corn syrup	1	tablespoon butter
¼	cup water	2	quarts plus 1 cup popped corn (9 cups)

Combine all ingredients except popped corn in a heavy 3 quart saucepan. Bring to a boil, stirring occasionally, and cook until thermometer registers 270°. Place popcorn in a large bowl. Pour syrup over and toss with a fork or wooden spoon until corn is coated. With buttered hands, form into 2½″ balls and place on waxed paper to cool.

Yield: 9 cups

Chocolate Popcorn

This is a change from the caramel corn. Nuts may be added to the mixture, if desired.

8	cups popped corn	⅓	teaspoon salt
¾	cup sugar	1½	cups semi-sweet chocolate
6	tablespoons butter or		morsels
	margarine	1½	teaspoons vanilla
¼	cup plus 2 tablespoons light	2	cups nuts (optional)
	corn syrup		

Combine sugar, corn syrup, butter and salt in heavy saucepan. Bring to a boil, stirring, until sugar is dissolved. Lower heat and simmer 5 minutes, stirring occasionally. Add the chocolate morsels and stir until morsels are melted and mixture is smooth. Remove from heat and add vanilla and the nuts, if desired. Pour over the popped corn on a buttered large cookie sheet with 1″ sides. Bake in a 250° oven for 1 hour, stirring 4 or 5 times. Remove from oven and spoon onto waxed paper. Separate into small clumps. Cool and store in a covered container.

Yield: 2 quarts

Chocolate Gelatin Squares

½	cup sugar	12	ounces semi-sweet
4	packages unflavored gelatin		chocolate morsels
1½	cup cold water	1	cup chopped pecans

Mix gelatin with sugar in a medium heavy saucepan, then blend in water. Let stand 1 minute, then place over low heat and stir constantly , until gelatin dissolves. Remove from heat and add chocolate morsels. Return to low heat and cook, stirring constantly, until chocolate is melted and mixture is smooth. Let mixture cool until lukewarm, then stir in nuts and pour into a buttered 8 or 9″ cake pan. Cool entirely, then refrigerate until firm. Cut into 1″ squares. Roll into sifted powdered sugar.

Yield: 1 (8 or 9″) pan

Aplets

1	cup unsweetened applesauce	3	envelopes unflavored gelatin
½	cup sugar	½ to ¾ cup finely chopped pecans	
1	cup water		

Mix applesauce, gelatin and sugar in heavy saucepan. Add water and mix again. Cook over low heat, stirring constantly, until gelatin and sugar are dissolved. Remove from heat and stir in nuts. Pour into a buttered 8" square cake pan. Let cool entirely, then place in refrigerator to harden. Cut into 1" squares and roll in sifted powdered sugar.

Yield: 8" cake pan

Cream Cheese Fondant

This recipe can be halved easily. However, fondant will freeze or will keep in the refrigerator in a covered plastic container for several weeks.

1	(8 ounce) package cream cheese, softened	1 to 1½ teaspoons extracts (vanilla, etc.) or ¼ teaspoon peppermint oil or concentrated oils
2	pounds powdered sugar, sifted	

Choice of food color

Place cream cheese, flavor and some of the color in bowl of mixer. Cream well, then add ¼ of the sugar, beat well, then add ¼ more, beating after each addition, add part of the remaining sugar. Mix. Add more color, if desired. Remove mixture to a board and knead in the rest of the sugar, making a stiff dough. If your mixer stalls at any time, remove mixture and knead rest of sugar in by hand. Cover or wrap with plastic to prevent drying out. Work with a small amount. Use molds for shaping.

Yield: 2½ pounds

For chocolate fondant, add 6 tablespoons cocoa and 1 teaspoon vanilla. My Mother used to stuff dates with the vanilla fondant and place a walnut or pecan half on top.

Almond Butter Brittle

1   cup blanched slivered   ½   cup sugar
     almonds   1   tablespoon light corn syrup
½   cup butter, do not substitute

Line the bottom of a 8″ or 9″ pie plate with aluminum foil. Butter foil heavily and set aside. Combine almonds, butter, sugar and corn syrup in an electric skillet. Bring to a boil over medium heat, stirring constantly. Boil, stirring constantly, until mixture turns a golden color, about 5 to 6 minutes. Spread quickly into prepared pan. Cool until firm. Lift candy out of pan by edges of foil. Peel off foil and let cool completely. Either leave whole or break into pieces.

Yield: About ¾ pound

Brickle Caramels

This is an easy, delicious candy

1   package Kraft Vanilla   9   ounces Heath Bits'O
     Caramels, 50 caramels   Brickle (1½ packages)
About ¾ pound white almond
     bark

Break bark up into pieces and place in top of a double boiler. Melt over simmering water, stirring, until melted and smooth. Remove from heat, but keep over the hot water. Place unwrapped caramels, one at a time, into melted mixture and dip out with a fork, drawing fork over edge of pan to remove excess. With another fork, ease into bowl of brickle and roll until covered. Place on cookie sheet lined with waxed paper or foil. Proceed with rest of caramels. When cold and bark has hardened, place in a container with a tight cover until served.

Yield: 50

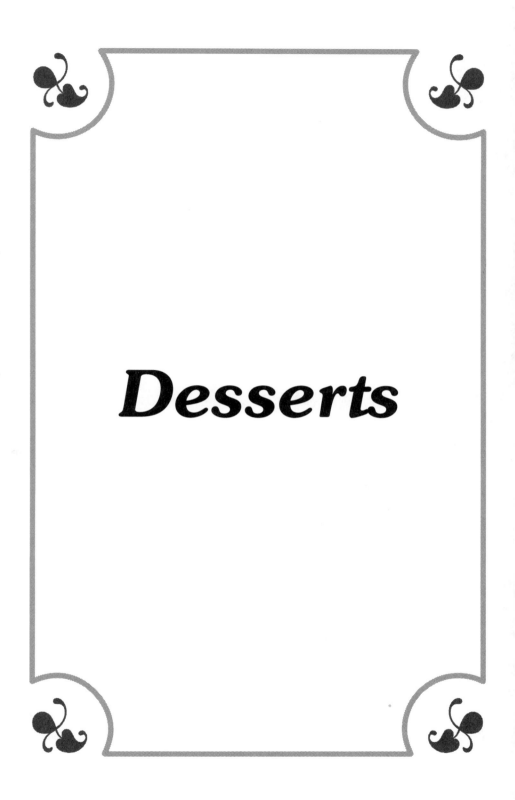

Desserts

Easy Cranberry Crunch

1   pound, 4 ounces canned or   1   tablespoon lemon juice
    frozen apple slices   1   teaspoon salt
1   (16 ounce) can whole
    cranberry sauce

Mix apples, cranberry sauce, lemon juice and salt in a bowl. Spread evenly in
a buttered 7″×11″ baking pan.

Topping:
1   teaspoon cinnamon   ¾   cup sugar
1   stick margarine or butter   ½   cup chopped pecans
½   cup flour

Mix cinnamon, flour, sugar and margarine or butter in a bowl. Cut in margarine with a pastry blender or the tips of your fingers until mixture is coarse
crumbs. Add pecans. Sprinkle over cranberry mixture and bake in a pre-
heated 350° oven for 35 or 40 minutes or until juices have thickened and
topping is golden brown. Serve warm with light cream.

Yield: 8 to 10 servings

Banana Nut Sundaes

⅓   cup chopped pecans   1   tablespoon butter,melted
⅓   cup shredded coconut   1   teaspoon lemon juice
2   tablespoons light brown   3   ripe bananas cut diagonally
    sugar, packed   in 1″ slices

Mix nuts and coconut together, then place in a 9″ pie pan. Broil 4″ from the
heat until coconut is toasted, stirring every 30 seconds. Transfer to shallow
dish. Mix light brown sugar, butter and lemon juice in a small bowl and place in
the 9″ pie pan, add the bananas, tossing to coat. Broil 4 inches from the heat
until bananas are lightly browned and sauce is carmelized. Spoon bananas into
4 dessert bowls, sprinkle with nuts and toasted coconut. Top with 2 balls of
vanilla ice cream.

Yield: 4 servings

Mrs. Sperring's Chocolate Cream Cheese Cake

This is a great dessert as it can be made days ahead of time and kept in the freezer. It is sinfully rich.

1½ cups finely crushed chocolate wafers	4 egg yolks, beaten
⅓ cup melted butter or margarine	12 ounce package semi-sweet chocolate morsels, melted
16 ounces cream cheese, softened	4 egg whites
½ cup sugar	½ cup sugar
2 teaspoons vanilla	2 cups whipping cream
	1½ cups chopped pecans

Combine the chocolate wafer crumbs and melted butter. Press onto bottom of a 9″ springform pan. Bake at 325° for 10 minutes. Set aside.

Combine cream cheese, sugar, vanilla in mixer. Mix until well blended and smooth. Add beaten egg yolks, the melted chocolate morsels, mix well. Beat the egg whites until soft peaks form, then gradually beat in the sugar by tablespoonfuls until firm, but not dry peaks form. Fold in chocolate mixture. Whip cream and add along with the chopped nuts. Pour mixture over crumbs and freeze overnight. Remove from freezer, loosen sides of pan with knife and remove sides. This dessert is very rich as it is, however, you may garnish with additional whipped cream, if you wish.

Yield: 8 to 10 servings

Cool Whip may be used instead of whipped cream.

Chocolate Pot de Creme Ice Cream

This is so rich, I usually serve it in small stemmed glasses.

½ cup water	3 egg yolks
1 (6 ounce) package semi-sweet chocolate morsels	1 (4 ounce) container whipped topping thawed

In small saucepan, heat water to boiling, Place chocolate into blender, add boiling water. Cover and blend until chocolate is melted. Add egg yolks; cover and blend until smooth, stopping to scrape sides of blender. Remove to a bowl and fold in whipped topping. Spoon into small stemmed glasses or small dessert dishes. Freeze. When serving, you may garnish with a fresh strawberry or candied violet if you wish.

Yield: 6 to 8 servings

Lemon-filled Crepes

Crepes:

3 eggs	⅛ teaspoon salt
¼ cup water	½ cup flour
½ cup milk	¼ cup oil

Place eggs, milk, water and salt in blender. Blend until mixed, then add flour and blend at high speed for 20 seconds. Turn off blender and scrape down sides with spatula. Blend at high speed for 15 seconds. Put in refrigerator for an hour. Pour 3 tablespoons batter in a heated oiled crepe pan, swirl pan to spread batter over bottom. Cook until bottom side is brown, turn out onto a towel and proceed with rest of batter. If you are using one of the new crepe pans that cook the crepe on the bottom, add 3 tablespoon more flour to batter when mixing.

Lemon filling:

2 eggs	⅔ cup sugar
1 additional egg yolk	Grated rind and juice of 1 large
½ cup butter, do not substitute	lemon

Beat eggs in a porcelain or ceramic saucepan. Do not use aluminum. Add butter, sugar, lemon rind and lemon juice. Mix well; then cook, stirring constantly, until mixture thickens. Place a crepe, brown-side down, on a cookie sheet and put a rounding teaspoonful on top. Roll up and place seam-side down on cookie sheet or shallow baking dish. Sprinkle filled crepes with mixture of ¼ cup melted butter and ¾ cup crushed almond or coconut macaroons. Warm in a 300 degree oven for 5 minutes. Serve lukewarm, 2 to a person.

Yield: 12 to 16 crepes

Jessie's Caramel Pears

4 large firm pears, peeled, cored and cut into 8ths	4 tablespoons sugar
¼ stick butter, melted	3 tablespoon heavy cream

Preheat oven to 450 degrees. Mix all ingredients together in a bowl. Put mixture in a glass or porcelain baking dish. Bake until sugar turns a light caramel color and pears are tender, about 12 minutes. Serve with light cream.

Yield: 6 servings

Greg's Nut Filling for Crepes

Filling:

16 (8″) crepes
¼   cup butter, divided
½   cup finely chopped walnuts
½   cup finely chopped
     blanched almonds

½   cup finely chopped pecans
½   cup honey

Sauté nuts in 2 tablespoons butter in medium skillet, stirring, about 5 minutes. Remove from heat and stir in the honey and remaining butter, mixing well. Place about 2 tablespoons in each crepe. Roll up. Arrange crepes, seam-side down, in sauce in chafing dish. Heat, then add rum and cognac and flame. Place 2 crepes on dessert plates and serve immediately.

Sauce:

¼   cup butter
6   tablespoons sugar
½   cup orange juice

2   tablespoons light rum
1   tablespoon cognac

Combine all except rum and cognac in a chafing dish or large skillet. Cook until sugar is dissolved.

Yield: about 16 crepes

Crepes with Strawberries and Kirsch

Quantities can be increased for more servings. Crepes can be filled ahead of time and kept in the refrigerator but should be taken out as you are serving dinner. They should be room temperature when served.

8   (8″) crepes
4   ounces cream cheese, room
     temperature
4   ounces sour cream

⅓   cup superfine sugar
¼   cup butter
1   box strawberries
2   ounces Kirsch

Mix cream cheese and sour cream in small bowl. Divide between 8 crepes. Roll up. Place 2 crepes on each of 4 dessert plates. In chafing dish, melt butter, add sugar and stir until sugar is melted. Add strawberries and heat, then add Kirsch and flame. Spoon over crepes and serve immediately.

Yield: 4 servings

Chocolate-Filled Crepes

You may also use a chocolate mousse to fill crepes. Fold 8" crepes in quarters and tuck a half cup of mousse into top layer, a sort of pocket. Sift powdered sugar over and garnish with grated sweet chocolate.

½	cup sugar	6	tablespoons cocoa
1	tablespoon cornstarch	2	tablespoons butter
2	egg yolks, beaten	10 to 12 (8 inch) crepes	
⅔	cup half and half, heated		

Beat egg yolks in a small bowl of electric mixer until thick and lemon-colored. Mix sugar, cornstarch and cocoa together and add to yolks. Mix, then add heated cream gradually, beating until light and fluffy. Pour into a heavy saucepan and cook, stirring constantly, until thickened. Add butter and stir until melted. Place about a tablespoon of chocolate filling in center of crepe and place, seam-side down in a buttered shallow baking dish. Heat in a 325 degree oven until just heated through. Sprinkle top with powdered sugar. Can be served with a dip of vanilla ice cream on the side.

Yield: 10 to 12 crepes

Apple Nut Pudding

This is a delicious pudding, good hot or cold. I like it with a topping of soft custard.

¾	cup sugar	1¼	cups finely chopped tart apple
2	eggs, beaten		
½	cup flour	½	cup chopped pecans
½	teaspoon baking powder	1	teaspoon almond extract

Gradually add sugar to beaten eggs, beating until sugar and mixture is light cream-colored and fluffy.Add dry ingredients that have been sifted together. Then stir in pecans, apples and extract. Pour into a buttered 8"×8" pan. Bake at 350° for about 30 minutes or until done in center. Serve warm with plain or whipped cream.

Yield: 6 servings

The secret of the success of this pudding is to beat the sugar and eggs together until they are almost white in color and fluffy, which gives it a macaroon-like texture. Also, be sure to cut the apple in small, thin pieces.

Chocolate Almond Torte

This is an excellent party dessert with a rich chocolate flavor. It is also pretty and should be presented at the table before it is cut.

2½ cups blanched whole
    almonds, toasted
9 ounces semi-sweet
    chocolate
¼ cup butter

6 eggs, beaten
¾ cup sugar
2 tablespoons flour
¼ cup brandy or bourbon
Chocolate glaze

In food processor, finely grind 1 cup of the toasted almonds; reserve remaining whole almonds for garnish. Generously butter a 9″ cake pan; sprinkle sides and bottom with 2 tablespoons of the ground almonds; set aside. Melt chocolate and butter in heavy pan over very low heat. In large bowl, beat eggs with sugar. Beat in chocolate mixture. Beat in flour, remaining ground almonds and brandy. Pour into prepared pan. Bake at 350° about 25 minutes or until toothpick inserted in center comes out nearly clean. Do not overcook. Cool 10 minutes. Invert torte onto wire rack. Cool completely. Meanwhile prepare chocolate glaze.

Chocolate Glaze:

6 tablespoons water
3 tablespoons sugar
3 ounces semi-sweet
    chocolate

1 tablespoon brandy or
    bourbon

In small saucepan, simmer water and sugar together until sugar dissolves. Add chocolate and brandy. Simmer a few minutes until mixture coats the back of a spoon. Pour glaze over torte, spreading over top and sides with a spatula. Transfer torte to a serving plate. Allow glaze to set. Arrange whole almonds, points toward center, around outer edge. Working toward center, repeat circles, overlapping almonds slightly.

Yield: 10 to 12 servings

Caledonian Cream

2 cups whipping cream
1½ cups small curd cottage
    cheese blended in a blender
    until smooth

⅔ cup finely cut orange
    marmalade
3 tablespoons bourbon
¼ cup sugar

Whip cream until it is stiff, fold in blended cottage cheese, the orange marmalade, bourbon and sugar. Spoon into 6 champagne glasses. Chill 2 or more hours.

Yield: 6 servings

Grand Marnier Chocolate Mousse

4½	teaspoons unflavored gelatin	½	cup plus 2 tablespoons Grand Marnier
¾	pounds bittersweet chocolate bits	2¼	cups chilled heavy cream
		¾	cup superfine sugar

In small bowl, sprinkle gelatin over ⅓ cup cold water. Soften for 5 minutes and heat in a small heavy saucepan over moderate heat until gelatin dissolves. In a double boiler over barely simmering water, melt chocolate, stirring until smooth. Whisk in gelatin mixture and a ¼ cup plus 2 tablespoons Grand Marnier until mixture is smooth. Remove from heat, keeping pan over hot water. Beat the cream in a mixer, adding the superfine sugar a little bit at a time. Add remaining ¼ cup Grand Marnier and beat until mixture holds stiff peaks. Transfer 1½ cups whipped cream to a bowl and reserve it, covered and chilled. Remove the chocolate mixture from over the hot water and let cool for 30 seconds. Add to the rest of the whipped cream, mixing well. Divide the mousse in 6 (1 cup) goblets and chill, covered with plastic, for 30 to 40 minutes, or until almost set. With a spoon, scoop out 1 tablespoon of mousse in center of each, transferring centers to small saucepan. Fill center with some of reserved whipped cream. Stir scooped mousse over low heat until smooth. Pour it over mousses and chill, covered with plastic for 2 hours. Garnish with rest of whipped cream.

Yield: 6 servings

Sabra Mousse

Sabra, the liqueur of Israel, is tangy with Jaffa oranges with a hint of chocolate.

4	(1 ounce) squares semi-sweet chocolate	⅛	teaspoon salt
¼	cup Sabra liqueur	⅛	teaspoon cream of tartar
4	eggs, separated	2	tablespoons sugar
		½	cup heavy cream, whipped

Melt chocolate over hot water. Cool about 5 minutes, then stir in Sabra liqueur. Beat egg yolks until thick and add to chocolate. Beat the egg whites with the salt, cream of tartar and sugar until stiff but not dry. Whip cream and fold into egg whites, then add chocolate mixture. Spoon into your prettiest sherbet glasses. Chill until thickened. Garnish with whipped cream, if desired.

Yield: 6 to 8 servings

Texas Ranch Pudding

This is a hearty dessert with a rich caramel flavor.

1	cup dark brown sugar, packed	½	teaspoon salt
¾	cup light corn syrup	1	cup pecans, toasted and chopped
4	eggs	1	cup raisins
¼	cup bourbon	1	cup whipping cream
½	stick margarine, melted	2	tablespoons bourbon
1	teaspoon vanilla	2	tablespoons powdered sugar

Butter a 9″ baking dish. Beat brown sugar, corn syrup, eggs, bourbon, melted margarine, vanilla and salt in mixing bowl. Beat until light and fluffy. Spread raisins and pecans in bottom of baking dish. Pour egg mixture over. Bake in a pre-heated 325 ° oven about 30 to 35 minutes or until done in center. Serve with cream that has been whipped with the 2 tablespoons bourbon and 2 tablespoons powdered sugar.

Yield: 6 to 8 servings

Sabra Ice Cream Pie

1	envelope unflavored gelatin	1	cup heavy cream, whipped
¼	cup cold water	2	tablespoons Sabra
½	cup Sabra		
1	pint chocolate ice cream, softened		

Soften gelatin in cold water in small saucepan. Add Sabra and heat until gelatin is dissolved. Stir in softened ice cream. Whip cream with the 2 tablespoons Sabra, fold into ice cream mixture. Spoon in chocolate crumb crust below. Cover and freeze. Remove from freezer about 10 minutes before serving or pre-cut and put back in freezer.

1½	cups chocolate wafer crumbs	¼	cup butter melted

Mix together and press into a 9″ pie plate. Bake at 350° for 5 minutes. Cool.

Yield: 6 to 8 servings

Mary's Frozen Chocolate Mousse

1⅔ cups graham cracker crumbs
⅓ cup margarine (⅔ stick), melted
6 (1 ounce) squares semi-sweet chocolate
3 eggs, separated
1 teaspoon vanilla
½ cup pecans, chopped
1½ cups whipping cream, whipped
⅓ cup sugar

Combine cracker crumbs and margarine; press into the bottom of an 8 or 9″ springform pan. Bake at 350° for 10 minutes. Set aside.

Mix together melted chocolate, egg yolks and vanilla. Stir in pecans. Reserve 1 cup whipped cream; fold remaining whipped cream into chocolate mixture. Beat egg whites until foamy; gradually beat in sugar by tablespoonsful, then beat until stiff but not dry. Fold into chocolate mixture. Pour into prepared crust. Garnish with rest of the whipped cream. Cover and freeze 6 hours or overnight.

Yield: 10 to 12 servings

Mother's Spanish Cream

This is a dessert I remember from my childhood. It is a not too rich, but satisfyingly sweet.

1 envelope unflavored gelatin
6 tablespoons sugar, divided
2 eggs, separated
2 cups whole milk, divided
1 teaspoon pure vanilla

In medium saucepan, mix unflavored gelatin with ¼ cup of the sugar. Mix egg yolks with 1 cup of the milk and add to gelatin mixture. Beat well and cook over low heat, stirring, until gelatin is dissolved. Add vanilla, pour into a bowl and add remaining cup of milk. Beat egg whites until frothy, then add remaining 2 tablespoons sugar by tablespoonfuls, beating after each addition, until soft peaks hold up when beater is lifted. Fold gently into custard which should be lukewarm by now. Place in either a 4 cup bowl or individual dessert dishes. Refrigerate. When dessert chills, it will have a clear layer on bottom, a frothy one on top so it is prettier in a clear glass dish. I like to serve this with a plain sugar cookie or tea cake.

Yield: 6 to 8 servings

Croquembouche Cointreau

When I was in Nice, France many years ago, we went to a restaurant in the hills. A wedding party was at a table near us. They were served a croquembouche for dessert. We were told it was a traditional wedding cake.

1   (9") circle of cooked pie
     pastry

Mini Cream Puffs:

½   cup butter   4   eggs
1   cup boiling water
1   cup flour sifted after
     measuring, so it is free of
     lumps

Bring butter and water to a boil, lower heat and add flour all at once, stirring rapidly until mixture makes a ball and leaves side of the pan. Remove from heat. Add one egg at a time, beating thoroughly after each. Beat until mixture adheres to the spoon when held up from bowl. Drop dough by level table-spoons onto an ungreased cookie sheet, an inch apart, making 24 puffs. Bake in a pre-heated 425° oven about 15 minutes, reduce heat to 325 and cook another 10 minutes or until puffs are golden brown.

Cream Filling:

1   (3½ or 3¾ ounce) package   1   cup whipping cream,
     instant vanilla pudding   whipped
1¼   cups cold milk   1   teaspoon almond extract

Make vanilla pudding as package directs only use the lesser amount of milk given in this recipe. Fold in whipped cream and flavoring. Refrigerate. About an hour and a half before serving, with a sharp knife, split cream puffs. Fill with the custard. Refrigerate.

Continued on next page

Syrup:

1½ cups sugar   1   cup water

Place ingredients in a large pan. Cook, stirring constantly, until syrup is thick and carmelized. To Assemble: Place pastry circle on your prettiest cake plate, a pedestal one is nice. Dip each filled puff into warm syrup and place a ring inside edge of crust. Continue layers as you would make a brick wall - one puff over place where lower layer of puffs join. Continue layering making a pyramid or tree-shape, until all puffs are used. Spoon rest of syrup over tops of puffs. Dust with sifted powdered sugar before serving, if desired. You can also flame the croquembouche with ¼ cup cointreau, heated, if you like.

Yield: 6 to 8 servings

It is composed of miniature cream puffs dipped in syrup, then stacked in a pyramid or tree-shape. 3 or 4 puffs are removed for each serving with a fork and spoon.

Orange Souffle

I like this recipe as it uses frozen orange juice eliminating the need to grate orange rind and squeeze orange juice.

1   cup cold water   2   (6 ounce) cans frozen
2   envelopes unflavored   orange juice, thawed
     gelatin   1   cup sugar
8   eggs, separated   1   cup heavy cream, whipped
½   teaspoon salt

Place water in top of double boiler and sprinkle gelatin over it to soften. Beat the egg yolks with salt until light. Add to gelatin, Mix well. Place over boiling water and cook, stirring constantly, until gelatin is dissolved and the mixture thickens a bit. Remove from hot water and stir in orange juice concentrate. Chill until mixture drops from a spoon in soft mounds. Beat the egg whites until foamy, gradually beat in sugar, and beat until stiff but not dry. Fold the orange mixture into egg whites, then fold in whipped cream. Arrange a collar of waxed paper around the top of a 2½ quart souffle dish. Collar should come 2″ above the top. Fasten it with gummed tape. Pour mixture into dish and chill until firm. Remove collar, bring to the table along with your prettiest crystal bowls and serve.

Yield: 6 to 8 servings

Dewberry Roll

I first tasted this at a Swedish farmer's house in Pennsylvania, the state where I spent my childhood.

1½	cups flour	2	tablespoons butter, melted
1	tablespoon sugar	4	cups fresh dewberries
1	teaspoon salt	1	cup sugar
½	cup shortening	¾	teaspoon sugar
3	tablespoons water	1	cup boiling water

Combine first 3 ingredients; stir well. Cut in shortening with pastry blender until mixture resembles coarse meal. Sprinkle water over surface; stir with a fork until dry ingredients are moistened. Shape into a ball; chill. On a floured board, roll dough to a 14" × 10" rectangle about ¼" thick. Brush pastry with butter.

Combine dewberries with 1 cup sugar; stir well. Spoon 3 cups dewberry mixture over dough. Starting with the short side, roll up jelly roll fashion. Place roll, seam side down on a greased 12" × 8" × 2" baking dish. Cut several small slits across top of pastry; sprinkle with ¾ teaspoon sugar. Spoon remaining dewberry mix around the roll. Bake in a 450° oven for 10 minutes; pour boiling water around roll. Reduce heat to 350° and bake for 35 minutes or until golden. To serve: slice roll and serve with cream. Serve warm.

Yield: 8 servings

It can be made with any fresh fruit.

Amaretto Torte

2	cups coarsely crushed Amaretti macaroons	¼	cup sugar
		¼	cup Amaretto
3	egg yolks	¾	heavy cream, divided
1	egg	¼	cup sliced toasted almonds

Spread macaroon crumbs on a cookie sheet; bake at 300° for 8 minutes. Cool. Combine egg yolks, egg and sugar in mixer bowl; beat at high speed until sugar is dissolved and mixture thickened. Reduce speed to low; gradually add Amaretto. Whip cream and fold in 1 cup. Spoon 2 tablespoons of crumbs into each of 8 stemmed dessert dishes. Top with ⅓ cup Amaretto mixture. Sprinkle remaining crumbs around outer edge of each dish, Freeze until firm. Top with remaining whipped cream and almonds.

Yield: 8 servings

Lucille's Cheese Cake

Crust:

1½ cups graham cracker
crumbs
¼ cup powdered sugar

1 teaspoon allspice
⅓ cup melted butter

Mix well and press in bottom of a 9″ springform pan, pressing up the sides to form a rim ½″ to ¾″ high.

Filling:

2 (8 ounce) packages cream
cheese, room temperature
2 eggs, beaten lightly

⅔ cup sugar
2 teaspoons vanilla

Stir cheese until soft and creamy. Add eggs, sugar and vanilla. Beat until thoroughly creamed and smooth. Pour into crust, bake at 350° for 25 minutes. Then top with sour cream mixture.

Topping:

1½ cups sour cream
4 tablespoons sugar

2 teaspoons vanilla

Mix all ingredients together and spread on top of cheese cake. Return to oven, increase temperature to 450° and bake for 7 minutes. Cool, then chill in refrigerator. When topping has hardened, cover with plastic film.

Yield: 8 servings

Easy Baklava

2 packages frozen puff pastry
patty shells, thawed
according to package
directions

3 cups finely chopped walnuts
or pecans
1 cup honey, warmed

Line an 8″ × 8″ × 2″ cake pan with foil. Butter lightly. Stack 3 patty shells, one on top of other. On lightly floured surface, roll into a 9″ square. Place in bottom of cake pan. Sprinkle with 1 cup of the chopped nuts and dribble with ¼ cup honey. Repeat this process 3 times making the top layer plain pastry. Mark top of pastry into diamond pattern with a sharp knife. Bake in a preheated 425° oven for 20 to 25 minutes. Let cool slightly in pan. Brush surface with the last of the honey. Remove from pan and peel away foil. Cut into diamonds. Serve with more honey and whipped cream.

Yield: 12 servings

Lemon Baked Alaska

This is one of my favorite desserts. It can be made several days ahead of time, kept in the freezer and then topped with meringue and browned.

Crust:
1 cup finely chopped pecans	¼ cup sugar
½ stick unsalted butter, softened	1 tablespoon flour

Mix all ingredients in a bowl, then press into the bottom of a 9″ springform pan. Bake in a pre-heated 350° oven until it is light brown. Let shell cool in the pan on a rack.

Filling:
1½ cups sugar	1 tablespoon grated lemon peel
9 tablespoons unsalted butter (1 stick plus 1 tablespoon) melted	¼ teaspoon salt
½ cup lemon juice	3 large eggs, well beaten
	3 large egg yolks, well beaten

Combine sugar, butter, lemon juice, lemon rind and salt in top of a double boiler. Beat in the eggs and egg yolks. Cook the sauce over simmering water, until it is thickened. Cool and chill, covered with plastic wrap.

To Assemble:
Spread 1 pint vanilla ice cream on crust (still in springform pan) and return to freezer until ice cream is hardened. Spread ½ the lemon filling over ice cream, return to freezer until it is frozen, then spread another pint of ice cream over, let it harden in freezer, then spread remaining lemon filling over. Return to freezer for several hours, preferably overnight. To serve, remove sides of springform pan , place on a wooden plank and spread with the following meringue. Bake as directed.

Continued on next page

Meringue:

6   egg whites, room temperature

1½   cups sugar

¼   teaspoon cream of tartar

¼   teaspoon salt

Have egg whites at room temperature, Beat with salt until frothy, add cream of tartar and beat until soft peaks form. Add sugar 2 tablespoons at a time, beating well after each addition. Beat whites until stiff, but not dry, peaks form. Pre-heat oven to 500°. Spread meringue over alaska making sure to seal crust to board. Bake until it begins to brown, Watch carefully as this takes only a few seconds. Remove from oven and cut into wedges with a heavy-bladed sharp knife. Serve immediately.

Yield: 12 servings

This recipe may be varied by using different fillings, such as fruit, Amaretto custard, etc.

Orange Angel Dessert

This was a popular dessert at church luncheons. It is delicious and easy to make for a crowd as it uses frozen orange juice and does not have to be cooked. Recipe can be doubled or tripled.

1   envelope unflavored gelatin

½   cup cold water

⅔   cup sugar

⅛   teaspoon salt

6   ounces frozen orange juice concentrate, undiluted

16   ounces Cool Whip

1   (14 ounce) bakery angel food cake, torn into small pieces

Additional Cool Whip for topping

Soften gelatin in cold water in small saucepan, stir over low heat until gelatin is dissolved, add sugar and salt and stir over the low heat until sugar is dissolved. Remove from heat, gradually add thawed undiluted orange juice. Mix and refrigerate until mixture is thickened but not set. Fold in Cool Whip. Pour a thin layer of the gelatin mixture in the bottom of a 13″ × 9″ × 2″ pan that has been rinsed out with cold water and then drained. Put about half the angel food pieces on top, then another layer of gelatin, then rest of angel food cake pieces. Top with rest of gelatin mixture. Press down gently to be sure cake pieces are covered. Refrigerate until firm. Then ice with a thin layer of additional Cool Whip. Cut into squares to serve.

Yield: 12 to 15 servings

Baked Alaska with Kahlua

3   pints coffee ice cream

Line a 7" plastic or stainless steel bowl with plastic wrap. Soften ice cream slightly and pack in bowl. Cover and put in freezer.

3 ounces unsweetened chocolate	**1¼ cups sugar**
	⅔ cup flour
7 tablespoons butter (⅞ Stick)	**¼ teaspoon salt**
2 eggs	**2 tablespoons Kahlua or**
½ teaspoons vanilla	**coffee-flavored liqueur**

Heat oven to 325°. Butter and flour a 9" round cake pan. Chop chocolate, melt butter; add chocolate to butter and melt over very low heat. Beat eggs and vanilla until foamy then gradually beat in the 1¼ cups sugar and continue beating until light. Add butter and chocolate mixture and beat until well combined. Stir in flour and ¼ teaspoon salt. Pour batter into prepared pan, bake at 325° until brownie pulls away from side of pan, 30 to 35 minutes. Cool 10 minutes, then stick holes in cake with a toothpick and brush with Kahlua. Loosen sides from pan with knife and let stand until cool. Remove brownie from pan to a wooden plank or oven-proof plate. Unmold ice cream onto brownie and return to freezer.

Meringue:

4 egg whites	**½ cup sugar**
¼ teaspoon cream of tartar	

Heat oven to 425°. Beat egg whites until foamy, add cream of tartar; beat until soft peaks form, add sugar by tablespoons, beating after each addition. Beat until stiff, but not dry, peaks form. Remove brownie and ice cream from freezer, ice with meringue making sure that meringue seals the brownie to the wooden plank or plate. Place on middle shelf of oven and bake until light brown. Watch carefully as this takes only a few seconds. Remove from oven and cut into wedges with a heavy, sharp knife. Place on plates and serve at once.

Yield: 6 to 8 servings

German Milk Rice

¾	cup uncooked rice	⅓	cup sugar
3	cups milk	1	egg, beaten (optional)
¾	teaspoon salt	¼	cup milk (optional)

Combine all ingredients in top of a double boiler, place over boiling water and cook until rice is tender. If mixture gets too thick, you may add a little more milk. When cooked, 1 egg beaten with ¼ cup milk may be added to rice and mixture cooked about 5 minutes more. Serve warm, sprinkled with a little cinnamon.

Yield: 8 to 10 servings

Crepe "Chips"

This is a different light dessert.

12 cooked 8 inch crepes cut
into 8 wedges

Apricot Sauce:

1½	tablespoons cornstarch	½	cup light corn syrup
2	tablespoons sugar	1	tablespoon butter
⅛	teaspoon salt	¼	teaspoon almond extract
1	cup apricot nectar		

Mix all ingredients except extract in heavy saucepan. Cook, over medium heat, stirring constantly, until thickened, Add almond extract. Refrigerate.

Strawberry sauce:

2	(10 ounce) packages frozen sliced strawberries, thawed.	½	cup currant jelly
2	tablespoons cornstarch	2	tablespoons Kirsch

Drain strawberries, saving juice. Place berries in blender and purée. Add enough water to juice to make 1½ cups. In small saucepan, mix cornstarch with juice, add currant jelly and puréed strawberries. Cook over medium heat, stirring constantly, until thickened. Remove from heat and add Kirsch. Refrigerate.

Place crepes on cookie sheet; bake at 375° until crisp and lightly browned. Watch carefully. Sift powdered sugar with a dash of cinnamon over. Pile into a bowl and serve with a sauce or variety of sauces.

Yield: 72 chips

Almond Cream Puff Ring

This is a dessert to be served at the table, so guests can see it before it is cut.

1	cup water	4	eggs
½	cup butter, room temperature	1	egg beaten with 1 tablespoon water (egg glaze)
¼	teaspoon salt		Almond Cream Filling
1	cup flour		Chocolate Glaze

In 2 quart saucepan over medium heat, combine the water, butter and salt, bring to a boil and boil until butter melts. Remove saucepan from the heat and add flour all at once, stir until mixed in. Return to heat and cook, stirring, until mixture leaves the sides of the pan and forms a ball. Remove from heat and add eggs, one at a time, beating well after each addition. Beat until mixture is smooth and shiny. Cool mixture slightly. Pre-heat oven to 400°. Lightly grease and flour a large cookie sheet. Using an 8" plate as a guide, trace a circle on flour on cookie sheet. Drop batter in 10 mounds on inside of circle to form a ring. Brush with egg wash, being careful not to let any roll down the sides. Bake for 40 minutes at 400° or until golden brown. Turn off the oven and prick ring with a small sharp knife in several places to let out the steam. Leave in closed oven for 15 minutes. Remove ring from oven and cool on wire rack. When ring is cool, slice horizontally with a very sharp knife. Spoon almond filling into ring, replace top and spread with chocolate glaze. Refrigerate until ready to serve. Cut into 10 puffs or into 5 servings of 2 puffs each.

Almond Cream Filling:

1	(3½ ounce or 3¾ ounce) package instant vanilla pudding	1¼	cups milk
		1	cup whipping cream
		1	teaspoon almond flavoring

Prepare pudding according to package directions but using only the 1¼ cups milk. Whip cream with almond flavoring and fold into pudding. Refrigerate until time to fill the ring.

Chocolate Glaze:

½	cup semi-sweet chocolate morsels	1½	teaspoons milk
1	tablespoon butter or margarine	1½	teaspoons light corn syrup

Heat all ingredients in top of a double boiler over hot, not boiling water, stirring until smooth. Dribble over ring.

Yield: 10 servings

Amaretto Stuffed Pears with Zinfandel Ice Cream

3	ripe pears, peeled, cored and halved	8	Amaretto macaroons or 32 Amaretti de Saronno
6	tablespoons butter, softened	6	tablespoons blanched almonds, crushed
1	tablespoon sugar plus 1 teaspoon	¼	teaspoon Kirsch
1	egg, beaten		

In a large bowl, cream butter until light and fluffy, add sugar and beaten egg, mix well. Crush macaroons and add crushed almonds with the Kirsch. Fill pears with a rounded tablespoon of the stuffing. Place in a buttered baking dish and bake in a pre-heated 350° oven until stuffing is lightly browned and pears are tender. Serve with Zinfandel ice cream.

White Zinfandel Ice Cream:

½	cup sugar	1½	cup heavy cream
½	cup half and half	1	cup White Zinfandel wine
2	eggs, beaten		

In a small saucepan, heat sugar with half and half. Remove from heat, add a little of the hot mixture to the beaten eggs, then add the rest, beating with a wire whisk. Return to saucepan and cook over low heat, stirring constantly, until mixture coats spoon. Strain into a bowl and add heavy cream and wine. Cool and freeze in ice cream maker. I use the Donvier. Makes 1 quart.

Yield: 6 servings

Orange Sherbet with Cointreau

This dessert can serve as both dessert and liqueur.

1	quart orange sherbet	3	tablespoons cointreau
3	tablespoons orange juice concentrate		

Soften sherbet in very cold bowl, add orange juice and cointreau. Working very quickly as sherbet melts fast, spoon into sherbet or parfait glasses. Cover and refreeze.

Yield: 6 servings

Sherbet looks pretty in glass so freeze in either glass sherbet dishes or parfait glasses.

Strawberry Fluff

This is another dessert that can be made days ahead of time and frozen.

Crumbs:

1 cup flour	½ cup chopped pecans
¼ cup brown sugar, packed	½ cup melted margarine

Combine flour, brown sugar. pecans and margarine. place on a cookie sheet and bake in a 350° oven for about 20 minutes, stirring occasionally, until light brown. Set aside and cool. Break into crumbs.

1 (10 ounce) package frozen sliced strawberries	2 egg whites
1 cup sugar	½ pint whipping cream, whipped or 1 pint whipped topping
2 teaspoons freshly squeezed lemon juice	

Combine strawberries, sugar, lemon juice and egg whites in mixer bowl, beat at high speed until light and fluffy. about 15 or 20 minutes. Mixture should almost fill mixing bowl. Fold in whipped cream or whipped topping. Spread ½ of the crumbs in a 13"×9"×2" cake pan. Pour whipped mixture over, then top with remainder of the crumbs. Place in freezer. To serve: cut into 12 or 15 servings.

Yield: 12 to 15 servings

You may make pies out of this strawberry mixture, if you like. Just use a graham cracker crust and sprinkle crumbs over top. Makes 2 very thick pies.

Ann's Swiss Chocolate Torte

1 (6 ounce) package semi-sweet chocolate morsels	½ teaspoon almond extract
1 cup toasted almonds, diced	1 (8") round layer cake, 1½ to 2" thick
1 cup dairy sour cream	½ cup pineapple-apricot jam
¾ cup powdered sugar	¼ cup diced toasted almonds for garnish
½ teaspoon vanilla	

Melt chocolate over very low heat or in a double boiler. Combine almonds with sour cream, powdered sugar and extracts. Blend into melted chocolate. Cut cake into 3 layers. Spread some chocolate cream over bottom layer, top with second layer and spread that with the chocolate cream, add top layer and spread chocolate cream only in center of layer. Melt jam over very low heat and spread over bare cake on top and sides. Garnish chocolate cream on top layer with the ¼ cup almonds.

Yield: 8 servings

Bob's Blueberry Dumplings

Bob Bennett was the organist at St.Luke's Methodist Church. I have several of his recipes, all good.

½	cup sugar	2	teaspoons baking powder
2	tablespoons butter	¼	teaspoon salt
1	cup flour	½	cup milk

Cream sugar and butter. Sift dry ingredients and add them alternately with the milk, beginning and ending with flour. Drop with a spoon into hot blueberry syrup, making 8 dumplings. Cook, covered, over medium-low heat for 15 to 20 minutes. Do not peek! Serve warm with cream.

Blueberry syrup:

2	cups fresh or frozen blueberries	¼	teaspoon cinnamon
		¼	teaspoon salt
3	tablespoons fresh lemon juice	1	cup sugar
		2	cups water

Grated rind of 1 lemon

Mix all ingredients in a heavy saucepan, 7" to 8" across the bottom. Bring to a boil, then simmer for 5 minutes. Bring syrup back to a boil and drop dumplings in. Follow preceeding directions. Serve warm dumplings and syrup into dessert dishes that leave plenty of room for light cream or ice cream.

Yield: 8 dumplings

Apple Crisp

A cook I once had always added ½ cup grated cheddar cheese to the crumbs for this dessert.

4	cups or 2 (1 pound cans) sliced apples	1	stick margarine
		½	cup grated cheddar cheese
¾	cup flour		
1	cup sugar or 1 cup brown sugar, packed		

Place apples in buttered 12"×8" casserole. Mix sugar, margarine and flour into crumbs, add grated cheese, Mix and spread over apples. If fresh apples are used, add 3 tablespoons water to casserole. Bake in a pre-heated 350° oven about 35 to 40 minutes or until syrup has thickened. Serve warm with cream or ice cream.

Yield: 6 servings

Brown Betty with Pears

This was my grandmother's recipe.

3 cups ¼" bread cubes made from firm-textured bread, crusts removed	⅔ cups plus 2 tablespoons dark brown sugar, packed
4 tablespoons butter, melted	1 teaspoon vanilla
2 (16 ounce) cans sliced pears, drained, reserving juice	

Drain pears, reserving ½ cup of the juice. In a medium bowl, mix pears, ⅔ cup of the brown sugar and vanilla together and stir until sugar dissolves. In a large bowl, mix bread cubes with melted butter. Scatter ⅓ of the bread cubes in bottom of a buttered 9" × 9" cake pan. Arrange ½ of the pear mixture on top, add another layer of bread, the remaining pear mixture and a final layer of bread. Pour reserved pear juice over all. Cover tightly with foil, Bake 30 minutes in a pre-heated 350° oven. Sprinkle remaining 2 tablespoons of brown sugar over top. Bake, uncovered, about 10 minutes or until top is lightly browned. Serve warm with light cream.

Yield: 6 to 8 servings

Ginger Snap Pear Crisp

4 medium pears, peeled, halved and cored	¼ cup orange juice
	2 tablespoons water

Place pear halves, cut-side up, in a baking dish just large enough to hold them in a single layer. Drizzle orange juice and water over them. Cover tightly with foil and bake in a 350° oven for 15 to 20 minutes or until pears are barely tender. Remove from oven and sprinkle with gingersnap mixture. Return to oven and bake until crumbs are crisp, about 15 minutes. Serve with light cream or whipped cream.

Ginger Snap Mixture:

¾ cups finely crushed ginger snaps	4 tablespoons chopped pecans
3 tablespoons sugar	3 tablespoons butter, melted

In a small bowl, combine gingersnap crumbs, sugar, pecans and butter.

Yield: 4 to 6 servings

Spicy Peach Crisp

This is a handy recipe to have when fresh peaches are not available.

4	tablespoons (½ stick) butter or margarine	3	tablespoons brown sugar, packed
6	gingersnaps, crushed	¼	teaspoon cinnamon
3	tablespoons old fashioned oats	1	(29 ounce) can peach halves, drained

Mix first 5 ingredients together. Place drained peach halves, cut-side up, in a buttered round or rectangular casserole just big enough to hold them. Sprinkle crumbs on top and bake at 350° until heated through, 20 to 25 minutes. Serve warm.

Yield: 6 servings

Apple Rolls

¾	cup butter, softened	1	egg, separated
1	(8 ounce) package cream cheese, softened	2	cups flour

Combine butter, cream cheese and egg yolk. Beat until smooth. Add flour, mixing well. Shape dough into 3 balls; wrap in film and chill.

6	medium apples, peeled, cored and thinly sliced	½	cup sugar
		2	teaspoons cinnamon

Combine apples, sugar and cinnamon in saucepan, cover and cook over low heat until apples are tender, stirring occasionally. Cool.

On a floured board, roll one portion of dough into a 10" × 13" rectangle about ⅛ inch thick; spread ⅓ of the apple mixture over dough. Starting with the short side, roll up jelly roll fashion, turning ends under. Repeat with remaining dough and apple mixture. Place rolls, seam-side down, on a greased 12" × 8" × 2" baking dish. Brush with beaten egg white. Bake in a pre-heated 375° oven for 40 minutes or until brown. Cut into slices to serve warm or cold with a wedge of cheddar cheese.

Yield: 12 servings

Wash Day Fruit Cobbler

My mother named it thus as it was a simple dessert to make on Monday, which was always wash day in the olden days.

½	cup butter, 1 stick	1	cup sugar
4	cups of fresh fruit of your choice		

Melt butter in a 13″ × 9″ × 2″ baking pan. Mix fruit with the 1 cup sugar. If you are using peaches, apples or pears, add a sprinkling of cinnamon; if using blueberries, sprinkle with lemon juice. Place fruit over the melted butter in baking dish. Pour the batter over but do not stir. Bake in a pre-heated 350° oven about 25 to 30 minutes until lightly brown and fruit is tender.

Batter:

1	cup sugar	2	teaspoons baking powder
1	cup flour	1	cup milk
¼	teaspoon salt		

Sift sugar, flour, baking powder and salt into a bowl, add milk and mix with a spoon until combined.

Yield: 8 servings

Russian Cream with Strawberries

This is a lower calorie version of Swedish Cream.

2	tablespoons unflavored gelatin	1½	cups sour cream
½	cup cold water	¾	teaspoon vanilla
¼	cup sugar	¼	teaspoon almond extract
1¼	cups light cream, heated		Fresh strawberries

Soak gelatin and sugar in cold water until softened. Add to heated cream and stir until dissolved. Refrigerate until mixture starts to congeal. Stir in sour cream, vanilla and almond extracts. Pour into a fluted tube mold that has been rinsed with cold water and drained. Refrigerate until firm. To serve, unmold on a serving plate and fill center with strawberries or fruit of your choice.

Yield: 6 servings

Swedish Cream

I like to mold this in heart-shaped molds, and garnish with fresh strawberries cut in half lengthwise and placed cut-side up around the heart. I have also used fresh peach slices and green grapes. Any fresh fruit can be used. It can be served plain, also.

3	cups sour cream		3	cups heavy cream
1½	cups sugar		1½	teaspoons vanilla
1½	tablespoons unflavored gelatin			Fresh fruit of your choice

Allow sour cream to warm to room temperature. Mix sugar, gelatin and heavy cream in saucepan. Heat and stir over low heat until gelatin is dissolved. Cool either at room temperature or in the refrigerator until slightly thickened. Carefully stir sour cream with the vanilla until mixture is smooth, then add to gelatin mixture until ingredients are well blended. Place in molds that have been rinsed with cold water and drained. Chill until firm. Unmold on crystal dessert plates and garnish with fruit.

Yield: 12 servings

Grand Marnier Parfait

This is a good dessert to serve after a heavy meal. The orange juice gives the parfait a tart flavor. It can be made days ahead of time in parfait glasses, and frozen. It is pretty served with a candied violet on top.

1	quart vanilla ice cream, softened a little		2	generous ounces Grand Marnier or to taste
12	ounces frozen orange juice, undiluted			

Fold all ingredients together and place in parfait glasses. Cover with film and freeze until needed.

Yield: 8 to 10 servings

Orange juice should be thawed, but still chilled so as not to melt ice cream.

Chocolate Soufflé

This souffle is unusual as it has no flour in it. The chocolate and cream thicken it enough.

4	(1 ounce) squares semi-sweet chocolate	2	additional egg whites making 5 in all
½	cup heavy cream	3	tablespoons sugar
3	eggs, separated		Confectioners sugar for sprinkling
½	teaspoon vanilla		
1½	tablespoons brandy		

Butter a 1 quart or 4 (1 cup) souffle dishes, and dust with confectioners sugar. In a heavy pan over low heat, heat the chocolate with the cream, stirring until chocolate is melted. Cook, stirring, until mixture is thick and will just fall from a spoon. Remove from heat and beat the egg yolks into the mixture. Return to heat for 2 or 3 minutes, stirring constantly. Remove from heat and stir in brandy and vanilla. The souffle can be prepared to this point 3 to 4 hours ahead. Keep covered at room temperature. 20 to 30 minutes before serving, set the oven at 425°. Beat the 5 egg whites with a pinch of salt until soft peaks form. Add the sugar by tablespoons and beat 20 seconds longer until glossy and just hold peaks when beater is lifted. The proper beating of the whites is crucial to the success of the souffle. If they are beaten too stiff, too much volume is lost in incorporating them into the first mixture. Heat the chocolate mixture until lukewarm, take from heat and stir in about a quarter of the egg whites. Add this mixture to rest of egg whites and fold in. Pour into prepared souffle dish or dishes. Bake the 1 quart souffle for 15 minutes, the smaller ones 7 to 9 minutes. Sprinkle with confectioners sugar, and serve immediately. When serving larger souffle, use 2 spoons and dip from inside to outside for servings.

Yield: 4 to 6 servings

Helpful Hint: *The best pastry bag is a reusable cloth one with a plastic lining. Wash it in warm sudsy water and rinse thoroughly. Do not store until completely dry. When metal pastry tips become clogged, they may be cleaned by boiling them in water for a few minutes.*

Chocolate Chiffon Pie

2	egg whites	½	cup sugar
⅛	teaspoon cream of tartar	½	cup chopped pecans
⅛	teaspoon salt	½	teaspoon vanilla

Beat the 2 egg whites, cream of tartar and salt until foamy. Add the ½ cup sugar slowly, a tablespoon at a time, beat until whites are stiff but not dry. Fold in pecans and vanilla. Spread in a 9″ buttered pie tin, heaping up around the edges to form a crust. Bake in a 300° oven for 1½ hours. Cool in pan.

Filling:

1	(6 ounce) package semi-sweet chocolate chips	4	tablespoons sugar, divided
3	tablespoons milk	4	eggs, separated

Melt chocolate chips, milk and 2 tablespoons sugar in heavy saucepan, beat a little of the chocolate mixture into egg yolks, then add yolks to rest of chocolate mixture. Stir over low heat for 1 minute. Cool. Beat egg whites until soft peaks form, add the 2 tablespoons sugar, 1 tablespoon at a time, beat until stiff, but not dry peaks form. Fold egg whites into cooled chocolate mixture. Fill meringue and refrigerate.

Yield: 8 servings

Angel Pie

4	egg whites, room temperature	1	tablespoon powdered sugar
½	cup granulated sugar	1	cup whipping cream
½	cup powdered sugar		Grated semi-sweet chocolate
			Heavy aluminum foil

Beat egg whites until they make soft peaks, then add both the granulated and powdered sugars about 2 tablespoons at a time and continue beating until mixture stands in stiff but not dry peaks. Line a 9″ glass pie plate with heavy aluminum foil well greased with margarine. Place meringue in prepared pan and put in cold oven. Turn on oven to 300° and bake for 1 hour. Remove from oven, turn upside down immediately on large plate, remove foil.

Whip cream with the 1 tablespoon powdered sugar. When meringue is cold, cover it with the whipped cream and sprinkle the grated chocolate over. Refrigerate for several hours or overnight before serving.

Yield: 8 servings

Chocolate or Lemon Supreme Tarts

These make small servings, but are adequate as they are rich. For a buffet, I make both kinds for a choice. If you are making 2 kinds from recipe, use vanilla for the flavoring of the meringue.

4	egg whites, room temperature		Slivered toasted almonds for garnish on chocolate filling
¼	teaspoon cream of tartar		
1½	cups sugar		
½	teaspoon almond flavoring for chocolate, lemon for lemon, depending on which filling you use		

Beat egg whites until frothy, add cream of tartar and beat until soft peaks form. Add sugar very gradually, beating well after each addition, until whites are stiff, but not dry.

Cut 18 circles of foil or brown paper 3″ in diameter. Place a rounding dessertspoonful on each making a depression in center with the bowl of the spoon. Bake 10 minutes in a 300° oven. Turn off oven, leaving door shut, and let meringues dry 5 minutes. Remove from paper while still warm. These are very delicate so handle carefully. If not using right away, place in a tightly covered container. Do not try to make these on a rainy day.

Chocolate filling:

2	egg whites, room temperature	4	ounces semi-sweet chocolate, melted
½	cup sugar	½	cup slivered toasted blanched almonds
2	tablespoons cocoa		
¾	cup butter		

Beat egg whites, sugar and cocoa until smooth in top of double boiler over hot water. Still beating constantly, add butter by spoonfuls. Finally, add melted chocolate. Remove from hot water and stir occasionally, until mixture thickens. This will take 20 to 30 minutes. Divide between the 18 meringues and sprinkle with the almonds.

Continued on next page

Lemon Filling:

4 egg yolks	2 tablespoons grated lemon rind
½ cup sugar	
¼ cup lemon juice	½ cup butter, softened

Beat egg yolks in a small mixing bowl until thick and lemon-colored. Gradually add ½ cup sugar. Blend in the lemon juice and lemon rind. Cook in the top of a double boiler over hot, not boiling water, stirring constantly until thick - 5 to 8 minutes. Add butter by spoonfuls, mixing until blended. Cool, stirring occasionally and spoon into meringues. Garnish with whipped cream, if desired. Enough filling for 18 meringues.

Yield: 18 Tarts

Patti's Easy Chocolate Mousse

1 (3¾ ounce) chocolate pudding mix, not instant	1 tablespoon Amaretto or 1 teaspoon vanilla or 1 teaspoon brandy for flavoring, whichever you prefer
1¾ cups milk	
8 ounces cream cheese, room temperature, broken into bits	

Combine pudding mix and milk in small saucepan. Cook over medium heat, stirring constantly, until mixture comes to a full boil. Remove from heat and add cream cheese, stirring constantly, until well blended in. Spoon into crystal dessert dishes. Garnish with whipped cream, if desired.

Yield: 4 servings

Lillian's Date Torte

This is a meringue-like dessert given to me about 60 years ago.

2 eggs, well beaten	1 cup chopped pecans
1 cup powdered sugar	1 teaspoon baking powder
1 cup chopped dates	2 tablespoons flour

Mix ingredients in order given. Place in buttered 9″ pie plate. Bake at 350 degrees about 20 minutes. Do not overbake as torte will become too chewy. Cool, cut into wedges and serve with whipped cream.

Yield: 6 to 8 servings

Chocolate Cream Roll

¾   cup (12 tablespoons) sugar,
    divided
6   eggs, separated
¼   cup cocoa
¼   cup flour
⅓   teaspoon baking powder

Pinch salt
½   teaspoon vanilla
¾   cup heavy cream, whipped
    with ¼ cup sugar and a
    teaspoon of vanilla

Beat egg yolks and 5 tablespoons sugar in mixer until light and lemon-colored. Sift cocoa, flour, baking powder, salt and 5 tablespoons sugar, add to yolks along with vanilla and beat well. Beat egg whites until frothy, then add 2 tablespoons sugar gradually, beating after each addition. Fold into egg yolk mixture. Pour onto a cookie sheet with 1" sides and lined with heavy waxed paper or foil, greased.

Bake in a pre-heated 350° oven for 20 minutes. Loosen edges with knife, then turn upside down onto a towel dusted with sifted powdered sugar. Remove paper or foil and roll from long end, jelly roll fashion. When cool unroll and spread with whipped cream. To serve, cut into slices and pour chocolate sauce over each portion.

Chocolate Sauce:

¼   cup butter or margarine
2   ounces unsweetened
    chocolate, broken into
    pieces

1¾ cup powdered sugar
¾   cup plus 1 tablespoon
    evaporated milk, not
    condensed

Melt butter and chocolate in double boiler, over hot, not boiling water; remove from heat and add sugar alternately with milk, stirring constantly, after each addition. Return to heat and cook in double boiler for 30 minutes, stirring frequently. Cool. If refrigerated, sauce might thicken, if so, add a little hot water to it and heat, if necessary. Makes 3 cups sauce.

Yield: 8 to 10 servings

Peanut Brittle Torte

Any nuts may be used in this recipe. I have even used broken up Heath bars.

8	egg whites, room temperature	3	cups heavy cream or whipped topping
2	cups sugar	½	pound peanut brittle
1	tablespoon vinegar		

Beat egg whites until soft peaks form, then add sugar gradually by tablespoonfuls, beating well after each addition, then add vinegar. Mix and beat whites until stiff, but not dry, peaks form. Line 2 (9") round cake pans with waxed paper or foil. Spoon meringue evenly into them, Bake 45 minutes in a preheated 325° oven. Turn off heat and let cool in oven with door closed. Remove from oven, peel off waxed paper or foil. Trim any rough edges off meringue with scissors and put scraps on top of the 2 layers.

Chop the peanut brittle into pea-sized pieces. Do not chop too fine or it will melt in the whipped cream and make the mixture runny. Whip cream, adding 5 tablespoons sugar and 1 teaspoon vanilla. Fold in chopped peanut brittle. Spread about a third over first layer, then divide the rest over top and sides of torte. Let set in refrigerator several hours or overnight before serving. Cut into wedges.

Yield: 6 to 8 servings

I never throw away any leftover egg whites, place them in a freezer-proof jar, 2 or 4 to a jar and freeze. In that way, you can have the exact amount you need for a recipe. Just let them thaw at room temperature and use. They beat like fresh ones.

Austrian Jam Tart

2	cups flour	1	tablespoon water
½	teaspoon baking powder	½	teaspoon almond extract
¼	teaspoon salt	1	(10 ounce) jar of apricot or strawberry preserves
1	stick margarine		
1	egg, beaten		

Combine dry ingredients; cut in margarine until mixture resembles coarse meal. Add egg, water and extract, mixing lightly with a fork. Chill ¼ of dough. Press remaining dough on bottom and ½ inch up sides of a 9" springform pan. Spread dough with preserves. On lightly floured board, roll out reserved dough. Cut into ½" wide strips. Place strips diagonally across preserves to form a lattice. Press edges to seal. Bake at 350° for 35 to 40 minutes or until lightly browned. Loosen crust from rim of pan. Cut into wedges to serve.

Yield: 6 to 8 servings

Mother's Lemon Mousse

3	egg yolks	¼	teaspoon grated lemon rind
½	cup sugar	2	egg whites, room
1½	tablespoons unflavored		temperature
	gelatin	2	tablespoons sugar
⅓	cup cold water	1	cup whipping cream
½	cup fresh lemon juice		

Beat egg yolks and sugar in top of double boiler until light and fluffy. Soften gelatin in cold water, mix in lemon juice and lemon rind. Add to egg mixture. Place over hot water and cook, stirring, until thickened. Remove from bottom of double boiler and cool for 8 minutes. Beat egg whites until frothy, then add sugar gradually, beating until egg whites are stiff, but not dry. Whip cream. Fold egg whites and whipped cream into egg mixture. Place either in individual dessert dishes or in a bowl. Refrigerate about 2 hours or until well chilled and firm.

Yield: 8 to 10 servings

Amaretto Macaroon Mousse

1	cup coarsely crushed	¾	cups sugar, divided
	Amaretti macaroons		Dash salt
2	tablespoons Amaretto	1	cup heavy cream
4	large eggs, separated		Green seedless grapes

Mix macaroons with Amaretto in small bowl. Let set for 5 minutes. Line a 9″ × 5″ × 3″ loaf pan with foil. Sprinkle half the crumbs in bottom of prepared pan. In large mixer bowl, beat egg yolks with ½ cup sugar until lemon-colored. Whip egg whites with salt in another bowl. until soft peaks form, then add ¼ cup of sugar by tablespoons, beating after each addition. Beat until stiff but not dry peaks form. Transfer to another bowl. Put cream into same bowl, no need to wash it or beaters. Whip cream until stiff peaks form. Stir about ¼ of whipped cream into yolk mixture to lighten it, then fold remaining whipped cream in and then the beaten egg whites. Pour half the mixture into prepared pan. Sprinkle remaining crumbs over and then pour remaining cream mixture into pan. Cover and freeze at least 6 hours. Invert onto serving plate and remove foil. Return to freezer until serving time. To serve: cut into slices and garnish with grapes. This melts fast, so serve immediately.

Yield: 10 to 12 servings

Chambord Souffle

If frozen raspberries are not available, frozen strawberries can be substituted. After being puréed, they do not have to be strained. Just be sure you do not have more than 1½ cups purée.

6	eggs, separated	1	teaspoon butter
4	ounces Chambord liqueur	Dash salt	
½	cup milk	2	(10 ounce) packages frozen
½	teaspoon sugar		raspberries with syrup

Thaw frozen raspberries, blend with their syrup in a blender or a food processor and put through a strainer. This makes 1½ cups of raspberry purée.

In a small bowl, beat egg yolks until thick and add Chambord, milk and puréed raspberries and blend. Pour mixture into a saucepan and cook over medium-high heat about 6 minutes, stirring constantly. Pour mixture into a large bowl and stir for about a minute and let cool. This mixture can be done before dinner for easy completion of souffle.

Immediately prior to placing souffle into oven, beat egg whites, room temperature, with dash of salt until egg whites form firm peaks but are not stiff. Using a spatula, gently fold the beaten whites in the cooled raspberry mixture. When all is blended, pour mixture into a 1 quart souffle dish which has been buttered and lightly coated with sugar. Place souffle on lowest rack of pre-heated 350° oven and bake for 25 minutes. Serve immediately from the souffle dish with two spoons, placed simultaneously into souffle, for one serving. The top will be slightly firm with a creamy center. For a firmer souffle, simply cook an extra minute or two.

Yield: 6 servings

If you wish to make a larger souffle, adjust time in oven by 5 minutes for every ⅓ adjustment in quantity.

Broiled Pears with Coconut

3	fresh pears, pared, halved and cored	2	tablespoons margarine, melted
½	cup Angel flake coconut	1	tablespoon milk
⅓	cup packed brown sugar		

Place pears, cut-side up, in baking dish just large enough to hold them in one layer. Cover and bake in a pre-heated 350° oven for 20 to 30 minutes or until tender. Combine coconut, brown sugar, butter and milk; spoon over pears. Broil, 4 to 5 inches from the heat, for 1 to 2 minutes or until golden.

Yield: 6 servings

Pear Almond Tart

1	sheet Pepperidge Farm frozen puff pastry thawed according to package directions	½	cup sugar
		2	tablespoons flour
		1	(29 ounce) can pear halves, drained well
½	cup ground, unblanched almonds	⅓	cup apricot preserves
		1	tablespoon light rum

Unfold pastry on a lightly floured board. Roll out to a 12½" square. Fit into a 9" pie plate; trim edges leaving a ¾" overhang. Crimp edges to make a rim.

Mix together almonds, sugar and flour; sprinkle evenly over pie shell. Cut each pear half into very thin slices, keeping pear in shape. Transfer to pie shell and arrange 4 pear half slices in spoke-fashion around edge. Arrange remaining pear half slices around center. Bake tart in a pre-heated 375° oven for 30 minutes. Remove from oven and let cool slightly. Heat apricot preserves and press through a sieve. Mix with rum; and, while tart is warm, brush apricot glaze over pears. Serve tart at room temperature.

Yield: 8 servings

Chocolate-Dipped Fruit

To dip cherries or strawberries, hold by stem; dip to coat a portion or the whole piece of fruit. Canned Mandarin oranges, maraschino cherries or dried fruit may be used. Dried fruit should be cut into ¼" strips.

½	pound chocolate or white chocolate bark or confectioners chocolate-flavored coating	**Fruit of your choice.**

Finely chop coating and place in top of a double boiler set over simmering water; stir constantly until melted. Remove from heat, but leave over hot water. With a fork, dip desired fruit, one at a time, into melted coating. do not pierce fruit as juice causes chocolate to lump. Draw fork over side of pan to remove excess coating. Use second fork to gently push morsels onto baking sheet lined with waxed paper. Let stand until coating hardens. Store fresh fruit in refrigerator. Serve within 24 hours.

Scandinavian Holiday Wreath

In Scandinavia, Christmas is especially wonderful and gay, celebrated by many until January 13th, St. Canute's Day. Guests are greeted with the Swedish greeting "Valkommen!." This wreath is one of the delicacies served.

Cream Puff Wreath:

1½ cups water	1½ cups flour
½ cup butter or margarine, softened	1½ tablespoons sugar
	6 eggs

In large saucepan, bring water and butter to a boil. All at once, add flour mixed with sugar; stir constantly until mixture no longer clings to sides of saucepan. Remove from heat; add eggs, one at a time, stirring vigorously after each addition.

Preheat oven to 400°. Reserve ¾ cup dough. To make wreath: on ungreased cookie sheet, place an 8 inch waxed paper circle. Drop heaping tablespoons of dough, forming about 18 puffs, ¼ inch apart, around edge of circle; remove wax paper. Inside circle, repeat procedure, forming about 12 puffs and allowing circles to touch slightly. Using reserved ¾ cup dough, form a "bow" at bottom of wreath. Bake 15 minutes; then reduce oven to 350° and bake an additional 30 minutes. Pierce in a few places with a pointed sharp knife to let out the steam. Cool completely on cookie sheet. Then remove to flat serving platter.

Scandinavian Cream Filling:

1 cup sour cream	2 tablespoons instant tea powder
½ cup milk	
½ teaspoon rum extract	½ cup finely chopped almonds
1 package (3¾ ounces) vanilla instant pudding mix	

In small bowl, combine sour cream, milk and rum extract, instant pudding and instant tea powder. Using electric mixer, mix at low speed to blend. Beat at high speed about 30 seconds or until slightly thickened; do not overbeat. Fold in almonds.

Glaze:

½ cup confectioners sugar	¼ teaspoon rum extract
2 teaspoons water	¼ cup chopped candied fruit

Combine all ingredients except fruit. Using a sharp knife, carefully slit tops from puffs; scoop out centers. Fill each puff with cream filling. Drizzle with rum glaze and decorate with candied fruit. Chill no longer than 2 hours before serving.

Yield: 1 wreath

Mother's Apple Dumplings

Apple dumplings were one of my father's favorite desserts. Soon after they were married, my mother attempted to make them. They were a disaster. She could not make the pastry stay around the apples. My father took one look at them and asked what on earth it was. My mother dissolved in tears. I take the easy way out by cutting squares of pastry to lay on top. Less calories, too.

Pastry:

2	cups flour	¾	cup shortening
½	teaspoon salt	5	or 6 tablespoons cold water

Mix flour and salt in a bowl, cut in shortening with two knives, pastry blender or tips of fingers until mixture resembles coarse meal. Make a well in center and add enough water to make dough into a ball. Divide in half. Roll out one half on a floured board. Cut into 5" squares. Prick each square 3 times with a fork. Do the same with the rest of the dough, until you have 6 squares.

6	medium-size baking apples, Roman Beauty, Granny Smith or Golden Delicious	1½	teaspoons cinnamon
½	cup sugar	2	tablespoons butter in small bits

Peel and core the apples. Place them in a rectangular pan large enough to hold them with at least a 2" space between. Mix sugar and cinnamon together and fill cavities in middle of apples with it, dot with the butter. Place squares of pastry over apples, pressing down over sides.

Syrup:

1	cup sugar	3	tablespoons butter
1½	cups water	¼	teaspoon cinnamon

Mix all ingredients in a saucepan. Bring to a boil and boil for 3 minutes. Pour around dumplings. Bake at 425° until apples are tender and pastry golden brown. Serve with juice in deep dishes with enough room for plenty of light cream.

Yield: 6 dumplings

Mrs. Dorman's Dessert

The toasted pecans in this dessert make it special.

6	eggs, separated	1	teaspoon vanilla
1	cup butter or margarine	2	cups vanilla wafer crumbs
1	(1 pound) box powdered sugar	1	cup heavy cream, whipped, for garnish
2	cups toasted pecans, chopped		

Cream butter or margarine and 1½ cups of the powdered sugar, add egg yolks, one at a time, beating after each addition. Add toasted pecans and vanilla. Beat egg whites to soft peaks, add the rest of the powdered sugar, gradually, and beat to stiff but not dry peaks. Add about ⅓ of whites to egg yolk mixture to lighten it, then fold in rest of beaten whites. Spread 1 cup of the vanilla wafer crumbs in bottom of a 13″×9″×2″ pan. Carefully pour filling over, smoothing top. Sprinkle rest of crumbs on top. Refrigerate for 24 hours before serving. Cut into squares and serve with whipped cream. This can also be frozen.

Yield: 12 to 15 servings

Sundae Pie

The original recipe called for a pie crust and the filling on top. We served this frequently at church functions and felt that the crust was superfluous. You may do as you like.

½	cup shortening	1	teaspoon vanilla
2	eggs	¾	teaspoon salt
1¼	cups brown sugar, packed	¾	cup flour
2	teaspoons light corn syrup	1	cup chopped nuts

Cream shortening and sugar until fluffy, add eggs, corn syrup, vanilla and salt. Mix well in mixer, then add flour and nuts. Place in a well buttered pie plate. Bake in pre-heated 300° oven until barely firm in center. Do not over bake. Cut into 8 wedges and serve with whipped cream. The amount of salt is correct since shortening is used instead of margarine or butter.

Yield: 1 9″ pie

Chocolate Crumb Dessert

30	vanilla wafers, crushed	3	(1 ounce) squares
1	cup finely chopped pecans		unsweetened chocolate,
6	eggs, separated		melted and cooled to
2	cups powdered sugar		lukewarm
2	sticks margarine	1	tablespoon Amaretto

Put half the crumbs in bottom of 9″×13″×2″ pan. Cream margarine and powdered sugar, then add egg yolks, melted chocolate, Amaretto, and chopped pecans and beat until fluffy. Beat egg whites until they hold soft peaks when beater is lifted. Fold about ¼ of the beaten whites into yolk mixture, then gently fold in the rest. Spread over crumbs. Sprinkle rest of crumbs on top. Chill overnight. To Serve: cut into 12 or 15 portions and garnish with whipped cream.

Yield: 12 to 15

Chocolate Pudding Cake

This was a dessert often served at church suppers or luncheons, since it could be increased in quantity and baked in large pans of 32 servings each.

1	cup flour	¼	teaspoon salt
¾	cup sugar	½	cup milk
½	cup chopped nuts	2	tablespoons oil
2	tablespoons cocoa	1	teaspoon vanilla
2	teaspoons baking powder		

Lightly spoon flour into measuring cup. Level off. In large bowl, combine flour, sugar, baking powder, salt, cocoa, milk, oil, nuts and vanilla. Mix at medium speed until well blended. Spread into a 9″ cake pan, ungreased.

Topping:

¼	cup firmly packed brown sugar	¼	cup cocoa
		1¾	cups hot water

Mix all ingredients together in a small bowl, then pour over cake, do not stir. Bake at 350° for 35 minutes . Spoon into serving dishes along with the chocolate sauce in the bottom of the pan. Serve warm with whipped cream or ice cream.

Yield: 6 servings

Caramel Pecan Pudding

This is similar to the Chocolate Pudding cake, but is a handy recipe to have for those who cannot eat chocolate.

2 cups brown sugar, packed	2 cups water

Blend sugar and water well and pour into a 9″ square or round pan.

Pudding:

3 tablespoons butter, melted	2 teaspoons baking powder
1 cup sugar	½ cup pecans, chopped
½ cup milk	1 teaspoon vanilla
1 cup flour	

Mix all ingredients together and pour into sugar mixture. Do not stir. Cook in a pre-heated 300° oven for 1 hour and 10 minutes. Serve warm with light cream or whipped cream.

Yield: 6 servings

Sour Cream Raisin Pudding Cake

1 cup flour	2 tablespoons oil
⅔ cup sugar	1 cup raisins
2 teaspoons baking powder	½ cup chopped nuts
¼ teaspoon salt	1 teaspoon vanilla
¾ cup sour cream	

Heat oven to 350°. Lightly spoon flour into measuring cup. Level off. In large bowl, combine flour, sugar, baking powder, salt, sour cream and oil. Mix well, add raisins, vanilla and nuts, then spread evenly in an ungreased 9″ square cake pan.

¾ cup brown sugar, packed	1½ cups hot water

Combine brown sugar and water in a bowl, stir well, then pour over batter. Do not stir. Bake at 350° for 50 to 60 minutes. Spoon into serving dishes along with sauce in bottom of pan. Serve warm with light cream.

Yield: 9 servings

English Apple Pudding

This is a very old recipe.

½	stick butter
½	cup sugar
1	egg, lightly beaten
½	cup milk
1	teaspoon baking powder

1¼	cups flour
3	medium apples, peeled, cored and sliced
¾	cup sugar
	Cinnamon

Cream butter and sugar. Add egg and mix well. Add milk. Sift baking powder and flour, mix with wet ingredients to form a batter. Place apples in buttered pie plate and sprinkle with sugar and cinnamon. Pour batter over apples and bake at 350° for 1 hour. Delicious served warm with ice cream.

Yield: 6 servings

Lemon Supreme Pudding

This is another recipe from the Guild Shop at Trinity Episcopal Church in Houston.

6	eggs, separated
¾	cup bottled lemon juice
1	cup sugar
	Pinch salt
1	envelope unflavored gelatin

¼	cup cold water
1	large homemade or bakery angel food cake torn into pieces.

Mix the egg yolks, lemon juice, sugar and salt in saucepan. Cook over low heat, stirring, until thickened. Soften gelatin in cold water and add to hot custard. Stir until gelatin is dissolved. Let cool until mixture starts to congeal. Whip egg whites until stiff, but not dry, and fold into lemon mixture with spatula. Place half of the cake pieces in an oiled 13″×9″×2″ cake pan. Pour half the lemon mixture over. Add rest of cake pieces and pour rest of lemon mixture over. Press cake into lemon mixture. Set into refrigerator several hours to firm up. "Ice" with either whipped cream or whipped topping. Cut into squares and serve.

Yield: 12 to 15 servings

The bottled lemon juice is fine in this recipe.

Cynthia's Brie Dessert Quiche

I was entertained in a home in Madrid, Spain. Fruit was served before the dessert of flan. A fingerbowl was in front of me. Luckily, the hostess, who was on my right, was served first. She dipped the fruit in the water before eating it, a new custom to me.

Egg Quiche Crust for 9″ quiche
    with fluted rim in pastry
    section of this book
4   eggs, separated
1½ cups half and half

1   pound Brie cheese, rind
    removed and broken into
    small pieces
Pinch of salt

Pre-heat oven to 375°. Place pastry in pan and line with foil. Weight foil down with uncooked dried beans or rice or the metal pellets made for this purpose. The rice and beans may be saved and used over and over again. Bake for 10 minutes. Remove from oven and remove foil and beans or whatever has been used. Cool and set aside.

Beat egg yolks and cream with a wire whisk until well combined, then add cheese and salt. Beat egg whites until stiff but not dry. Stir in about ¼ of the whites to lighten the mixture, then fold in rest of whites with a spatula. Pour into cooled crust, bake in pre-heated 350° oven for 45 to 55 minutes, or until knife inserted in center comes out clean. This is a thick quiche and should be cooked in a shell with a fluted rim. Let cool for 20 minutes before serving.

Yield: 8 servings

This is a delicious way to serve cheese and fruit for dessert. Pears are especially good with this, but you can serve any fruit of your choice. This can also be served as a first course on salad plates with a fork or as an appetizer with cocktails.

Easy Chocolate Ice Cream

I freeze this in a Donvier freezer.

2   cups fresh cream
1   cup milk
½   cup chocolate syrup
2   eggs

⅛   teaspoon salt
1   cup sugar
½   teaspoon vanilla extract

Beat all ingredients in mixer until well combined. Pour into freezer and freeze.

Yield: About 4 cups

Merry Christmas Ice Cream

My mother always made this ice cream for Christmas or special occasions. The candied cherries add a delicious "chewy" touch with the crisp almonds.

6	egg yolks	1	tablespoon vanilla
⅔	cup sugar	1	cup slivered blanched
⅛	teaspoon salt		almonds
1⅔	cups milk	1	cup quartered candied
2⅔	cups heavy cream		cherries

Combine egg yolks, sugar and salt in mixer bowl, beat until creamy and lemon-colored. Heat milk in medium heavy saucepan until it begins to boil. It will have little bubbles around the edges. Do not boil. Stir a little of the hot milk into the egg mixture, Mix well, then add yolk mixture to rest of milk. Cook, stirring constantly, until mixture thickens enough to lightly coat the spoon. Draw your finger over the back of the spoon, if it leaves a track, it is done. Do not boil. Cool for 20 minutes, then stir cream and vanilla into custard. Refrigerate. Put custard in ice cream freezer and freeze until it is a soft ice cream, add cherries and almonds and finish freezing. Remove dasher and pack in extra ice to harden or place in freezer.

Yield: about 1½ gallons

This ice cream is good without the almonds and cherries. Serve plain or with brandied fruit, strawberries macerated in Kirsch or topping of your choice.

Lime Sherbet

You may substitute lemon juice for the lime, if you wish.

1½	cups sugar	1	teaspoon grated lime rind
⅔	cup fresh lime juice	2	cups milk, scalded
1	envelope unflavored gelatin	3	cups half and half

Combine sugar and gelatin, then add scalded milk. Stir until gelatin is dissolved. Add half and half, lime juice and lime rind, mixing well. Mixture will curdle slightly. Pour into freezer, freeze; then remove dasher and pack in additional ice to harden.

Yield: About 1½ gallons

This is richer than most sherbets.

Lemon Sherbet

This is the sherbet my mother used to make.

1	envelope unflavored gelatin	½	cup lemon juice
1	cup sugar	1	teaspoon grated lemon rind
1½	cups boiling water	2½	cups milk

Mix gelatin and sugar in large bowl, add boiling water and stir until gelatin is completely dissolved. Add lemon juice and rind. After mixture has cooled, add milk and freeze.

Yield: About 1½ gallons

Lemon Sherbet II

I serve this in lemon rind halves on an ivy leaf for an intermezzo between a rich first course and the entree, to clean the palate. Pretty and delicious.

1¾	cups lemon juice	2¼	cups water
1½	cups sugar	1	envelope unflavored gelatin

Mix sugar and gelatin in small saucepan, add water and stir over low heat until gelatin is dissolved. Remove from heat and stir in lemon juice. Cool, then freeze.

Yield: 1 quart

This recipe is ideal to freeze in a Donvier freezer.

Easy Cranberry Sherbet

This is only 177 calories per ½ cup.

1	(16 ounce) can cranberry sauce	2	tablespoons fresh lemon juice
¼	cup orange juice		White of 1 egg

Put cranberry sauce and juices in blender. Add egg white and blend about 30 seconds at high speed until smooth. Pour into small freezer and freeze according to directions.

Yield: 4 servings

Cranberry Orange Sherbet

This is another tart sherbet suitable for an intermezzo.

3	cups fresh cranberries	½	cup cold water
2	cups water	¼	cup orange juice
1½	cups sugar	1	egg white, beaten until
1	envelope unflavored gelatin		foamy

Combine cranberries and water in saucepan, bring to a boil and simmer for 5 minutes until berries burst. Press through a sieve. Add sugar to pulp. Soften gelatin in cold water and add to warm cranberry mixture. Stir until gelatin is dissolved. Stir in orange juice.Pour into freezer and freeze until mushy, add egg white and freeze. Take out dasher and either put in freezer or pack in additional ice to harden.

Yield: About 1½ gallons

Raleigh House Chocolate Mousse

In French, mousse means froth or foam. This recipe can be used as a cold mousse or hot souffle.

6	ounces unsweetened chocolate, broken into pieces	6	large eggs, room temperature, separated
1	cup sugar, divided	¼	teaspoon cream of tartar
⅓	cup water	1	tablespoon vanilla extract

Place chocolate into bowl of processor fitted with a metal blade. Turn machine on and off a few times, then process until chocolate is very finely chopped. Dissolve ½ cup sugar into water and bring to a rolling boil. With machine running, pour boiling mixture through feed tube and process until smooth. Let mixture remain in processor. Add egg yolks and vanilla to cooled chocolate mixture. Turn machine on and off, scrape down sides and mix for 3 to 4 seconds. Remove mixture to large bowl. Beat egg whites in mixer with cream of tartar to soft peaks, then add sugar gradually, beating until stiff, but not dry peaks form. Add about ¼ of egg whites to chocolate mixture to lighten, then fold rest of the whites in with a rubber spatula. It does not matter if a few streaks of egg white remain. Spoon into 1½ quart serving dish. Refrigerate several hours or until firm.

For a hot souffle, spoon mixture into 6 or 8 ounce souffle dishes that have been buttered and dusted with sugar, filling them ⅔ full. Place on an aluminum baking sheet that has been heated in a 425° oven. Bake for 12 to 15 minutes or until puffed. Serve immediately.

Yield: 8 to 10 servings

Cranberry Relish Sherbet

This is good with some Grand Marnier dribbled over before serving.

1	envelope unflavored gelatin	¼	cup orange juice
¼	cup cold water	½	teaspoon almond extract
2	cups buttermilk	1	egg white, beaten until
¾	cups frozen or canned		foamy
	cranberry-orange relish	2	tablespoons sugar
½	cup sugar		

Soften gelatin in water in small saucepan, cook over low heat, stirring, until gelatin dissolves. Transfer to a large mixing bowl, add about ¼ cup buttermilk to the dissolved gelatin very slowly, stirring constantly, then add the rest of the buttermilk, the relish, sugar, orange juice and almond extract. Place in freezer and freeze until mushy; add egg white mixed with the 2 tablespoons sugar, continue to freeze to ice cream consistency. Remove dasher and either place in freezer or pack in additional ice to harden.

Yield: about 1 gallon

Fresh Peach Ice Cream

This is a must when peaches are in season.

5	peaches (about 1¼ pounds)	1½	cups heavy cream
1½	cups sugar	½	teaspoon almond extract
1½	cups milk		

Blanch peaches in boiling water, peel and pit them. Place in a blender or food processor and purée them. In a large bowl, mix milk, sugar and cream, stirring until sugar is dissolved. Stir in the peach purée and almond extract, and freeze.

Yield: About 1½ quarts.

I like almond extract in this recipe. However, you may substitute vanilla, if you prefer.

Helpful Hint: *My Pennsylvania Dutch mother used to say: if, after a rain, you can see enough blue sky to make a Dutchman a pair of pants, the rain is over.*

Raleigh House Cheese Cake

This dessert was another popular one at Raleigh House. In the first years Raleigh House was open, there were very few places that served breakfast. Many of the camp parents bought a cheesecake for breakfast in their motel rooms.

12 ounces cream cheese, room temperature	2 eggs, room temperature
½ cup sugar	½ teaspoon vanilla

Place cream cheese in bowl of mixer and beat until fluffy, add eggs, sugar and vanilla. Beat until smooth. Pour into a 9″ graham cracker crust. Bake in a 325° oven about 20 minutes or until edges are firm, but center is a little shaky. Remove from oven and cool 20 minutes.

Topping:
1½ cups sour cream	½ teaspoon vanilla
2 tablespoons sugar	

Fold all ingredients together in a small bowl, and gently spread over cooled cheesecake. Return to 325° oven and bake for 5 minutes. Remove, cool, and refrigerate before serving.

Yield: 8 servings

Be careful not to overcook the cheesecake. Let it still be a little shaky in the middle as you would when baking custard. It will firm up when cold, but will still be creamy in the center.

Dessert Fudge

2 cups sugar	1 cup chopped pecans
4 eggs, room temperature	2 teaspoons vanilla
½ cup flour	1 cup heavy cream, whipped,
½ cup cocoa	for garnish
1 cup butter or margarine, melted	

Pre-heat oven to 325°. Beat sugar and eggs until mixture forms a ribbon when beaters are lifted. Sift flour and cocoa into egg mixture and beat well. Stir in melted butter, nuts and vanilla; do not overmix. Spread batter in a buttered 8″ × 10″ pan. Place that pan in larger pan with enough boiling water to come half-way up the sides. Bake until knife inserted in center comes out slightly moist, but clean, about 1 hour. Let cool. Cut into squares and serve with whipped cream or ice cream.

Yield: 12 to 16 squares

Strawberry Sherbet Chambord

This is a light tart sherbet suited for a dessert or for an intermezzo.

½   cup water
⅔   cup sugar
3   pints stawberries, hulled
     and sliced
¼   cup fresh lemon juice

2   or 3 tablespoons Chambord
     liqueur
1   large egg white, room
     temperature

Place sugar and water in a heavy saucepan, bring to a boil, covered, then uncover and boil for 3 minutes until sugar is dissolved. Let cool. Place strawberries in food processor and purée. Press purée through a strainer, discard pulp. Add lemon juice, chambord and syrup. Place in refrigerator and chill for 1 hour. Beat egg white until it is frothy and fold into strawberry mixture. Place in freezer and freeze. This is the right amount for a Donvier freezer, or any small freezer.

Yield: 1 quart

Liqueur may be omitted, add ½ teaspoon almond extract instead.

Apple and Peach Crisp

1   cup finely chopped dried
     peaches
6   tablespoons bourbon
¾   cup flour
9   tablespoons dark brown
     sugar, packed
½   teaspoon salt
1   stick butter plus 1
     tablespoon, cut into bits

1   cup Quick Quaker oats
6   tablespoons sliced,
     blanched almonds
6   golden delicious apples,
     peeled, quartered and sliced
     thin crosswise

Let peaches soak in bourbon for 5 minutes. In a bowl, mix flour, brown sugar, salt and butter until mixture makes coarse crumbs, add oats and almonds. Combine well. In another bowl, combine the apples and peach and bourbon mixture. Place in a buttered 8" × 10" pyrex or ceramic baking dish. Spread the crumbs over the top. Bake in pre-heated 350° oven for about 30 to 35 minutes or until apples are tender and topping browned.

Yield: 6 generous servings

Hettie's Cranberry Nut Pudding

This recipe may be doubled to make a 13" × 9" oblong pan to serve 12. It can be used as a dessert or as a side dish when serving any kind of fowl.

3 cups peeled, diced apple	1½ cups sugar
2 cups cranberries, raw (½ pound)	

Mix all ingredients and place in a 9"square × 3" deep buttered baking pan. Spread oat crumb mixture evenly over top. Bake at 350 degrees for about an hour or until juices have thickened as in a fruit pie. Serve warm or cold.

Oat Crumb Mixture:

1½ cups quick oats	½ cup coarsely chopped pecans
½ cup brown sugar, packed	
⅓ cup flour	1 stick butter or margarine, melted
⅛ teaspoon salt	

Mix all ingredients except butter or margarine in a bowl. Spread mixture over unbaked pudding. Drizzle melted butter over top. Bake as above.

Yield: 6 servings

Parfait Houston

1 quart coffee ice cream, softened slightly	3 ounces (6 tablespoons) brandy
1 cup heavy cream, whipped	
2 tablespoons instant coffee powder	

Add ¾ of the whipped cream to ice cream. Add instant coffee and gently blend in. Fill 6 parfait glasses. Put in freezer for several hours. Make a hole about the size of a lead pencil almost to the bottom of each parfait. Fill with brandy and top with rest of whipped cream. Return to freezer until ready to serve.

Yield: 6 servings

Poundcake Pudding

This is a great way to use leftover pound cake. No one will know it is a leftover. It can be fixed ahead of time, put in the refrigerator and baked just before dinner. I like it served lukewarm with whipped cream or light cream.

About 5 ounces stale poundcake, preferably homemade	¼	teaspoon salt
	2	teaspoons vanilla
4 eggs, beaten	2	cups milk
½ cup sugar	1	cup light cream

Butter a 6″ × 10″ × 1½″ baking pan. Cut poundcake into ¼″ slices. Place in a single layer in prepared pan.

Beat eggs, sugar, salt and vanilla together in a large bowl. Scald milk and cream until small bubbles begin at edge of pan. Pour slowly over egg mixture, beating with a wire whisk. Pour over poundcake, cake will rise to the top. Let it set for 10 minutes. Sprinkle a little sugar over the top. Place pan in one a little larger and pour enough boiling water in larger pan to come up an inch on pudding pan. Place in a 350° oven and bake for 25 to 30 minutes or until a table knife inserted in the center comes out clean. Remove from hot water and set aside to cool. If not eating within an hour, be sure to refrigerate. Bring to room temperature before serving.

Yield: 6 to 8 servings

Chambord Mousse

This is a delicious frozen dessert.

6	egg yolks	4	ounces (½ cup) Chambord liqueur
1	cup heavy cream		
3	tablespoons sugar		

Beat the egg yolks, sugar and Chambord together until thick and pale yellow. In another bowl, beat cream until stiff. Fold cream, gently, into egg yolk mixture until mixture is completely blended. Spoon into your prettiest freezer-proof dessert dishes and freeze at least 1 hour, covered. Serve straight from the freezer.

Yield: 4 servings

Orange Cream Trifle

This dessert just takes 30 minutes to prepare. It is a pretty dessert and should be served at the table.

11 ounce can Mandarin oranges, drained, reserve syrup	4 cups milk
	1 cup heavy cream
	1 teaspoon almond extract
3½ or 3¾ ounce package vanilla instant pudding mix	2 (3 ounce) packages ladyfingers (2 dozen)
1 (3 ounce) package dessert topping mix (2 envelopes)	¼ cup sugar

Place oranges sections on paper-lined baking pan or pie plate and freeze to chill quickly. Meanwhile, in large bowl with mixer at low speed, beat instant pudding, dessert-topping mix, milk, cream and extract just until blended. Increase speed to medium-high, beat 5 minutes or until fluffy, occasionally scraping sides of bowl with rubber spatula.

Split ladyfingers and line bottom and sides of a 2 quart bowl or trifle dish. Drizzle with half the reserved orange syrup. Spoon half the pudding mixture into bowl; arrange remaining ladyfingers on pudding and drizzle with remaining syrup. Spoon remaining pudding mixture into bowl; arrange orange sections on top. Refrigerate. About an hour before dinner, melt the ¼ cup sugar in a small heavy saucepan over high heat until amber-colored. Remove from heat and let stand 2 minutes. With spoon, quickly drizzle sugar over pudding by waving spoon back and forth for thin strands. If making ahead of time, do not put caramelized sugar on until an hour before serving as it will tend to melt. This can be served without the spun sugar topping, if you like.

Yield: 12 servings

Serve in trifle dish or crystal bowl.

Amaretto Chocolate Mousse

This is another beautiful dessert that should be served at the table or from a buffet.

6	ounces (1 cup) semi-sweet morsels	4	egg yolks, beaten
18	whole blanched almonds	⅓	cup sugar
½	cup Amaretto	2	cups milk
2	envelopes unflavored gelatin	4	egg whites, stiffly beaten
		2	cups heavy cream, whipped
¼	cup water	2	packages (3 ounces each) lady fingers, split

Place chocolate pieces in a bowl. Place in another bowl of hot water. Stir until chocolate is melted. Dip bottom half of almonds into chocolate and place on waxed paper. Chill until firm. Gradually add Amaretto to remaining melted chocolate. Set aside.

Combine gelatin and water in a saucepan, add egg yolks, sugar and milk. Stir over low heat until mixture thickens slightly and coats a spoon. Stir in chocolate mixture. Chill until mixture mounds. Fold in beaten egg whites. Remove 1 cup of the whipped cream and set aside for decorating the top. Fold remaining into chocolate mixture. Chill until mixture mounds.

Line the bottom and sides of an ungreased 9″ springform pan with split lady fingers. Pour in chocolate mixture. Chill until firm. Remove sides of pan and pipe rosettes of whipped cream around outer edge of cake. Press an almond into each rosette. Chill until ready to serve.

Yield: 1 9″ Cake

Alma's Swiss Rice

2	cups whipping cream	⅓	cup cold water
½	cup sugar	⅓	cup boiling water
2	teaspoons vanilla		Fresh crushed strawberries or peaches
2	cups boiled rice		
1	tablespoon unflavored gelatin		

Whip cream until stiff, add sugar and vanilla and beat again to mix. Add rice gradually, folding in after each addition. Soak the gelatin in cold water to soften, then dissolve in the hot water. Add to rice mixture. Place in mold that has been rinsed out with cold water. Place in refrigerator. When firm, turn out on serving plate. Serve with strawberries, peaches or fruit of your choice.

Yield: about 8 servings

French Apple Turnovers

1   (17½ ounce) package
     Pepperidge Farm frozen
     puff pastry thawed
     according to package
     directions
½   cup sugar
1   tablespoon flour

1   teaspoon cinnamon
3   cups apples, peeled and cut
     into ½ inch pieces
1   egg beaten with 1
     tablespoon water for egg
     wash

Mix sugar, flour, cinnamon and apples. Set aside. On a lightly floured board, gently unwrap thawed puff pastry sheets. Roll each sheet into a 12" square. Cut each square into 4 6" squares. Place about ⅓ cup of the apple mixture on each square, Fold over to make a triangle, press edges together with a fork to seal. Brush each turnover with the egg wash. Place on cookie sheet and bake at 375° until golden brown. Cool. Brush with glaze made of ¾ cup powdered sugar and 1 tablespoon milk mixed together.

Yield: 8 turnovers

Strawberry Frozen Yogurt

This is another easy recipe.

1   quart plain yogurt
10   ounces frozen sliced
     strawberries

¼   cup honey
½   teaspoon almond extract

Put all ingredients in blender, blend until well mixed, then freeze according to directions.

Yield: about 6 cups

Helpful Hint: *Wine, in moderate quantities, has a mellowing property. A good man concerns himself, not with getting drunk, but with drinking in all the natural flavors of wine, its power to turn evenings into occasions, to lift eating beyond nourishment to companionship and to bring us, for a short time, to that happy state where men are wise, women are glamorous and even one's children begin to look promising.*

Gateau St. Honore

This is a little different presentation of Gateau St. Honore as it has the addition of fresh strawberries.

Cream Puff Dough:

¾   cup butter or margarine   6   large eggs
1½ cups flour

Preheat oven to 400°. In medium saucepan, combine 1 cup water and butter. Bring to boiling over medium heat, remove from heat and beat in flour all at once. Return to low heat and continue beating until mixture forms a ball and leaves side of pan. Remove from heat and add eggs, one at a time, beating hard after each addition. Continue until mixture is smooth and breaks into strands. Spread a dusting of flour on an ungreased cookie sheet and, with an 8" plate as a guide, draw a circle in the flour. Spread ⅓ of the dough evenly in the 8" circle, ¼" thick. On the same cookie sheet, for 12 medium-size puffs, drop another ⅓ of the dough by rounded tablespoons, 2 inches apart. Bake 30 to 35 minutes or until puffed and brown. Make a small slit in the top of each puff with a small sharp knife to let the steam out. Cool on a wire rack. For small puffs, drop rest of dough by level tablespoons, 2" apart, on ungreased cookie sheet. Bake 25 to 30 minutes or until puffed and brown. Slit and cool on wire rack.

Place 1¼ cups sugar and ¼ cup water in a medium-size heavy skillet, cook over medium heat until mixture forms a light-brown syrup, about 8 minutes. Stir to blend, Remove from heat.

Dip medium puffs into syrup and arrange around edge of cream puff round to make a border, puffs should touch one another. Dip the smaller puffs into the syrup and place on top of where first row of puffs join. Make a third row in same manner. Spoon rest of syrup over each cream puff.

Filling:

2   (3½ ounce) or 3¾ ounce)   2   cups whipping cream,
    vanilla-flavored instant   whipped
    pudding   1   teaspoon almond extract
2½ cups milk

Make instant pudding according to directions on the box, only use amount of milk in above recipe. Then fold in whipped cream and almond extract.

Just before serving, turn filling into the center of Gateau. Mound whole strawberries on top of filling and dust with sifted powdered sugar. Serve 2 or more puffs with some of the filling and strawberries to each guest.

Yield: 12 to 16 servings

Apricot Bombe

This is a showpiece dessert you can make in minutes, and put in the freezer.

1 (1 pound) can whole apricots	1 pint vanilla ice cream
⅓ cup apricot preserves	7 to 8 ladyfingers, split
	Frozen whipped topping

Drain apricots, reserving 1 tablespoon syrup. Heat preserves with syrup in small heavy saucepan until melted.

Unmold ice cream in one piece, onto a chilled serving plate. Press ladyfingers onto top and sides of ice cream to cover completely, cutting to fit where necessary. Brush melted preserve mixture over ladyfingers until absorbed. Return to freezer.

Just before serving, arrange 6 apricots on plate and garnish with rosettes or dollops of whipped topping between them. Cut into wedges to serve.

Yield: 6 servings

Blender Chocolate Souffle

1 cup evaporated milk, heated	½ teaspoon salt
1 cup semi-sweet chocolate chips	6 egg yolks
2 (3 ounce) packages cream cheese, cubed	6 egg whites
	⅓ cup powdered sugar

Heat oven to 325°. Put evaporated milk and chocolate chips into blender container, cover and blend at stir setting for a few seconds, then increase speed and process until smooth. Remove feeder cap and drop in cream cheese pieces one at a time; process a few seconds after each addition. Add salt and egg yolks, one at a time, replace feeder cap and continue processing until very smooth. In mixer bowl, beat egg whites until soft peaks form. Gradually add sugar and continue beating until stiff, but not dry, peaks form. Pour chocolate mixture over egg whites and fold in gently but thoroughly. Pour into ungreased 2 quart souffle dish and bake 45 minutes or until knife inserted in the center comes out clean. Dust with sifted powdered sugar and serve.

Yield: 8 to 10 servings

Flora's Peach Coconut

When fresh peaches are not available, this is a handy recipe to have.

1 (2½ size) can sliced peaches in light syrup	½ cup shredded coconut
2 tablespoons butter	¼ cup brown sugar, packed
1 cup fresh bread crumbs, lightly packed	¼ teaspoon cinnamon

Drain peaches, reserving juice and placing it in small saucepan. Spread peaches in buttered 9″ pie plate. In hot butter in a skillet, heat crumbs until light brown. Add coconut, sugar and cinnamon; heat until sugar begins to melt. Spread over peaches. Bake at 375° about 10 minutes or until crisply toasted and bubbling. Serve with peach sauce.

Peach Sauce:

1 cup peach juice	2 tablespoons butter
½ cup brown sugar, packed	¼ teaspoon ground nutmeg
Dash salt	
1 tablespoon fresh or frozen lemon juice	

Combine all ingredients, bring to a boil in small saucepan; cook, stirring, until sugar is melted. Serve warm over peaches.

Yield: 4 servings

Pear Crisp

This is another recipe made with canned fruit for off-season use.

1 (2½) can pear halves, drained	¼ teaspoon salt
½ cup brown sugar, packed	¼ teaspoon cinnamon
½ cup flour	¼ cup butter or margarine

Arrange pears, cut-side down, in a 9″ pie plate. Mix sugar, flour, cinnamon and salt. Work in butter until crumbly. Sprinkle thickly over and around pears. Bake 15 to 20 minutes in a 375 degree oven or until crumbs are golden brown. Serve warm with light cream or ice cream.

Yield: 4 servings

Peach Blueberry Crisp

I had an abundance of frozen blueberries so I tried this combination. My guests liked it.

2	cups sliced fresh or frozen peaches	1½	cups frozen blueberries
		½	cup sugar

Mix peaches, blueberries and sugar together in a small bowl, Place in a buttered 9 inch round casserole.

Topping:

1½	cups quick oats	½	cup pecans, coarsely
½	cup brown sugar, packed		chopped
⅓	cup flour	1	stick margarine, melted
⅛	teaspoon salt		

Mix topping ingredients together, except for the melted margarine. Spread dry mixture on top of fruit. Pour melted margarine over and bake at 350° for about an hour or until juices have thickened and topping is brown.

Yield: 6 servings

Twice this recipe will make a 9" × 13" × 2" pan.

Pear Turnovers

1	cup chopped fresh pears	1	tablespoon orange or
1	teaspoon lemon juice		apricot preserves
1	tablespoon flour		Make 1½ times the recipe for
1	tablespoon melted butter		pastry for a 9 inch pie

Toss pears with lemon juice, then with flour. Combine butter and marmalade or preserves.Add pears and mix. Roll pastry into a rectangle about 12" × 8". Cut into 6 4" squares. Divide pear mixture on squares, leaving a margin on edge. Fold over making a triangle. Press edges of pastry together firmly with a fork. Prick tops twice with a fork. Bake at 400° about 20 minutes or until golden brown.

Yield: 6 turnovers

Eggs & Cheese

Jane's Frittata

This is a great way to use leftover meat and vegetables. You can improvise however you like. Always use onion, then you can add fresh tomato sautéed in butter and drained, leftover meat or vegetables.

1	cup thinly sliced onion	¼	cup grated Parmesan
¼	cup olive oil		Cheese
2	tablespoons butter or	1	teaspoon salt
	margarine	¼	teaspoon pepper
8	eggs	2	cups thinly sliced zucchini
½	cup milk		

In a 10″ skillet, sauté zucchini in 2 tablespoons of the olive oil and 1 tablespoon butter or margarine, until limp but not brown. Remove from pan and drain off the fat. Beat eggs and milk, then add cheese, onion, salt, pepper and zucchini. Mix thoroughly. Heat remaining oil and butter in skillet. When very hot, pour in egg mixture; cook 5 minutes until bottom and sides are set. Loosen sides with a spatula. Place a plate over skillet; flip frittata onto plate then slide back into skillet, uncooked side down. Cook 4 minutes longer or until bottom is set. Serve immediately with boiled new potatoes and mustard on the side.

Yield: 6 to 8 servings

Frittata made with fresh spinach torn into pieces and beaten in with the eggs, raw, is delicious.

Brunch Casserole

This casserole has to be made the day before serving.

2	pounds sausage	6	eggs
½	cup chopped green onions	3	cups milk
1	(2 ounce) can chopped	¼	teaspoon dry mustard
	pimientos	1	tablespoon Worcestershire
12	slices bread		sauce

Cook sausage until crumbly, drain well. Add onions and pimento. Layer 6 slices of bread, crusts removed, in a buttered 13″ × 9″ × 2″ casserole. Spoon meat, onions and pimento over bread. Top with rest of bread. Beat together the eggs, milk, mustard and Worcestershire sauce. Pour over casserole. Place in refrigerator overnight. Next day, bake in a 350° oven for 1¼ hours. Mushrooms may be added, if desired.

Yield: 8 to 12 servings

Ham Breakfast Casserole

This casserole has to be prepared the day before cooking.

¼	cup diced green pepper	1	pound cooked ham, diced in bite-sized pieces
⅓	cup minced onion		
2	cups sliced fresh mushrooms, 6 ounces	7	eggs
		3	cups milk
2	tablespoons butter	1½	teaspoons dry mustard
16	slices sandwich bread, crusts removed	1	teaspoon salt
		¼	teaspoon white pepper
1	pound cheddar cheese, grated	2	cups cornflakes, crushed
		1	tablespoon butter

Grease a 13″×9″×2″ pan well. Sauté pepper and onion and mushrooms in butter until tender, but not brown. Place 8 slices bread in bottom of pan. Spread 8 ounces of the grated cheese on top of bread. Place ham over cheese and spread sautéed vegetables over ham. Place remaining cheese on top of vegetables and remaining 8 slices of bread over the top.

Mix eggs, milk, mustard, salt and pepper together and pour over bread. Let set overnight in refrigerator. Before baking the next day, spread cornflakes over and dot with the butter. Bake at 350° for 1½ to 2 hours or until custard is set in the center when knife is inserted.

Yield: 12 servings

Macaroni and Cheese Frittata

2	tablespoons butter	1	cup grated cheddar cheese, 4 ounces
8	eggs		
½	cup milk		
⅛	teaspoon pepper		
1	cup cooked elbow macaroni, about ½ cup, uncooked		

Melt butter in 10″ skillet. Beat together the eggs, milk and pepper. Stir in the macaroni and cheese. Pour into skillet and cook over medium heat until eggs are almost set, 3 to 4 minutes. Broil 6 inches from heat until eggs are completely set and top is browned. Serve from skillet or invert on serving plate.

Yield: 4 servings

Spinach Ricotta Quiche

This book has a number of crust recipes. However, you can always use a frozen crust or prepared crusts of various kinds for your quiche. Be sure to pre-bake them as directed.

2	tablespoons minced green onions, white only	⅛	teaspoon pepper
2	tablespoons butter or margarine	⅛	teaspoon nutmeg
1	(10 ounce) package frozen chopped spinach, thawed and squeezed dry	½	cup Ricotta cheese
		3	eggs
		½	cup heavy cream
¼	teaspoon salt	¼	cup coarsely grated Swiss cheese
		Cherry tomatoes, optional	

Sauté onions in butter, add spinach and stir over moderate heat a few minutes to evaporate all the water. Remove from heat, add salt, pepper, nutmeg and ricotta. Beat eggs and cream until well mixed but not frothy. Stir in spinach mixture and Swiss cheese. Pour into prepared shell and bake in a pre-heated 375° oven for 25 to 30 minutes or until set. Serve with tomatoes, if desired.

Yield: 6 servings

Rice Frittata

1	tablespoon butter	4	drops Tabasco
½	cup minced onion	2	cups cooked rice
8	eggs	1	(4 ounce) can chopped green chilis, undrained
½	cup milk		
1	teaspoon salt	1	medium tomato, chopped
1	teaspoon Worcestershire sauce	½	cup grated cheddar cheese

In 10″ skillet, over medium heat, sauté onion in butter until limp but not brown. Remove from skillet with a slotted spoon.

Beat together eggs, milk and seasonings. Stir in rice, chilis, tomato and sautéed onion. Pour into skillet and cook over medium heat, until eggs are almost set, 12 to 15 minutes. Sprinkle with cheese, cover, remove from heat and let stand about 10 minutes. Cut into wedges and serve.

Yield: 4 servings

White Cheese Casserole

The combination of cheeses in this recipe is unbeatable and different from most casseroles of its kind. It would be delicious served for a luncheon with a generous green or fruit salad.

6   **(½ inch) slices of firm-textured bread, crusts removed**
1½ **cups whole milk**
4   **large eggs**
8   **ounces Monterey Jack cheese**

4   **ounces cream cheese**
½   **cup creamed small curd cottage cheese**
½   **of ¾ of a stick of butter or margarine**

Cut bread into ½ inch cubes and cut the Monterey Jack and cream cheese in the same manner. Cut the butter in ¼ inch cubes. Set aside.

Beat eggs in a large bowl, add milk and mix again. Then add bread, cheeses, cottage cheese, butter and mix well. Pour into a buttered 11″ × 7″ × 2″ casserole. Place in the refrigerator, covered, overnight.

Next day, bake in a pre-heated 350° oven for 45 to 50 minutes or until a knife inserted in center comes out clean. Let set 10 minutes before serving. Cut into portions or spoon onto plates.

Yield: 6 servings

Recipe can be doubled for a 13″ × 9″ × 2″ casserole that serves 12.

Helpful Hint: *Mark quart or cup capacity on bottom of much-used casseroles or bowls with a permanent marking pen. Marking will survive dishwashing and take the guesswork out of matching recipes to casserole size.*

Brie Cheese Strata

Good for a luncheon dish with a fruit salad and white wine.

1	stick butter, do not substitute	1½	cups milk
6	slices firm textured bread, such as French or homemade bread, crusts removed	1	teaspoon salt
			Dash Tabasco
		4	eggs
		1	pound Brie Cheese, rind removed

Butter a 1½ quart soufflé dish. Butter one side of bread slices and cut each into 3 fingers. Mix milk, eggs, salt and tabasco with wire whisk. Grate Brie on coarse grater.

Put 3 slices (9 strips) bread into bottom of dish, butter-side up. Sprinkle with half the Brie. Repeat using rest of Brie and bread. Gently pour milk mixture over the bread and let stand, covered, in the refrigerator overnight or 8 hours. Pre-heat oven to 350°. Bake for 25 to 30 minutes or until golden brown and set in middle.

Yield: 4 to 6 servings

Carrot Frittata

Great for a late evening snack, brunch or lunch.

1	cup grated carrots	½	teaspoon celery salt
½	cup chopped onion	¼	teaspoon thyme or marjoram, crushed
½	cup water		
8	eggs	½	teaspoon pepper
½	cup milk	2	tablespoons butter
½	teaspoon dry mustard		

Combine carrots, onion and water in a 10″ skillet with an oven-proof handle. Cover and cook over medium heat about 5 minutes or until crisp-tender. Drain and set aside.

Beat eggs, milk and seasonings together . Stir in onion-carrot mixture. Melt butter in same skillet over medium heat. Pour mixture into skillet and cook until eggs are almost set, 8 to 10 minutes. Place in oven and broil, 6 inches from heat, until eggs are set, 3 to 4 minutes. Or, you can cover the skillet, remove from heat and let stand 5 to 7 minutes. Cut into wedges and serve from skillet or invert onto serving plate and serve. Garnish with halved cherry tomatoes.

Yield: 4 to 6 servings

Cheesy Egg Casserole

¼	cup flour	1	(4 ounce) can chopped green chilis, drained
¼	teaspoon salt		
¼	cup margarine or butter, melted	2	cups (8 ounces) Monterey Jack cheese, grated
4	eggs, beaten	1	(4 ounce) jar pimientos, chopped
1	cup creamed small curd cottage cheese		

Combine flour, salt and butter in a large bowl. Add next 4 ingredients. Mix well. Pour mixture into a buttered 10″×6″×2″ casserole. Garnish with pimientos. Bake, uncovered, for 30 minutes in a 350° oven.

Yield: 6 servings

Beef-Vegetable Quiche

	Pastry for a 9″ pie, pricked and pre-baked for 10 minutes, cooled	1	cup sliced mushrooms, fresh or canned
1	pound lean ground beef	2	medium tomatoes, skinned and cut into thin wedges
1	tablespoon margarine	1	teaspoon leaf basil, crumbled
1	tablespoon cooking oil		
½	cup chopped onion	½	teaspoon salt
1	large clove garlic, finely minced	¼	teaspoon pepper
2	cups pared, cubed egg plant	1½	cups grated Swiss cheese, divided
1	cup thinly sliced zucchini		

Brown beef in skillet, stirring to break up; pour off drippings. In another skillet or saucepan, melt margarine and oil and, over medium heat, sauté the onion and garlic a few minutes. Add eggplant and zucchini and cook, stirring constantly, about 5 minutes; reduce heat and add mushrooms and tomatoes, cooking 5 minutes, stirring constantly. Add beef, basil, salt and pepper. Sprinkle ¾ cup cheese in bottom of prepared pie shell and add beef mixture. Top with the rest of the cheese and bake in a 350° oven about 25 minutes or until pastry is browned and filling bubbling.

Yield: 6 servings

Brunch Cheese Pudding

This has the same cheeses in it that the White Cheese Casserole has. The difference is that this version is like a soufflé and has to be served at once, by inserting two spoons and lifting out the soufflé. It is superb. Please try it.

6	large eggs	1	cup small curd cottage
1	cup milk		cheese
1	pound Monterey Jack	½	cup flour
	cheese, cut into ½″ cubes	1	teaspoon double-acting
8	ounces cream cheese, cut		baking powder
	into ½″ cubes		
¾	stick unsalted butter, cut		
	into ½″ cubes		

In a large bowl, beat eggs and the milk. Add the Monterey Jack cheese, cream cheese, butter and cottage cheese. Combine well. Sift the flour and baking powder together, add to cheese mixture. Place in a 2 quart soufflé dish, or a casserole with straight sides, that has been buttered and dusted with fine bread crumbs. Bake in a preheated 350° oven for 1 hour or until it is puffed and golden. It will still be a little trembly in center. Serve at once.

Yield: 8 servings

Chicken Bacon Quiche

Any quiche can be served as an appetizer. Served on small plates in the living room with drinks is a good way to use it as a first course. In that way, it eliminates clearing the table one time. Salad can be served with the entree.

2	cups chopped cooked	1	tablespoon cornstarch
	chicken	1	teaspoon salt
½	teaspoon onion salt	Dash tabasco sauce	
1	cup shredded Swiss cheese	2	tablespoons grated
4	eggs		Parmesan cheese
1	cup milk	2	slices bacon, cooked crisp
¼	cup corn oil		and crumbled

Sprinkle onion salt in pre-baked 9″ pie crust. Mix chicken and cheese and put in crust. In mixing bowl, beat eggs slightly; stir in milk and corn oil. Add cornstarch, salt and tabasco until well blended. Pour over chicken mixture. Sprinkle with Parmesan cheese and bacon. Bake in a pre-heated 350° oven about 40 minutes or until delicately browned and custard is set. Let set a few minutes before serving.

Yield: 6 to 8 servings

Cottage Cheese Spinach Quiche

Baked in a china quiche dish, this is a pretty dish to serve at the table. It is topped with slices of fresh tomato.

1 unbaked 9″ pie crust, pre-baked for 10 minutes in a 375° oven, weighted down with foil lined with unbaked dried beans. Remove foil and beans midway of baking.	¼ cup whole milk
	Dash nutmeg
	½ teaspoon salt
	Dash white pepper
	4 large eggs, beaten
	1½ cups creamed small curd cottage cheese
⅓ cup minced onion	½ cup grated Parmesan cheese
2 tablespoons unsalted butter	
1 (10 ounce) package chopped frozen spinach, thawed and squeezed dry	2 fresh tomatoes, thinly sliced
	2 tablespoons butter.

In a heavy saucepan or skillet, sauté onion in butter until it is limp. Add the spinach and cook for 2 minutes. Remove from heat and stir in milk, nutmeg, salt and pepper, cool. In a bowl, beat eggs, cottage cheese and the Parmesan cheese; stir in spinach mixture. Pour into prepared pie shell. Arrange slices of tomato around edge and in the middle. Sprinkle them with salt and white pepper and dot with butter.

Bake in a pre-heated 350° oven for 35 to 40 minutes or until quiche tests done in middle. Let set 5 or 10 minutes before serving.

Yield: 6 servings

You may use a regular pie tin, if you prefer.

Helpful Hint: *Quick Quiche Crusts: Press a thin layer of cooked spaghetti on bottom and sides of a well-buttered quiche pan. Pour in the quiche of your choice and bake as usual. Crust browns nicely and is much quicker to make than pastry. Cut with a sharp knife. Another quick crust is to unroll a package of crescent rolls and press into a quiche pan, fill with your favorite filling and bake.*

Zucchini Quiche

This quiche has a rice shell which may also be used in other quiches if you like. I think it is a nice change from the pastry crust. A vegetable cooking spray is used instead of butter which makes it lower in calories.

Rice Shell:

1½ cups cooked rice
1   egg, beaten

¼ cup shredded Swiss cheese
   (1 ounce)

Spray a 10″ pie plate with vegetable cooking spray. Combine rice, egg and cheese. Stir well. Press into pie plate; bake at 350° for 5 minutes. Press rice mixture back up sides of pie plate, if necessary, with the back of a spoon. Cool.

Filling:

1½ cups zucchini, sliced in ⅛″
     slices
¼   pound fresh mushrooms,
¼   cup chopped onion
3   eggs, beaten
½   cup evaporated skim milk

¼ cup water
½ teaspoon salt
¼ teaspoon white pepper
¾ cup grated swiss cheese,
   divided

Cook zucchini in a small amount of salted water for 3 minutes. Drain well. Spray a small skillet with vegetable cooking spray. Sauté mushrooms and onion over low heat until limp. Set aside.

Combine milk, water, eggs, salt and pepper in a bowl and mix well. Add zucchini, mushroom mixture and ½ cup cheese. Stir well. Pour into prepared rice shell, and top with remaining ¼ cup grated cheese. Bake about 35 to 40 minutes or until set in middle in a 375° oven.

Yield: 6 servings

You may use butter to sauté and grease pan, if you like.

Quiche Au Fromage

The first time I ate this quiche was at a Chef's Training School in Zurich, Switzerland. They were served as a first course in individual size. The rich taste of cheese without any vegetables or meats was delicious. They graciously served us seconds.

Crust:

1	cup flour	1	tablespoon ice water
¼	teaspoon salt	1	teaspoon lemon juice
⅓	cup butter or margarine, chilled	2	cups dried beans or rice (for pre-baking shell)
1	egg		

Stir together flour and salt in a bowl, then cut butter in with a pastry blender or 2 knives until it resembles coarse crumbs. With a fork, beat together egg, water and lemon juice until blended. Sprinkle over flour mixture. Toss with a fork; then with your hand, gather mixture into a ball. If mixture is too dry to make a ball, add 1 or 2 teaspoons more ice water. Wrap airtight and put in the freezer for 10 minutes. On a lightly floured board, roll out to a circle 1 to 1½ " larger than quiche or pie pan. Roll up on your rolling pin and place in the pan, being careful not to stretch the dough. Trim and crimp the edges. Prick pastry with a fork about 10 times. Cover with a circle of waxed paper and fill with beans. Bake in a pre-heated oven at 425° for 12 minutes. Cool slightly, remove paper and beans.(save beans for future pastry making.) Fill shell with preferred quiche filling and bake as directed.

Filling:

2	cups (1 pound) grated Swiss or Gruyere cheese	¼	teaspoon salt
1	tablespoon flour		Dash nutmeg
4	eggs	2	cups light cream
		2	tablespoons butter

Toss the cheese with the flour and spread in the pastry shell. Beat the eggs, salt and nutmeg, then beat in the cream. Slowly pour into the shell, so as not to disturb the cheese. Dot with the butter. Bake in a pre-heated 375° oven on the middle shelf for 25 minutes or until a knife inserted in the center comes out clean. Let set 10 minutes before cutting into wedges.

Yield: 6 servings

Crustless Quiche Lorraine

This recipe is given for the microwave, however you can cook it in a conventional oven at 350°.

½ pound bacon, diced	1 cup evaporated milk
1 cup shredded Swiss cheese	½ teaspoon salt
¼ cup minced onion	¼ teaspoon sugar
4 eggs	Dash Tabasco sauce

Place diced bacon in wreath shape on several layers of paper towels on a paper plate. Cover with a paper towel and microwave on high for 5 to 6 minutes, rotating plate once during cooking. Sprinkle bacon, cheese, and onion into a glass pie plate.

Beat remaining ingredients together in a bowl and pour over bacon mixture, Microwave 11 to 12 minutes on 70% power until knife inserted center comes out clean. Rotate once or twice during baking, if needed. Let stand 10 minutes before serving.

Yield: 4 to 6 servings

French Quiche

1 9″ pastry shell baked until light brown	1 cup grated Swiss cheese
4 slices bacon	3 eggs
1 medium onion, sliced	¼ teaspoon dry mustard
1 tablespoon bacon drippings	1 cup half and half, heated
1 cup baked or boiled ham, shredded	Dash nutmeg

Cook bacon over low heat until crisp. Drain and crumble over bottom of pie shell. Sauté onion in bacon grease until soft. Arrange over bacon. Place half the shredded ham and half the cheese over onions, repeat layers of ham and cheese. Beat eggs and mustard together, add to warm cream and beat again., Pour into pie shell. Sprinkle with nutmeg. Bake in a pre-heated 350° oven for 35 minutes or until a knife inserted in center comes out clean. Let set 10 minutes before serving.

Yield: 4 generous servings

Ann's Scallop Quiche

My granddaughter gave me this recipe. This is an easy way to serve seafood.

9″	pastry shell precooked for 10 minutes. Place foil in crust, fill bottom with dried beans or uncooked rice, bake at 375° for 5 minutes, remove foil then bake for another 5 minutes. Remove from oven and cool	¼	cup dry vermouth
		3	tablespoons butter
		¼	cup finely chopped onion
		¼	finely chopped celery
		4	eggs
		¾	cup whole milk
¾	pound scallops, washed and cut in slices if large	1	cup half and half
		¼	teaspoon salt
		¼	teaspoon white pepper
		½	teaspoon dillweed

Mix scallops and vermouth in glass or plastic bowl. Refrigerate 1 hour. Sauté onions and celery in the butter until limp. In a bowl, beat eggs with a whisk, then add milk, half and half and seasonings. Add scallop mixture and pour into prepared crust. Bake in a pre-heated 375 ° oven 25 to 30 minutes or until knife inserted in middle comes out clean. Let set for 10 minutes before serving.

Yield: 6 servings

Crabmeat Quiche

This makes a pretty dish when served; delicious, too.

1	9″ pastry shell	4	eggs
1	large avocado, sliced, and sprinkled with lemon juice	1	(12 ounce) can evaporated milk
2	teaspoons lemon juice	¼	cup dry white wine
⅓	teaspoon salt	⅛	teaspoon salt
7	ounces white crabmeat		Dash white pepper
	Dash Tabasco		

Prebake pastry shell. Line with foil and fill bottom with dried beans or uncooked rice. Bake for 5 minutes, remove foil and beans and cook for 5 minutes more in a 375° oven. Cool.

Lay avocado slices in bottom of prepared crust, sprinkle with the ⅓ teaspoon of salt. Mix crabmeat with Tabasco and place on avocado. Beat eggs with a wire whisk, then add rest of ingredients. Mix well, then pour over crabmeat. Bake in a pre-heated 375° oven 30 to 35 minutes or until a knife inserted in center comes out clean. Let cool 10 minutes before serving.

Yield: 6 servings

Sour Cream Quiche

This quiche has a crust made of frozen hashed brown potatoes, which makes it a perfect breakfast or luncheon dish.

Crust:

3 cups frozen hashed brown potatoes	⅓ cup butter, melted

Thaw potatoes and press between paper towels to remove all moisture. Press potatoes into a 10" pie pan, drizzle melted butter over, Bake in a 425° oven for 25 minutes. Remove from oven and reduce heat to 350°.

Quiche:

½ cup cooked bacon, crumbled	¼ teaspoon salt
1 cup Swiss cheese, grated	Dash nutmeg
1 cup sour cream	Dash white pepper
4 eggs	1 cup evaporated milk

Sprinkle bacon and cheese in bottom of prepared shell. Beat sour cream, eggs and seasonings together. Stir in evaporated milk, pour into shell and bake for 35 to 40 minutes in 350°oven, or until knife inserted in center comes out clean. Cool for 10 minutes before serving.

Yield: 6 servings

The potato crust can be used in other ways. I have lined individual casseroles with it and filled them with creamed chicken, creamed ham or creamed hard boiled eggs.

Tuna Quiche

In another recipe in this book, I mentioned that my Mother always put tuna in a colander or fine sieve and ran hot water over it to remove the oil. I do this with the tuna in this recipe. It makes a milder tasting product, more like chicken.

1	(9 ounce) can tuna, drained and flaked	3	eggs
1	cup Swiss cheese in ¼″ dice	1	cup milk
		½	teaspoon salt
¼	cup grated Parmesan cheese	⅛	teaspoon white pepper
			Parsley and lemon wedges for garnish
¼	cup chopped green onions, with tops	1	(9″) pastry shell, pre baked
2	tablespoons chopped pimiento		

Sprinkle tuna, then Swiss cheese, Parmesan, onions and pimiento evenly in prepared pastry shell. Beat eggs, milk, salt and pepper until well mixed but not frothy. Pour into shell. Bake in a pre-heated 375° oven for 25 to 30 minutes or until set. Garnish with parsley and lemon.

Yield: 6 servings

Appetizer Quiche Lorraine

This quiche is made in a jelly roll pan, then cut into squares.

	Crust for 3 (9″) pie shells	4	cups light cream
1	pound sliced bacon	1½	teaspoons salt
2	cups finely chopped onion	1	teaspoon sugar
3	cups grated Swiss cheese, ¾ pound	¼	teaspoon nutmeg
		¼	teaspoon white pepper
6	eggs		Dash Tabasco sauce

Roll out pastry to a 18″×15″ rectangle. Use to line a cookie sheet with 1″ rim. Flute edges and refrigerate until needed.

Fry bacon until crisp. drain well and crumble. Sauté onion in 2 tablespoons bacon drippings. Sprinkle cheese over bottom of shell. Sprinkle bacon and onion over cheese. Beat eggs with cream, salt, sugar, nutmeg, pepper and tabasco. Pour over cheese and bacon. Bake in a 375° oven for 35 to 40 minutes or until firm in center. Cool 10 minutes before cutting into squares. Serve warm.

Yield: 25 appetizer, 60 cocktail

Individual Cheese Soufflé

When I attended La Varenne in Paris, I ate at the La soufflé Restaurant. The menu consisted only of soufflés (entree and dessert) salad and, of course, wine. I ordered a chicken soufflé, salad and a hazelnut soufflé for dessert. White wine was a must.

1½	tablespoons butter	¼	cup grated Gruyere or
2	tablespoons flour		Swiss cheese
½	cup milk	2	egg whites
¼	teaspoon salt	½	tablespoon grated cheese
Dash pepper			for sprinkling on top before
⅛	teaspoon dry mustard		baking
2	egg yolks		

Melt butter, stir in flour and cook until foamy. Remove from heat and gradually add milk, stirring constantly. Return to heat and bring to a boil, stirring, simmer 2 minutes. Season with salt, pepper and mustard. Remove from heat and beat in the egg yolks. Let cool slightly, then add cheese. Taste for seasoning. This can be done 3 to 4 hours ahead of time. However, sauce has to be lukewarm before proceeding.

Preheat oven to 400°. Beat egg whites until soft peaks hold their shape when beater is lifted. This is the secret of a good soufflé. Very stiffly beaten whites are too hard to mix in without losing some of their volume. Add ¼ of the whites to custard to lighten mixture. Mix well with spatula, then gently fold in remaining whites with spatula. Pour mixture into a 2 cup soufflé dish that has been buttered and dusted with fine bread crumbs. Sprinkle the ½ tablespoon cheese on top. Bake 12 to 15 minutes or until soufflé is puffed and brown. It should be slightly trembly in center. Serve at once. The saying goes, the customer can wait on the soufflé, but the soufflé waits on no one.

Yield: 1 serving

To finish my story, the waiter brought a cheese soufflé, separated it with two spoons and spooned in delicious creamed chicken. On my return home, I invested in a dozen 2 cup soufflé dishes, which were the size they used, and loved fixing this for friends.

Filled Cheese Roll

This is a soufflé-like cheese roll filled with spinach. However, you may fill it with mix of chicken or ham using much the same ingredients.

Spinach filling:

2 (10 ounce) packages frozen chopped spinach, thawed and squeezed dry
2 tablespoons butter or margarine
¼ cup minced onion
¼ teaspoon salt
¼ cup grated sharp Cheddar cheese
½ cup sour cream
¼ pound thinly sliced processed cheese for topping

Melt butter in medium skillet, add onion and spinach. Cook over low heat until moisture is gone. Add salt, the grated sharp cheese, then the sour cream. Keep warm until needed.

Soufflé Roll:

7 eggs, separated
Butter or margarine
6 tablespoon unsifted flour
Dash cayenne pepper
¾ teaspoon salt
1¼ cups milk
½ cup grated Parmesan cheese
½ cup coarsely grated cheddar cheese
¼ teaspoon cream of tartar

Place yolks and whites in separate bowl. Let whites come to room temperature. Grease bottom of jellyroll pan, 15″ × 10½″ × 1″. Line bottom with waxed paper; then grease with butter or margarine. Heat oven to 350°. Melt ⅓ cup butter in saucepan, remove from heat.

With wire whisk, stir in flour, cayenne pepper and ½ teaspoon salt. Beat until smooth, gradually stir in milk. Bring to a boil, stirring, reduce heat to simmer. Cook, stirring, until thick and mixture leaves bottom of pan. Beat in ½ cup of Parmesan cheese and ½ cup cheddar cheese. With whisk, beat egg yolks into cheese mixture.

Continued on next page

In mixer, beat whites at high speed until foamy, add cream of tartar and beat until stiff peaks form when beater is lifted. With over and under motion, fold ⅓ of whites into cheese mixture. Carefully fold in remaining whites. Spread into prepared pan and bake for 15 minutes or until puffed and firm when pressed with the fingertips With metal spatula, loosen edges of soufflé, invert on waxed paper sprinkled lightly with grated Parmesan cheese. Peel off waxed paper on under side. Spread spinach filling evenly over surface. From long side, roll up. Place, seam-side down, on greased cookie sheet. Arrange slices of processed cheese over top. Broil 4 inches from the heat until cheese melts. Transfer to serving dish. Cut into 1½" slices to serve.

Yield: 8 servings

This can be made ahead, wrapped in film and refrigerated. To heat, place on cookie sheet, cover with foil and place in a 300° oven until warm, then uncover and put cheese slices on top and heat in oven until cheese melts. Serve warm.

Raleigh House Spinach Quiche

Evaporated milk makes a richer, more firm quiche than whole milk does.

Pre-bake a 9" pie crust, lined with foil weighted down with uncooked rice or dried beans, for 4 minutes in a 400° oven. Remove foil and beans and bake for 6 minutes more. Cool.

1	(10 ounce) package frozen, chopped spinach, thawed and squeezed dry	1	(12 ounce) can evaporated milk
2	tablespoons butter or margarine	4	eggs, beaten
¼	cup finely chopped green onion, white part only	½	teaspoon salt
			Dash white pepper
		1½	cups grated swiss cheese

Melt butter in heavy saucepan or skillet. Sauté onions and spinach. Sauté until spinach is dry. Mix milk, eggs, salt, pepper and cheese, add spinach mixture and pour into prepared pastry shell. Bake in a 350° oven about 35 to 40 minutes or until set in middle.

Yield: 6 servings

Always save the dried beans or uncooked rice that you use to weight down the foil in pre-baking crust, and use them over and over.

Basil Cheese Tart

Crust:
1	cup flour
¼	teaspoon salt
⅛	teaspoon garlic salt

⅓   cup plus 1 tablespoon
      shortening
3 to 4 tablespoons water

Combine first 3 ingredients in a bowl, cut in shortening until coarse crumbs form. Add water, 1 tablespoon at a time until mixture makes a dough. Form into a ball and chill, wrapped in film, for ½ hour. Roll dough out on lightly floured board to ⅛" thickness. Trim dough to an 11" circle and place in the bottom of an 8" springform pan. Prick with a fork. Cover and chill 30 minutes. Place piece of foil over pastry, weight it down with uncooked dried beans. Bake at 450° for 8 minutes. Remove foil. If pastry has drawn away from sides, press back up gently with the back of a spoon. Bake another 5 minutes until lightly browned. Remove from oven. Cool.

Filling:
8   ounces cream cheese, room
      temperature
⅓   cup Ricotta cheese
¼   cup butter or margarine,
      softened
2   eggs
2   tablespoons flour

½   teaspoon salt
¼   teaspoon pepper
½   teaspoon dried leaf basil,
      crumbled
Cherry tomatoes for garnish
(optional)

Combine cream cheese, Ricotta cheese and butter. Beat until light and fluffy, add eggs, one at a time. Beat well after each addition. Add the flour and next 3 ingredients. Beat just until blended. Pour into pastry shell and bake in a 350° oven for 35 to 40 minutes or until set. Remove from oven and serve either hot or at room temperature. Garnish with cherry tomato wedges, if desired.

Yield: 8 inch tart

Baked French Toast

This was a favorite way that my mother made french toast. She usually doubled this recipe as there were 5 of us. She baked it in two baking pans, much easier than frying them.

3	large eggs, beaten	8	(1″ thick) slices of
⅔	cup milk		homemade bread or French
3	tablespoons sugar		bread
¼	teaspoon cinnamon	½	stick butter, do not
¼	teaspoon vanilla		substitute

In a square, flat dish, beat the egg, milk, sugar cinnamon and vanilla together. Soak the bread in a single layer for 2 minutes, then turn it over and soak other side until all the custard is absorbed. In a flat baking dish, melt the butter in a 300° oven. Remove from oven and increase heat to 400°. Add soaked bread to buttered pan in one layer and bake it for 15 minutes. Turn it over and bake 10 minutes more. Serve with powdered sugar or syrup.

Yield: 4 to 8 servings

Tomato Quiche

2	large ripe tomatoes cut into 6 slices, ½″ thick	1	cup minced scallions, divided
¼	cup flour	3	slices Provolone cheese
½	teaspoon salt	2	slightly beaten eggs
⅛	teaspoon coarse pepper	1	cup grated aged cheddar
2	tablespoons cooking oil		cheese
1	cup sliced ripe olives	1	cup heavy cream.

Prebake a 9″ pastry shell for 8 minutes in a 400° oven with dried beans on foil in shell. Remove from oven and remove foil and beans. Cool.

Mix the flour, salt and pepper together in a flat small pan. Dip tomato slices in the mixture and sauté them quickly in the oil. Arrange the ripe olives and all but 2 tablespoons of the scallions in bottom of prepared pastry shell. Add 3 slices of the provolone cheese and the sautéed tomatoes. Stir the slightly beaten eggs. the 1 cup of grated cheddar cheese and the cream together. Carefully pour into the pie.

Bake in a 325° oven 40 to 45 minutes or until filling is set in the center. Cool 5 minutes before cutting.

Yield: 6 servings

Quiche Lorraine

I am including a recipe for pastry in this recipe. It makes enough for 3 pie shells. I like to make it as it enables me to put 2 of the shells in the deep freeze for later needs.

Egg Pastry (3 quiche shells):

3   cups flour, spooned into cup
    and leveled off
1   teaspoon salt
1   cup shortening

1   large egg, beaten
1   tablespoon lemon juice
4 to 6 tablespoons ice water,
    divided

In large bowl, stir together the flour and salt. Cut in the shortening until particles are about the size of navy beans. Flour mixture should still look dry. If moist, shortening has been cut in too much and pastry will not be as flaky. Beat egg, lemon juice and 4 tablespoons ice water in small bowl. Sprinkle over flour mixture and toss with a fork until dough gathers into a ball. Add 1 to 2 tablespoons more water, if necessary. Make a ball with your hands. Wrap airtight and place in freezer 10 minutes. Divide dough into 3 pieces. Keep only one piece out of refrigerator at a time. On lightly floured board, roll out piece of dough into a circle 1 to 1½" larger than quiche pan. Fold in quarters and place in quiche pan. Unfold and fit loosely into pan being careful not to stretch the dough. Trim and crimp edges.

To prebake, Cover bottom and up the sides about 1" with a circle of foil. Fill it with dried beans or uncooked rice. Bake in a preheated 425° oven for 12 minutes. Cool slightly, then remove beans and foil. Fill with desired filling and bake as directed.

Quiche:

8   slices bacon, cooked crisp
    and crumbled
3   eggs
1½ cups half and half,
    evaporated milk or whole
    milk

½   teaspoon salt
Dash pepper
Dash nutmeg
1   cup Swiss cheese in ¼"
    dice
Minced parsley

Sprinkle bacon evenly over prepared quiche shell. Beat eggs, half and half, salt, pepper and nutmeg until mixed but not frothy. Stir in cheese, then pour over bacon. Bake in a preheated oven at 350° for 30 to 40 minutes or until set.

Yield: 6 servings

Entrées

Graves Grandchildren

(Mrs. Johnson's Great-Grandchildren)

From left to right:

Standing
Ashley Gray and Bryan Graves

Seated
Kristen Calame, Meagan Graves, Emily Graves, and Andrew Gray

Almond Chicken

2	cups raw chicken cut into bite-sized pieces	8	fresh large mushrooms, sliced
1	tablespoon soy sauce	1	stalk celery, cut diagonally in ⅛″ slices
1	tablespoon cornstarch		
1	tablespoon sherry	Salt	
½	teaspoon salt	15	snow peas, ends and strings removed
1	clove garlic, minced		
1	teaspoon grated ginger root	¾	cup water
6	tablespoon oil for cooking	1	tablespoon soy sauce
¾	cup blanched whole almonds	1	tablespoon cornstarch
½	cup sliced bamboo shoots, rinsed in cold water	½	teaspoon sugar

Marinate chicken in mixture of soy sauce, cornstarch, sherry, salt, garlic and ginger for 15 minutes. Heat 1 tablespoon oil in wok over medium heat; sauté almonds until lightly browned, Remove. Heat 2 tablespoons oil over high heat, add mushrooms, bamboo shoots and celery, stir-fry for 2 minutes or until vegetables are crisp tender. Remove from pan. Heat 1 tablespoon oil in wok, sprinkle with salt, add snow peas, stir-fry 1 minute. Remove. Heat 2 tablespoons oil over high heat, add marinated chicken and stir-fry about 4 minutes or until meat is white. Scrape bottom of wok with turner to prevent sticking. Return vegetables and nuts to wok. Mix water, cornstarch, soy sauce, and sugar, add to wok and cook, stirring gently, until thickened. Serve immediately.

Yield: 4 to 6 servings

Chicken and Almonds with Sherry

2	cups milk	1	tablespoon butter
4	tablespoons butter	½	cup slivered almonds
4	tablespoons flour	3	tablespoons sherry wine
2	cups diced cooked chicken	2	tablespoons grated Parmesan cheese
1	cup sliced fresh mushrooms		

Melt the 4 tablespoons butter in saucepan, add flour and cook over medium heat, until bubbling; add milk slowly, stirring constantly, and cook until sauce is smooth and thick. Sauté the mushrooms in the 1 tablespoon butter, add the wine and cook 1 minute. Add cream sauce and chicken and cook until well blended. Pour into 1½ quart casserole, sprinkle with the almonds and Parmesan cheese. Bake at 300° until bubbly. Serve over cooked asparagus or broccoli or over wild rice.

Yield: 4 to 6 servings

Marjorie's Supreme de Volaille

Marjorie was a fellow student of mine in a French course. She prepared this for the "graduation dinner." The recipe can be doubled or tripled. It is a great way to entertain small as well as large parties.

5 whole chicken breasts, split in half or 10 (6 to 8 ounce) frozen boneless, skinless chicken breasts	4 tablespoons flour
3 tablespoons lemon juice	2 cups chicken stock or 3 teaspoons chicken base dissolved in 2 cups boiling water
Salt and freshly ground pepper	½ cup dry white wine
Dried thyme, crushed	1 bay leaf
3 tablespoons olive oil	Cooked white rice dressed with butter and chopped parsley
3 tablespoons butter, do not substitute	
½ pound fresh mushrooms, sliced	

On the morning of the party or the day before, wash the chicken breasts, boned or not, as desired; Dry them well and sprinkle them with the lemon juice, salt, pepper and thyme. Do not hesitate to sprinkle them generously with the thyme. Cover well and place in the refrigerator.

At the cooking time, heat the olive oil to sizzling in large deep skillet. Pat the chicken breasts dry and sauté them in a single layer, until they take on a deep, gold color on all sides. As the chicken breasts brown, remove them to a deep casserole or baking dish that has a tight-fitting cover. When all the breasts are browned and removed from skillet, add the butter, melt it and sauté the mushrooms. Blend in the flour and add the chicken stock and wine, a little at a time. Cook, stirring constantly, until mixture thickens. Add the bay leaf and pour this sauce over the chicken breasts, making certain first to have blended all the pan glaze from the skillet into the sauce. Although sauce may seem rather thick and not too ample at this point, it will increase in volume and thin to proper consistency as chicken simmers in it. Cover the casserole and bake at 325 degrees about an hour or until chicken breasts are tender. Serve with white or wild rice.

Continued on next page

Note: The menu was: Mixed green salad with a vinaigrette dressing, the chicken and rice, broccoli florets dressed with a lemon butter sauce, spiced baby carrots, monkey bread and crepes Fitzgerald for dessert. A French Chablis was served throughout the dinner. Three of the ladies helped prepare the dinner. To simplify the serving to four tables of eight, we set a bowl of salad in the middle of each table with a stack of eight plates so the guests could help themselves. The chicken, rice and broccoli was arranged on silver trays, the rice in the center, then the chicken with the broccoli as a border. The carrots were served from a small dish. I prepared the crepes in a French chafing dish and guests came up to get them. Thus the "cooks" could sit and enjoy their meal. I should mention that the men cleared the tables. Everyone had a great time.

Yield: 10 servings

Marjorie cooked the 32 servings of chicken in a large heavy aluminum roaster. She stacked the chicken breasts on top of each other, then poured the sauce over all. The finished sauce was exactly the right thickness and heavenly in flavor.

Raleigh House Chicken

This chicken was always served at noon at Raleigh House on Sundays only. The original recipe came from Mabel Sterling, a loyal member of the kitchen committee at my church in Houston.

1 3½ pound fryer, cut into quarters	Pepper
	Paprika
Salt	Margarine

Place chicken quarters on sheet of waxed paper, skin-side down. Season with salt and pepper, turn skin-side up and season with salt, pepper and paprika. Paprika helps the chicken to brown. Melt enough margarine in a baking pan, just large enough to hold chicken snugly, to the depth of 1½". Place seasoned chicken in pan skin-side down and bake, uncovered, at 350° for 45 minutes, turn skin-side up and bake 25 or 30 minutes more, until chicken is tender and golden brown. Drain well and put on platter. Strain the margarine and place in a container with a cover. Set in refrigerator. It will keep at least 6 weeks to be used again and again for chicken, which makes this recipe more economical than fried chicken.

Yield: 4 servings

We cooked 20 or more fryers at a time in large baking pans, but recipe can be used for only 1 fryer or as many as you need to serve your family. It is good hot or cold and leftovers are delicious boned and cut into bite-size pieces in casseroles or salad.

Chicken with Lime Sauce

This is one of my favorite chicken dishes.

6	(6 to 8 ounce) boneless, skinless chicken breasts	2	egg whites
	Salt and pepper	1	cup finely chopped pecans

Season chicken with salt and pepper. Beat egg whites until frothy. Dip chicken into egg whites, coating well on both sides, drain, then roll in the finely chopped pecans. Place in a well buttered baking dish with a little space between and bake at 350° for 20 or 25 minutes or until just tender. Do not overcook or chicken will be dry. Serve with lime sauce.

Lime Sauce:

2	tablespoons butter		Dash white pepper
2	tablespoons flour	2	egg yolks
1	cup chicken broth	½	teaspoon grated lime rind
¼	teaspoon salt	2	tablespoons fresh lime juice

Melt butter, add flour; mix, then add chicken broth, salt and pepper. Cook, stirring, until sauce thickens. Beat egg yolks until lemon-colored. Stir about 4 tablespoons of the sauce into the egg yolks, then add yolks to rest of the sauce. Return to low heat and, stirring constantly, cook until thickened. Remove from heat and add lime juice and rind. Taste for seasoning and serve over chicken.

Yield: 6 servings

Chicken and Pasta Casserole

1	cup uncooked elbow macaroni, I like the smaller size	1	cup milk
		4	ounces Velveeta cheese, diced
2	cups diced cooked chicken	2	hard boiled eggs, sliced
1	(10¾) can cream of mushroom soup, undiluted	2	tablespoons chopped pimiento

Combine all ingredients, stirring well. Spoon into a lightly buttered 1½ quart casserole, cover and put in the refrigerator overnight. Next day, remove from refrigerator and allow to sit at room temperature 30 minutes. Cover and bake at 350° one hour or until heated through and bubbly.

Yield: 6 servings

This is another casserole that is prepared the day before baking.

Chicken Green Rice Casserole

This is a quick casserole to make as the rice is put in raw and bakes with the other ingredients.

6   (4 ounce) boneless, skinless chicken breasts or 3 cups cubed, cooked chicken
1   cup uncooked rice
1   can cream of mushroom soup
1   can chicken broth (10¾ ounces)
1½   cups milk
½   cup chopped celery

¼   cup minced onion
2   tablespoons butter or margarine
1   teaspoon Worcestershire sauce
1   (10 ounce) package frozen chopped spinach, thawed and squeezed dry
1½   cup grated sharp cheese

If using uncooked chicken breasts, cut chicken into strips and sauté in 2 tablespoons butter over medium-low heat, until opaque and firm to touch. Remove with slotted spoon to mixing bowl, add onions and celery to skillet and sauté just until crisp tender. Add to mixing bowl along with rest of ingredients except cheese. Place in a 2 ½ quart oblong casserole, bake, covered, at 350° for 40 to 45 minutes, or until rice is tender, then sprinkle grated cheese over top. Return to oven until cheese is melted. Let casserole set 10 minutes before serving. For the cooked chicken, simply add it to the rest of the ingredients, and bake.

Yield: 6 servings

Chicken Almond Cutlets

1   cup fresh bread crumbs
1   cup blanched slivered almonds, toasted and chopped
2   tablespoons chopped parsley
½   teaspoon ground ginger

¼   teaspoon salt
⅛   teaspoon pepper
6   (4 ounce) boneless, skinless chicken breasts
1   cup Lite Creamy Italian dressing

Preheat oven to 350°. In medium bowl, combine bread crumbs, almonds, parsley. ginger, salt and pepper. Dip chicken in creamy Italian dressing, then in bread crumb mixture, coating well. In a shallow baking pan, arrange chicken about ½″ apart. Bake, uncovered, for about 20 minutes or until firm when touched with your finger.

Yield: 6 servings

Bavarian Chicken

½ cup chicken broth
½ cup chopped onion
½ cup chopped celery
1 (3 to 4 pound) fryer, skinned
1 cup dry white wine
1½ teaspoons salt, divided
⅛ teaspoon pepper
6 cups finely shredded cabbage
1 tablespoon lemon juice
¼ cup chopped pimiento, drained (optional)

Wash and remove giblets from chicken. Heat chicken broth in small saucepan over low heat, add onion and celery and cook until crisp tender, stirring occasionally. Place whole chicken in a deep 3 quart casserole. Combine onion celery mixture, undrained, wine, 1 teaspoon salt and pepper. Pour over chicken. Bake, uncovered, in a 350° oven, basting occasionally, for 45 minutes or until chicken is tender. Add cabbage, ½ teaspoon salt, pepper and lemon juice to chicken. Cover and bake 15 more minutes, or until cabbage is just tender. If pimiento is used, add just before serving.

Yield: 6 servings

This recipe is delicious and pretty to serve. The trick is not to overcook the cabbage.

Cornish Game Hens Veronique

This makes a delicious gourmet dish.

6 (12 ounce) Cornish Game hens, split in half
½ cup olive oil
1 teaspoon salt
1 teaspoon powdered thyme
½ teaspoon pepper
½ cup butter
2 cups fresh small, button mushrooms
2 cups green seedless grapes (½ pound)
½ teaspoon salt
¼ cup cognac

In a small bowl, combine olive oil, salt, thyme and pepper. Mix well and brush over game hens. Bake in a shallow, oblong pan just large enough to hold them, for about 30 minutes in a pre-heated 350° oven. Check after 30 minutes to see if they are tender.

Just before serving, sauté the mushrooms in the butter, cooking until just tender. Add the grapes, sprinkle with the salt, and sauté just until heated through. Pour the cognac over and flame. Pour sauce over game hens and serve with either brown or wild rice.

Yield: 12 servings

Chicken Breast en Croute

1	package frozen puff pastry patty shells	1	(10 ounce) package frozen broccoli florets, thawed and drained well
1	tablespoon butter		
6	(4 ounce) skinless, boneless chicken breasts	1	egg, beaten with 1 tablespoon cold water for egg wash
6	thin slices boiled ham		

Melt butter in a skillet and sauté chicken over very low heat for 1½ minutes on each side. Set aside to cool. Defrost patty shells according to package directions. Roll each patty shell on a lightly floured board, to an 8″ circle. Place cooled chicken breast on lower half of pastry. Fold a slice of ham in fourths and place on top of chicken. Divide broccoli between the chicken breasts, fold top half of pastry over broccoli. Brush under edge with egg wash being careful not to let any run onto baking pan. Crimp with a fork to seal. Prick tops with a fork. Bake in a pre-heated 400° oven for 35 minutes. Serve with sauce.

Sauce 2:

2	tablespoons butter, melted	¼	cup dry vermouth
2	tablespoons flour	⅓	cup grated imported Swiss cheese
1½	cups chicken broth		

Stir flour into melted butter in a small saucepan, add chicken broth and vermouth. Place over low heat and stir with a wire whisk until thickened. Remove from heat and add grated cheese, stirring until melted. Serve.

Yield: 6 servings

Chicken Mushroom Casserole

This is one of my favorite casseroles. The pasta does not have to be pre-cooked, but cooks along with the other ingredients.

3	cups diced cooked chicken	1	cup chopped celery
2	cups grated cheddar cheese	¼	cup grated onion
2	cups milk	1	(6 ounce) can sliced mushrooms
7	ounces macaroni, uncooked		
1	can cream of celery soup	1	(8 ounce) can water chestnuts, sliced
1	can cream of mushroom soup		

Mix all ingredients together and set in refrigerator over night. Next morning, stir well and put in a lightly buttered 13″×9″ oblong casserole. Bake, covered, for 30 minutes in a 350° oven, then uncover and put buttered bread crumbs on top. Bake about 20 minutes longer or until crumbs are browned.

Yield: 10 servings

Turkey Cutlets

Ground turkey is low in calories as it is ground without the skin.

1	pound ground raw turkey	½	teaspoon salt
¼	cup soft bread crumbs	¼	teaspoon whole thyme, crumbled between palms of the hands
2	tablespoons evaporated milk		
1	egg, slightly beaten	¼	teaspoon whole rosemary, crumbled
3	tablespoons grated onion		
2	tablespoons chopped fresh parsley		

Combine turkey and next 8 ingredients, stirring well with a fork. Do not use a mixer as it will make the cutlets tough. Shape into 6 cutlets. Place into a 12″×8″×2″ baking pan that has ¼″ of melted margarine in it. Bake, uncovered, at 350° for about 25 to 30 minutes, or until done. Time depends on how thick the cutlets are. Spoon rosemary sauce over and sprinkle with chopped parsley.

Rosemary Sauce:

1	tablespoon margarine	½	teaspoon chicken base
½	cup chopped onion	⅓	cup plus 2 tablespoons water
1	clove garlic, minced		
1	tablespoon flour	¼	cup plus 2 tablespoons milk
¼	teaspoon whole rosemary, crumbled		

Melt margarine in small saucepan. Add onion and garlic. Sauté until tender, add flour and rosemary. Cook, stirring constantly, 1 minute. Gradually add chicken base, water and milk. Cook over medium heat, stirring constantly, until thickened. Spoon over hot cutlets and serve.

Yield: 6 servings

You may spray the baking pan with vegetable spray and omit the margarine, if you want to cut calories.

Turkey and Wild Rice Casserole

1	cup wild rice, precooked according to instructions below
3	cups hot water
¼	teaspoon salt
2	cups diced cooked chicken or turkey
½	pound fresh mushrooms, sliced, about 3 cups
2	tablespoons butter
1	cup heavy cream
1½	cups chicken or turkey broth or 2 chicken boullion cubes dissolved in 1½ cups water
2	tablespoons finely chopped green onions or chives
2	tablespoons chopped pimiento
1	teaspoon salt
¼	teaspoon pepper
2	tablespoons grated Parmesan cheese
1	tablespoon butter

Put wild rice in small saucepan, pour 1 cup boiling water over, cover and let set for 1 hour. This is the "quick-soak" method and shortens the cooking time considerably. After soaking, drain thoroughly; then cook, covered, in the 3 cups boiling water and salt, until until rice is tender. Drain, if necessary, and place in mixing bowl. Sauté the mushrooms for 3 minutes in the 2 tablespoons butter and add to rice, then add the turkey stock or dissolved boullion cubes. chives or onions, pimiento, salt and pepper and heavy cream. Add turkey and toss well. Place in a 1½ quart casserole. cover and bake at 350° for 1 hour. Uncover, sprinkle casserole with Parmesan cheese, dot with the 1 tablespoon butter and brown the topping under broiler.

Yield: 4 servings

Helpful Hint: *To prevent a burned, smoky smell in the oven when foods spill during roasting or baking, sprinkle the area with salt mixed with a little cinnamon.*

Turkey Loaf

Turkey makes good health sense to avoid high cholesterol and fat, particularly because the skin is removed before the turkey is ground.

2	pounds raw ground turkey	2	teaspoons salt
3	slices day old bread crumbled	1	teaspoon dry mustard
2	eggs, lightly beaten	⅓	cup evaporated milk, not condensed milk
1	medium onion, chopped	¾	cup ketchup, divided
¼	cup green pepper, chopped		
2	tablespoons prepared horseradish		

Combine turkey, bread, eggs, onion, green pepper, horseradish, salt, mustard, milk and ¼ cup of the ketchup. Mix with a spoon or fork. Do not use mixer as it will make the loaf too solid. Mold gently in loaf pan. Spread with rest of ketchup. Bake at 350° about 1¼ hours. Unmold onto serving platter and use pan juices for gravy.

Yield: 6 to 8 servings

The addition of evaporated milk keeps the loaf from getting too dry and insulating with the ketchup topping during baking serves to keep it moist. This is also good cold for sandwiches.

Chicken Almondine

This is a good, low calorie dish; about 235 calories per serving.

1	tablespoon flour	2	tablespoons olive oil
½	teaspoon salt	⅓	cup sliced almonds
¼	teaspoon pepper	2	tablespoons lemon juice
4	skinless, boneless 4 ounce chicken breasts		Parsley for garnish

Mix flour, salt and pepper on a piece of waxed paper; use to coat chicken breasts. Heat 1 tablespoon olive oil in a 10″ skillet, cook chicken breasts over medium-low heat until lightly browned and firm to the touch, do not overcook or chicken will be dry. Remove to platter. In same skillet over medium-low heat, cook almonds in 1 tablespoon olive oil until lightly browned. Stir in lemon juice. Spoon over chicken. Garnish with parsley.

Yield: 4 servings

Creamed Avocado and Chicken

6 (4 ounce) boneless, skinless frozen chicken breasts
Salt and pepper
1 tablespoon butter
1 tablespoon olive oil
¼ pound fresh mushrooms, sliced

2 tablespoons chopped green onions, white tops only
2 tablespoons brandy
1½ cups heavy cream
1 avocado, peeled, seeded and cut into cubes

Cut each chicken breast into 5 or 6 strips. Sprinkle with salt and pepper. Heat butter and olive oil in heavy skillet, add the chicken and cook over low heat, turning every minute, until it is opaque and firm to the touch, about 3 or 4 minutes. Do not overcook or chicken will be dry.

Remove chicken with slotted spoon and set aside. Add the green onions and mushrooms to skillet and cook a few minutes. Sprinkle with the brandy. Add cream and cook over medium heat, about 5 minutes, until thickened. Taste for seasoning. Add chicken and gently cook in the sauce, add avocado and cook until barely heated. Serve with brown or wild rice. When you use heavy cream, no flour is needed as the cream thickens without it.

Yield: 6 servings

Lemon Chicken with Mushroom Sauce

This recipe can be increased easily to suit your needs. Just follow this recipe for each additional chicken you want to cook

1 (3½ pound chicken) cut into quarters
4 tablespoons butter
4 cloves garlic, crushed

1 cup water
2 tablespoons lemon juice
1 (8 ounce) can sliced mushrooms

Melt butter and crushed garlic. Place chicken, skin-side up, in baking dish just large enough to hold it. Brush it well with the butter-garlic mixture. Place in a pre-heated 400° oven and bake until browned. Mix the water with the lemon juice and pour over chicken. Cover chicken, lower oven to 350° and bake about 35 to 45 minutes or until tender. Remove chicken from pan. Strain drippings and skim off fat. Mix 2 tablespoons of the fat with 2 tablespoons flour. Add a tall can of sliced mushrooms and 1 tablespoon grated onion. Cook until thickened, pour over chicken and enjoy!

Yield: 4 servings

Chicken Breasts with Whole Wheat Stuffing

8 (4 or 6 ounce) boneless, skinless chicken breasts
¼ pound (1 stick) butter
2 tablespoon minced onion
1⅓ cups thin diagonally sliced celery
1⅓ cups whole wheat bread crumbs, dried in a 250° oven
⅔ cup cooked rice

½ teaspoon dried basil leaves, crumbled between the palms of the hands. (the heat of your hands brings out the flavor.)
½ teaspoon salt
⅔ cup canned apricot halves, drained well and cut into thirds.

Sprinkle chicken on both sides with paprika. Place on greased baking pan just large enough to hold them snugly, this keeps them from drying out. Heat half the butter in a large skillet, add onion and celery; sauté 6 to 8 minutes until limp. Add remaining butter, when melted, stir in bread crumbs, rice, basil and salt. Cook 1 minute longer, stirring constantly. Remove from heat; stir in the apricot halves cut in thirds. Lightly pile ⅓ cup stuffing on top of each chicken breast. Bake in 350° oven about 20 minutes for the 4 ounce breasts, 30 to 35 minutes for the 6 ounce, or until just done. Do not overcook or breasts will be dry.

Yield: 8 servings

Emerald Chicken

1 tablespoon cornstarch
2 teaspoons sherry
2 teaspoons soy sauce
¼ teaspoon MSG (optional)
½ teaspoon salt
½ teaspoon sugar
1 clove garlic, minced
1 teaspoon grated ginger root

1½ cups raw chicken breast, cut into bite-sized pieces
Salad oil for cooking
1 cup seedless green grapes
⅓ cup water
1 teaspoon cornstarch
1 tablespoon water
½ teaspoon sugar

Combine cornstarch, sherry, soy sauce. MSG, salt, sugar, garlic and ginger; add chicken and let stand 15 minutes. Heat 2 tablespoons oil in a wok, drain chicken, reserving marinade. Cook over medium-low heat for 3 to 4 minutes, or until meat is opaque, turning often to prevent sticking. Add cornstarch mixture and stir until thickened. Add green grapes and cook just until grapes are heated. Serve with Chinese Fried Rice or steamed white rice.

Yield: 4 servings

Chicken Stew with Rosemary Dumplings

If you do not have chicken broth on hand, either use canned broth or buy chicken necks and make your own. I always freeze any chicken broth I have left over, to use in other recipes.

¼	cup oil	¾	cup flour
2	(3 pound) chickens cut into serving pieces or 6 pounds chicken parts of your choice	2	cups chopped onion
		8	cups chicken broth
		1	cup chopped celery
		Cayenne and salt to taste	

In a large skillet, preferably cast iron, heat the oil over moderate heat until it is hot but not smoking, brown the chicken, that has been patted dry and seasoned with salt. Chicken will have to be browned in batches and placed in a large bowl. Pour off all but ¼ cup of fat, stir in flour and cook mixture over low heat, stirring constantly, until it is a light brown.

In a large stock pot, bring the chicken broth to a boil, whisk in the flour mixture until it is well blended, then add the celery, onion and chicken with any juices that have accumulated in the bowl. Bring the liquid to a boil, then simmer, covered partially, for 30 minutes. Transfer the chicken with a slotted spoon to a serving bowl or turéen. Boil the gravy until mixture is reduced to 6 cups. Add the chicken and season with cayenne and salt.

Rosemary Dumplings:

1	cup all purpose flour	Dash white pepper	
2	teaspoons double-acting baking powder	¼	teaspoon dried rosemary, crumbled
½	teaspoon salt	½	cup milk

Sift flour, baking powder, salt and pepper into a bowl, add rosemary, then add the milk and stir with a fork until just combined. Drop the batter by spoonsful into 8 mounds onto simmering stew. Cover tightly and cook for 20 minutes. Sprinkle the stew with finely chopped green onions and serve with steamed rice.

Yield: 8 servings

Chicken Tortilla Casserole

2   tablespoons oil
6   (4 ounce) boneless, skinless chicken breasts, cut into thin strips
½   cup thinly sliced green onion
1   clove garlic, minced
3   tablespoons cornstarch
4   cups cold chicken broth
1½ cups grated Monterey Jack cheese, divided
½   cup mayonnaise
½   cup sour cream
1   (4 ounce) can chopped green chilis, undrained
½   cup sliced ripe olives, divided
12 (7 inch) tortillas
¼   cup chopped parsley or cilantro

Heat oil in large skillet over medium heat. Add chicken, onions and garlic; cook over medium heat, stirring, until chicken is firm to the touch and lightly browned. Do not overcook. In saucepan, stir together the cornstarch and chicken broth; bring to a boil over medium heat, stirring constantly. Boil 1 minute then stir in 1 cup of the cheese, mayonnaise, sour cream, chilis, cilantro and ¼ cup olives. Remove 1 cup of the sauce and stir in chicken mixture. Spoon 2 tablespoon chicken mixture into each tortilla and roll to enclose. Place tortillas, seam-side down in a 13″×9″ baking pan. Spoon remaining sauce over tortillas. Top with remaining cheese and olives. Bake at 350° until bubbly, about 25 minutes.

Yield: 6 servings

Helpful Hint: *To remove the odor of onion or garlic from a wooden cutting board or wooden spoon, rub the surface with lemon juice. To remove the odor of onion or garlic from your hands, place them flat on a stainless steel sink and let cold water run over them.*

Stir-Fry Chicken

This same recipe can be made with shrimp, cut in half lengthwise, and substituting frozen small green peas for the snow peas.

4	(4 ounce) boneless, skinless chicken breasts	2	slices fresh ginger root, 1″ diameter, ⅛″ thick
2	teaspoons cornstarch	1	tablespoon dry sherry
1	egg white	1	teaspoon salt
½	pound fresh mushrooms, washed and sliced	1	teaspoon cornstarch dissolved in
½	package frozen snow peas	1	tablespoon chicken broth
4	tablespoons oil		

Slice chicken in strips 2″ × 1″. Combine cornstarch and chicken and toss until each piece is coated. Add egg white and toss until chicken is coated, set aside. Mix wine and salt, set aside. Heat a wok or skillet until hot, pour in 1 tablespoon oil. Add mushrooms, snow peas and ½ teaspoon of the salt. Stir-fry about 2 minutes. Remove vegetables, add 3 tablespoons oil to wok, drop in ginger, cook 30 seconds and discard. Add chicken, stir-fry 2 minutes or until it is white and firm. Stir in wine and salt. Add vegetables and cook a few seconds. Add cornstarch mixed with chicken stock or water and cook, stirring, a few seconds until ingredients are coated with a thin glaze. Serve at once.

Yield: 4 servings

I use only half the ginger called for as I am not too fond of it. Use your own discretion.

Helpful Hint: *Cook mushrooms either quickly — usually not more than 2 minutes, to retain shape — or very slowly until very dry. Since mushrooms are 75 percent water, they cook down and reduce in size in a very short time. Cook chopped mushrooms slowly over low heat until they become dry and are reduced by more than half for a duxelle — a mushroom paste that stores well in the refrigerator and can be used as an addition to stuffing for poultry, fish and vegetables, and as a flavor base for many dishes.*

Turkey Lasagna

Ground raw turkey is substituted for beef in this dish, but it is still very good, with less calories. I make various versions of Lasagna often as it is a favorite of my family, even the great grandchildren love it.

2	tablespoons olive oil	1	(10 ounce) package Mozzarella cheese, coarsely grated
2	pounds ground raw turkey		
1	large onion, chopped		
1	package Lawry's or McCormick's spaghetti seasoning	1	(12 ounce) container creamed small curd cottage cheese
2	(16 ounce) cans tomatoes, broken up in juice	1	large egg, beaten
		¼	cup grated Parmesan cheese
1	(15 ounce) can tomato sauce	¼	teaspoon dried basil, crumbled
8	ounces Lasagna noodles, cooked according to directions		
1	(10 ounce) package frozen chopped broccoli or spinach thawed and squeezed dry		

Sauté turkey and onion in olive oil, over low heat, in a heavy large pan, until onion is limp and turkey is light brown. Add tomatoes, tomato sauce, spaghetti seasoning mix and ¼ cup water. Heat to boiling, then turn heat to low and simmer, uncovered, until sauce thickens; about 30 minutes, stirring occasionally.

Grate cheese and reserve ½ cup for top of the lasagna. In a large bowl, mix the Mozzarello cheese, cottage cheese, the beaten egg, Parmesan cheese and basil. Pre heat oven to 350°.

Spoon about ½ cup turkey sauce on bottom of a 13″×9″×2″ baking pan, spreading evenly. Layer ⅓ of the noodles over sauce, overlapping to fit. Spread ⅓ cheese mixture over noodles. Spoon about 2 cups turkey sauce over cheese mixture. Spread all of the broccoli or spinach over, then continue layering twice with remaining noodles, cheese mixture and sauce. Sprinkle top layer of sauce with reserved ½ cup cheese. Bake for about 45 minutes in a 350° oven or until hot and bubbly. Serve with extra Parmesan cheese, if desired.

Yield: 12 servings

Chicken Ole Casserole

This is a favorite casserole of mine. With the oregano, it is a combination of Italian and Mexican food.

2 cups cooked rice (¾ cup uncooked)
3 cups cooked chicken, cubed
8 ounces zucchini sliced very thin
⅓ cup grated onion
2 tablespoons butter or margarine
8 ounces Monterey Jack cheese, grated and divided
1 (4 ounce) can chopped green chilis
2 medium tomatoes, sliced thin, then halved
1 cup sour cream
⅛ teaspoon garlic powder or 1 clove fresh garlic, crushed
¼ teaspoon oregano, crumbled between palms of hands
Salt and pepper to taste

Sauté zucchini and onion in butter over medium heat about 5 minutes, stirring. Set aside. Butter a 2 quart oblong baking dish. Spread cooked rice over bottom, top with chicken, then zucchini and onion mixture, ¾ of the grated cheese, chilis and then tomato slices. Mix the sour cream, garlic, oregano and salt and pepper to taste. Spread over tomatoes, then top with the rest of the cheese. Bake in a 350° oven about 30 minutes or until lightly browned and bubbly. This casserole can be frozen after baking.

Yield: 12 servings

Chicken Breasts with Wine Sauce

8 (4 ounce) boneless, skinless chicken breasts
2 tablespoons olive oil
2 tablespoon butter
1 medium onion, chopped
1 (10¾ ounce) can cream of chicken soup, undiluted
⅔ cup dry white wine
1 tablespoon chopped parsley
1 teaspoon paprika
Pepper to taste
1 tablespoon lime juice
1 tablespoon soy sauce
No salt, soy sauce is salty

Heat butter and olive oil in heavy skillet, add chicken breasts and roll in oil and butter. Lower heat to low and let meat whiten slowly on both sides. Using tongs, turn chicken over every 2 minutes, cooking just until it is firm to the touch, about 4 to 5 minutes. Remove and place in a rectangular baking pan just large enough to hold them snugly. Add onion to the skillet and cook over medium heat just until limp, do not brown. Add soup, wine, seasonings, soy sauce and lime juice. Blend thoroughly and pour over chicken. Bake at 325° until tender, about 20 to 25 minutes. Serve on a bed of mixed wild and white rice.

Yield: 8 servings

Chicken in Lettuce

This is similar to the Chinese dish served in Chinese pancakes.

1	cup stir-fry sauce
1	teaspoon steak sauce
1	pound chicken breasts, boned and diced or 3 (4 ounce) boneless, skinned chicken breasts, diced
1	tablespoon cornstarch
1	tablespoon soy sauce

2	tablespoons oil
1	cup chopped celery
1	cup fresh bean sprouts
1	(8 ounce) can water chestnuts, sliced
1	head iceberg lettuce, separated in leaves

Combine stir-fry sauce with steak sauce. In a bowl, combine cornstarch and soy sauce and dip chicken in it. Heat oil in wok and place chicken in it, stir fry 1 minute, add celery and stir fry 30 seconds. Add bean sprouts and water chestnuts. Add stir-fry sauce and cook until mixture thickens. To serve: Place about 2 tablespoons of chicken mixture on a lettuce leaf. Roll up and serve immediately or you may serve chicken mixture on a platter and guests may fill lettuce leaves themselves.

Yield: 4 servings

The recipe for stir-fry sauce is in the Sauce section of this cookbook.

Chicken and Vegetable Stir-Fry

3	tablespoons oil
1	pound boneless skinless chicken breasts, cut into thin strips
½	cup broccoli florets, cut in half or fourths, if large
2	ounces snow peas (about ½ cup)
1	medium carrot, very thinly sliced on the diagonal

½	medium red or green pepper cut into very thin strips
1	teaspoon cornstarch
⅛	teaspoon ground ginger
1	tablespoon chicken stock
2	teaspoons soy sauce
1	tablespoon dry sherry
	Hot cooked rice

In wok or skillet, heat 1 tablespoon of the oil, add chicken and stir-fry until chicken is firm. Remove with a slotted spoon to a bowl and set aside. Add remaining 2 tablespoons oil to wok and add vegetables. Stir-fry until crisp tender. Add chicken to wok. Mix cornstarch, ginger, broth, soy sauce and sherry in a bowl and add to chicken-vegetable mixture. Cook, tossing, until sauce makes a glaze. Serve with boiled rice and thinly sliced green onion, if desired.

Yield: 4 servings

Chicken and Spanish Rice

This is another one-dish meal with the bonus that the rice is cooked along with the other ingredients.

2	(2½ pound) frying chickens, cut into pieces or 5 pounds chicken parts of your choice	1	teaspoon dried leaf basil, crumbled
½	cup olive oil	1	teaspoon salt
4	cloves garlic, minced	¼	teaspoon pepper
2	large onions, grated	2	(8 ounce) cans sliced mushrooms, drained
1	green pepper, chopped fine	1	(7 ounce) can chopped pimientos, drained
1	bay leaf, crushed	1	(1 pound) can peas, drained or equivalent of frozen peas, (optional)
1	(15 ounce) can tomato sauce		
1½	quarts water (6 cups)		
2	cups uncooked Uncle Ben's white rice		

Sprinkle chicken with salt and pepper, then brown in sections in olive oil, removing to roaster as browned, (chicken does not have to be fully cooked). In same pan, sauté garlic and onions in olive oil, adding more oil as needed. Add next 8 ingredients to chicken in roaster. Cover and bake in a 325° oven until rice is done, 1½ to 2 hours.

Stir in salt, pepper, mushrooms, pimientos and peas and put back in oven a few minutes to heat. Serve.

Yield: 8 servings

Helpful Hint: *Rice and mushrooms: Add lemon juice to the water when cooking rice. It makes it white and added to the butter you sauté mushrooms in gives them a high gloss.*

Chicken Broccoli Casserole

1   cup Uncle Ben's converted
     rice
1   small onion, chopped
¾   cup celery cut into thin
     diagonal slices
1   (6 or 8 ounce) can water
     chestnuts, sliced
2   (10 ounce) packages frozen
     broccoli florets, thawed
2   (10½ ounce) cans cream of
     mushroom soup

1   cup mayonnaise
3   cups cooked chicken, cut
     into bite-sized pieces
2   teaspoons lemon juice
¼   to ½ teaspoon curry
     powder, according to your
     taste
1½   cups grated Cheddar cheese

Cook rice according to directions on box. Place in a 9" × 13" casserole. Add thawed and well drained but not cooked, broccoli. Sauté celery and onion in a little butter until tender-crisp, then sprinkle over broccoli. Add chicken. Mix the soup, mayonnaise, lemon juice, chestnuts and curry, heat and spread over chicken. Bake in a 350° oven for 20 to 30 minutes. Turn off oven and sprinkle grated cheese on top. Leave in oven until cheese melts. Serve.

Yield: 10 to 12 servings

Glazed Chicken Breasts

This is another dish that lends itself to cooking for a crowd. The chicken does not have to be precooked, is baked in a sauce that serves as a gravy when chicken is served over rice.

6   (6 or 8 ounce) boneless,
     skinless chicken breasts
¼   cup brown sugar
¼   cup cider vinegar
2   tablespoons soy sauce

2   tablespoons cornstarch
½   teaspoon salt
1   clove garlic, minced or
⅛   teaspoon garlic powder, not
     garlic salt

Place chicken breasts in a baking pan just large enough to hold them snugly. Mix the rest of ingredients well and place in a heavy saucepan. Bring to a boil and cook, stirring constantly, until it just begins to thicken. Remove from heat, and pour over chicken. Bake in a 325° oven about 20 to 30 minutes or until chicken is just tender, time depends on size of breasts. Do not overbake or chicken will be dry. Serve over rice. Note: Chicken does not need to be salted as the soy sauce is salty. Serve over steamed rice.

Yield: 6 servings

Cazuelo Sabrosa

This is a tasty one-dish recipe to serve the family or, increased, to serve a crowd. The pasta is cooked in the casserole. It is a change from spaghetti or lasagna.

1	medium onion, chopped	1	cup uncooked macaroni
2	cloves garlic, minced	1	tablespoon chili powder
1	cup chopped celery	1	teaspoon salt
½	cup chopped green pepper (optional)	1	cup buttermilk
		4	ounces Neufchatel cheese
1½	pounds lean ground beef	6	ounces grated Cheddar cheese
1	(16 ounce) can whole kernel corn, drained		
1	(16 ounce) tomatoes, undrained		

Sauté onion, garlic and celery in olive oil until limp. Place beef in heavy saucepan and cook, stirring, just until beef falls apart. Mix beef with the rest of ingredients except the cheeses and place in a 13″×9″×2½″ oblong baking pan. Dot with the Neufchatel cheese, then top with the grated Cheddar cheese. Bake, covered, at 350° about 45 minutes or until macaroni is done and liquid absorbed. Let set about 15 minutes before serving.

Yield: 8 to 10 servings

This can be baked and frozen.

Sauce for Linguine

½	cup margarine	1⅔	cups grated Parmesan cheese
¼	cup olive oil		
½	cup chopped parsley	½	cup heavy cream
½	cup pine nuts	2	tablespoons butter
3	tablespoons dried sweet basil, crumbled	1	egg, beaten
2	cloves garlic, crushed	1	teaspoon salt
½	teaspoon salt		Cooked Linguine or pasta of your choice
¼	teaspoon freshly ground pepper		

Put first 8 ingredients in blender and blend until smooth, scraping down sides several times with rubber spatula. Toss cooked linguine with cheese, cream, butter, egg and salt. Serve piping hot with sauce from blender.

Yield: Sauce for ¾ to 1 pound

Pot Roast with Spring Vegetables

This is a colorful entree, delicious, too.

2½ teaspoons salt, divided	2 tablespoons dried parsley
¼ teaspoon freshly ground pepper	flakes
	1 bay leaf
5 pound bottom round of beef roast	2 cloves garlic, minced
1 (1 pound,12 ounce) can whole tomatoes, broken up	6 medium carrots, peeled and sliced
¾ cup dry red wine	1½ pounds zucchini, sliced
2 medium onions, minced	2 cups cherry tomatoes

Rub 1½ teaspoons of the salt and the black pepper into surface of the meat. Place meat, fat side down, in a heavy, ovenproof casserole or Dutch oven. Brown well on all sides on top of the stove. Drain off all fat. Combine tomatoes, wine, onion, parsley flakes, bay leaf, minced garlic and remaining teaspoon of the salt. Pour over meat. Cover and place in a 325° oven; bake for 2½ to 3 hours, adding carrots 40 minutes before cooking time is up, zucchini and cherry tomatoes 10 minutes before the cooking time is up. Remove meat and slice, then serve with vegetables.

Yield: 8 to 10 servings

Russian Meat Balls

These are delicious, tender meat balls. I have made these using half venison and half beef.

2 pounds lean ground beef	1⅓ cup water
1 teaspoon salt	1 cup sour cream
½ teaspoon pepper	1 teaspoon lemon juice
1 teaspoon MSG (optional)	½ teaspoon Worcestershire
⅓ finely chopped onion	1 teaspoon chopped parsley
2 eggs, well beaten	¼ teaspoon paprika
¼ cup shortening	½ teaspoon salt
¼ cup flour	

Combine meat, salt, pepper, MSG, chopped onion and beaten eggs. Mix lightly with a fork until well combined. Make 1½ " balls. Add ¼ cup cooking oil in a skillet and brown meat balls. Remove to a baking pan.

Add flour to remaining grease in skillet, blend; add water and remaining seasonings. Cook, stirring, until thickened, then add sour cream and heat, but do not let mixture boil. Taste for seasoning, then pour over meat balls and bake at 350° 20 minutes. Serve over parsley rice or noodles.

Yield: 50 small balls

Sauce for Pasta

⅔ cup chopped walnuts
½ cup chopped ripe olives
⅓ cup chopped pimiento
½ cup chopped parsley
¾ teaspoon dried basil leaves, rubbed between palms of hands to bring out the flavor

2 or 3 tablespoons oil
8 ounces cooked pasta, any kind
Salt and pepper to taste
1 clove garlic finely minced
¼ cup heavy cream
Grated fresh Parmesan cheese

Mix first 5 ingredients in a bowl. Put the oil in a heavy pot, add cooked pasta, salt and pepper, garlic and cream. Mix well and heat over very low heat, then pour onto a heated platter. Spread olive mixture on top and serve with a bowl of Parmesan cheese.

Yield: Sauce for 8 ounces pasta

Scalloped Potatoes and Pork Chops

This is my Mother's recipe. It is a delicious way to cook pork chops. The milk tenderizes them and they taste like chicken. It can also be made with serving portion thick slices of ham.

4 cups pared, thinly sliced raw potatoes
⅔ cup minced onion (optional)
2 tablespoons flour
1 teaspoon salt
⅛ teaspoon pepper
3 tablespoons butter or margarine

1½ cups hot milk
4 (½ to ⅓ inch thick) pork chops, lightly salted on one side or
4 (½ thick slices) cooked ham
Paprika

Place ½ of the potatoes and onion in bottom of a 3 quart casserole, one large enough to hold pork chops in a single layer. Mix flour, salt and pepper in a small bowl. sprinkle half of the mixture over the potatoes, then place pork chops over potatoes. Sprinkle with rest of flour mixture, Then add remaining potatoes and onion. Pour hot milk over all, dot with the butter and sprinkle with paprika. Bake, covered, in a 350° oven for 30 minutes, then uncover and bake 30 minutes longer or until potatoes and chops are tender. Thick apple sauce or Waldorf salad are a must with this entree.

Yield: 4 servings

This recipe can be doubled satisfactorily. Just use a pan large enough to hold the chops in a single layer and increase rest of ingredients. This dish can be prepared early in the day and refrigerated, covered.

German Pot Roast

This is a delicious recipe for pot roast, given to me by Mrs. Drucker, a friend in the Hill Country.

4	pound beef rump or pike's peak roast	4	large white onions, sliced thin
2	slices bacon, chopped	2	cups cold water or beef consomme
1	tablespoon dry mustard		
2	teaspoons salt	3	fresh tomatoes, peeled and chopped fine
½	teaspoon freshly ground pepper		
⅓	cup shortening	2	tablespoons red wine vinegar

Place onions and bacon in Dutch oven; cook, over low heat, until onions are limp. Remove with a slotted spoon and set aside. Rub meat with the salt, pepper and mustard until it is well-rubbed in. Add the shortening to Dutch oven and let melt. Place roast in and brown on all sides. Add the water or consomme, scraping up any brown bits left in pan. Add onion and bacon mixture and cook, covered, for 3 hours in a 325° oven. Add the tomatoes and the wine vinegar. Cook until meat is tender, and the liquid is boiled down to a thin gravy. Serve with boiled whole potatoes or partly peeled new potatoes sprinkled with finely chopped parsley and melted butter.

Yield: 6 to 8 servings

Beef with Burgundy

1	pound top sirloin steak or round steak, 1 to 1½ inches thick	¼	teaspoon dried tarragon, crumbled
¼	pound fresh mushrooms, sliced	¼	teaspoon salt
		⅛	teaspoon marjoram, crumbled
½	cup burgundy or dry red wine	1½	tablespoons flour
1½	tablespoons butter or margarine		

Cut steak in ¼" slices across the grain; place in a bowl with the wine. Let stand in the refrigerator at least an hour or more. Then drain thoroughly, saving marinade. Melt butter with herbs and salt in skillet. Add meat and mushrooms; stir and cook over medium heat until meat loses red color but is still slightly pink. Do not overcook. Sprinkle with the flour and blend in marinade. Cook until slightly thickened.

Yield: 4 servings

Marinated Pork Roast

Using a plastic bag is an easy way to marinate, no pots to wash.

½ cup soy sauce
½ cup dry sherry
2 cloves garlic, minced
1 tablespoon dry mustard
1 teaspoon ground ginger

1 teaspoon leaf thyme, crumbled
1 (4 to 5 pound) boned, rolled and tied pork loin roast

Combine soy sauce, sherry, garlic, mustard, ginger and thyme. Place roast in large, clear plastic bag; set in a deep bowl to steady roast. Pour in marinade and close bag tightly. Let stand 2 to 3 hours at room temperature or overnight in the refrigerator. Occasionally press bag against meat in several places to distribute marinade evenly. Remove roast from marinade, place it on rack in a shallow baking pan. Roast, uncovered, at 300° for 2½ to 3 hours or until meat thermometer registers 175°, basting occasionally with marinade during the last hour of roasting. Serve with juices.

Yield: 10 to 12 servings

Ham, Egg and Potato Casserole

1 small onion, minced
6 tablespoons melted margarine
6 tablespoons flour
½ teaspoon salt
¼ teaspoon pepper
2½ cups milk

1½ cups grated cheddar cheese, divided
6 hard boiled eggs, diced
2 cups diced cooked potatoes
1 (12 ounce) can cooked ham, diced, or leftover cooked ham

Sauté onion in margarine until limp, Add flour, salt and pepper and cook over low heat until bubbly. Gradually add milk; cook, stirring constantly, until smooth and thickened. Add 1 cup of the grated cheese to sauce, stirring until melted. Remove from heat; stir in potatoes, eggs and ham. Spoon into a lightly buttered shallow casserole, sprinkle with rest of grated cheese. Bake at 400° for 15 to 20 minutes or until bubbly and hot.

Yield: 6 servings

Ham with Strawberry Pineapple Sauce

Allow 3 to 4 servings per pound of boned, cooked ham.

1   whole or half boneless fully-cooked ham
3   tablespoon honey or white corn syrup
¼   cup sugar
1   tablespoon cornstarch

1   (12 ounce) can unsweetened pineapple juice
2   teaspoons grated orange rind
1   cup sliced fresh strawberries

Put ham on rack in shallow baking pan. Bake, uncovered, in a slow oven, 325°, as directed on package label, or until thermometer reads 130°. It takes about 2½ hours to heat a 10 to 12 pound whole ham, 1½ hours to heat a 6 or 8 pound half ham. Thirty minutes before the end of baking time, increase oven temperature to 375°. Brush ham with honey or corn syrup 2 or 3 times during final baking period. Combine cornstarch and sugar, add pineapple juice; cook, stirring constantly, until thickened and smooth. Very gently fold in orange rind and strawberries, heat. Pour a little of the sauce over ham. Place the rest in a bowl for guests to help themselves.

Yield: Servings depend on ham size

This entree would be delicious with a tomato aspic salad, sweet potatoes, a green vegetable, Sally Lund bread and Spanish Cream with Butter Drops for dessert.

Mexican Oven-Cooked Brisket

This recipe came from the Texas Department of Agriculture. They recommended a brisket not less than 8 pounds. The smaller ones usually come from young animals and do not have the maturity for a juicy, flavorful piece of meat.

1   (10 pound) brisket
1   bottle Sangria wine
1   finely sliced onion
1   finely sliced green pepper

¼   cup picante sauce or to taste
Salt and pepper to taste

Place brisket in a large pyrex, ceramic or stainless steel container. Pour wine over meat and marinate, covered and refrigerated, 24 hours, turning occasionally with a wooden spoon. Remove brisket from marinade and place in roaster pan. Pour marinade over meat, add onion, green pepper, picante sauce, salt and pepper. Cover and cook at 275° for 7 to 8 hours or until tender. When brisket is done, remove to serving platter. Pour off liquid and serve as a sauce.

Yield: About 25 servings

A brisket baked at 275° will yield up to 17% more meat than one cooked at 450°.

Roast Beef With Red Wine

This is one of the most satisfactory roasts I know of. It is expensive but there is no waste to it and it slices easily. Be sure to get the roast with the tip removed. The tip is composed mostly of fat.

1 (8 to 10 pound) choice grade boneless beef ribeye	Salt and pepper to taste
16 large mushrooms, sliced	Pan juices from roast with fat skimmed off
2 tablespoons sliced green onions	2 tablespoons butter or margarine
2 tablespoons butter, do not substitute	2 tablespoon flour
1 cup Bordeaux or Burgundy wine, reduced to ½ cup by rapid boiling	

Roast ribeye, uncovered, at 325° about 1 hour and 25 minutes or until medium rare in center. Remove from oven and let rest for 15 minutes before carving. This waiting time is a must to let juices go back into meat.

Sauté mushrooms and green onions for 1 to 2 minutes in butter until limp. Add remaining sauce ingredients and bring to a boil. If a thicker sauce is desired, cream 2 tablespoons butter or margarine with 2 tablespoons flour and add by bits to hot juices; cook, stirring constantly, until thickened.

Yield: 20 to 24 servings

This recipe has the mushroom, wine sauce, but a choice grade ribeye is delicious without any sauce, just season the juices and serve.

South of the Border Meat Loaf

3 pounds lean ground beef	2 (4 ounce) cans chopped green chilis
1 (15 ounce) can Hunt's tomato sauce	2 eggs, beaten
2 cups broken corn tortilla chips	2 tablespoons chili powder
1 cup finely chopped onions	1 teaspoon salt

In a large bowl, mix beef with ½ can of the tomato sauce. Set rest of tomato sauce aside. Add all the remaining ingredients and mix lightly with a fork. Do not use mixer. Shape into 2 loaves in shallow baking dishes. Bake at 375° for 1 hour. Drain off any fat in pans. Divide remainder of tomato sauce between the 2 loaves and return to oven for 5 minutes. Let stand 10 minutes before slicing.

Yield: 8 to 10 servings

Beef Stroganoff

This is one of my grandson's favorite dishes. Recipe can be doubled.

3½ pounds top sirloin steak or tenderloin, if you want to be extravagant, top round steak can also be used	6 tablespoons flour
	¼ teaspoon dry mustard
	2 cups hot water
	3 beef boullion cubes
2 teaspoons salt	½ cup sour cream
1½ teaspoons pepper	8 ounces canned mushrooms, drained, may be added, if desired
½ cup butter or margarine	
¼ cup minced onion	

Cut beef into strips (¼ × 1½" long). Sprinkle with salt and pepper. Let stand at room temperature for one hour. Heat half the butter in an electric skillet. Cook beef, ⅓ at a time, until still slightly pink in the middle. Place in a bowl until all meat is cooked. Return all meat to the skillet with any juices that have accumulated, add onions and cook 2 to 3 minutes at low heat. Add mushrooms. In top of a double boiler or in a heavy saucepan, melt remaining butter, add flour and mustard and cook until foamy. Gradually add the hot water in which the boullion cubes have been dissolved. Cook, stirring constantly, until smooth and thickened. Add to beef in skillet, add sour cream, Mix, then heat just until hot. Do not boil as sour cream has a tendency to separate over high heat. Serve over steamed white rice.

Yield: 8 to 10 servings

The meat and gravy can be cooked the day before serving, refrigerated, then reheated. However, do not add sour cream until just before serving.

Sweet and Sour Pork Chops

This is the easiest entree you will ever make. Serve with Chinese rice or plain white rice dressed with melted butter and chopped parsley.

6 (6 ounce) center cut pork chops	Catalina salad dressing
	Grape jelly or peach preserves

Lightly brown pork chops in a little oil in a skillet just large enough to hold them. Spread 3 tablespoons of Catalina Salad Dressing over each chop, then place a dessertspoonful (2 teaspoonsful) of either grape jelly or peach preserves on top of each chop. Lower heat to simmer and cook, covered, until chops are tender.

Yield: 6 servings

Super Meat Loaf

2	eggs	¼	teaspoon pepper
1	cup milk	1	tablespoon chopped parsley
¾	cup quick oats		or ¼ teaspoon dried
1	teaspoon salt	1	tablespoon butter
1	teaspoon MSG (optional)	½	cup finely chopped onion
½	teaspoon dried marjoram, crumbled between palms of hands	2½	pounds lean ground beef

Beat eggs and milk together, stir in oats, salt, MSG, marjoram, pepper and parsley. Set aside. In melted butter, sauté onions until tender but not brown. Add to egg mixture along with the meat. Mix well with a fork or with clean hands, but do not use mixer as loaf will not be fluffy. Line a loaf pan with waxed paper or plastic wrap. Turn meat mixture into pan, packing it down gently. Refrigerate, covered, at least 2 hours. Turn out onto shallow baking pan and bake at 325° for 30 minutes. Spread following glaze over and bake for 45 more minutes. Spread rest of glaze over in two parts during this last 45 minutes of baking.

Glaze:

½	cup ketchup	¼	teaspoon dry mustard
2	tablespoons brown sugar, packed	½	teaspoon Worcestershire sauce

Mix all ingredients together and spread over meat loaf in 3 bastings.

Yield: 6 to 8 servings

Ham Balls in Sour Cream Gravy

2	pounds ground cooked ham	1	cup water
½	cup finely chopped onion	2	cups sour cream
½	teaspoon pepper	½	teaspoon dill weed
2	eggs, beaten	½	teaspoon marjoram, crumbled
¼	cup margarine		
¼	cup flour		

Combine first 4 ingredients, form into 16 balls. Place in baking pan and bake at 350° about 20 minutes.

Melt margarine in skillet, add flour; Mix well, then add water; mix, and cook over medium heat until smooth and thickened. Add sour cream, dill weed and marjoram. Heat but do not boil or sour cream will get thin. Add salt to taste. Serve over ham balls.

Yield: 8 servings

Italian Spaghetti

This recipe was given to me 65 years ago by a very dear friend. I like it because it has more vegetables in it than the traditional Italian sauce. I have often tripled it to serve larger groups.

2	pounds lean ground beef
4	tablespoons olive oil
½	cup chopped celery
1	large carrot diced
2	large onions, chopped
1	large clove garlic, minced
1	(6 ounce) can tomato paste, not tomato sauce
1	(16 ounce) can whole tomatoes, broken up in juice
1	bay leaf
¾	teaspoon oregano, crumbled
¼	teaspoon basil leaves crumbled
	Salt and pepper
	Grated Parmesan cheese
¾	pound spaghetti, cooked according to directions

Lightly brown meat and onions in olive oil in heavy stock pot or sauté pan. Then add rest of the ingredients except Parmesan cheese and spaghetti. Bring to a boil, then simmer slowly for 2 or 3 hours, stirring occasionally, or until sauce thickens.

To combine: place a layer of sauce in bottom of a 13″×9″×3″ baking pan, then about ⅓ of the spaghetti, sprinkle a generous amount of Parmesan cheese; then sauce, spaghetti, cheese and so on leaving some sauce for the top. Sprinkle top with Parmesan cheese. Place in 350° oven and bake until bubbly. Serve with additional Parmesan cheese and garlic bread.

Yield: 12 servings

I combine the sauce and spaghetti in a casserole and make it a day ahead. It freezes well, too.

Mexican Lasagna

This is an attractive casserole, with toppings to be served as the guests desire.

1½	pounds lean ground beef	1	(16 ounce) can tomatoes
1½	teaspoons ground cumin	2	cups small curd cottage cheese, drained
1	tablespoon chili powder		
1	clove garlic, crushed or ⅛ teaspoon garlic powder	1	cup Monterey Jack cheese, grated
¼	teaspoon red pepper	1	egg, beaten
1	teaspoon salt		About 15 tortillas
1	teaspoon pepper		

In a heavy skillet, cook meat until it breaks up, drain thoroughly. Add cumin, chili powder, garlic, red pepper, salt, pepper and tomatoes. Heat through. Cover bottom of a lightly greased 13″ × 9″ baking pan with half of the tortillas, overlapping slightly. Pour meat mixture over tortillas, Place rest of tortillas on top. Cover while you mix topping so they will not get dry. Mix cottage cheese, grated Monterey Jack cheese and beaten egg together, and spread on top of tortillas. Bake at 350° for 30 minutes. Serve with garnishes.

Garnishes:

1	cup grated Cheddar cheese	6	green onions, chopped
2	cups shredded lettuce	½	cup ripe olives, sliced
1	cup chopped tomatoes		

Place each item in a separate bowl to serve at table or, if you are serving the plates in the kitchen, sprinkle some of each on each plate. I always make some extra for a second helping of the garnishes.

Yield: 8 servings

Ham Loaves

I am indebted to another dear friend for this recipe.

2	pounds ground ham	½	cup milk
1½	pounds freshly ground pork	1	cup cracker crumbs
1	cup tomato juice	1	cup brown sugar, packed
2	eggs, beaten	½	cup cider vinegar

Mix first 6 ingredients together lightly. Do not use mixer. Form into 8 or 10 small loaves. Place in ovenproof pan. Bake in 300° oven for 1 hour. Mix brown sugar and vinegar and baste loaves three times during baking.

Yield: 8 to 10 servings

Western Burgers

The meat filling has to be made the day ahead for easier handling. The completed burgers can be frozen before cooking. These are good to have on hand for emergencies. They only need to thaw about 30 minutes before baking.

Burger Filling:

2	pounds lean ground beef	3	tablespoons mayonnaise
2	tablespoons prepared mustard	1	tablespoon dehydrated onion
2	teaspoons Worcestershire sauce	10	ounces sharp cheddar cheese, grated

Cook meat in skillet until it breaks apart, then mix in remaining ingredients. place in covered container and refrigerate overnight. Next day, make dough.

Dough for Burgers:

1¾	cups water, 105 to 115°	½	cup dry milk
2	packages dry yeast	¾	teaspoon salt
⅓	cup sugar	¼	cup oil
4 to 5 cups flour			

Place hot water in mixer bowl and sprinkle yeast and 1 teaspoon sugar over. When yeast has foamed up, add sugar, salt and oil. Mix well, then add dry milk and 2 cups of the flour. Beat well, then add 2½ to 3 cups more flour to make a fairly stiff, not sticky. dough. On a floured board, knead dough about 10 times. Oil mixer bowl with 1 tablespoon oil and place dough in it, turning over so that top is oiled. Cover well and let rise until more than doubled. Divide dough in half, then roll one half about ⅛″ thick into a rectangle 20″×8″. Cut rectangle in half, lengthwise, then cut each strip into five 4″ squares, making 10 squares. Place about ¼ cup (an ice cream scoop that holds ¼ cup is good for this) of meat filling in center of square. Flatten meat slightly and bring opposite corners of dough together, then crimp dough together at seams, around meat. Press to seal. Roll out other half of dough and make 10 more burgers. Bake in pre-heated 350° oven about 30 to 40 minutes or until hot and golden brown. These can be frozen on a cookie sheet then placed in plastic sacks. To cook, let thaw at room temperature for 30 or 40 minutes, then bake. These are fairly small, so I count on 2 to a person. If you want to glamorize them, brush tops with an egg wash of 1 egg beaten with 1 table-spoon water, before baking. Do not let any of the egg wash run down onto pan, or they will stick.

Yield: About 20 to 22 burgers

Hamburger Casserole

1½ pounds lean ground beef
½ cup chopped onion
¾ cup milk
1 can cream of mushroom
    soup
8 ounces cream cheese
1 (10 ounce) package frozen
    broccoli florets, thawed

8 ounce can mushroom stems
    and pieces with the juice
¼ cup chopped pimiento
6 ounces noodles, cooked
1½ teaspoon salt
Dash pepper

Cook meat in skillet until it breaks apart. Add onion and cook until onion is limp, but not brown. Add milk, soup and cream cheese, that have been combined well in a bowl. Add rest of ingredients. At this point, you can either heat in the skillet or place in a 13″ × 9″ × 2″ casserole and bake at 350° until bubbly.

Yield: 8 servings

I usually divide this recipe into 2 casseroles and freeze one.

Barbecued Beefies

These could be made in the form of hamburger patties and used for hamburgers, baked in the oven instead of broiled.

1 egg, beaten
1 cup milk
1 cup soft bread crumbs
1 teaspoon salt
¼ teaspoon pepper
1 teaspoon celery seeds
½ teaspoon Worcestershire
    sauce

2 tablespoons minced onion
2 pounds lean ground beef
6 to 8 very thin slices onion,
    depending on the number of
    loaves you are fixing

Mix all ingredients lightly. Make into 6 or 8 individual loaves. Place in lightly greased baking pan, just large enough to hold them, place a slice of onion on top of each. Cover and bake in a 350° oven about 15 minutes, then uncover, brush with the barbecue sauce in this cookbook and bake until browned. The length of baking depends on how thick the loaves are. Mine were a scant inch thick. I made 3 to a pound or 6 in all. Serve with additional sauce, if desired.

Yield: 6 to 8 servings

An easy way to get uniform burgers is to make a roll of the ground meat, then cut into uniform slices and mold into patties.

Pork and Broccoli

The recipe for the stir-fry sauce is in the recipe section of this cookbook.

1	pound pork, trimmed of fat and cut into ⅛" thick slices about ¾" long. Pork will cut easier if partially frozen first	1	cup stir-fry sauce
		2	tablespoons corn starch
		1½	pounds fresh broccoli
		1	pint cherry tomatoes
		3	tablespoon oil

Flatten pork slices with a cleaver. In a bowl, toss with ¼ cup of sauce and the cornstarch. Set aside. Cut broccoli in small flowerets. Peel and slice stalks. Set aside. Put the oil in a wok, heat until hot but not smoking. Add pork slices, a few at a time, cook until lightly browned. Remove to a bowl and set aside. Next add broccoli to wok, adding more oil, if needed, stir fry until it turns bright green. Add tomatoes and cooked pork, stir to combine; then add rest of sauce, stir until heated through and sauce has thickened. Serve immediately.

Yield: 4 servings

Chili Relleno Casserole

Original recipe called for 2 (4 ounce) cans of green chilis. If your taste dictates, you may use the extra can of green chilis.

½	pound lean ground beef	2	cups grated sharp cheese, divided
½	pound pork sausage		
1	medium onion, chopped	4	eggs
2	cloves garlic, minced or ¼ teaspoon garlic powder	¼	cup flour
		1½	cups milk
1	(4 ounce) can chopped green chilis, divided	½	teaspoon salt
			Dash Tabasco

In large skillet, crumble together the beef and sausage. Cook over medium heat, stirring, until meat is lightly browned. Add onion and garlic, cook until onion is limp. Drain off fat. Line a lightly greased 9"×9" pan with half the chilis, top with 1½ cups of the grated cheese. Add meat mixture, then rest of chilis. Beat eggs and flour until smooth, add milk, salt and Tabasco. Pour over meat mixture in pan. Bake, uncovered, in a 350° oven about 40 minutes or until knife inserted in center comes out clean. Sprinkle rest of cheese over top. Let stand 5 minutes before serving.

Yield: 6 servings

Mrs. Dorman's Tamale Pie

This casserole can be made ahead and refrigerated. Just increase baking time to about 60 minutes or until bubbling.

¼ cup olive oil	1 teaspoon salt
1½ pounds lean ground beef	1½ teaspoons chili powder
1 cup chopped onions	¼ teaspoon pepper
1 clove garlic, minced	1 cup yellow cornmeal,
½ cup chopped green peppers (optional)	divided
	1 cup water
1 (18¾ ounce) can tomatoes, broken up with juice, 2½ cups	1½ cups milk
	1 teaspoon salt
	2 tablespoons margarine
1 (12 ounce) can whole kernel corn, drained	1 cup grated Longhorn cheese
	2 eggs, slightly beaten

Pre-heat oven to 375°. In a deep skillet, brown meat in the olive oil, add onion, garlic and peppers (if used). Cook, stirring, until onions are limp. Add corn, tomatoes, chili powder, salt, pepper; simmer 5 minutes. In a saucepan, bring the 1 cup water to a boil, add ½ cup cornmeal slowly and cook, stirring constantly, over low heat for 10 minutes. Mix with meat mixture and place in a 3 quart casserole.

Heat the 1½ cups milk with the salt and margarine. Slowly stir in the last ½ cup of cornmeal; cook, stirring constantly, until thickened. Add eggs and cheese. Mix well, then pour over meat mixture in casserole. Bake, uncovered, 30 to 40 minutes or until top layer is cooked.

Yield: 6 to 8 servings

Tamale Casserole

1 medium onion, chopped	10 to 12 canned tamales, reserve the juice
1 small green pepper, chopped	2 cups fresh or frozen whole kernel corn
1 (2 ounce) jar chopped pimientos	1½ cups grated Cheddar cheese
1 tablespoon margarine, melted	

Steam tamales. Lightly sauté onion, pepper and pimiento in margarine, then simmer briefly in 4 tablespoons tamale juice. Remove tamale husks and cut tamales in 1″ pieces. Toss vegetable mixture with corn, salt and pepper to taste. Fold in tamales and place in a 1½ quart casserole. Bake at 350° until mixture thickens, about 1 hour. Top with cheese, then return to oven just until cheese melts.

Yield: 6 servings

Comida Mexicana

This recipe came from the Texas Department of Agriculture.

1½ pounds lean ground beef	2 teaspoons salt
1⅓ cups chopped onion	4 cups cooked rice
1⅓ cups chopped green pepper	1⅓ cups canned tomato sauce
2 small cloves garlic, minced	1 cup milk or 1 cup creamed cottage cheese
1 tablespoon plus 2 teaspoons chili powder	1⅓ cup cubed Cheddar cheese

Cook beef, onion, green pepper, garlic and seasonings until vegetables are tender but not brown in an electric skillet or top-of-the-stove skillet over medium-low heat.

Stir in rice, tomato sauce, milk or cottage cheese. Heat thoroughly, then fold in cheese. Serve with chopped green onions and corn chips, if desired.

Yield: 8 servings

Mexican Casserole

This recipe came from the Texas Department of Agriculture.

1 pound lean ground beef	1 (10 ounce) can enchilada sauce
1 large onion, chopped	2 dozen corn tortillas, cut into 8ths
1 (10 ounce) can tomatoes with green chilis	2 cups grated cheddar cheese
1 (10¾ ounce) can cream of mushroom soup, undiluted	

Sauté beef and onion, stirring to crumble meat. Cook until onions are limp. Stir in remaining ingredients except tortillas and cheese. Alternately layer meat mixture and tortillas in a 13″×9″×2″ pan, beginning and ending with meat mixture. Sprinkle with cheese. Bake at 350° for 35 minutes or until bubbly. This can be divided in 2 smaller casseroles with one saved for another meal.

Yield: 8 servings

Stir-Fry Beef with Vegetables

½	pound fresh mushrooms, washed and sliced	2	teaspoons cornstarch
½	package frozen snow peas	½	(8 ounce) can water chestnuts, sliced
1	pound beef tenderloin or top sirloin steak	3	tablespoons peanut oil
1	teaspoon sugar	4	thin slices peeled fresh ginger, about 1" diameter and ⅛" thick
1	tablespoon dry sherry		
2	tablespoons soy sauce	½	teaspoon salt

Cut meat into thin strips. This is easier if meat is frozen slightly. In a bowl, combine sugar, soy sauce, wine and cornstarch, mix thoroughly. Add beef slices and toss them in the mixture until they are well coated. Heat a wok or skillet until hot, pour in 1 tablespoon oil. Add mushrooms, snow peas and water chestnuts and stir-fry at medium heat about 2 minutes. Stir in the salt, then remove vegetables with a slotted spoon and set aside in a dish. Pour remaining 2 tablespoons oil in wok, add the ginger and turn to high. Drop in beef and stir-fry for 2 to 3 minutes until they are lightly browned. Pick out the ginger and discard. Return vegetables to meat in wok and cook for about 10 seconds or until they are heated through. Serve immediately.

Yield: 4 generous servings

Easy Pot Roast

1	large cooking bag 14" × 20"	3	medium carrots, peeled and quartered
½	cup flour		
1	(8 ounce) can tomato sauce	5	stalks celery, cut in 1" pieces
½	cup water		
1	teaspoon instant beef boullion	1	medium green pepper, cut into squares
1	teaspoon salt	8	whole new potatoes, washed
¼	teaspoon pepper	2	medium onions, peeled and quartered
4	pound beef rump roast, boneless		

Preheat oven to 325°. Shake flour into bag, place in a 13" × 9" × 2" baking pan. Roll down top of bag, add tomato sauce, water, instant boullion, salt and pepper, squeeze bag gently to blend. Trim fat from roast; place roast in bag. Add carrots, celery, green pepper, potatoes and onions. Turn bag gently to coat ingredients with sauce. Close bag with nylon tie; make 6 (½ inch) slits in top. Bake 1¾ to 2¼ hours or until roast is done and tender. To serve, place roast and vegetables on platter and pour over gravy from bag.

Yield: 6 to 8 servings

Stir-Fried Pork with Vegetables

1	pork tenderloin, about ¾ pound, cut crosswise into ⅛" slices	½	pound fresh mushrooms, washed and sliced
3	tablespoons soy sauce	1	medium carrot very thinly sliced on the diagonal
1	tablespoon dry sherry	¼	teaspoon salt
2½	teaspoons cornstarch	2	tablespoons water
1¼	teaspoons sugar	5	tablespoons oil, divided
⅛	teaspoon ground ginger		
1	(10 ounce) package frozen broccoli florets or equivalent fresh florets, cut into ¾" size pieces		

In medium bowl, combine pork with next 5 ingredients. In wok with 3 table-spoons oil, cook broccoli, carrot, mushrooms and salt, stirring, until vegetables are coated with oil. Add water and stir-fry until vegetables are tender-crisp. Drain and remove to a bowl. Wipe out wok, then add the 2 remaining tablespoons of oil. Heat and add pork and cook until done, 2 or 3 minutes, stirring frequently. Return vegetables to wok and heat through. Serve immediately.

Yield: 3 to 4 servings

Cantonese Casserole

I love recipes where the pasta or rice is cooked along with the rest of the ingredients. This is a tasty dish that lends itself to large groups. It can be doubled or tripled or whatever.

1½	pounds lean ground beef	2	ounces (¼ cup) soy sauce
1	cup finely chopped onion		No salt, soy sauce is salty
1	cup thin sliced celery, sliced diagonally	¾	cup uncooked Uncle Ben's rice
1	can cream of mushroom soup	8	ounce can sliced water chestnuts (optional)
2	soup cans water		

Cook meat, stirring with a fork until it breaks apart. Add rest of ingredients. Mix well. Place in a 13"×9"×2" pan. Cover tightly with foil and bake in a 350° oven for 1 hour, or until rice is tender. Serve with a bottle of soy sauce on the table for those who want it. If you want to be extravagant, you may add snow peas during the last 10 minutes of cooking.

Yield: 8 servings.

Be sure to use Uncle Ben's rice.

Pork in Lettuce Cups

¾ pound boneless pork, cut into ⅛″ thick slices then cut slices into match-like thin pieces
1 tablespoon cornstarch
2 tablespoons soy sauce
¼ teaspoon salt
¼ teaspoon ground ginger
⅛ teaspoon cayenne pepper
¼ teaspoon sugar
1 (6 ounce) package pea pods or thinly sliced zucchini or broccoli stems

3 tablespoons oil
1 medium carrot, cut in 3″ match-like strips
1 medium onion, very thinly sliced
1 small clove garlic, minced
4 large Boston or iceberg lettuce leaves

Place pork slices in freezer until they are slightly frozen, then cut into match-like thin pieces. In medium bowl, mix pork strips, cornstarch and next 5 ingredients; set aside. In 10″ skillet or wok, heat oil and add carrot, onion, garlic and vegetables. Cook, stirring frequently, until crisp tender. Remove with a slotted spoon to a small bowl. In drippings remaining, over high heat, cook pork until meat is brown and tender, about 5 minutes, stirring. Return vegetables to wok, heat through. Spoon ¼ of mixture onto each lettuce cup. Serve immediately.

Yield: 4 servings

Beef Tenderloin

I have used this marinade for a trimmed brisket weighing 4 pounds. I put the brisket in an oven bag and poured the marinade over it, then tied it with the twist provided. I marinated it for 4 hours turning occasionally. It was baked for 12 hours at 200°.

1 beef tenderloin, oven ready, fat trimmed
2 tablespoons grated fresh ginger or ¼ teaspoon ground ginger

½ cup dry sherry wine
¼ cup soy sauce
1 medium onion sliced thin

Rub tenderloin with ginger. Marinate in the sherry, soy sauce and onion for at least 1 hour. Roast at 450° for 25 minutes for rare, 40 minutes for medium. Use a meat thermometer for accuracy. Baste with marinade during cooking. Slice and serve with the juices.

Yield: 6 to 8 servings

For the brisket, I thickened the juices with 1 tablespoon of cornstarch dissolved in 3 tablespoons water. you may do the same with the tenderloin, if you like.

Stuffed Leg of Lamb

You may put carrots, potatoes on bottom of roasting pan, if you like, pouring 1 cup chicken or beef broth over.

1 (5 to 6 pound) leg of lamb, trimmed of all but a thin layer of fat, boned and butterflied	½ cup olive oil 1 cup chicken or beef stock Pepper Salt

Place lamb on work surface, cut ¼ to ½" deep slits in thick muscles of lamb. With a meat mallet, pound lamb into a 1½" thick rectangle. Sprinkle with salt and pepper. Spread spinach filling over surface, leaving a 1" border. Starting from the long side, roll up into a roll. Tie roll with string at 1" intervals, then tie with string lengthwise twice. Place in a roaster and add 1 cup chicken or beef broth. Bake in a 325° oven, basting with Galliano butter frequently, and adding stock as needed. Bake until thermometer registers 135° for medium-rare or to your taste.

Transfer to platter; place roasting pan over medium heat and degrease juices, scraping up any brown bits. Transfer to a saucepan and cook over medium heat, stirring, until sauce measures 1⅛ cups. Taste for seasoning and serve with lamb.

Galliano Butter:

½ pound unsalted butter 1 teaspoon salt ¼ teaspoon each pepper and oregano	½ cup Galliano Liqueur

Heat all ingredients together for basting lamb.

Spinach Stuffing:

1 (10 ounce) package frozen chopped spinach, thawed and squeezed dry ⅔ cup minced parsley 2 tablespoons minced shallots ½ clove garlic, crushed 3 tablespoons fresh bread crumbs	¼ cup ground raw veal or raw chicken ½ cup pine nuts or coarsely chopped pecans 1 egg, beaten

Mix all ingredients and add the beaten egg. Stuff the lamb. Bake per directions.

Yield: 8 to 10 servings

This stuffing could also be used to stuff chicken breasts.

Deviled Meat Loaf

1	pound lean ground beef	1	teaspoon Worcestershire
1	cup bread crumbs		sauce
3	tablespoons prepared	1	teaspoon salt
	mustard	¼	teaspoon freshly ground
2	tablespoons prepared		pepper
	horseradish	1	egg, beaten
1	tablespoon grated onion	¼	cup ketchup

Mix all ingredients together and press lightly into a 1 quart loaf pan. Cover with foil and bake 45 minutes in a 350° oven. Remove foil and bake 10 minutes longer.

Yield: 4 or 5 servings

Leg of Lamb with Red Wine

1	(6 to 7 pound) leg of lamb	1	teaspoon thinly sliced
	boned and butterflied		peeled garlic
¾	cup dry red wine	3	bay leaves
½	cup vegetable oil	1	teaspoon dried oregano,
1	cup thinly sliced peeled		crumbled
	onion	1	teaspoon salt
2	tablespoons lemon juice		
2	tablespoons chopped		
	parsley		

Mix all ingredients together except leg of lamb. Place leg of lamb in large plastic bag. Set in a bowl and pour marinade into bag. Fasten with tie. Press bag gently to distribute marinade. Set into a stainless steel, ceramic or glass pan. Refrigerate 8 to 24 hours, turning lamb two or three times.

Remove from refrigerator 1 hour before putting in oven. Remove lamb from bag and place, fat-side up, in roasting pan. Strain marinade and pour a little over lamb. Roast at 350° about 1 hour or to desired doneness, basting occasionally with marinade. Remove lamb and place on cutting board or platter. Strain juices, season to taste and serve with lamb.

Yield: 8 to 10 servings

Tenderloin en Croute

1   oven-ready tenderloin, 6 or
    7 pounds

2   packages (2 sheets each)
    Pepperidge Farm frozen
    puffed pastry, thawed
    according to package
    directions

Marinade:

⅓   cup olive oil
½   cup sliced onions
½   cup sliced carrots
½   cup sliced celery

¼   teaspoon dried thyme
¼   teaspoon dried marjoram
1   cup dry vermouth

Place above ingredients, except the vermouth, in a small saucepan and cook over medium heat, covered, until vegetables are tender. Place tenderloin in a large cooking bag. Spread vegetables on top of meat, then pour the 1 cup of vermouth over all. Close bag with tie provided. Place in a pan and refrigerate for 24 hours, turning over bag and pressing against meat at least 4 times during that time.

Mushroom Duxelles:

2   tablespoons butter
1½ pounds fresh mushrooms,
    washed and minced
⅓   cup dry Madeira or
    Cabernet Sauvignon

2   tablespoons finely chopped
    green onions
2   ounces foie gras

Sauté mushrooms in the butter along with the onions until the mushrooms begin to separate from each other. Add the wine and simmer until liquid has evaporated. Add salt and pepper to taste. Cool, then beat in 2 ounces foie gras. Refrigerate. I usually make this the day before when I marinate the meat. Stir well the next day before using.

On the day of your dinner, scrape off the vegetables and liquid into a bowl and dry the tenderloin with paper towels. Strain the marinade and reserve for sauce.

Continued on next page

Rub the tenderloin with 1 tablespoon olive oil, fold under the thin end and tie with string. Bake at 425° in the upper third of the oven for 25 minutes. Baste with oil three times during the baking. However, if the butcher saves the large piece of suet from the tenderloin for you, you can lay it over the tenderloin and you won't have to baste the meat. Remove from oven and let cool at least 30 minutes. You may cook the tenderloin the day before and refrigerate, well covered. However, it must be at room temperature before proceeding.

Have the puff pastry thawed according to directions in refrigerator. Remove 1 package (2 sheets) and press the sheets together end to end. Roll into a rectangle 16" × 10" Place pastry on oven proof platter or cookie sheet. Place meat on pastry and trim pastry leaving a 1½" margin around the meat. Remove meat and spread about ⅓ of the duxelles over pastry, leaving a 2" border. Remove string from tenderloin and place meat over duxelles. Turn up pastry on sides of meat. Brush outer edges with an egg wash made of 1 egg beaten with 1 tablespoon water, making sure that none rolls down on pan. Place rest of duxelles over top of meat. Roll remaining 2 sheets of pastry into a rectangle 16" × 10" or one large enough to come over the meat and meet the lower pastry with a 1" overlap. Press edges of pastry firmly together. Use any trimmings for decoration, you should have some from the corners and sides.

Brush top pastry with egg wash. Cut out leaves, flowers or whatever you wish from pastry trimmings; lay on top and then brush them with egg wash. Make 3 vent holes in top of pastry to vent steam. Bake in a 425° oven for 25 minutes, then lower temperature to 375° and bake 20 to 25 minutes longer to 140° for medium rare beef. Let rest for 20 minutes before serving. Remember, meat will continue cooking some during standing time, so medium rare will come close to medium by the time it is served.

Sauce:

Marinade	2	tablespoons cornstarch
2 cups canned beef boullion	¼	cup dry red wine
1 tablespoon tomato paste		

Place marinade and boullion in saucepan, add tomato paste; simmer until reduced to 2 cups. Thicken with the cornstarch dissolved in the red wine. Taste for seasoning and serve in a bowl for guests to help themselves.

Yield: 8 servings

Ask the butcher to remove all fat and membrane. It will save you a lot of time, if he will do it. If not, you will need a very sharp boning knife.

Pork-Noodle Bake

This is a dish where noodles or pasta does not have to be pre-cooked.

1½ pounds boneless lean pork, cut into bite-sized pieces	½ teaspoon salt
1 cup thin diagonally sliced carrots	¼ teaspoon garlic powder, not garlic salt
1 cup celery diagonally sliced	¼ teaspoon dried whole basil, crumbled
½ cup finely chopped onion	¼ teaspoon pepper
15 ounce can tomato sauce	4 ounces uncooked medium noodles
2 cups water	
⅓ cup ketchup	
1 cup fresh mushrooms, washed and sliced	

Spray a large electric skillet with vegetables spray. Set heat to medium. Add pork and cook until lightly browned. Remove from skillet. Add carrots, celery and onion; sauté until crisp tender. Stir in tomato sauce and remaining ingredients, including pork. Bring to a boil; cover, reduce heat to simmer and cook 30 minutes, stirring occasionally.

Yield: 4 servings

Beef may be used instead of pork, if desired.

California Pork Stew

2 pounds pork shoulder, cubed	½ teaspoon freshly ground pepper
2 tablespoons olive oil	1 bay leaf
1 cup chopped onion	1 cup dry red wine
2 cloves garlic, minced	2 medium zucchini, cut into 1" pieces
2 (3 ounce) cans Italian tomatoes	¼ cup flour
3 teaspoons salt	¼ cup red wine
2 teaspoons mixed Italian herbs, crumbled	¼ cup water

Brown pork in olive oil. Remove and set aside. Sauté onion and garlic in same pan; return pork to pan and add tomatoes, herbs, salt, pepper, bay leaf and 1 cup wine. Simmer 1 hour. Add zucchini and cook 15 minutes longer or until meat and vegetables are tender. Remove bay leaf. Stir flour into the wine and water and add to bubbling liquid. Cook, stirring gently, until thickened and bubbly about 3 minutes. Serve hot over spaghetti and top with Parmesan cheese.

Yield: 6 servings

Gourmet Beef Stew

This stew has to be made the day before serving, baked, and reheated the next day. This enhances the flavor.

3	pounds lean beef, cut in bite-size pieces	1½	cups thinly sliced carrots
Flour seasoned with salt and pepper		6	peppercorns
		4	whole cloves
6	strips bacon	1	bay leaf, crumbled
2	cloves garlic, minced	3	tablespoons chopped parsley
16	whole small mushrooms	¼	teaspoon marjoram, crumbled
1	cup condensed beef broth		
1½	cup dry red wine	¼	teaspoon thyme, crumbled
16	small white onions, peeled		

Place seasoned flour in a paper bag, add beef cubes and shake until well covered with flour. Fry bacon in skillet, until it begins to brown, remove from pan, saving drippings. Then cut into 1″ pieces and put in large heavy baking dish. Cook garlic slightly in same pan, then add beef cubes and brown on all sides. Remove meat and garlic and place in casserole. Put mushrooms in skillet and cook only 3 minutes over medium heat, add to casserole. Put boullion and 1 cup red wine in skillet and bring to a boil. Stir from bottom to loosen any brown particles. Pour liquid into casserole. Add onions, carrots, peppercorns, cloves, bayleaf, parsley, marjoram and thyme. Pour over remaining ½ cup wine, Cover casserole tightly and bake at 300° for 2 hours. Cool and place in refrigerator. When ready to serve the next day, spoon some of the liquid from the bottom over meat and bake, covered, at 300° for 1 hour, or until piping hot.

Yield: 6 to 8 servings

Helpful Hint: *Do not crowd the pan when cooking cubes for meat for stews or casseroles. Overcrowding causes the moisture in the meat to evaporate slowly, which produces steam and turns the meat gray. Also be sure the meat is completely dry before browning it in order to prevent steam.*

2 K's Hobo Stew

You may want to serve this for a large party. The recipe was given to me by the owner of the 2 K Sandwich Shop in Houston.

12	pounds lean beef, cut into 1" cubes	2	cups celery, coarsely chopped
Flour as needed		6	sprigs parsley, stems removed
1	cup beef drippings or shortening	¼	cup salt
3	quarts boiling water	Pepper to taste	
2	quarts diced turnips	1	teaspoon peppercorns
2	quarts diced carrots	6	bay leaves
2	quarts green peas	12	whole cloves
6	medium onions, sliced thin		

Dredge meat in flour. Brown in drippings or shortening in a heavy large stockpot. Add remaining meat and water. Simmer 4 or more hours. Two hours before serving, stir in vegetables and seasonings, and simmer for the 2 hours. If additional liquid is needed, add a little beef broth.

Leftover roast or steak may be used in which case, meat does not have to be browned again. This freezes well. Since it is "Hobo Stew," it is appropriate to serve it from an old black iron kettle.

Yield: 36 to 40 servings

For a "Hobo" luncheon, the menu was baked potatoes with the skins on, this stew, cornbread and apple dumplings for dessert. As the guests arrived, they were given bandannas, tied to a stick, containing crackers, cheese, carrot and celery sticks for an appetizer.

Oven Barbecued Brisket

2	partially trimmed 5 or 6 pound brisket	2	cups Worcestershire sauce
Salt and pepper to taste		1	cup liquid smoke
		Water, as needed	

Combine all ingredients except brisket; place in a baking pan, pour sauce over adding just enough water to cover. Bake at 275° about 6 or 7 hours, covered. Add more water, if necessary. Take off cover to let brown towards end of cooking.

Yield: 24 servings

Roast with Red Wine

This is a deluxe pot roast.

1	(3 or 4 pound) rump roast	1	teaspoon salt
1½	cups red wine	1	teaspoon ground ginger
2	large onions, sliced	12	peppercorns
1	lemon, sliced	4	tablespoons shortening
2	tablespoons sugar	2	tablespoons flour

Place roast in a deep bowl and add remaining ingredients except shortening and flour. Cover and refrigerate for 18 to 24 hours, turning at least 4 times. Remove roast from marinade and drain well. Heat 2 tablespoons shortening in a dutch oven or heavy deep pan. Brown the roast in the hot fat. Strain marinade and pour over roast. Cover and simmer for 3 to 4 hours, adding a small amount of water, if necessary.

To serve: Lift roast out of the dutch oven and pour off and reserve remaining liquid. Melt remaining fat in the dutch oven and stir in flour, Brown lightly, then add reserved pan juices, and cook over low heat until thickened. Taste for seasoning. Place roast back in the sauce and cook for 5 minutes, then remove and slice on a hot platter. Serve with sauce.

Yield: 6 servings

Priest's Goulash

This recipe calls for beer and carraway seed, which adds an individual taste to this dish.

2	pounds chuck steak, cut into bite-sized pieces	¼	teaspoon dried leaf basil, crumbled
1	tablespoon flour	3	cups beer
½	teaspoon salt	1	cup beef stock or boullion
¼	teaspoon pepper	2	onions, chopped
2	teaspoons paprika	3	carrots, chopped
¼	cup cooking oil	4	tomatoes, peeled and chopped
1	clove garlic,minced		
1	bay leaf	½	teaspoon carraway seeds

Mix flour, salt, pepper and paprika and toss meat in it. Heat oil in large, heavy pan, add meat and cook over medium heat until browned. Add garlic, bay leaf, basil, beer and stock. Stir until boiling, then transfer to a casserole. Cover, and cook in a 325° oven for 2 hours. Add onions, carrots, tomatoes and carraway seeds and continue cooking for 1½ to 2 hours. Correct seasonings before serving.

Yield: 4 servings

Baked Shortribs

Marinade
2   cloves garlic, finely minced
½   cup olive oil
¼   cup red wine vinegar
1   teaspoon dried thyme, crumbled

1   teaspoon salt
½   teaspoon finely ground pepper

Combine the garlic, oil, vinegar, thyme, salt and pepper in a large bowl. Add the ribs and toss well. Chill, covered, overnight.

5   pounds lean beef shortribs, cut into 3" pieces
2   large onions, halved lengthwise and sliced thin crosswise
1½   pounds California boiling potatoes, cut into 1" pieces and put in a bowl of cold water
¾   pound carrots, halved lengthwise, cut into ½" pieces and put in a bowl of cold water

1½   cups brown stock or canned beef broth
1½   cups dry red wine
½   cup minced parsley leaves
1   tablespoon grated lemon peel
1   tablespoon minced garlic

Drain the ribs, reserving the marinade. In a shallow 3 to 4 quart baking dish, arrange the onions and drained ribs. Bake them, uncovered, in a pre-heated 450° oven for 30 minutes. Pour off all but ⅓ cup of the fat in the dish and add the drained potatoes and carrots, tossing them to coat them with the fat. Sprinkle them with salt and pepper, pour the reserved marinade over and bake in a 350° oven, basting occasionally, for 40 minutes. Combine the stock and wine in a saucepan and reduce liquid to about 2 cups. Add the lemon peel and garlic then pour the liquid over the vegetables. Bake for 15 to 20 minutes more until vegetables and meat are very tender. Sprinkle parsley over dish and serve.

Yield: 6 servings

Pot Roast with Buttermilk Gravy

1	(3 pound) beef pot roast or pork shoulder
2	tablespoons cooking oil
Salt and pepper	
1	(10½ ounce) can beef or chicken broth
1	teaspoon dried thyme, crushed
½	teaspoon dried rosemary, crushed
2	bay leaves
3	medium potatoes, peeled and sliced ¼″ thick or sweet potatoes in chunks
1	(8 ounce) can small whole onions or 1 medium onion cut into small wedges
1	(10 ounce) package cut broccoli
1	recipe buttermilk gravy

In a large kettle, brown meat in hot oil on all sides. Drain off fat. Sprinkle with salt and pepper. Add broth, thyme, rosemary and bay leaves. Cover and bake at 325° 1 to 1½ hours or until meat is tender. Add potatoes and vegetables, except broccoli, and cook until vegetables are tender. Add broccoli and cook about 7 minutes. Remove meat and vegetables to a warm platter; cover and keep warm. Skim fat from juices, remove bay leaves. Measure 1½ cups pan juices, adding water if necessary, and put back into pan. In a screw top jar, combine ½ cup buttermilk and ¼ cup flour and shake well. Stir into pan juices and cook, stirring, until thickened. Cook 1 minute more. Season to taste with salt and pepper. Spoon some over meat and pass the rest.

Yield: 6 servings

Simmered Pot Roast

Recipe for the stir-fry sauce is in sauce section of this book. It is good with any oriental dish and is similar to Teriyaki sauce.

1	tablespoon oil
3	pounds beef chuck pot roast about 1½ inches thick
½	cup stir-fry sauce
½	cup dry red wine
½	pound fresh mushrooms, sliced
3	tablespoons cornstarch
¼	cup water

Heat oil in Dutch oven or skillet with a cover, over medium heat. Add beef and brown on all sides. Combine stir-fry sauce and wine; pour over beef. Cover and reduce heat to simmer; simmer for 1 hour and 40 minutes. Add mushrooms and simmer, covered, 10 minutes longer. Combine cornstarch and water; set aside. Remove beef to serving platter and keep warm. Add cornstarch mixture to pan drippings, bring to a boil and cook until gravy thickens slightly. To serve, cut roast across the grain into thin slices and serve with the hot mushroom gravy.

Yield: 4 to 6 servings

Shrimp and Wild Rice Casserole

This makes an attractive entree. I have served this many times on a buffet table with a mixed vegetable salad and hot rolls for a complete meal. A lemon or fruit dessert tops off the meal.

½ cup uncooked wild rice	¼ cup diced pimiento
¾ cup uncooked Uncle Ben's white rice	8 ounces fresh mushrooms, sliced
½ teaspoon salt	2 pounds medium size shrimp, peeled, cleaned and cooked
5 stalks celery, cut diagonally into thin slices	
2 medium onions, minced	
1½ sticks margarine or butter, melted	

Place wild rice in small saucepan with 1½ cups boiling water and parboil for 5 minutes only. Let set, covered, for 1 hour. Drain, then place in a 9″ × 13″ × 2″ baking pan, add white rice and 1 teaspoon salt. Pour 3¼ cups boiling water over rice and stir with a fork. Cover tightly with foil, crimping edges, and bake at 400° for 25 to 35 minutes. Foil will puff up slightly when rice is done. However, after 25 minutes, you can peek to see if it is done, if you like. Remove from oven and place in a large mixing bowl and set aside. In a heavy skillet or sauté pan, sauté onion and celery in ½ stick butter or margarine until celery is crisp-tender and onion is limp. Add to rice. Sauté mushrooms in same pan, adding a little more margarine or butter, just 5 minutes. Add to rice along with any juices in skillet. Add pimiento and cooked shrimp to rice. Add melted margarine or butter, toss well and check the seasoning. If mixture seems dry, add a little more melted butter or margarine. Place in a shallow casserole, cover and bake in 325° oven until just hot. Garnish with parsley sprigs and serve.

Yield: 8 servings

Helpful Hint: *Fresh celery leaves dropped in the pot while cooking shrimp helps destroy the odor.*

Seafood Gruyere

¾	cup plus 2 tablespoons butter, divided	2	teaspoons tomato paste
¾	cup flour	3	teaspoons lemon juice, divided
3	cups milk	1	pound scallops, washed well and cut in half if large
12	ounces Gruyere cheese		
¼	teaspoon garlic powder, not garlic salt	½	pound fresh mushrooms, sliced
1½	teaspoons salt, divided	1	pound cleaned cooked shrimp
¼	teaspoon white pepper		
¼	teaspoon Accent	2	tablespoons diced green pepper (optional)
¼	teaspoon dry mustard		

Cream the ¾ cup butter and flour together in a bowl. Heat milk in top of a double boiler and add the flour-butter mixture gradually by tablespoonsful, stirring constantly with a wire whisk. Add the cheese cut into cubes, cook and stir until cheese melts. Add garlic powder, 1 teaspoon of the salt, pepper, Accent, mustard, tomato paste and 2 teaspoons of the lemon juice. Poach washed scallops in water to which you have added the ½ teaspoon salt and 1 teaspoon lemon juice, cooking just until tender. Take ½ cup of the broth and add to the cream sauce. Sauté mushrooms in remaining 2 tablespoons butter for just 3 minutes and add to sauce. Drain scallops and shrimp and add to sauce. Taste for seasoning. Heat through. Garnish serving dish with the green peppers which have been sautéed until tender with a little butter. Serve over rice or in patty shells or over toast.

Yield: 8 to 10 servings

Baked Red Snapper

I am fond of any fish almondine. This same recipe may be used for trout.

5	fillets of red snapper	¾	cup thin sliced almonds
¼	cup olive oil	½	cup melted butter
	Salt, pepper		Juice of 1 small lemon
	Flour		

Wipe fillets with a damp cloth, season with salt and pepper and lightly dredge with flour, shaking off excess. Sauté the fillets in heavy sauté pan in the olive oil until they are nicely browned on both sides. Lay the fillets in a shallow baking dish that will hold them in one layer. Mix almonds, lemon juice and melted butter and pour over them. Bake in a 400° oven until almonds are nicely browned.

Yield: 5 servings

Barbecued Cod Fillets

2	pounds cod fillets or other fresh or frozen fish fillets about 1″ thick	1	(8 ounce) can tomato sauce
1	clove garlic minced	2	tablespoons dry sherry
2	tablespoons chopped onion	½	teaspoon salt
2	tablespoons fat or oil	¼	teaspoon oregano, crumbled
		3	drops tabasco sauce
			Dash pepper

Cook onion and garlic in oil until tender. Add remaining ingredients and simmer for 5 minutes, stirring occasionally. Cool. Cut fillets into serving size portions. Place in a single layer in a shallow baking dish. Pour sauce over fish and let it stand for 30 minutes, turning once. Remove fish, reserving sauce for basting. Place fish in well-greased hinged wire grills. Cook about 4″ from moderately hot coals for 8 minutes. Baste with sauce. Turn and cook 7 to 10 minutes longer or until fish flakes easily when tested with a fork. Serve with any sauce left. Note: Time of cooking depends on thickness of fillets.

Yield: 6 servings

Cod Filet Piquant

2	pounds cod fillets	1	tablespoon lemon juice
¾	cup bread crumbs	½	cup butter, melted
1	tablespoon vinegar	1	teaspoon prepared mustard
1	tablespoon Worcestershire sauce	⅛	teaspoon pepper
		1	teaspoon salt

Sprinkle the bottom of a greased shallow baking dish with bread crumbs. Wipe fish with a damp cloth. Place cod in dish. Mix together remaining ingredients and pour over fish. Baste several times, sprinkle with paprika. Bake in hot oven, 450° about 10 minutes for each inch the fish is thick. Serve with any sauce left in the dish.

Yield: 6 servings

Codfish in Sour Cream

2	pounds codfish, fresh, in one piece, or other firm-fleshed fish	1	teaspoon fresh parsley, minced
1	bay leaf	1	large tomato, skinned and diced
1	slice lemon	1	cup sour cream
2	whole cloves		Pinch marjoram, crumbled
2	tablespoons olive oil		Pinch sweet basil, crumbled
4	green onions, cut fine		Salt and pepper to taste

Wrap the fish, together with bay leaf, lemon and cloves in cheesecloth to keep it from breaking, and cook it in gently simmering water until it flakes. Remove from cheesecloth and place in shallow baking dish. Cook the onions in the oil, add parsley, tomato, herbs, salt, pepper and sour cream. Pour this over fish and heat it under the broiler for just a minute or two. Delicious with small new potatoes seasoned with minced parsley, butter, salt, pepper and grated lemon peel.

Yield: 8 to 10 servings

Individual Shrimp Casseroles

6	tablespoons melted butter, divided	1	pound cooked shrimp
4	tablespoons flour	½	pound fresh mushrooms, sliced
2	cups milk	1	cup crushed Ritz Crackers, divided
1	tablespoon dry sherry	3	tablespoons melted butter or margarine
½	teaspoon salt		
	Dash pepper		
¼	teaspoon mace		

Combine 4 tablespoons butter and flour, blending until smooth. Cook until bubbly over low heat, stirring. Slowly add milk and sherry and cook until thickened. Add salt, pepper, mace and shrimp. Set aside. Sauté mushrooms in 2 tablespoons butter a few minutes, and add to sauce. Cover bottoms of four buttered individual casseroles with ⅓ of the cracker crumbs. Divide shrimp mixture into casseroles. Add melted butter or margarine to the rest of the crumbs and sprinkle on top of casseroles. Bake at 375° until brown and bubbly.

Yield: 4 servings

Fish with Spinach

Recipe can be halved to serve 2 or 3 generously.

2   (10 ounce) packages frozen
    chopped spinach, thawed
    and squeezed dry
1   stick butter
Salt and white pepper

4   tablespoons flour
1½   cups milk
1½   pounds white fish (cod, sole
    or haddock)
1   tablespoon lemon juice

Melt butter in heavy saucepan or skillet and sauté spinach with salt and pepper to taste, just until moisture evaporates. Remove from heat. Mix flour with spinach, then add milk. Return to heat and cook, stirring, until mixture thickens. Taste for seasoning, remove to heated serving platter and keep warm. Cut fish into 6 portions, poach in salted water with 1 tablespoon fresh lemon juice just until fish flakes. Place on top of creamed spinach and top with the following shrimp sauce or hollandaise sauce.

Shrimp Sauce:

½   pound small sized boiled
    shrimp
¼   stick butter (2 tablespoons)
2   tablespoons flour
1   cup milk
¼   cup dry white wine

½   teaspoon paprika
¼   teaspoon dry mustard
½   teaspoon Worcestershire
    sauce
Dash tabasco
Salt to taste

Melt butter in heavy saucepan, blend in flour and cook, stirring, until bubbly. Remove from heat, add milk and wine slowly. Blend well, return to heat and cook over medium heat, stirring constantly, until thickened. Add seasonings and shrimp. Check seasoning and serve hot over fish.

Yield: 6 servings

Make shrimp sauce before cooking fish, set aside and warm before serving.

Helpful Hint: *Frozen fish: Cook frozen fish while it is still a bit icy in the middle. It takes only a few minutes longer and stays moist and juicy.*

Shrimp Casserole

This recipe was given to me many years ago by a friend. It is easy to prepare and very good.

2 tablespoons margarine	1½ cups grated cheddar cheese
1 (4 ounce) can sliced mushrooms	½ cup evaporated milk
1 pound cooked shrimp, cut in half lengthwise	3 tablespoons ketchup
1½ cups cooked rice	½ teaspoon Worcestershire sauce
	Salt and pepper to taste

Sauté mushrooms in margarine for 5 minutes. Place other ingredients in a bowl and add mushrooms. Place in buttered casserole and bake at 350° until bubbly and golden, about 25 to 30 minutes.

Yield: 4 servings

Superb Crabmeat Casserole

1 pound cooked crabmeat or a combination of cooked shrimp and crabmeat	4 tablespoons flour
4 tablespoons butter, do not substitute	1 cup cream
	4 tablespoons dry sherry
	¾ cup grated sharp cheese
	Salt and pepper to taste

Make a cream sauce with the butter, flour and cream. Add salt, pepper and sherry and heat. Remove from heat and add crabmeat. Pour into a square or oval baking dish. Sprinkle with grated cheese and bake in a 350° oven until cheese melts.

Yield: 4 servings

Shrimp or Crawfish Etouffé

This recipe was given to me by a young man from Louisiana, who made it for us when he was visiting one summer. It is a simplified version and is very good.

1   pound fresh cleaned peeled shrimp or crawfish
1   stick butter
2   medium onions, chopped
1   can Rotel tomatoes with green peppers

1   (10¾ ounce) can cream of celery soup
1   can cream of mushroom soup

Sauté onions in the butter until golden and transparent, stirring constantly. Add Rotel tomatoes, mushroom and celery soups. Then add shrimp or crawfish. Cook only 15 minutes. Remove from heat. If not serving immediately reheat over medium heat just before serving. Serve on boiled rice. You will need 6 cups.

Yield: 8 to 10 servings

Scallops with Spinach Pasta

¼   stick butter, do not substitute
2   tablespoons olive oil
1   pound bay scallops, washed and cut in half, if large
1   tablespoon cornstarch
2½ tablespoons water

½   cup teriyaki sauce
¼   cup lemon juice
½   pound spinach pasta, cooked al dente
½   pound frozen peas, thawed and drained

Melt butter and olive oil in heavy sauté pan, cook half of the scallops at a time, cooking just until they become opaque. Do not overcook. Remove with slotted spoon to a bowl. Reserve liquid in pan. Mix cornstarch and water; set aside. Add teriyaki sauce and lemon juice to reserved juices in the sauté pan. Bring mixture to a boil, then add cornstarch mixture. Cook, stirring constantly, until thickened. Add cooked pasta, peas and scallops to sauce. Garnish with lemon slices.

Yield: 6 servings

Fish with Stir-Fry Sauce

This stir-fry sauce can be used many ways and is a handy recipe to keep.

1	pound fish fillets, partially thawed, cut into 2″ × 1″ × ½″ pieces	¼	cup oil, divided
		½	pound fresh green beans sliced diagonally
1	egg white, beaten until slightly frothy	½	pound fresh mushrooms, sliced
3	tablespoons cornstarch	1	cup stir-fry sauce

Coat fish, a few pieces at a time with egg white and toss into cornstarch. Heat wok, add 3 tablespoons of the oil, heat on medium heat. Add fish, cook a few at a time, until opaque, turning carefully to prevent crumbling. Cook remaining fish and set aside in a bowl. Heat remaining 1 tablespoon oil in wok and add beans. Stir fry for 30 seconds, add mushrooms and stir fry 30 seconds. Add stir-fry sauce and heat, then fold in fish, heat and serve.

Sauce:

3	tablespoons dark brown sugar, packed	½	cup dry sherry
		¼	teaspoon Tabasco sauce
3½	tablespoons cornstarch	3	tablespoons red wine vinegar
2	teaspoons ground ginger		
4	garlic cloves, crushed	2½	cups beef or chicken broth
½	cup soy sauce		

Combine all ingredients, except broth in blender, cover and process until smooth. Pour in a jar and add broth, shake well. Store up to 2 weeks in refrigerator or freeze in 1 cup portions up to 2 months.

Yield: 4 servings

Shrimp Luncheon Casserole

3	tablespoons butter	½	cup canned chopped mushrooms, drained
1	medium onion, minced		
1	green pepper, minced (optional)	1	pound peeled and cleaned fresh shrimp
1	clove garlic, minced	1	teaspoon salt
¼	cup pimiento, drained and chopped	1	bay leaf
		1	(8 ounce) can tomato sauce
1	cup uncooked rice	1	cup chicken broth

Combine butter, onion, green pepper, garlic, pimiento and uncooked rice in an electric skillet; mix well. Stir in mushrooms, salt, bay leaf, tomato sauce and broth. Cover and simmer 25 minutes. Add uncooked shrimp and cook for 5 or 10 more minutes, or until rice is tender.

Yield: 4 servings

No oven to turn on for this casserole. It is made on top of the stove in an electric skillet.

Fish Cooked in a Bag

This recipe is for a whole fish, freshly dressed.

1	whole fresh fish, freshly dressed	3	tablespoons chopped celery
		2	tablespoons lemon juice
1	tablespoon flour	3	tablespoons melted butter
1	small onion, chopped	1	tablespoon dill weed

Preheat oven to 400°. Shake flour into oven bag and add onion and celery, lemon juice and melted butter. Shake bag to mix all together and place bag in shallow baking pan. Rinse the fish and pat dry with paper towels. Sprinkle with dill weed, salt and pepper. Add a sprinkling of paprika on top. With a spatula, slip fish into the bag on top of vegetables; close bag with tie provided. With a sharp, small knife, make 6 small slits in top of bag to let steam escape. Do not let bag touch sides of pan. Bake for 45 minutes, or until fish flakes. Remove pan from oven and allow to cool a few minutes, then slit bag open with knife or scissors being careful of escaping steam. Place fish on platter and spoon vegetables and juice over, if desired.

Pies

Almond Fudge Pie

2	squares unsweetened chocolate	½	teaspoon salt
		3	eggs, beaten slightly
2	tablespoons butter or margarine	1	teaspoon vanilla
			Unbaked 9″ pie shell
1	cup sugar	¾	cup toasted, diced blanched
¾	cup light corn syrup		almonds

Melt chocolate and butter in small, heavy skillet over very low heat. In a heavy saucepan, combine sugar, corn syrup and salt and heat to boiling, stirring. Stir in chocolate mixture, cool slightly, then pour mixture slowly over beaten eggs. Mix well. Stir in vanilla and pour into pie shell. Bake in a pre-heated 375° oven for 45 to 50 minutes. Cover edges of pie crust with foil if crust gets too brown. Sprinkle almonds over top of pie before serving.

Yield: 6 to 8 servings

Apple Coconut Pie

This is a delicious open-faced pie.

1	9″ unbaked pie shell	3	tablespoons butter, cut in ¼″ cubes
3	medium tart baking apples, peeled, cored and cut into ¼″ slices	2	cups coconut
		½	cup evaporated milk
1	cup sugar, divided	1	egg, beaten
½	teaspoon cinnamon		

Heat oven to 425°. Arrange apples in a single layer in unbaked pie shell. Combine ½ cup of the sugar with the cinnamon and sprinkle over the apples. Dot with butter. Bake until crust is golden, about 25 minutes. Combine coconut, milk, egg and the remaining ½ cup sugar and mix well. Remove pie from oven and pour coconut mixture over top. Reduce oven temperature to 325° and bake 20 more minutes until coconut is toasted.

Yield: 6 to 8 servings

Plum Tart

I ate this tart at a restaurant on a hill overlooking Vienna, It was served with the famous Viennese coffee. The tarts in Europe are not usually as sweet as those we make in the United States. The only sweetening in this tart is the glaze.

Pastry:

1⅓ cups plus 2 tablespoons flour	1 stick plus 1 tablespoon unsalted butter, softened
1 tablespoon sugar	2 teaspoons finely grated fresh lemon peel
3 egg yolks, freeze egg whites for future use	

Combine the 1⅓ cups flour and the sugar. Sift them into a deep bowl. Make a well in the center, drop in the egg yolks and, stirring gently, gradually stir the flour into the yolks. Beat in the stick of butter, 1 tablespoon at a time, then add the lemon peel and beat until the dough is smooth and pliable. Gather the dough into a ball, wrap in film and refrigerate for at least 30 minutes.

With a pastry brush, brush the 1 tablespoon butter over the bottom and sides of a fluted 9″ quiche pan with a removable bottom. Sprinkle 2 tablespoons flour over the butter and tilt the pan from side to side to spread the flour evenly. Invert the pan and tap the pan on the bottom to remove the excess flour.

On a lightly floured board,pat the dough into a circle about 1″ thick. Dust a little flour over and under it and roll it out to a circle about 13 to 14″ in diameter and ⅛″ thick. Drape the dough over the rolling pin, lift it up and unroll it slackly over the prepared pan. Gently press into pan, being careful not to stretch the dough. Roll the rolling pin over the top of the pan, pressing down hard to remove the excess pastry. Chill the pastry-lined pan for 30 minutes or more.

3 pounds firm ripe purple plums	½ cup red or black currant jelly

Preheat oven to 375°. Wash and pit plums, then cut in half lengthwise. Arrange plum halves, cut-side up in concentric circles in the pastry-lined pan. If plums are small, it may be necessary to arrange them in two layers. Bake in the middle of the oven for 1 hour or until the plums are tender and tart is brown.

Continued on next page

Remove tart from the oven, set the pan on a large jar or can and slip down the outside rim. Let cool at room temperature, then run a metal spatula under the tart to loosen the bottom, and slide the tart off onto a serving plate. Before serving, heat the jelly in a small saucepan until it melts. With the back of a spoon,rub the jelly through a fine sieve into a small bowl. Then, with a pastry brush, glaze the surface of the plums with the jelly while it is still warm. Set the tart aside to cool to room temperature but do not refrigerate.

Yield: 6 servings

Carrot Pie

This is similar to the pumpkin pie, but is made with brown sugar, and has a brown sugar glaze on top. Delicious!

2	eggs	½	teaspoon ginger
2	cups cooked mashed carrots	¼	teaspoon cloves
¾	cup brown sugar, packed well	1	(13 ounce) can evaporated milk
½	teaspoon salt	9″	unbaked pie shell with high fluted edge
1	teaspoon cinnamon		

Beat eggs in a mixing bowl then add rest of ingredients in order given. Mix with a spoon until well combined. Pour into pie shell and bake at 425° for 15 minutes. Lower heat to 350° and bake until knife inserted in the middle comes out clean. Spread hot pie with following glaze.

Glaze:

⅓	cup brown sugar, packed	¾	cup pecans, chopped coarsely
3	tablespoons heavy cream		

Bring mixture to a boil in a small heavy saucepan. Boil 1 minute. After spreading on hot pie, sprinkle with the chopped pecans. Cool before serving.

Yield: 6 to 8 servings

Chocolate Cream Cheese Pie

This pie is frozen so it can be made in advance.

1½ packages (4 ounces each) German sweet chocolate
⅓ cup milk
2 tablespoons sugar (optional)
3 ounces cream cheese, softened

3½ cups thawed whipped topping
1 9" graham cracker pie crust

Finely chop the ½ package chocolate. Heat remaining chocolate and 2 tablespoons of the milk in a heavy saucepan over low heat, stirring until melted. Beat sugar into cream cheese; add remaining milk and chocolate mixture. Beat until smooth. Fold in whipped topping and blend gently until smooth. Fold in chopped chocolate. Spoon into crust and freeze until firm, about 4 hours. Let stand ½ hour out of freezer before serving.

Yield: 6 to 8 servings

Toasted Coconut Pie

I ate this pie at a restaurant in Lisbon, Portugal. It was served with a glass of Port wine. We were told to take a bite of pie, then a sip of wine. The one complimented the other.

3 eggs
1½ cups sugar
1 stick butter, softened

4 teaspoons lemon juice
1 teaspoon vanilla
1½ cups coconut (3½ ounces)

Thoroughly combine the eggs, sugar, butter, lemon juice and vanilla. Stir in coconut. Pour into an unbaked 8" pie shell. Bake in a 350° oven about 40 minutes or until a light brown. Notice, this is for an 8" pie. Do not use a larger shell as filling will be too thin.

Yield: 8" pie

Chocolate Mint Pie

4 ounces German sweet
chocolate, broken up
⅓ cup milk
2 tablespoons sugar
3 ounces cream cheese,
softened

½ teaspoon peppermint
extract
8 ounces whipped topping,
thawed
9″ graham cracker crumb
crust

Heat chocolate and 2 tablespoons of the milk in a heavy saucepan over low heat, stirring until chocolate is melted. Beat sugar into cream cheese; add remaining milk, the chocolate mixture and peppermint extract. Beat until smooth. Fold chocolate mixture into whipped topping. Spoon into crust and freeze until firm, about 4 hours. Remove from freezer about 20 minutes before serving.

Yield: 6 to 8 servings

German Chocolate Pie

This pie has both coconut and pecans in it similar to the German chocolate cake.

4 ounces German sweet
chocolate, broken up
¼ cup (½ stick) butter
1 (12 ounce) can evaporated
milk
1½ cups sugar
3 tablespoons cornstarch

⅛ teaspoon salt
2 eggs
1 teaspoon vanilla
½ cup chopped pecans
1⅓ cups coconut
Unbaked 9″ pie shell

Combine chocolate, evaporated milk and butter in a heavy saucepan. Place over low heat until chocolate melts, stirring constantly. Remove from heat. Combine next 7 ingredients; stir into chocolate mixture and pour into pie shell. Bake in a 375° oven for 45 minutes or until barely done in middle. Pie will be soft but will set while cooling.

Yield: 6 to 8 servings

Chocolate Pecan Pie

⅔ cup evaporated milk
2   tablespoons margarine
6   ounce package semi-sweet
     chocolate morsels
2   eggs, beaten
1   cup sugar

2   tablespoons flour
⅛ teaspoon salt
1   teaspoon vanilla
1   cup chopped pecans
Unbaked 9" pie shell

Combine evaporated milk, margarine and chocolate morsels in a heavy saucepan. Place over low heat until chocolate melts, stirring constantly. Remove from heat. Combine next 6 ingredients; stir into chocolate mixture. Pour into pie shell and bake in a 375° oven for 35 to 40 minutes or until almost firm in center. Serve cooled.

Yield: 6 to 8 servings

Chocolate Cake Pie

1   cup sugar
2   tablespoons flour
⅛ teaspoon salt
3   eggs, separated
2   (1 ounce) squares
     unsweetened chocolate,
     melted

1   cup half and half or rich
     milk
1   unbaked 9" pie shell

Beat egg yolks until light and fluffy. Sift dry ingredients together and add to beaten yolks. Stir in melted chocolate, then milk. Beat egg whites until soft peaks form when beater is lifted then fold into chocolate mixture. Pour into pastry shell. Bake in a 350° oven about 30 minutes or until slightly trembly in center.

Yield: 6 to 8 servings

Lemon Syrup Pie

5   eggs, beaten well
1½   cups white corn syrup
1   cup sugar
Juice of 2 lemons

Grated rind of 1 lemon
¼   cup (½ stick) butter,
     softened
Unbaked 9″ pie shell

Add corn syrup to beaten eggs, then add sugar, lemon juice and rind. Add softened butter, beat until well mixed. Pour into pie shell and bake in lower half of a 375° oven for 10 minutes, then move to middle shelf and bake at 350° for about 30 minutes or until a knife inserted in the middle comes out clean.

Yield: 6 to 8 servings

Pumpkin Pie

This is the pie my mother used to make, rich with eggs and milk. I like to eat it room temperature as it is. However, a dollop of whipped cream on top doesn't hurt.

2   eggs, slightly beaten
1   (16 ounce) can pumpkin
¾   cup sugar
½   teaspoon salt
1   teaspoon cinnamon

½   teaspoon ginger
¼   teaspoon cloves
13   ounce can evaporated milk
1   unbaked 9″ pie shell with
     fluted edge

Beat eggs in mixing bowl, then add rest of ingredients in order given. Mix well with a spoon, then place in unbaked crust and bake in a pre-heated 425° oven for 15 minutes. Reduce temperature to 350° and bake for 45 more minutes or until a knife inserted in center comes out clean. Cool and garnish with whipped cream, if desired.

Yield: 6 to 8 servings

This mixture can also be made in custard cups for those who want to cut calories.

Toffee Pie

Another rich but very delicious pie.

Crust:

1	cup flour	3	(1 ounce) squares
½	cup shortening		unsweetened chocolate,
¼	cup brown sugar, packed		melted
	well	1	teaspoon vanilla
¾	cup chopped nuts	1	tablespoon water

Combine first 5 ingredients, then stir in vanilla and water. Press into a greased 9" pie pan. Be sure to have crust the same thickness over entire pan. Bake in a 350° oven for 15 minutes. Set aside.

Filling:

1	stick butter	2	teaspoons instant coffee
¾	cup sugar	2	eggs
1	(1 ounce) square		
	unsweetened chocolate,		
	melted		

Beat butter and sugar together until fluffy, blend in coffee and chocolate, then add eggs, one at a time, beating 5 minutes after each addition. Pour into pie shell, chill.

Topping:

1	cup whipping cream	2	tablespoons coffee liqueur
½	cup powdered sugar		

Beat all ingredients together until mixture holds stiff peaks. Spread on pie and refrigerate at least 2 hours. Garnish with shaved chocolate or a dusting of cocoa.

Yield: 6 to 8 servings

Petite Derby Tarts

These are nice to serve at teas or coffees.

Pastry:

2	(3 ounce) packages cream cheese, softened
½	cup solid vegetable shortening
½	cup butter or margarine, softened
2	cups all-purpose flour

Combine cream cheese, shortening and butter in a large mixer bowl; blend in flour. Divide dough into 4 dozen 1″ balls and place in 1¼″ ungreased muffin cups. Shape balls into pastry shells by pressing dough against bottom and sides of each cup. Set aside.

Filling:

2	eggs
1	cup sugar
¼	cup cornstarch
½	cup butter or margarine melted
¼	cup bourbon
½	cup finely chopped pecans
¾	cup semi-sweet mini chocolate chips

In small mixer bowl, beat egg slightly, gradually add sugar and cornstarch. Add melted butter and bourbon. Mix well. Stir in pecans and chocolate chips. Spoon about 1 tablespoon mixture into pastry-lined muffin cups. Bake at 350° about 20 minutes or less, until done in center. Cool in pans 20 minutes. Tarts come out best when warm. Cool and garnish with Derby topping.

Derby Topping:

⅔	cup whipping cream or 1⅓ cups non-dairy whipped topping, thawed
¼	cup powdered sugar (eliminate if topping is used)

1 to 2 teaspoons bourbon

Whip cream with sugar. Add bourbon and whip to stiff peaks. If whipped topping is used, fold bourbon into it.

Yield: 48 small tarts

Super Pecan Pie

This pie is caramel-like in flavor due to the brown sugar and dark corn syrup.

1½	cups dark corn syrup	2	teaspoons vanilla
4	eggs, lightly beaten	2	cups broken pecans
½	teaspoon salt	1	(9″) unbaked pie shell
½	cup brown sugar, packed		

In mixer bowl, combine syrup, eggs, salt, sugar and vanilla. Stir briskly until well blended. Beat at medium speed as you do not want to make foam. Stir in nuts. Pour into unbaked pie shell, bake in a pre-heated 400° oven for 10 minutes, then reduce temperature to 350° and bake about 40 minutes more or until edges are set and center trembles slightly. Remove from oven and cool.

Yield: 6 to 8 servings

Crunchy Crust Frozen Pie

This is a versatile crust. It can be used with almost any filling and is a nice change from the graham cracker crumb crust.

Crust:

2	cups rice cereal, cornflakes or any combination of cereals, crisped in the oven	⅔	cup brown sugar, well packed
½	cup chopped nuts	1	quart vanilla ice cream
½	cup coconut		Chocolate, butterscotch, or fruit toppings of your choice; pie fillings are good, too
½	cup butter or margarine		

Mix cereal, nuts and coconut. In saucepan, melt butter and sugar over low heat, stirring until sugar is melted. Pour over cereal mixture. Toss to coat evenly. Press into a 9″ pie tin making sure it is an even thickness. Fill with 1 quart of ice cream. Freeze about 2 hours. Cut with a sharp knife dipped in warm water. Spread with any topping you desire.

Yield: 6 to 8 servings

Lemon Swirl Pie

Lemon curd is folded into ice cream to make a refreshing dessert.

1½	teaspoon grated lemon rind	1	quart vanilla ice cream,
6	tablespoons lemon juice		softened
½	stick butter or margarine	1	(9″) graham cracker pie
¼	cup sugar		crust
Dash salt		¼	cup toasted, blanched
2	eggs plus 1 yolk		almonds, chopped or sliced

Cook first 5 ingredients in heavy saucepan over low heat until hot. Beat eggs and egg yolk until thick. Stir a little of the hot mixture into the eggs, then gradually add the rest, beating with a wire whisk. Return to saucepan and cook until thickened. Cool. Fold into softened ice cream and place in crumb crust. Freeze. To serve: cut into wedges and top with the toasted almonds.

Yield: 6 to 8 servings

Raleigh House Buttermilk Pie

This pie was a popular dessert at Raleigh House. Many of my customers bought several for their freezers. They freeze well.

1	stick margarine, melted	1	cup buttermilk
2	cups sugar	Dash nutmeg	
3	eggs	1	teaspoon vanilla
3	rounded tablespoons flour	9	or 10″ unbaked pie shell

Mix melted margarine and sugar in mixer, beat well. Add eggs, one at a time, alternately with flour, beating after each addition. Add buttermilk, nutmeg and vanilla. Mix again and pour into pie shell. Bake on the lower rack of a 375° oven for 30 to 35 minutes or until edges are firm but center is still a little trembly. This pie is good hot or cold. We always heated it in the microwave before serving.

Yield: 6 to 8 servings

Almond Tart

Crust:

1	cup flour	1	large egg, beaten lightly
2	tablespoons sugar	1	tablespoon water
¼	teaspoon baking powder		
3	tablespoon cold, unsalted butter cut into bits		

Sift together the flour, sugar, and baking powder, then blend in the butter until mixture resembles coarse meal. Add the beaten egg and the 1 tablespoon water or enough to form the mixture into a ball. Knead the dough lightly with the heel of your hand against the board to distribute the fat evenly. Re-form it into a ball. Flatten the ball slightly, dust it with flour, and wrap it in film. Chill for an hour.

Roll dough into a 13″ circle ⅛″ thick. Fit it in a 10½″ fluted flan pan with a removable bottom, and crimp the edge decoratively. Chill the shell for 30 minutes or until firm.

Filling:

1	stick unsalted butter, softened	¼	cup heavy cream
1	cup sugar	1½	cups sliced blanched almonds, toasted lightly
5	tablespoons flour	¼	teaspoon almond flavoring

Mix the butter, sugar and flour in the mixer until it is light and fluffy, add cream and mix. Stir in the almonds and flavoring. Spread the mixture evenly in the shell. Bake the tart in the lower third of a pre-heated 450° oven for 20 minutes. The filling will not be set. Let the tart cool on a wire rack for at least 2 hours, or until filling is set. Remove sides of pan, cut into wedges and serve.

Yield: 6 to 8 servings

Kahlua Pecan Pie

¼ cup butter	½ cup dark corn syrup
¾ cup sugar	¾ cup evaporated milk
1 teaspoon vanilla	1 cup whole or chopped
2 tablespoons flour	pecans
3 eggs	½ cup heavy cream, whipped
½ cup Kahlua	

Line a 9″ pie pan with your favorite pastry. Chill. Set oven at 400°.

Cream together butter, sugar, vanilla and flour. Mix well, then beat in eggs, one at a time. Stir in Kahlua, corn syrup, evaporated milk and pecans. Mix well, then pour into crust. Bake for 10 minutes. Then reduce heat to 325° and bake until firm, about 40 minutes. Chill. When ready to serve, garnish with whipped cream and pecan halves, if desired.

Yield: 6 to 8 servings

Chocolate Nut Pie

3 egg whites, room temperature	½ cup chopped pecans
⅛ teaspoon salt	1 teaspoon vanilla
½ cup sugar	1 cup heavy cream, whipped with 1 tablespoon brandy
¾ cup fine chocolate wafer crumbs (12 wafers)	and 2 tablespoons powdered sugar

In large bowl, beat egg whites and salt until soft peaks form, gradually beat in sugar until stiff but not dry, peaks form. Lightly, but thoroughly, fold in crumbs, nuts and vanilla. Spread evenly in lightly buttered 9″ pie plate. Bake in pre-heated 325° oven about 35 minutes or until wooden pick inserted in center comes out clean. Cool on wire rack; spread with whipped cream mixture on top and chill well. Garnish with grated semi-sweet chocolate.

Yield: 8 servings

Pecan Praline Tart

New Orleans style Praline Liqueur is delicious flavoring for recipes containing brown sugar or caramel, too.

Pastry for 9″ tart pan
⅓   cup butter, melted
1   cup sugar
1   cup light corn syrup
4   eggs, beaten

2   teaspoons Praline liqueur
1   teaspoon vanilla
¼   teaspoon salt
1   cup pecan halves

Place pastry in a tart pan with a removable bottom. Set aside. Combine butter, sugar and corn syrup in medium saucepan. Cook over low heat, stirring constantly, until all the sugar dissolves. Let mixture cool slightly, then add beaten eggs, vanilla, liqueur and salt; stir well. Pour filling into pie shell and top with pecan halves. Bake at 325° for 50 to 55 minutes. Let cool.

Topping:
½   cup whipping cream, whipped
1   teaspoon praline liqueur

½   teaspoon vanilla
2   tablespoons powdered sugar

Whip whipping cream, vanilla and praline liqueur together until foamy, gradually add powdered sugar, beating until soft peaks form. Place about 2 tablespoons of whipped cream on dessert plate, place a piece of pie on top and serve immediately.

Yield: 6 to 8 servings

Chocolate Chess Pie

This is one of my granddaughter's favorites. It is made with cocoa instead of chocolate, but is deliciously rich and very easy to make.

2   eggs
1½   cups sugar
2   tablespoons flour
3   tablespoons cocoa
⅛   teaspoon salt

1   small can evaporated milk
1   teaspoon vanilla
1   stick margarine, melted
1   unbaked 9″ pie shell

Beat eggs slightly, set aside. Mix dry ingredients together, then add milk and melted margarine. Mix well, then add beaten eggs and vanilla. Mix thoroughly, then pour into pie shell. Bake at 350° for 35 to 45 minutes or until barely firm in the center. Do not overbake.

Yield: 6 to 8 servings

Mother's Butterscotch Pie

The filling in this pie is much richer than most. It is a family favorite.

2	cups brown sugar, packed (1 pound less ⅓ cup,packed)	3	eggs separated
3	tablespoons cornstarch	2	teaspoons vanilla
3	tablespoons flour	⅔	stick butter, softened (Mother's recipe read butter the size of an egg)
½	teaspoon salt		
2	cups warm milk	1	10" baked pie shell

Mix sugar, cornstarch, flour and salt in a heavy saucepan. Gradually add warm milk, beating with a wire whisk until blended. Place over medium heat and cook, stirring constantly, until very thick. Remove from heat. Beat egg yolks and add some of the hot custard, mix, then add to rest of custard in saucepan, beating well. Place over heat and cook about 5 minutes more until eggs are cooked. Remove from heat and add butter and vanilla. Mix again and set aside to cool. When cold, place in baked crust and spread meringue over and bake in a 400° oven until light brown. Refrigerate until served. Cream pies should be eaten the same day they are baked.

Meringue:

3	egg whites, room temperature	6	tablespoons sugar
¼	teaspoon cream of tartar	¼	teaspoon vanilla

Beat egg whites and vanilla until frothy, add cream of tartar. Beat until soft peaks form, then add sugar by tablespoonfuls, beating well after each addition. Continue beating until whites are stiff and glossy, not dry. Spread meringue around edge of pie making sure that meringue is sealed to crust, then spread meringue over rest of pie. Bake in a 400° oven until light brown. As with most cream pies, this is best eaten the day it is made.

Yield: 6 to 8 servings

Mother's Apple Pie

My Mother was Pennsylvania Dutch. She loved apple pie for breakfast, always with a wedge of cheese. She said apple pie without cheese is like a kiss without a squeeze.

¾ to 1 cup sugar
1   tablespoon cornstarch
1   teaspoon cinnamon
6   cups sliced, peeled and
     cored apples

½   stick margarine or butter
1   unbaked 10″ pie crust plus
     top crust

Mix sugar, cornstarch and cinnamon in a bowl. Toss with apples. Place apples in an unbaked pie crust and dot with butter or margarine. Place top crust over, prick with a fork, spread with a little milk or cream, then sprinkle sugar over the top. Bake in a 400° oven 35 to 45 minutes or until apples are tender. We like it served warm with melted cheese, of course.

Yield: 6 to 8 servings

Be sure to use baking apples for your pie, Granny Smith's, Roman Beauty or Golden Delicious are some of the varieties. We always had 3 barrels of apples in our cellar — two were eating apples, the third cooking.

Pear Pie

Pears are rather bland, so this recipe calls for dark brown sugar and ginger.

½   cup firmly packed dark
     brown sugar
3   tablespoons cornstarch
½   teaspoon ginger
⅛   teaspoon salt
4½   cups thinly sliced, pared,
     cored pears

1   tablespoon lemon juice
3   tablespoons margarine
1   unbaked 10″ crust plus a
     top crust

Mix dry ingredients together in a bowl, then toss with pears and lemon juice. Place in piecrust and dot with the margarine. Place top crust on and crimp to bottom crust. Bake at 425° for 15 minutes, then reduce temperature to 350° and bake 40 minutes longer or until pears are tender.

Yield: 6 to 8 servings

Cherry Pie

Cherry pie always needs a little almond flavoring. If you use prepared cherry pie filling, do add ¼ to a ½ teaspoon almond extract, or to taste.

¾ cup sugar
3   tablespoons cornstarch
½ teaspoon salt
2   (1 pound) cans pitted sour cherries, drained, with ⅓ cup of juice reserved

¼ teaspoon almond flavoring
2   tablespoons margarine
1   unbaked 10″ pie crust plus top crust

Mix dry ingredients; toss with cherries, juice and almond extract. Place in pie crust, dot with margarine; top with crust, crimp edges well and prick with a fork. Spread a little milk or cream over top crust and sprinkle with sugar. Bake in 425° oven for 15 minutes, lower heat to 350° and bake 40 minutes longer.

Yield: 6 to 8 servings

Peach Pie

Peaches need a touch of almond extract to bring out the flavor.

¾ cup sugar
2½ tablespoons cornstarch
½ teaspoon cinnamon
6   cups sliced, peeled and pitted fresh peaches

¼ teaspoon almond extract
2   tablespoons butter or margarine, cut into bits
Unbaked crust for 10″ pie plus top crust.

Toss mixed dry ingredients with peaches and almond extract. Place in an unbaked 10″ crust. Dot with butter or margarine. Place top crust over, sealing edges, and pierce several times with a fork. Brush with milk or light cream and sprinkle with granulated sugar. Bake in a 425° oven for 40 minutes.

Yield: 6 to 8 servings

Blueberry Pie

Blueberries need lemon juice to bring out the flavor.

1 cup sugar	2 teaspoons lemon juice
2½ tablespoons cornstarch	2 tablespoons butter or
4 cups fresh or frozen	margarine cut into bits
blueberries (If using frozen	9″ unbaked pie shell plus top
berries, put in pie still	crust
frozen, add 5 minutes more	
baking time.)	

Mix sugar and cornstarch and toss with berries, add lemon juice. Place in an unbaked 9″ pastry shell, dot with butter or margarine. Place top crust over, sealing edges. Prick crust several times with a fork so steam can escape, and bake in a 425° oven for 40 minutes.

Yield: 6 to 8 servings

Apple Molasses Pie

This pie is a deep-dish pie with only a top crust. Delicious!

6 cooking apples, about 3	½ cup light molasses
pounds, pared, quartered	½ cup apple juice
and sliced thin. (10 cups)	4 tablespoons butter or
¾ cups sugar	margarine
4 tablespoons flour	Heavy or light cream
½ teaspoon cinnamon	1 package pie crust mix or
¼ teaspoon salt	homemade pie crust for
¼ teaspoon nutmeg	double crust pie

Mix sugar, flour, cinnamon, nutmeg and salt in small bowl. Sprinkle over apples in large bowl; toss gently to mix; turn mixture into an 11¾″ × 7½″ × 1¾″ baking dish or a shallow 10 cup baking dish.

Heat molasses and apple juice in small saucepan. Boil, uncovered, 5 minutes; stir in butter or margarine until melted. Pour over apples in baking dish.

Prepare pie crust mix according to directions. Roll out on a lightly floured board to a rectangle 13″ × 9″; cut a few slits near the center to allow steam to escape. Fit over top of baking dish; press edges firmly against side of dish. Bake in a 375° oven 50 to 60 minutes or until juice starts to bubble through slits. Serve warm with cream poured over top or topped with whipped cream or ice cream.

Yield: 6 to 8 servings

Mother's Mock Mincemeat Pie

When Mother ran out of mincemeat, she improvised with this pie.

1½ cups raisins	1½ cups apples, peeled, cored and finely chopped
1½ cups grated carrots	
1 cup water	1 small navel orange, finely chopped
¾ cup sugar	
1 tablespoon cornstarch	1 package pie crust mix or pastry for 2 crust pie
1 teaspoon cinnamon	
¼ teaspoon cloves	
2 tablespoons butter or margarine	

Combine raisins, carrots and water in small saucepan; bring to boiling; simmer, covered, for 5 minutes. Mix cornstarch, sugar, cinnamon and cloves; stir into boiling mixture; cook, stirring, for 5 minutes. Remove from heat. Stir in butter or margarine until melted; stir in apple and orange. Set aside to cool.

Prepare pie crust mix or homemade pastry. Roll out ⅔ of dough to a 12" round; fit into a 9" pie tin. Trim overhang to ½". Spoon in cooled filling. Roll out remaining pastry to a 10" round. Moisten pastry edges with water and place over filling. Turn under pastry edges flush with rim and flute edge. Make slits in top crust to allow steam to escape. Bake in a 400° oven for 45 minutes, or until pastry is golden. Serve warm.

Yield: 6 to 8 servings

A friend in Kerrville always added a small, finely chopped orange to prepared mincemeat bought at the grocery. It adds a pleasing flavor.

Chocolate Coconut Pie

This is easy to prepare and wickedly rich!

4 (1 ounce) squares semi-sweet chocolate	1⅓ cups coconut
	3 eggs, slightly beaten
¼ cup (½ stick) butter or margarine	½ cup sugar
	1 unbaked 9" pie shell
1 (13 ounce) can evaporated milk	1 cup thawed Cool Whip or ½ cup heavy cream, whipped

Melt butter and chocolate in heavy saucepan over low heat. Add milk, coconut, eggs and sugar. Stir until well blended. Pour into unbaked pie shell, bake at 400° for 30 minutes. Cool. Serve with whipped cream or topping, if desired.

Yield: 6 to 8 servings

Fried Apple Pies

We always used dried apples, cooked until tender, then mixed with sugar and cinnamon to taste for the filling of fried pies. However, prepared pie filling of whatever fruit you like can be used. Notice that the crust does not have as much shortening.

Crust:

2 cups flour, sifted after measuring	⅓ cup shortening
1 teaspoon salt	2 tablespoons water or more

Mix flour and salt together in a bowl, cut in shortening until the consistency of coarse meal, add enough water to form dough into a ball. Knead gently a few times. Roll out dough as thinly as possible on a lightly floured board. Cut into circles, using a 5 to 6″ saucer as a pattern and using a fluted cutter instead of a knife, for fancy edges.

Place 2½ to 3 tablespoons cooked, cooled pie filling in center of each circle of crust. A few suggestions are: cherry pie filling made a wee bit thicker; dried apricots cooked with a little sugar to consistency of preserves; pie-sliced apples, drained well, and glazed with sugar and cinnamon and dotted with butter or margarine. Canned pie filling needs to be drained of thickened juice or more thickening added. Moisten edges of pastry with water and fold over like pocket books; press together firmly with a fork. Drop 1 or 2 pies at a time in deep skillet containing 1½″ fat - preheated to 365°. Fry, turning once, until browned, about 5 minutes. Drain on brown paper and dust with powdered sugar. Serve hot or cold.

Yield: 6 pies

I had a black nurse, when my daughter was born, who made the most delicious fried pies I had ever tasted. My mother found out that she fried them in butter. You can do it, too, if you feel extravagant.

Glazed Cherry Pie

I like a one-crust pie. This one has a delicious glaze in lieu of a top crust.

	Pastry for a 9″ pie	4	tablespoons flour
⅔	cup pecans, finely chopped	¼	teaspoon almond extract
2	(number 2) cans sour cherries	2	tablespoons butter or margarine
1	cup sugar	¾	cup red currant jelly
⅛	teaspoon salt		Dash cinnamon

Heat oven to 450°. Line pie pan with pastry and sprinkle chopped nuts over bottom. Besides tasting good, this prevents sogginess.

Mix drained cherries with the sugar, salt, flour and almond extract and spoon into unbaked crust. Dot with butter or margarine and bake 10 minutes at 400°. Then reduce oven heat to 350° and bake 30 minutes longer. Remove from oven and cool. Melt currant jelly and cinnamon in heavy saucepan and spoon over the cherries. Cool and serve.

Yield: 6 to 8 servings

Apples and Cream Pie

This pie does not have a top crust, but a custard topping instead.

6	cups cooking apples, unpeeled, cored and sliced in thin sliced rounds	¼	cup flour
		½	teaspoon cinnamon
¾	cup sugar		Unbaked 9″ pastry shell

Mix apple slices, sugar, flour and cinnamon in a bowl. Then arrange slices in circles in pie shell.

Custard topping:

2	eggs	1	teaspoon vanilla
1	cup heavy cream	¼	cup sugar

In a bowl, beat eggs, cream, vanilla and sugar until well blended. Pour mixture evenly over top of apples. Bake in a pre-heated 375° oven for 40 minutes, covered with a piece of foil. Remove foil and continue baking another 20 to 30 minutes or until apples are tender. Serve slightly warm.

Yield: 6 to 8 servings

Apple Pie in a Paper Bag

This is a fool-proof way to bake an apple pie. This is also a one-crust pie with oatmeal crumbs on top.

6	medium apples, pared, cored and coarsely chopped, 6 or 7 cups	½	teaspoon nutmeg or cinnamon
½	cup brown sugar, well packed	1	unbaked 9″ pie shell
2	tablespoons regular rolled oats	2	tablespoons water
			Topping

Mix apples, sugar, oats and nutmeg or cinnamon in a bowl. Toss to coat well. Spoon into unbaked pie shell. Sprinkle with water.

Topping:

½	cup sugar	1	tablespoon flour
½	cup oats	½	cup butter

Combine sugar, oats and flour in mixing bowl. Cut in butter and mix until crumbly. Sprinkle on top of filling. Slide pie into a heavy brown paper bag to cover loosely. Fold open end over twice and fasten with paper clips. Place on cookie sheet. Bake at 425° for 1 hour. Split bag open carefully, watch for steam coming out. Remove pie to cooling rack. Serve warm.

Yield: 6 to 8 servings

Lemon Yogurt Pie

⅔	cup boiling water	1	tablespoon lemon juice
1	(3 ounce) package lemon jello	2	(8 ounce) containers plain yogurt
1	tablespoon grated lemon rind	9	inch graham cracker crust

Pour boiling water over jello; stir to dissolve. Place in a bowl of ice water; stir occasionally until slightly thickened, the consistency of unbeaten egg whites. With wire whisk, beat in lemon rind, lemon juice and yogurt until combined. Turn into graham cracker pie crust. Refrigerate until firm, about 4 hours. To serve: garnish with thin lemon slices and mint, if desired.

Yield: 6 to 8 servings

Deep Dish Mince-Apple Pie

This is a one-crust pie spiked with a little brandy. Great for the holidays.

Filling:
1   (28 ounce) jar prepared
    mincemeat
2   tart apples, pared, cored
    and chopped

¼   cup brandy

Mix all ingredients in a bowl and place into a buttered 10″ pie plate. Follow directions for completing pie.

Pastry:
1½   cups flour, sifted after
    measuring
½   teaspoon salt

6   tablespoons unsalted butter
3   ounces cream cheese,
    softened

Combine flour and salt in medium bowl. Cut in butter and cheese with a pastry cutter or rub quickly with finger tips until mixture clings together and forms a ball. Wrap in waxed paper and chill an hour. Then roll into a 12″ round on a lightly floured surface. Cut decorative vents near center. Fit pastry over filling. Fold edge under; pinch to make a stand-up edge, flute.

Glaze:
1   egg yolk
2   tablespoons milk

2   teaspoons sugar

Combine egg yolk and milk in a cup, brush over pastry and sprinkle with sugar. Bake at 400° for 30 minutes or until crust is brown and glazed. Cool on wire rack, Serve at room temperature.

Yield: 6 to 8 servings

"Schloss Herblingen" Apple Pie

I was fortunate to participate in a number of tours for restauranteurs while I owned Raleigh House. We were served this pie at the Schloss Herblingen Restaurant located in an old castle in Germany. They graciously gave us the recipe.

6	cups unpeeled, cored cooking apples (about 4 large) cut into thin rounds	2	tablespoons finely chopped unblanched almonds
¾	cup sugar	2	eggs, beaten
¼	cup flour	1	teaspoon vanilla
½	teaspoon cinnamon	¼	cup sugar
	Unbaked 9″ pastry shell	1	cup heavy or light cream
2	tablespoons soft bread crumbs		

Mix bread crumbs and almonds and place in bottom of pastry shell. Mix apple slices, sugar, cinnamon and flour in a bowl. Arrange apple slices in circles in pie shell.

Mix eggs, vanilla, cream and sugar in a bowl until well blended. Pour mixture evenly over apples. Bake in a pre-heated 375° oven, covered with foil, for 40 minutes. Remove foil and continue baking another 30 minutes. Serve slightly warm.

Yield: 8 servings

Their recipe was for a 12″ pie. This is a pared down version for a 9″ pie. This pie can also be made with fresh peaches or peaches frozen without sugar. Omit vanilla and use ½ teaspoon almond extract.

Pecan Crunch Pie

3	eggs	11	graham crackers
½	teaspoon baking powder	1	cup chopped pecans
1	cup sugar	1	teaspoon vanilla

Beat eggs and baking powder, add sugar very slowly. Beat until very stiff. Crush graham crackers, mix with pecans into egg mixture. Add vanilla. Spread in a heavily buttered 10″ pie tin. Bake at 350° for 30 minutes. Chill about 4 hours. Serve with either whipped cream or ice cream.

Yield: 6 servings

Mrs. Colvin's Date Pie

This is an easy, delicious dessert given to me by a dear friend many years ago.

2 eggs, separated	2 teaspoons baking powder
1½ cups powdered sugar	1 cup chopped dates
4 tablespoons flour	1 cup chopped pecans

Beat egg yolks until lemon colored. In another bowl, beat the whites until they hold soft peaks when beater is lifted. Fold beaten whites into yolks. Sift sugar, flour and baking powder together and fold into egg mixture. Gently mix in dates and nuts and place in a well-buttered 9″ pie tin. Bake at 300° about 35 or 40 minutes. Cool and cut into wedges. Serve with whipped cream.

Yield: 6 servings

Sour Cream Pie Crust

This is the crust used in the Apple Cream Tart. Very easy to make.

1 cup flour	½ cup butter, 1 stick
¼ teaspoon salt	7 to 8 tablespoons sour cream

Combine the flour and salt; cut in butter with a pastry blender or with tips of fingers until mixture resembles coarse meal. Add 7 tablespoons sour cream, one tablespoon at a time, stirring with a fork until dry ingredients are moistened. Stir in an additional tablespoon of cream if mixture is too dry. Shape into a ball and chill 30 minutes. Roll dough to ⅛″ thickness and fit into tart pan or pie plate.

Yield: 9″ crust

Quick Puff Pastry

The pastry scraper mentioned in this recipe is a handy tool. It is an almost square piece of metal with wood on one side. It is used to cut rolls, some cookies, and also to clean the pastry board of flour.

1 **cup butter, chilled and cut into ⅜″ cubes**	½ **cup cake flour**
1¼ **cups flour plus 2½ tablespoons**	¼ **teaspoon salt**
	½ **cup ice water**

Freeze cubed butter for 10 minutes. Combine flour and salt. Mound on a smooth surface and make a well in the center. Put chilled butter in well. Working quickly, cut butter coarsely into flour using pastry scraper, until cubes are halved and quartered. Sprinkle ice water evenly over mixture; stir with a fork until dry ingredients are moistened. Quickly shape into a ball and wrap in waxed paper. Dough will be very lumpy with pieces of butter showing. Chill 15 minutes.

Working quickly, roll dough on floured surface into a ⅛″ thick rectangle about 13″×8″. Fold short sides inward to meet in the center; fold in half along center where the sides meet. Lightly flour surface and roll dough out again into a ⅜″ thick rectangle; fold as before. Repeat rolling and folding process one additional time. Chill 15 minutes, then roll out to the shape you desire. This is enough pastry for an oblong pastry shell.

For an oblong pastry shell 11½″×6½″, roll pastry to ⅛″ thickness; trim edges to form a 13″×8″ rectangle. Place dough on a cookie sheet lined with waxed paper. Chill 15 minutes. Then cut a ¾″ strip from each of the 4 sides of dough. Brush strips with egg wash made of 1 egg mixed with 1 tablespoon water. Place them egg-side down on top of each side of rectangle, edges flush together and overlapping corners to form a border. Brush top of border with egg wash. Chill 30 minutes.

Bake at 400° for 15 or 20 minutes or until puffed and golden brown. Reduce temperature to 300°. Open oven door and prick bottom of pastry with a fork in several places to let steam escape. Close oven door and bake at 300° for 15 minutes. Gently remove pastry to wire rack. Cool and fill as you desire.

Pastry must be cold when put in the oven to bake in order to puff up properly. Round tart shells, individual tart shells or any shape you wish may be made.

Yield: 1 oblong tart shell

The pastry scrapers can be obtained at gourmet kitchen supply stores. They are a good investment.

Hot Water Pie Crust

¾   cup shortening
¼   cup boiling water
1   tablespoon milk

2   cups flour
1   teaspoon salt

Put shortening in medium bowl, add boiling water and milk; with a fork, break up shortening. Tilt bowl, then beat with a wire whisk, in rapid strokes, until mixture is smooth and thick like whipped cream and holds soft peaks when whisk is lifted. Sift flour and salt onto shortening mixture. With vigorous. round-the-bowl strokes, stir quickly forming a dough that clings together and cleans the bowl. Pick up dough and work into a smooth, flat round. Divide in half; form into 2 rounds. Roll into a crust. Makes enough pastry for 2 pie shells or 1 two crust pie.

Yield: 2 pastry shells

Short Bread Tarts

⅓   cup butter (⅔ of a stick), do
     not substitute
¾   cup flour

3   tablespoons sugar
¼   teaspoon vanilla

Mix flour and sugar, cut in butter until mixture resembles fine crumbs. Add vanilla. Form into a ball and knead until smooth. Divide into 6 portions, roll each into a ball. Press into the bottom and up the sides of regular size muffin tins or tart pans. Flute edges, if you like. Bake at 300° for 25 to 30 minutes or until edges are very light brown. Cool in pans. Remove and fill each with fresh fruit or filling of your choice. These shells should be kept chilled if you want a crisp shell.

Yield: 6 tart shells

Basic Short Pastry

I usually use partially baked crusts for open pies and quiches and fully baked crusts for tarts filled with pastry cream and fresh fruit or berries.

1	cup cake flour	1	tablespoon vegetable
⅛	teaspoon salt		shortening
2	teaspoons sugar	1½	tablespoons ice water
5	tablespoons butter, ½ stick plus 1 tablespoon		

Sift flour, sugar and salt, mix well. Add butter and shortening and blend thoroughly with your fingers or pastry blender. Stir in the water and rapidly work dough into a ball. Refrigerate for 2 or 3 hours. When dough is cold, it will roll out more easily.

Place dough on floured board; then press it into a fairly flat circle. Work fast because if the dough gets soft, it will be difficult to handle. While dough is still cold, roll it into a 12" circle about ⅛" thick and fit into pie plate.

Yield: 9" pastry shell

When baking the pastry, you can either line crust with foil and partially fill it with uncooked rice or beans or you can place a smaller pie tin inside the pastry-lined one, which keeps the pastry from rising during cooking. Remove pan after 10 minutes.

Mrs. Tucker's Pie Crust

I found this recipe on a can of Mrs. Tucker's shortening and have used it many times at Raleigh House. I continue to use it as it is foolproof. I make the whole recipe and put the pie shells in the freezer. This recipe is also great for making Stick-Tights

2	cups flour	5	cups shortening
2	cups cold water	11	cups flour
3½	tablespoons salt		

Mix the 2 cups flour, 2 cups water and the salt in mixing bowl. Beat until smooth. Place the 11 cups flour in a large mixing bowl and cut in the shortening until mixture resembles coarse meal. Add the flour-water mixture. Mix until combined, then roll out as you wish.

Yield: 18 pie shells

At Christmas, I make Stick-Tights for my family. Mother made them. Roll pastry into a rectangle, spread with softened margarine and sprinkle with a mixture of sugar and cinnamon. Make a roll about 1" thick, cut into rounds. Bake on greased pan at 300°.

Coconut Pecan Crust

½ **pound shredded coconut**
½ **pound coarsely chopped pecans**

½ **pound butter or margarine, melted**

Combine coconut and pecans. Add melted butter or margarine and mix well. Press into buttered pie tins and refrigerate until firm. Fill with ice cream or whatever you wish.

Yield: 2 9″ crusts

Chocolate Coconut Crust

I ate a crust like this at a restaurant recently filled with coffee ice cream. You can let your imagination dictate what you would like as a filling.

4 **ounces German sweet chocolate. broken into pieces**

2 **tablespoons margarine or butter**
2 **cups coconut**

Melt chocolate and butter or margarine in heavy saucepan over very low heat. Add coconut and mix well. Press into bottom and sides of a 9″ pie tin. Freeze until needed.

Yield: 1 9″ crust

Be sure to press mixture evenly into pan, If it is too thick where the sides begin, it is very hard to cut.

Easy Crumb Crust

This same recipe can be used for a chocolate cracker or gingersnap crumb crust, just eliminate the sugar.

1¼ **cups graham cracker crumbs**
2 **tablespoons sugar**

¼ **cup melted butter or margarine**

Combine all ingredients and press firmly on bottom and sides of a 9″ pie tin. Chill at least an hour, then fill.

Yield: 1 9″ pie shell

Some recipes call for this crust to be pre-cooked; others, as for cheese cake, cook the crust with the filling. I make the graham cracker crust in quantity. It keeps almost indefinitely in a covered container in the refrigerator.

Almond Flavored Pastry Shells

1 cup butter, softened	1½ teaspoon almond extract
1 cup sugar	2½ cups flour
1 egg	2 tablespoons water

Cream butter and sugar, add egg and almond extract. Stir in flour, mix well; then add water. Press gently into tart pan. Bake at 350° about 15 minutes. Remove from pans while still warm. If not using right away, keep in a tightly covered container.

Yield: 16 to 24 tarts

Crisco Pie Crust

This recipe has different directions for rolling out crust.

2 cups all purpose flour	1 teaspoon salt
¾ cup Crisco	5 tablespoons water

Cut Crisco into flour and salt using a pastry blender or two knives, to form pea-sized chunks. Sprinkle water over 1 tablespoon at a time. Toss lightly with a fork until dough forms a ball. Divide in half, press to form 2 (5 to 6") "pancakes." Flour each side. Slide one into a 13" × 15" storage bag or between 2 pieces of waxed paper. Do not close bag. Center "pancake." Place on dampened counter top. Roll dough into a circle 1" larger than up-side-down pie plate. Sprinkle flour on pastry, if it sticks. Turn for even rolling. Repeat for second crust. If using bag, slit on all three sides. Remove top sheet, flip into pie plate, remove plastic. Press pastry into pie plate being careful not to stretch it. Trim edge even with pie plate. Add filling and moisten edge with water. Cover with top crust and trim 1" larger than pie plate. Fold under bottom crust and flute edges. Prick top crust with a fork for vents. Bake according to recipe.

Yield: 2 crust pie

Nut Crumb Crust

1⅓ cups chocolate cookie crumbs	⅓ cup finely chopped pecans
⅓ cup brown sugar, packed	⅛ teaspoon nutmeg
	¼ cup melted butter, ½ stick

Blend together and press into a 10" pie tin. Bake at 325° for 10 minutes. Fill with ice cream or any filling you desire.

Yield: 10" crust

Apple Cream Tart

This is baked in the sour cream pie crust. Recipe is in Pastry Section of cookbook.

2 medium golden delicious apples, peeled, cored and sliced into 16 slices apiece	3 egg yolks, beaten
¾ cup sugar	⅓ cup sour cream
½ teaspoon cinnamon	2 tablespoons apple jelly, melted
¼ cup flour	Recipe for Sour Cream pie crust
Pinch salt	rolled and placed in 9″ tart pan with removable bottom.

Arrange apples in tart shell. Combine sugar, ¼ cup flour, cinnamon, salt, egg yolks and the ⅓ cup sour cream; mix well. Pour evenly over apples; Bake for 55 to 60 minutes in lower half of a 350° oven or until filling is set and apples tender. Let cool. Brush with melted apple jelly. Serve hot or cold.

Yield: 6 to 8 servings

Okley's Buttermilk Pie

1 stick margarine, melted	1 cup buttermilk
2 cups sugar	1 teaspoon vanilla
3 tablespoons flour	½ cup coconut
4 eggs	

Beat eggs well, add flour and sugar and beat again, then add melted margarine and beat until fluffy. Stir in buttermilk and vanilla, then stir in coconut. Pour into 10″ unbaked pie crust and bake at 350° about 45 minutes or until firm on the sides, but still trembly in the middle. Cool slightly, serve warm.

Yield: 6 to 8 servings

This is similar to the Raleigh House buttermilk pie, a recipe which Okley also gave me, with the addition of coconut. Very good.

Chocolate Oatmeal Pie

Any flavor of cookie can replace the oatmeal.

Oatmeal Cookie Crust:

4 cups oatmeal cookie crumbs	½ cup plus 2 tablespoons
1½ sticks butter or margarine, melted	brown sugar, packed

Combine all ingredients, mix well and press into a lightly buttered 9″ pie plate, making sure that crumbs are the same thickness all over the pan. Fill shell with chocolate ice cream or any flavor you desire. Freeze for 2 or 3 hours. Cut in wedges and serve topped with hot fudge sauce. Note:Dip knife in hot water between cuts for smooth, clean edge.

Yield: 6 servings.

Sabra Chiffon Pie

Sabra, the liqueur of Israel, is tangy with Jaffa oranges with a hint of chocolate.

1 9″ pie shell, baked	½ cup sugar
1 envelope of unflavored gelatin	Pinch salt
¼ cup cold water	¼ cup Sabra liqueur
4 egg yolks	2 teaspoons grated orange rind
¼ cup orange juice	4 egg whites

Soften gelatin in cold water. Beat egg yolks until thick and lemon-colored; beat in orange juice and sugar. Add pinch of salt and softened gelatin. Cook over low heat, stirring, until gelatin is dissolved. Stir in Sabra and grated orange rind. Cool. Beat egg whites until stiff, but not dry. Fold into cooled gelatin mixture and turn into cooked pie shell. Chill until firm.

Yield: 6 to 8 servings

Raspberry Tart

The custard pies served at a hotel buffet in Austin had a thin coating of chocolate on the pie shell which prevented the custard from soaking the crust, a very practical, as well as delicious,idea. It was also used in a raspberry tart.

¼	cup blanched, sliced almonds	¼	teaspoon almond extract
¼	cup sugar	2½	ounces semi-sweet chocolate, finely chopped or grated
1¼	cups flour		
⅛	teaspoon salt	1	pint raspberries or small strawberries
¾	of a stick of unsalted butter, room temperature	⅓	cup currant jelly

Grind the almonds and sugar to a meal in food processor. Add flour and salt and pulse just to blend. Add butter and almond extract. Blend again. With processor running, add 2 to 3 tablespoons ice water through the feed tube. Process until a dough is formed. Press dough evenly in an ungreased 9″ tart pan with a removable bottom. Prick with a fork. Bake the crust at 400° until golden brown. Remove from oven and immediately sprinkle chocolate evenly over the bottom of crust. When chocolate melts, spread evenly over bottom of crust with the back of a spoon. Cool completely.

To serve: Remove tart shell to serving plate. Arrange raspberries or strawberries, top sides up, in the shell. Melt the currant jelly over low heat, stirring constantly; and, using a small pastry brush, brush jelly over berries. Serve at room temperature.

Yield: 6 to 8 servings

Lemon Pecan Pie

3	eggs	¾	cup pecan pieces
⅓	stick margarine, melted	1	teaspoon lemon extract
1½	cups sugar		Juice of ½ a lemon

Mix ingredients in order given, but do not use mixer or beat until frothy. Pour into an 8″ unbaked pie shell. Put in pre-heated 350° oven and bake 10 minutes. Lower oven to 300° and bake until crust is brown and filling set. Cool before serving. If pie is cooked at too high a temperature, pecans will scorch before center of pie is done.

Yield: 6 servings

Amaretto Chocolate Pie

This recipe can be made in individual pies by placing a tablespoon of the crumb mixture in the bottom of muffin cups, then adding the filling. When frozen, they are easily unmolded by running a table knife around the edge and lifting out. 6 or 8 pies.

⅔ cup semi-sweet chocolate morsels	1 tablespoon Amaretto
⅓ cup whole milk	8 ounces frozen whipped topping, thawed in refrigerator
2 tablespoons sugar	
3 ounces cream cheese, softened	

Heat chocolate and 2 tablespoons milk in heavy saucepan or skillet over low heat, stirring constantly, until chocolate is melted and smooth. Beat sugar into cream cheese; add remaining milk, the chocolate mixture and Amaretto and beat until smooth. Fold in whipped topping. Spoon into prepared crust. Freeze until firm. Garnish with toasted almonds, if desired.

Chocolate Crumb Crust:

1½ cups oreo chocolate cookies, crushed	3 tablespoons melted butter or margarine

Mix ingredients together in a bowl, then press into a 9″ pie tin.

Yield: 6 to 8 servings

Frozen Caramel Pie

This was another popular dessert at Raleigh House.

24 Kraft Vanilla Caramels	8 ounces whipped topping, thawed in refrigerator
⅓ cup water	
½ cup sour cream	

Combine water and caramels in heavy small skillet. Heat over low heat, stirring constantly, until caramels are melted and mixture is smooth. Let cool about 15 minutes, then stir in sour cream thoroughly. Fold in whipped topping. Pour into a 9″ graham cracker crust and freeze. When serving: Dip the knife in hot water for a smoother edge.

Yield: 6 to 8 servings

We made the pies in large muffin tins. Put 1 tablespoon of the graham cracker crust mix in bottom of muffin cups. Use an ice cream scoop to dip up filling. Freeze. When ready to serve, run a table knife around edge and lift out. Recipe makes 6 or 8.

Heath's Brickle Pecan Tart

Heath's Brickle Pecan Pie:

18 Ritz crackers, crushed to
    fine crumbs
3   egg whites, room
    temperature
1   cup sugar

½   teaspoon baking powder
1   cup chopped pecans
1   teaspoon vanilla
½   teaspoon almond flavoring

Beat egg whites until soft peaks form. Combine baking powder and sugar, then add by tablespoonfuls to beaten whites, beat to stiff, but not dry, peaks form. Fold in crumbs, pecans and flavorings. Pour into a buttered 9″ pie plate and bake at 350° for 30 minutes. Let cool, then spread whipped topping or whipped cream topping over.

Topping:

1   cup frozen whipped topping,
    thawed, or ½ cup whipping
    cream, whipped

½   cup Heath's Brickle

Fold brickle into whipped topping or whipped cream and spread over cool pie.
Yield: 6 or 8 servings

Deluxe Apple Pie

8   medium apples, pared,
    cored and sliced
1⅔ cup sour cream
⅓   cup flour

1   cup sugar
1   egg
2   teaspoons vanilla
½   teaspoon salt

Combine all ingredients in a large bowl, mix well. Then place in unbaked pie crust and bake at 450° for 10 minutes, lower heat to 350° and bake until filling is puffed and brown, about 40 minutes.

Topping:

1   cup chopped pecans
⅓   cup sugar
½   cup flour

1   teaspoon cinnamon
Pinch salt
1   stick butter or margarine

Combine all ingredients except margarine. Then blend in margarine until crumbly. Sprinkle over pie and return to oven for 15 minutes longer.
Yield: 9 inch pie

Shell-Shaped Tarts

Each of these recipes is baked or molded in fluted, 4 to 5 " baking shells usually used for seafood dishes. You can find these in kitchen specialty shops. You can also use real shells, which is what I do as I have a number of them.

Chocolate Sandwich Shells:

½ cup water	⅛ teaspoon salt
¼ cup margarine	¼ cup buttermilk
¼ cup cocoa, plus 1 tablespoon cocoa	1 egg, beaten
¼ cup oil	½ teaspoon soda
1 cup sugar	½ teaspoon vanilla extract
1 cup flour	Chocolate or vanilla ice cream or any flavor you wish

Combine water, butter and cocoa in a small saucepan; cook over medium heat, stirring, until mixture comes to a boil. Remove from heat; stir in oil.

Combine flour, sugar and salt in a large bowl; add cocoa mixture, stirring well. Stir in buttermilk, egg, soda, and vanilla.

Grease 8 shells and set on top of muffin pans, making sure they are setting level. Spoon batter evenly into prepared shells to within ¼ " of edges. Bake at 350° for 15 to 20 minutes or until toothpick placed in center comes out clean. Immediately invert cakes on a wire rack and let cool.

To serve: cut shells in half horizontally and spread ice cream on cut surfaces, replace top. sprinkle with powdered sugar or ladle hot fudge sauce over.

Pastry Shells with Lemon Filling:

1½ cup flour	1 egg, beaten
2 tablespoons sugar	1 tablespoon water
½ cup butter, do not substitute	

Combine flour and 2 tablespoons sugar; cut in butter with pastry blender or with finger tips until mixture resembles coarse crumbs. Stir in egg, then sprinkle water evenly over surface; stir with a fork until dry ingredients are moistened. Shape dough into a ball; cover and chill.

Divide dough in 8 equal portions. Roll each portion to ⅛" thickness on lightly floured board. Press each portion firmly onto back of ungreased shell. Trim dough with scissors ⅛" smaller than shell. Bake, dough-side up, on cookie sheet in 400° oven about 12 minutes, first pricking pastry well with a fork. Bake until lightly browned. Remove from shell while warm. Cool and fill with lemon filling. Refrigerate until served.

Note: Regular pie crust dough may be shaped over shells and baked, then filled with creamed seafood or chicken for an entree.

Continued on next page

Lemon filling:

4   eggs, beaten

1   cup butter or margarine

1¾ cups sugar

Grated rind of 1 lemon

Juice of 2 lemons

Mix butter, sugar, lemon juice and lemon rind in a heavy ceramic, glass or stainless steel pan. Cook over low heat, stirring constantly, until butter melts. Add a little of the hot mixture to the beaten eggs, mix and then add to rest of hot mixture in saucepan. Cook, stirring constantly, until mixture thickens. Chill, covered tightly with film about 2 hours.

To serve, divide lemon filling between shells and top with a mound of whipped cream. You can use other cake recipes or crust recipes in this way. Let your imagination guide you.

Chocolate Shells with Amaretto Cream:

12   ounces chocolate bark,
      broken up

Melt bark in top of double boiler over simmering water until melted. Remove from bottom of double boiler. Spread plastic over bottoms of 8 shells, pressing into ridges smoothly, then fold under the top of shell securely. Let chocolate cool slightly and thicken, then spread with a thin spatula or knife over bottoms of shells, leaving about ¼″ margin. Do not try to spread over "handle" of shell, just smooth chocolate in even line under it. Let set about 30 minutes. then gently lift plastic up, and place shell on plate, then remove plastic from inside shell. This chocolate does not have to be refrigerated. When ready to serve, spoon or pipe in Amaretto whipped cream. Sprinkle with toasted nuts, if desired.

Amaretto Cream:

2   cups heavy cream

¼   cup powdered sugar

2   tablespoons cocoa

2   tablespoons Amaretto

½   teaspoon vanilla

Combine powdered sugar and cocoa, add to heavy cream in mixer and beat until soft peaks form, add Amaretto and vanilla and beat until stiff peaks form. Spoon ½ of mixture into shells. Place rest in a pastry bag and pipe on the tops of the tarts. Serve immediately or refrigerate and serve within 2 hours. Note: The chocolate bark comes in either 1½ ounce cubes or 2 ounce ones. Either size is easy to use for the 12 ounces called for.

Yield: 8 servings

Be sure to grease the shells as directed in the recipe before pouring in cake-like batters. Do not grease the shells when shaping pastry dough around them.

Egg Pastry

This is a delicious pastry for pies or quiche. Make into shells, use 1 and put the others, well-wrapped, in the deepfreeze.

3	cups flour, spooned into cup and leveled off with a straight knife	1	large egg, beaten
		1	tablespoon lemon juice
1	teaspoon salt	4	or 6 tablespoons ice water, divided
1	cup shortening		

In large bowl, stir together the flour and salt. Cut in the shortening until particles are about the size of navy beans. Flour mixture should still look dry. If, moist, shortening has been cut in too much and crust will not be as flaky. Combine beaten egg, lemon juice and 4 tablespoons water in a bowl. Sprinkle over flour mixture and toss with a fork until dough gathers into a ball. Add 1 to 2 tablespoons more water, if necessary. Make a ball in your hands. Wrap airtight in plastic film and place in freezer 10 minutes. Divide dough into 3 pieces keeping only 1 piece out at a time and placing rest in refrigerator.

On lightly floured board, roll out piece of dough into a circle 1½″ larger than pan you are using. Fold into quarters and place in pan, Unfold and fit loosely into pan being careful not to stretch the dough. Trim and crimp edges.

To pre-bake for quiche, Place circle of foil in shell and put about ½″ uncooked dried beans or rice or the metal pellets made for this purpose on top of foil. Bake in a pre-heated 425° oven for 12 minutes. Cool slightly, then remove beans and foil and let cool completely. Fill with desired filling and bake as directed.

Yield: 3 pie shells

Lemon Cake Pie

½	cup butter, do not substitute		Grated rind of 1 lemon
1	cup sugar plus 2 tablespoons		Juice of 2 lemons
4	eggs, separated	1	cup rich milk
2	tablespoons flour	1	unbaked 9″ pastry shell

Cream sugar and butter. Beat egg yolks until light and then stir into butter mixture along with flour and grated lemon rind. Add lemon juice and milk and mix thoroughly. Beat egg whites until stiff but not dry and fold into lemon mixture. Turn into pastry shell. Bake at 350° for 15 minutes, then lower oven to 300° and bake for another 30 minutes.

Yield: 6 to 8 servings

Polly's Walnut Molasses Tart

½ stick butter, melted
½ cup sugar
3 large eggs
1 cup molasses
½ teaspoon vanilla
⅛ teaspoon salt

1 cup coarsely chopped
   walnuts or pecans
1 unbaked 9″ pastry shell
   with a 1″ overhang folded
   over the rim and crimped
   decoratively

In electric mixer, cream butter, then beat in sugar a little bit at a time until mixture is light and fluffy. Beat in the eggs, one at a time, then the molasses, vanilla and salt. Combine well. Scatter nuts over bottom of the pie shell, carefully pour in molasses mixture. Bake in pre-heated 325° oven for 45 to 50 minutes or until it is puffed and browned lightly. Let pie cool and serve it plain or with whipped cream or ice cream.

Yield: 6 to 8 servings

Grasshopper Pie

This is another dessert that can be made a day ahead of time. It is attractive and delicious. Useful, too, when you need a green dessert.

1 chocolate cookie crumb
   crust
½ pound marshmallows
⅓ cup whole milk
¼ teaspoon salt
3 tablespoons creme de
   menthe

3 tablespoons white creme de
   cocoa
1½ cup heavy cream, whipped
Additional chocolate crumbs for
   garnish

In a heavy saucepan, heat milk and salt over medium heat, until bubbles start to form around edge of pan, Remove from heat, turn heat to low. Add marshmallows to milk, stirring, and return to heat. Continue stirring until marshmallows are melted. Remove from heat and add liqueurs, stirring to blend. Chill until mixture is like unbeaten egg whites. Whip cream and fold in. Pour into prepared chocolate crumb shell. Sprinkle with additional chocolate cookie crumbs. Chill at least an hour before serving.

Yield: 6 to 8 servings

Potpourri

Raleigh House Orange Butter

This is the butter for the orange rolls. However, it is also good spread over hot gingerbread or spice cake and delicious on waffles or pancakes. It will serve as an icing when spread on warm cake.

1	pound powdered sugar	2	ounces (¼ cup) frozen
1⅓	stick margarine, room temperature		orange juice, undiluted

Beat margarine and sugar together until fluffy, then add orange juice and mix well. Refrigerate in covered container, or place in the freezer.

Yield: About 2½ cups

This will keep for weeks in the refrigerator and months in the the freezer. I store it in either a stainless steel or non-metallic container.

Chocolate Amaretto Butter

1	ounce semi-sweet chocolate	½	cup blanched almonds,
1	teaspoon sugar		toasted and chopped
1	tablespoon Amaretto		
1½	sticks unsalted butter, room temperature		

Melt the chocolate and sugar and Amaretto in the top of a double boiler over simmering water, stirring constantly. Do not let water touch bottom of top pan. Cool to room temperature. Mix in the butter and almonds. Place in a covered container and let set in a cool place, not the refrigerator, for at least an hour before serving on croissants, hot rolls or pound cake.

Yield: 2 cups

Maitre d'Hotel Butter

Use on grilled steaks, poultry and fish

2	tablespoons dried parsley flakes	¼	teaspoon ground white pepper
2¼	teaspoons lemon juice	2	sticks butter
¼	teaspoon salt		

Mix parsley flakes and lemon juice; let stand 10 minutes for parsley to soften. Combine with salt and white pepper. Beat butter until creamy, add parsley mixture gradually. Mix thoroughly. Shape into 1 inch rolls on waxed paper. Refrigerate until firm. Slice as needed.

Yield: 12 servings

Herbed Lemon Butter

Serve with broiled fish, baked potatoes or hot biscuits.

1	stick butter	1	tablespoon fresh lemon juice
½	teaspoon grated lemon rind		

Small pinch each of dried rosemary, oregano and thyme, crushed between palms of the hands

Cream butter in mixer, add grated lemon rind and herbs. Mix, then gradually add lemon juice. Mix until all liquid is absorbed. Form mixture into sticks or blocks; chill until firm. Slice into pats and serve with fish.

Yield: ¼ pound

Lemon-Garlic Butter

Serve on broiled steaks or chops or for garlic bread

1	stick butter	¼	clove garlic, crushed or
½	teaspoon grated lemon rind	$^1/_{16}$	teaspoon garlic powder, not garlic salt
½	teaspoon paprika		

2 tablespoons fresh lemon juice

Cream butter in mixer, add rind and paprika. Gradually add lemon juice. Mix until liquid is absorbed. Add juice from crushed garlic or garlic powder. Mix well.

Yield: ¼ pound

Jellied Orange Slices

My mother always made these on Thanksgiving and Christmas. They were placed on the table in a beautiful cut glass bowl, along with the turkey and all the trimmings, for the family to help themselves.

6	large navel oranges	½	cup light corn syrup
1	tablespoon salt	1	cup water
2	cups sugar		

Wash oranges and place in a saucepan big enough to hold them in one layer. Cover them with cold water to which the tablespoon of salt has been added. Bring to a boil and simmer for 30 minutes. Add more water, if needed, to keep oranges covered, bringing to a boil again then lowering to simmer. Remove oranges and place in cold water. Let stand for 30 minutes. Remove to a flat dish and chill in the refrigerator at least an hour, Then slice into ⅓" slices.

Combine sugar, corn syrup and water in a heavy saucepan. Cook over medium heat, stirring constantly, until sugar is dissolved. Cook, stirring, about 10 minutes or until mixture is syrupy. Add orange slices and continue to cook without stirring, about 5 minutes more or until mixture forms heavy drops when spoon is lifted. Spoon into a heat-proof bowl, cool, then refrigerate, covered. To serve; place in your prettiest crystal bowl.

Yield: 24 to 36 slices

Rosy Pears

6	ripe pears	1	(2" long) stick of cinnamon
2	cups cranberry-raspberry juice	½	cup water

Wash and peel pears, leaving stems on. Combine pears, cranberry-raspberry juice, water and cinnamon stick in a 3 quart saucepan. Bring to boiling, uncovered, reduce heat and simmer, turning occasionally, until pears are tender, about 20 minutes, depending on size of pears. Remove from heat and lift pears out, with a slotted spoon, to a bowl that just fits them and allows them to stand upright. Discard cinnamon stick and boil juice down to 1½ cups. Pour over pears. Refrigerate until well chilled. Serve with juice spooned over pears.

Yield: 6 servings

Spiced Plums

1½	pounds purple plums, washed, seeded and halved	1	stick cinnamon
1½	tablespoons fresh lemon juice	½	teaspoon ground ginger
		4	peppercorns
1½	cups water	2	whole cloves
¾	cup sugar	¼	cup light rum (optional)

Boil all ingredients, except plums and rum, for 6 minutes in saucepan large enough to hold plums comfortably. Add plums and cook for 5 minutes or until barely tender. Remove from heat and add rum, if desired. Remove to a bowl. Serve slightly warm or cold with following topping.

Topping:

8	ounces cream cheese, at room temperature	½	cup sour cream
½	teaspoons vanilla	¼	cup powdered sugar
			Grated rind of half a lemon

Mix all ingredients in a bowl and refrigerate until needed.

Yield: 4 to 6 servings

Oranges with Strawberry Sauce

This makes a refreshing dessert, particularly after a heavy dinner. I like to serve it at the table from a crystal bowl into crystal dessert dishes.

4	large navel oranges, peeled, removing rind and white membrane	1	pint fresh strawberries
		1	tablespoon sugar
		1	tablespoon Kirsch liqueur

Slice oranges into 6 slices. Place sugar, Kirsch and strawberries in a blender or food processor and purée. Spoon over oranges in a pretty crystal bowl. Chill until served. If fresh strawberries are not available, individually unsweetened frozen strawberries may be used.

Yield: 6 servings

Oranges with Cognac

This is pretty, delicious dessert, easily prepared.

Sectioned oranges   **Cognac**
Sifted powdered sugar

Place orange sections around the edge of champagne glasses or footed dessert dishes, like the petals of a flower.It will take about 6 to 8 sections, depending on size. Place about a tablespoon of the powdered sugar in the center. Place Cognac in liqueur glasses. Serve with cocktail forks. Guests are to dip an orange segment into Cognac, then into powdered sugar, eat and enjoy.

Orange segments can be placed in serving dishes ahead of time and refrigerated, adding sugar just before serving.

Spiced Orange Wedges

These are pretty and good to serve with chicken, turkey or ham.

3	medium or 4 small thin-skinned oranges	2	tablespoons white corn syrup
1½	cups sugar	2″	long piece stick cinnamon
½	cup white vinegar	6	whole cloves
¼	cup water		

Place oranges, unpeeled, in a saucepan with cold water to cover. Bring to a boil, then lower heat and simmer for 10 minutes. Drain and repeat the procedure 2 more times, using fresh cold water each time. Carefully remove from pan- they will be very soft- and refrigerate 2 hours, until completely chilled, then cut into wedges with a very sharp knife, 4 wedges for the smaller orange, 5 or 6 wedges for the medium.

Combine rest of ingredients in a 3 quart heavy saucepan. Bring to a boil, stirring, and boil 5 minutes. Add orange wedges and simmer for 20 minutes. Carefully lift out wedges with a slotted spoon and place in a deep bowl. Simmer syrup over low heat, until heavy drops fall when spoon is lifted. Watch very carefully as syrup is apt to scorch at this point. Pour over orange wedges. cool and refrigerate.

To serve: place in a serving dish, a crystal one is nice, and place on the table for guests to help themselves.

Yield: 9 to 12 servings

Spiced Peaches

This is an inexpensive way to make spiced peaches, if you need them in an emergency, or even if you do not.

1   **(29 ounce) can peach**   3   **sticks cinnamon**
    halves, drain and save juice   1   **teaspoon whole cloves**

Place peach juice in saucepan, add spices and bring to a boil. Add peaches and simmer 15 minutes more. Cool and remove spices. Place in refrigerator in covered non-metallic container. Let set overnight before serving.

To serve: Place peach half on dinner plate with entree and put 1 teaspoon currant jelly in center. When serving turkey, chicken or ham around the holidays I like a dessertspoon (2 teaspoons) cranberry relish or jelly in the center.

Yield: 8 to 12 servings

Minted Pears

1   **(29 ounce) can pear halves,**   ⅓   **teaspoon mint extract**
    drain reserving juice   ⅓   **teaspoon green coloring**

Drain syrup from pears and place in a saucepan, add coloring and bring to a boil. Remove from heat and add mint extract. Mix and pour over pears, covering completely. Store over night in refrigerator. Serve warm with lamb or cold as a salad.

Yield: 8 servings

Oranges with Grand Marnier

I ate these oranges many years ago at a hotel in London. They were served in the cocktail lounge for a late-afternoon pick-up. They could also be served as a dessert, plain, or garnished with candied violets.

6	large navel oranges	2	tablespoons white corn
2	cups sugar		syrup
1	cup water	2	tablespoons Grand Marnier

Remove thin, bright-colored rind from each orange with vegetable peeler, no white. Cut into julienne strips. Simmer in 4 cups water for 8 minutes, drain and reserve rind. Cut remaining white membrane from oranges with a very sharp or serrated knife, and remove center core. Place in a bowl just large enough to hold them in a single layer.

Combine sugar and corn syrup with water in a heavy saucepan; cook over medium heat, stirring constantly, until sugar is dissolved. Then cook, without stirring, until mixture is syrupy, about 10 minutes. Add blanched orange peel, cook about 5 minutes or until peel is translucent. Remove from heat, add Grand Marnier and pour hot syrup, with peel, over oranges. Cool, then place in the refrigerator several hours or overnight.

Yield: 6 servings

These have to be served with fruit knife and fork.

Orange Slices Cassis

Cassis is one of my favorite liqueurs. It can be used to macerate any variety of fruits.

8	medium navel oranges	4	tablespoons Cassis
¾	cup orange juice	1	tablespoon lemon juice

With an orange zester or potato peeler, remove surface skin from 3 of the oranges in long, thin strips. There should be about ½ cup. Place in a pan of cold water and bring to a boil, then drain immediately. Set aside. Cut off top and bottom of each orange and remove skin and white membrane from all oranges. Remove sections by placing a table knife close to the connecting membrane between sections, then gently lifting section out. Place sections in a bowl along with the orange juice, Cassis, lemon juice and reserved peel. Toss gently so as not to break sections. Cover tightly and refrigerate at least 2 hours.

Yield: 8 servings

Chambord Cranberry Relish

This relish is perfect with hot or cold fowl.

3   ounces Chambord liqueur
1   pound fresh cranberries (4 cups)

2   large oranges, peeled and quartered
½   cup sugar

Wash and drain cranberries and combine with oranges in food processor. Process to obtain a coarse mixture. Add the sugar and Chambord and mix well. Place in a jar and refrigerate.

Yield: About 5 cups

Dilly Onion Rings

1   large mild onion, cut into thin slices
⅓   cup sugar
2   teaspoons salt

1   teaspoon dried dillweed
½   cup white vinegar
¼   cup water

Cut onion into thin slices, separate into rings. Combine salt, sugar, dillweed, vinegar and water. Pour over onion rings. Cover and refrigerate at least 5 hours, stirring occasionally.

Yield: About 2 cups

Cranberry Mincemeat Relish

The addition of mincemeat and pecans make this an unusual relish.

1   cup sugar
½   cup water
2   cups fresh cranberries, washed

⅓   cup prepared mincemeat
¼   cup chopped pecans

In medium saucepan, combine sugar and water. Heat to boiling over medium heat, add cranberries and cook just until the skins pop, about 5 minutes. Remove from heat and let cool to room temperature. Stir in mincemeat and pecans. Cover and refrigerate.

Yield: About 2 cups

Pickled Carrots

I like to use the baby carrots for this, if possible. However, you may use larger carrots cut into ½" slices. They are a colorful addition to any plate. This is a sweet-sour dish.

4	pounds small baby carrots, either fresh or frozen	8	sticks cinnamon
4	cups sugar	8	bay leaves
6	cups white vinegar	24	peppercorns
4	teaspoons whole cloves	6	teaspoons salt
		4	dashes Tabasco sauce

Cook baby carrots in boiling, salted water until barely tender. Drain and place in gallon jar or smaller jars. Bring sugar and vinegar to a boil. Wrap spices in cheesecloth and drop them in hot vinegar. Add salt and Tabasco and boil 10 minutes, Remove spice bag and pour hot mixture over carrots. Cool and refrigerate. Let stand overnight before using.

Yield: About 12 cups

These keep well in the refrigerator and are simple to make.

Marinated Carrot Sticks

6	cups carrot sticks	1½	teaspoons pepper
¾	cup Green Goddess Dressing	3	teaspoons dill seed
¾	cup Wishbone French Dressing	½	cup grated onion (optional)
¾	teaspoon salt	3	teaspoons dried parsley flakes

Boil carrots in salted water until crisp-tender. Mix remaining ingredients and pour over carrots. Place in a non-metallic container and refrigerate over night before using.

Yield: 18 servings

Carrot and Pineapple Relish

This is delicious with ham or pork.

1	pound carrots, frozen or fresh, cut into 1½″ pieces	1	cup sugar
1	(1 pound) can cubed pineapple, undrained		Scant teaspoon salt
		½	stick butter or margarine

Cook carrots in a small amount of water in a saucepan until almost tender. Add pineapple, then sugar, salt and butter. Cook over low heat until almost candied. Serve warm.

Yield: About 6 servings

Spiced Pineapple Sticks

1	(20 ounce) can pineapple spears	½	cup sugar
¼	cup vinegar	5	whole cloves
		1	stick cinnamon

Drain pineapple, saving syrup. Combine syrup in saucepan with remaining ingredients; boil 5 minutes. Remove cloves and cinnamon stick. Pour syrup over pineapple and place in a covered container, cool and store in refrigerator.

Yield: 6 servings

Jeweled Relish

This is also an attractive relish.

2	(8 ounce) jars applesauce	2	tablespoons orange juice
1	cup fresh cranberries, ground in a blender or food processor	2	teaspoons grated orange rind
1	tablespoon grated orange rind	1	tablespoon honey
		⅔	cup toasted slivered almonds

Mix all ingredients except almonds in a mixer, then add almonds and place in covered container in refrigerator.

Yield: 3 cups

Salads

Egg and Olive Loaf

This is a recipe from the Guild Shop that the women of Trinity Episcopal Church operated for many years. It is a good dish for a ladies luncheon.

2	envelopes unflavored gelatin	2	cups mayonnaise
1	cup cold water	1	tablespoon grated onion
1	teaspoon salt	1½	cups finely diced celery
¼	cup lemon juice	½	cup finely cut stuffed green olives
½	teaspoon Tabasco	8	hard boiled eggs, chopped

Soften gelatin in cold water. Place over boiling water and stir until dissolved. Add salt, lemon juice and Tabasco; cool. Gradually add gelatin mixture to mayonnaise, stirring until blended. Mix in remaining ingredients. Turn into a 6 cup lightly oiled loaf pan; chill until firm. To serve: unmold on platter and slice into 8 to 10 slices. Place on lettuce-lined plates and garnish with tomato slices and olives. This salad can be made in small molds, if desired.

Yield: 8 to 10 servings

Doris' Molded Chicken Salad

2	large (3½ pound) fryers, cooked, boned and cubed or 2½ cups cooked chicken, diced	1	tablespoon Worcestershire sauce
		1	tablespoon sweet relish
2	cups celery, chopped	1	can green peas, drained
1	cup mayonnaise	1	envelope gelatin
1	cup chopped almonds	¼	cup cold water
3	hard boiled eggs, chopped	1	cup boiling chicken stock

Dissolve gelatin in cold water then dissolve in boiling chicken stock. Cool, then pour over other ingredients. Mix well, then add mayonnaise. Mix again and pour into an oiled 9″ × 13″ pan or in individual molds.

Yield: 12 to 15 servings

Mrs. Giraud's Jellied Chicken Loaf

Mrs. Giraud was a beloved member of Trinity Church. She was also a loyal helper in the Guild Shop there. I treasure her recipes.

2½ cups cooked chicken, diced	1 teaspoon lemon juice
2½ tablespoons unflavored gelatin	1½ cups finely diced celery
3½ cups chicken stock	3 hard boiled eggs, sliced
1 cup mayonnaise	1 teaspoon salt
1 teaspoon onion juice	1 tablespoon chopped pimento

Soften gelatin in a little cold chicken stock. Then dissolve in rest of stock that has been heated. Chill in refrigerator. When it begins to thicken, stir in mayonnaise and add other ingredients that have been chilled. Mold in a loaf pan or individual molds.

Yield: 18 small or 12 larger molds

Cheese Salad Mold

This mold has a small amount of Bleu cheese to give it zip.

3 envelopes unflavored gelatin	1 teaspoon Worcestershire sauce
1 cup cold water	⅛ teaspoon paprika
1 cup milk	¾ teaspoon salt
2 ounces Bleu cheese, crumbled	Dash pepper
½ cup mayonnaise	2 cups creamed small curd cottage cheese
1 teaspoon onion juice	

Sprinkle gelatin over cold water. Set bowl over boiling water, stir until gelatin is dissolved, gradually stir in milk, chill until very thick. Meanwhile place rest of ingredients in a food processor bowl with metal blade. Process until creamy and smooth. Whip thickened gelatin with a wire whisk until foamy, then combine with cheese mixture. Place in a 7 cup ring mold that has been rinsed with cold water and turned upside down a moment to drain. Place in refrigerator to firm up , then unmold on a plate lined with salad greens. Surround with avocado slices and tomato wedges.

Yield: 10 to 12 servings

Tomato Aspic Ring Salad

This is a 3 layer salad. Very attractive on a buffet table.

2	envelopes unflavored gelatin	1	tablespoon chopped pimiento
4	cups tomato juice (32 ounces)	1	tablespoon chopped green pepper
½	teaspoon onion juice	½	cup chopped pecans
Salt and pepper		4	teaspoons lemon juice
½	cup mayonnaise	2	teaspoons gelatin
8	ounces cream cheese, softened	¼	cold water
1	cup finely chopped celery	Lettuce	

For first layer, soften 2 envelopes gelatin in ½ cup cold tomato juice. Heat the remaining 3½ cups tomato juice and pour over softened gelatin, stir until dissolved. Add onion juice and seasonings. Pour half the mixture into a 2 quart ring mold that has been rinsed in cold water and turned upside down, chill until firm.

For second layer, blend mayonnaise into cream cheese. Add the celery, pimiento, green pepper, pecans, lemon juice and the 2 teaspoons gelatin softened in ¼ cup cold water, then dissolved in a bowl over hot water. Spread this mixture over firm tomato aspic, and chill until it is firm. Pour the remaining tomato aspic over the cream cheese layer and chill until firm. Unmold on crisp lettuce and fill center with torn lettuce leaves.

Yield: 10 to 12 servings

Meredith's Broccoli Salad

This dish serves as both a vegetable and salad.

1	large bunch broccoli	½	cup mayonnaise
10	strips bacon, cooked until crisp and crumbled	¼	cup sugar
3	green onions	2	tablespoon cider vinegar

Wash broccoli and separate into small florets. Use stems for another purpose. Wash and chop green onions. Combine mayonnaise, sugar, and vinegar in a large bowl, add broccoli, bacon and onions. Let stand in the refrigerator at least an hour before serving in your prettiest bowl.

Yield: 6 to 8 servings

Pea Pod Salad

1 cup fresh or frozen pea pods or sugar snap peas	½ teaspoon sugar
1 cup yellow squash, sliced thin	¼ teaspoon dried basil, crushed between palms of hands
1 cup sliced fresh mushrooms	Fresh watercress or spinach leaves
½ cup salad oil	Alfalfa sprouts
⅓ cup white wine vinegar	
¾ teaspoon salt	

Cook pea pods or sugar snap peas in salted water for 1 to 2 minutes; drain, cover and chill. Cook squash in a small amount of boiling salted water 1 to 2 minutes or until crisp tender; drain. In bowl, combine squash and mushrooms. In a screw-top jar, combine salad oil, vinegar, salt, sugar and basil. Cover and shake well. Pour dressing over squash and mushrooms; toss gently to coat vegetables. Cover and chill overnight or several hours. Just before serving, add pea pods or sugar snap peas, tossing gently to coat. Arrange watercress or spinach leaves on platter or individual plates; spoon vegetables on top. Garnish with sprouts.

Yield: 4 servings

Petite Frozen Cranberry Salads

This is salad for the summer. It is slightly tart and a good substitute for a fresh fruit salad.

1 cup whipping cream	1 pound can whole cranberry sauce in small dice
¼ cup sugar	
2 tablespoons mayonnaise	3 ounces frozen orange juice, thawed, undiluted
Dash salt	

Whip cream to soft peaks, fold in mayonnaise, sugar and salt. Fold in cranberry sauce and orange juice. Line muffin pans with paper liners. Fill with salad and freeze until firm. Remove to refrigerator. To serve: remove from paper cups onto salad plates 15 minutes before serving on a lettuce leaf. This salad needs no dressing.

Yield: 6 to 8 servings

Eggplant Caviar

I like to serve this as a first course on a thick slice of tomato. No additional dressing is needed.

1	medium-size eggplant	1	teaspoon sugar
⅓	cup grated onion		Salt and freshly ground pepper
1	clove garlic, crushed		to taste
1	large tomato, peeled and chopped fine	4	tablespoons chopped fresh parsley
3	tablespoons olive oil		
2	tablespoons red wine vinegar		

Bake eggplant at 400° for 30 minutes. Cool and peel, chop fine and mix with sugar, onion, garlic, tomato, oil and vinegar. Season with salt and pepper. Garnish with chopped parsley. Serve cold.

Yield: about 3 cups

This can also be served as an appetizer with dark rye bread or Latvash.

Melon Ring Salad

I serve this salad with poppyseed dressing or fresh strawberry dressing. The amount of fruit varies with the variety of fruit you want to use and the number you wish to serve. It is an attractive dish for a first course or for a luncheon entree.

Medium size cantaloupe
Pineapple chunks in natural juice
Strawberries
Blueberries
Green grapes
Leaf lettuce

Cut cantaloupe into ¾″ slices, peel and take out seeds. Drain pineapple; wash strawberries, remove hulls and slice in half lengthwise; cut grapes in half, lengthwise; wash blueberries. Lay melon ring on lettuce, fill center with whatever variety of fruit you wish. I sometimes use just the green grapes in the center with the poppyseed dressing. It makes a cool looking summer salad. Pick fruit to blend in with your color scheme, china, placemats or whatever. If you want to use this for a luncheon entree, you may want to use larger cantaloupes.

If you use the canned pineapple in its own juice, save and freeze the juice. It will keep apples and peaches from turning dark the same as lemon juice.

Strawberry and Avocado Salad

Salad:

1	avocado	½	cup medium mushrooms
2	tablespoons lemon juice	1	cup strawberries

Dressing:

¾	cup salad oil	½	cup fresh or frozen whole
3	tablespoons red wine		strawberries
	vinegar	1	tablespoon sugar
1	tablespoon orange juice	½	teaspoon salt

Peel and slice avocado, dip slices in lemon juice; wash and slice mushrooms lengthwise; wash and cut strawberries in half, lengthwise. Divide on 4 lettuce-lined plates and add dressing.

Place all ingredients except oil in blender. Blend at high speed 5 minutes, then add oil in driplets. The slower the oil is added, the thicker the dressing will be. Refrigerate. This dressing is good on any fruit salad.

Yield: 4 servings

Squash, Zucchini Salad

You will have plenty of the lemon vinaigrette left over from this salad. Keep it refrigerated to use on other salads.

2	small young yellow squash, sliced thin		Leaf or romaine lettuce torn into pieces
2	small zucchini, sliced thin	½	cup lemon vinaigrette
¼	pound mushrooms, sliced thin	¼	cup white vinegar
1	small red pepper, in julienne strips		

Place all vegetables in heat proof bowl or serving dish.

Lemon Vinaigrette (3 cups):

1½	cups lemon juice	½	teaspoon sugar
1½	cups vegetable oil	¼	teaspoon pepper
¾	teaspoon salt		Pinch basil leaves, crushed

Place salad dressing ingredients in screw-top jar; shake well. To serve, add the vinegar to the lemon vinaigrette, heat just before serving and pour over salad. Serve warm.

Yield: 4 to 6 servings

Tomato, Zucchini Salad

2½ pounds zucchini, trimmed
    and washed in salt water
1   pint cherry tomatoes,
    halved
1   cup olive oil
⅓   cup red wine vinegar
½   teaspoon salt

1   tablespoon sugar
2   teaspoons Dijon-type
    mustard
1   small garlic clove, minced
¼   cup chopped fresh basil or
    1 teaspoon dried basil
    leaves, crumbled

In a food processor with a coarse grating blade, grate the zucchini in long strands, then combine it with the tomatoes in a large bowl. In a blender or food processor with a steel blade, combine oil, vinegar, sugar, salt, mustard and garlic. Process or blend the mixture until smooth. Add the basil and pepper to taste and blend dressing for 30 seconds. Pour the dressing on the zucchini mixture, toss until it is combined well. Transfer with a slotted spoon to a serving bowl.

Yield: serves 6

Hot Red Cabbage Slaw

1   large red onion, thinly
    sliced
2   cloves garlic, minced
1   stick unsalted butter
1   medium-size red cabbage,
    2½ pounds

3   medium tart apples, 1½
    pounds
1   teaspoon salt
½   teaspoon pepper

Quarter cabbage, cut into quarters then into ½" slices. Peel and quarter apples and cut into ½" slices. Sauté onion and garlic in butter in a 12" skillet until onion softens. Add cabbage, cover and cook, stirring occasionally, for about 10 minutes, until tender crisp. Add apples and cook 5 minutes. Season with salt and pepper. Serve warm.

Yield: 8 servings

Antipasta Salad

This salad is sufficient for a main dish at a luncheon.

3	pounds Rotelle pasta	2	cups black olives, sliced
½	pounds sliced salami, cut into julienne strips	¾	cup freshly grated Parmesan cheese
4	cups broccoli florets	2	cups olive oil vinaigrette dressing
3	cups cherry tomatoes		

Cook pasta according to package directions. Combine all ingredients, mix well with dressing and refrigerate 2 to 3 hours before serving.

Vinaigrette Dressing:

½	cup red wine vinegar	2	cups olive oil
3	tablespoons lemon juice	½	teaspoon dried basil, crumbled between the palms of your hands to bring out the flavor
2	teaspoons dry mustard		
3	cloves garlic, crushed		
2	teaspoons salt		
1	teaspoonful freshly ground black pepper		

Combine all ingredients except oil in a quart jar, shake to combine; add olive oil and shake vigorously. Shake again before pouring over salad.

Yield: 12 servings

Strawberry and Spinach Salad

1	pound fresh strawberries, washed and cut in half	10	ounces fresh spinach, washed in salt water, rinsed and drained well

Lemon dressing:

¼	cup sugar	1	egg yolk
	Juice of 1 lemon, (scant 3 tablespoons)	6	tablespoons salad oil

Place sugar in medium mixing bowl. Add lemon juice and mix with a wire whisk until most of the sugar is dissolved. Add egg yolk and whisk until sugar is completely dissolved. Add oil, 1 tablespoon at a time, whisking constantly until dressing is thick and creamy. Cover and refrigerate.

To serve: Tear spinach into medium-size pieces. Place in salad bowl, arrange strawberries on top and chill well. When ready to serve, rewhisk dressing, if necessary, and pour over salad. Toss gently.

Yield: 6 servings

Potato, Zucchini and Chicken Salad

6   cups cooked cubed
    potatoes, about 1 pound
3   cups cooked, finely chopped
    chicken
4   small zucchini, washed well
    and shredded, about 4 cups
6   coarsely chopped hard
    boiled eggs
½   cup finely chopped green
    onions
¼   cup chopped parsley
Salt and pepper to taste
¾   cup mayonnaise
¼   cup chicken broth,
    homemade or canned
1   tablespoon white vinegar

Sprinkle shredded zucchini with salt in a colander and let it set about 30 minutes, then drain well and squeeze dry in a clean towel. In a large bowl, toss potatoes, chicken, zucchini, eggs, onions, parsley, salt and pepper. In a small bowl, whisk mayonnaise, chicken broth, and vinegar until well blended. Pour over salad, toss well and refrigerate until ready to serve.

Yield: 10 to 12 servings

Vegetable Salad

2½ cups hot cooked potatoes,
    cubed, about 1 pound
½   cup white vinegar
¼   cup olive oil
Salt and pepper to taste
2   cups cauliflower florets
2   cups broccoli florets
1   cup sliced mushrooms
½   cup frozen green peas
3   chopped green onions
1   carrot, peeled and grated
16 cherry tomatoes, halved

Place hot potatoes in a bowl. Combine vinegar, oil, salt and pepper in a screw-top jar; shake well. Pour over hot potatoes and toss lightly. Cover and refrigerate. Steam cauliflower and broccoli separately for 5 minutes or until crisp tender. Pour boiling water over peas, let set 5 minutes, but do not cook. Chill with cauliflower and broccoli. Just before serving, combine potato mixture with rest of vegetables. Toss lightly.

Yield: 6 to 8 servings

Molded Avocado Salad

1   package lime gelatin
1½ cups boiling water
1   cup mashed avocado
½   cup mayonnaise

½   cup whipped cream
3   cups grapefruit and orange
     sections

Dissolve gelatin in hot water, chill until it begins to congeal, fold in avocado and mix well. Fold mayonnaise and whipped cream together and add to gelatin mixture. Pour into ring mold that has been rinsed in cold water and turned upside down to drain. To serve: unmold on plate lined with salad greens. Fill center with grapefruit and orange segments.

Yield: 6 to 8 servings

Avocado Cheese Salad

1   cup mashed avocado
8   ounces cream cheese, room
     temperature
2   tablespoons onion juice
1   tablespoon Worcestershire
     sauce

1   package lime gelatin
½   tablespoon unflavored
     gelatin
1½ cups boiling water
Salt and pepper to taste
8   stuffed olives, sliced

Mash avocado, cream cheese, onion juice,Worcestershire together. Dissolve lime and unflavored gelatins in boiling water. When cool, add avocado mixture and sliced olives and congeal in molds. Serve on lettuce and garnish with mayonnaise.

Yield: 4 to 6 servings

Mother's Waldorf Salad

Mother always served this salad when we had macaroni and cheese, with bacon on top, during the war as a meatless day.

2   cups diced, unpeeled red
     apples
1   cup thinly sliced celery
½   cup chopped walnuts

½   cup quartered candied red
     cherries
¼   cup orange juice

Mix all ingredients together and add ¼ cup orange juice and enough mayonnaise to moisten.

Yield: 4 servings

Carrot Salad

I make this salad for myself very often. It is an easy way to make sure I get vitamin C, some iron and raw fruit.

1	pound carrots, scraped and washed	½	cup raisins
2	apples, unpeeled and diced	¼	cup frozen orange juice, undiluted

Cut carrots in pieces and put them in food processor with metal blade. Process until finely chopped. Transfer to a medium-size bowl and add the apples, raisins and enough orange juice to moisten. Refrigerate in covered container.

Yield: 4 to 6 servings

This salad can be varied by adding crushed pineapple with its juice instead of orange juice and by adding sliced green grapes and nuts. Suit your fancy.

Mother's Boiled Salad Dressing

Mother combined this dressing with 1 cup whipped cream for fruit salads and added 2 tablespoons sour cream, 1 teaspoon snipped parsley and ½ teaspoon grated onion to 1 cup dressing for vegetable salads.

2	tablespoons flour	1	teaspoon prepared mustard
2	tablespoons sugar	1	cup water
3	tablespoons butter	2	eggs, beaten
1¼	teaspoons salt	6	tablespoons cider vinegar
Dash cayenne pepper			

In heavy saucepan, combine flour, sugar, salt, cayenne pepper, and mustard. Gradually blend in water and vinegar. Cook over direct low heat, stirring constantly, until mixture thickens and boils. Boil 1 minute and remove from heat. Add ½ cup of cream sauce gradually to beaten eggs, then combine with rest of sauce. Add butter and return to heat , stirring, for 3 minutes, enough to cook the eggs. Store in covered container in refrigerator.

Yield: 1½ cups

Raleigh House French Dressing

My customers liked this dressing as it contained no sugar.

¾ cup white vinegar
2¼ cups oil
1½ teaspoon salt
¾ teaspoon pepper

3 tablespoons lemon juice
1 clove garlic crushed or ⅛
teaspoon garlic powder

Shake all ingredients together in a screw-top jar.

Yield: 2¼ cups

Raleigh House Dressing

We always made this dressing 2 gallons at a time. This recipe makes about 1 quart plus 1 cup. It keeps for months in the refrigerator. My customers say that this dressing is good with shrimp, fish, hamburgers and hot dogs.

1 quart Kraft or Hellman's
mayonnaise
½ cup plus 2 tablespoons
Heinz ketchup

⅛ teaspoon garlic powder or 1
clove garlic, crushed
⅓ teaspoon dry mustard
¾ cup evaporated milk

Mix well by hand or in mixer. Replace in jar the mayonnaise came out of plus a smaller jar for the overage.

Yield: 1 quart plus about 1 cup

Some of my college employees even ate this dressing on their baked potatoes.

Mrs. Giraud's Poppyseed dressing

This is also the poppyseed dressing we served at Raleigh House on fresh fruit salads.

1½ cups sugar
2 teaspoons salt
2 teaspoons dry mustard
⅔ cup white vinegar

2 teaspoons onion juice
2 cups salad oil
2 tablespoons poppyseed

Mix first 5 ingredients in blender. Let blend at medium speed until sugar is dissolved. Gradually add oil. The slower you add the oil, the thicker the dressing will be. Add poppyseed last and stir in. Refrigerate, but do not put in coldest part of refrigerator or it might separate.

Yield: scant quart

Creamy French Dressing

¾ cup salad oil
¼ cup white wine vinegar
2 teaspoons Dijon mustard
1 tablespoon water

1 egg
½ teaspoon salt
Freshly ground pepper to taste

In a blender or covered jar, combine all ingredients. Blend for 30 seconds or shake vigorously until well blended. Refrigerate. Serve chilled dressing on greens of your choice.

Yield: 1½ cups

Italian Dressing

1 cup salad oil
⅓ cup red wine vinegar
2 tablespoons lemon juice
1 teaspoon garlic salt
1 teaspoon sugar
¼ teaspoon dry mustard
¼ teaspoon dried oregano, crumbled between palms of hands

¼ teaspoon dried leaf basil, crumbled between palms of hands
Freshly ground black pepper

Combine all ingredients in a blender, blend for 30 seconds. Store in refrigerator. Shake before using.

Yield: 1½ cups

Strawberry Dressing

¾ cup fresh or unsweetened whole frozen strawberries
2 tablespoons light corn syrup

½ cup Miracle Whip salad dressing

Place thawed or fresh berries in mixer bowl. Mix just until broken up. Stir in corn syrup, then add salad dressing, folding in well. Chill about an hour to develop flavor and color. Good on fruit salads.

Yield: 1¼ cups

Buttermilk Salad Dressing

2	cups mayonnaise	2	tablespoons snipped parsley
2	cups buttermilk	¼	teaspoon garlic powder
2	tablespoons minced onion		

Mix all ingredients together and place in glass jar.

Yield: 3¾ cups

Slim Spinach dressing

1	cup low-fat plain yogurt	¼	teaspoon pepper
2	cups chopped fresh spinach		Pinch garlic powder
2	tablespoons sliced green onions with green tops	1	teaspoon Worcestershire sauce
½	teaspoon salt		

Put all ingredients in blender. Blend at high speed until smooth. Serve over salads, sliced tomatoes, cold sliced meat or chicken. 3 calories per teaspoonful.

Yield: 1¼ cups

Bobby's Bacon Dressing

This is particularly good on fresh spinach salad with fresh mushrooms and hard boiled egg slices.

4	slices lean bacon	¼	teaspoon salt
1	egg	2	tablespoons cider vinegar
2	tablespoons sugar	1¼	cups milk
1	tablespoon flour		

Cook bacon until crisp, drain well, then break into small pieces. Beat the egg slightly, add the sugar, flour and salt. Blend well. Add vinegar and milk. Wipe out skillet the bacon was cooked in with a paper towel. Place flour mixture in. Cook over low heat, stirring constantly, until it is the consistency of thin custard, add bacon. Serve over spinach salad while hot.

Yield: About 2¼ cups

Tarragon Dressing

1 egg	¼ teaspoon tarragon leaves, crumbled
2 teaspoons water	Dash pepper
⅓ cup tarragon vinegar	Bacon bits
1½ cup salad oil	Paprika
½ teaspoon garlic salt	½ cup grated Parmesan cheese
¼ teaspoon sweet basil leaves, crumbled	

In blender, mix egg, water and vinegar. Add oil slowly while blending, add the garlic, salt, basil, tarragon and pepper. Blend to creamy consistency. Top greens with bacon bits, paprika and Parmesan cheese.

Yield: About 2½ cups

Easy Cheddar Cheese Salad Dressing

1½ cups mayonnaise	1 tablespoon red wine vinegar
½ cup buttermilk	Pinch salt
½ cup finely grated Cheddar cheese	Pinch pepper
Dash Worcestershire sauce	Dash Tabasco

Combine all ingredients in medium bowl and blend thoroughly. Store in refrigerator in tightly covered jar.

Yield: 2½ cups

Strawberry Vinaigrette

This dressing is good on spinach-lined salad plates, topped with avocado slices around the edge and lengthwise sliced strawberries, placed, cut-side up, in center.

¾ cup oil	½ cup fresh or individually frozen strawberries
3 tablespoons red wine vinegar	3 tablespoons sugar
1 tablespoon lemon juice	¼ teaspoon salt

Put all ingredients except oil in blender. Blend at high speed for 5 minutes, then start adding oil in driblets. After all the oil is added, blend an extra few minutes. Keep in covered container in refrigerator.

Yield: 3 cups

Lime Salad Dressing

This dressing is delicious on a fresh spinach salad with toasted slivered almonds and mandarin oranges.

¾ cup oil
2 tablespoons cider vinegar
3 tablespoons fresh lime juice
¼ cup orange juice

2 tablespoons sugar
½ teaspoon salt
⅛ teaspoon paprika

Mix all ingredients in a screw-top jar. Refrigerate. Shake well before using.

Yield: about 1⅓ cups

Apricot Dressing

This dressing can also be made with dried peaches.

½ cup cooked dried apricots, drained and puréed in food processor
1 tablespoon lime juice

3 tablespoons mayonnaise
1 cup whipping cream, whipped

Mix apricots with lime juice, add mayonnaise, then fold in whipped cream. Delicious on fruit. Store in covered container in refrigerator.

Yield: 2¼ cups

Strawberry Cream Dressing

2 cups sour cream or creme fraiche
½ cup frozen sliced strawberries

½ teaspoon salt

Fold sour cream into strawberries. Add salt and store in covered container in refrigerator.

Yield: 2½ cups

Pineapple Daiquiri Mold

2	envelopes unflavored gelatin	½	cup sugar
½	cup fresh or frozen lime juice	¼	teaspoon salt
1	(14 ounce) can pineapple tidbits	1	cup orange juice
1½	teaspoons grated lime or lemon rind	½	cup light rum
		1	avocado

Soften gelatin in lime juice. Drain syrup from pineapple and add enough water to make 1⅓ cups. Combine with lime peel, sugar and salt. Heat, stirring to dissolve sugar. Add softened gelatin; heat to dissolve, stirring. Cool; stir in orange juice and rum. Chill until mixture begins to congeal. Meanwhile, cut avocado into cubes, fold pineapple and avocado into thickened gelatin. Pour into a 1½ quart ring mold that has been rinsed with cold water and turned upside down to drain. Chill until firm (4 or 5 hours) or overnight. Turn out on lettuce-lined plate. Garnish with additional pineapple and avocado, if you like.

Yield: 8 to 10 servings

Layered Fruit Salad

This is a beautiful salad for a buffet table and delicious to eat.

1	(8 ounce) package Philadelphia cream cheese, softened	¼	cup powdered sugar
2	tablespoons lemon juice	2	cups peach slices
1	teaspoon grated lemon rind	2	cups blueberries
½	cup whipping cream	2	cups strawberry slices
		2	cups green grapes
		½	cup chopped nuts

Combine cream cheese, lemon juice and rind, mixing until well blended. Whip whipping cream until soft peaks form, gradually add sugar, beat until stiff peaks form. Fold into cream cheese mixture. Chill. Layer fruit in order given, in 2½ quart trifle or crystal bowl. Spoon cream cheese mixture over and garnish with the nuts. Note: You may vary the fruit, but try to have 4 different colors to make an attractive presentation.

Yield: 8 servings

Jellied Ham Loaf

This is a main dish salad. Serve it with sliced tomatoes or carrot and celery sticks.

1	can tomato soup
1	cup water
1½	tablespoons unflavored gelatin
1	(3 ounce) package cream cheese, softened
½	cup mayonnaise
2	teaspoons prepared mustard
2	tablespoons cider vinegar
2	cups ground cooked ham

Heat soup and water. Soften gelatin in ¼ cup cold water, then add to hot soup mixture, stir until gelatin is dissolved. Add softened cream cheese and stir until blended. Cool, then add mayonnaise, mustard, vinegar and ham. Pour into 2 quart salad mold that has been rinsed in cold water, then turned upside down to drain or into individual molds. Serve on lettuce with a sour cream or horseradish dressing.

Yield: 6 to 8 servings

Orange Salad Dressing

1	tablespoon flour
¼	cup sugar
1	egg, beaten
2	tablespoon white vinegar
3	tablespoon frozen orange juice concentrate with enough water added to make ¾ cup
2	tablespoons melted butter

Mix sugar and flour in a small, heavy saucepan; mix well, then add beaten egg, vinegar and orange juice mixture. Cook over low heat, stirring with a wire whisk, until mixture is thickened. Add melted butter. Mix well. Refrigerate until ready to use.

Yield: 1½ cups

Grand Marnier with Fruit

This salad has only 130 calories per serving

Juice of 1 lemon
¼ cup sugar
3 tablespoons Grand Marnier
2 tablespoons peach jam
1 cup orange sections
1 cup seedless grapes
1 cup hulled strawberries
1 cup blueberries
1 cup peeled, thin sliced apples
1 cup peeled sliced pears
1 cup sliced nectarines
Or fruit of your choice

In medium bowl, combine lemon juice, sugar, Grand Marnier and peach jam. Add fruit and toss until well coated. Chill until ready to serve.

Yield: 8 servings

Molded Potato Salad

1 tablespoon unflavored gelatin
3 hard-boiled eggs, sliced in French dressing
4 cups cooked new potatoes, peeled and sliced
2 cups thinly sliced celery
2 tablespoons chopped pimento olives
1 cup sour cream
1 cup mayonnaise
Salt and pepper to taste

Brush a 2 quart ring mold with French dressing. put 6 slices of hard boiled egg in bottom of mold. Combine the rest of the sliced eggs with potatoes, celery and olives.Soften the 1 tablespoon gelatin in 1 tablespoon cold water, melt over hot water and then mix a little of the mayonnaise in. Then add to the rest of the mayonnaise, and add the sour cream. Taste for seasoning. Add to potato mixture. Pack firmly into mold and chill for several hours. Garnish with cherry tomatoes and leaf lettuce.

Yield: 8 servings

Pickled Peach Salad

This salad is particularly good with baked ham.

1	(2½ size) can pickled peaches, drained, saving juice
4	ounces cream cheese, softened
2	envelopes unflavored gelatin
½	cup cold water
1	cup mayonnaise

Soften gelatin in cold water, Add enough water to the peach juice to make 1½ cups. Heat peach juice and water and add to gelatin, stir until dissolved. Cool. Add cream cheese and mix until very smooth. When mixture begins to thicken, add peaches, which have been cut into medium-size pieces, and the mayonnaise. Pour into a large ring mold or individual molds.

Yield: 8 servings

Chicken Salad with Fruit

4	cups diced cooked chicken
1	(15½ ounce) can pineapple chunks, drained
1	(11 ounce) can Mandarin oranges, drained
1	cup chopped celery
½	cup sliced ripe olives
1	cup mayonnaise
1	teaspoon prepared mustard
1	small can chow mein noodles

Combine first 5 ingredients in large bowl; mix well. Combine mayonnaise and mustard. Toss with chicken mixture. Cover and chill. Just before serving, stir in noodles. Serve on leaf lettuce.

Yield: 8 servings

Chicken and Spinach Salad

24 ounces raw boneless,
    skinless chicken breasts
1   pound fresh spinach,
    washed in salt water, rinsed
    and dried

3   small zucchini, washed in
    salt water, and rinsed

Poach chicken breasts in small amount of salted water until opaque and firm to the touch. Cut into thin strips, You should have 4 cups. Tear spinach into bite-sized pieces. Thinly slice zucchini on the diagonal.

Lemon Dill dressing:

2   medium-size green onions,
    chopped
½   cup olive oil
5   tablespoons fresh lemon
    juice
2   tablespoons fresh dill or ¼
    teaspoon dried dill weed.

1   medium clove garlic,
    minced
Salt and freshly ground pepper
    to taste

Combine all ingredients in a small bowl and mix well. Pour over chicken in shallow dish and let marinate in refrigerator overnight. Combine spinach and zucchini in large serving bowl, add chicken strips with dressing. Toss well and serve.

Yield: 6 to 8 servings

Beans with Sour Cream Dressing

1   (1 pound) can whole Blue
    Lake green beans
1   tablespoon vinegar
1   tablespoon oil
⅔   teaspoon dry mustard

½   teaspoon lemon juice
3   tablespoons mayonnaise
5   tablespoons sour cream
1   teaspoon onion juice

Mix vinegar and oil together, then add beans. Marinate overnight in refrigerator. Mix mustard, lemon juice, mayonnaise, sour cream and onion juice, toss with beans. Serve cold.

Yield: 8 servings

Mushroom Zucchini Salad

This salad is only 35 calories per half-cup serving. Recipe may be varied by using green or yellow squash instead of zucchini and cider vinegar instead of the wine vinegar. The small amount of oil and vinegar is sufficient to marinate the vegetables.

8 ounces fresh mushrooms, washed, drained and thinly sliced	¼ cup minced onion
	1 tablespoon vegetable oil
	3 tablespoon red wine vinegar
1 medium zucchini, thinly sliced	½ teaspoon salt
	¼ to ½ teaspoon white pepper
1 medium tomato, chopped, or 12 cherry tomatoes, cut in half	¼ teaspoon dried marjoram, crumbled between palms of hands

In salad bowl, combine mushrooms, zucchini, tomato and onion. In screw-top jar, combine oil, vinegar, salt, pepper and marjoram. Cover and shake well. Toss with vegetables. Cover and chill for 4 hours.

Yield: 6 to 8 servings

I like to serve this salad on leaf lettuce.

Golden Dressing

This is exceptionally good with fruit salads. You may serve it with or without the whipped cream. Chopped nuts may be added, if you like.

4 eggs	2 cups canned pineapple juice
1 cup sugar	2 cups cream whipped
1½ tablespoons flour	¼ teaspoon salt
8 tablespoons lemon juice	

Beat the eggs, then add sugar, flour and lemon juice. Mix well, then add pineapple juice. Cook, stirring constantly over medium heat until thickened. Cool and keep in a covered container in the refrigerator. Just before serving, fold in whipped cream, if desired.

Yield: About 3 cups

The 3 cup yield is without the addition of the whipped cream. You would have about 6 cups with the whipped cream.

Ham Mousse

1 package lemon jello
1½ cups hot water
¼ cup cider vinegar
Dash salt
1 teaspoon onion juice
2 tablespoons water
½ cup chopped sweet pickle
   relish

2 tablespoons diced pimento
⅓ cup mayonnaise
⅓ cup heavy cream, whipped
1 cup ground cooked ham,
   firmly packed
½ cup finely diced celery
½ teaspoon Worcestershire
   sauce

Dissolve jello in hot water. Add vinegar, salt and onion juice. Pour 1 cup of the jello into a small bowl, add 2 tablespoons cold water, mix and chill until syrupy, then add pickles and pimento. Turn into 1½ quart ring mold that has been brushed with mayonnaise. Chill until firm.

Chill remaining jello in large bowl until thick and syrupy, Place in bowl of ice water and whip until fluffy and thick like whipped cream. Fold in the ham, celery and Worcestershire sauce. Mix mayonnaise and whipped cream together and fold into jello mixture. Place over firm jello layer in mold. Chill until firm. Unmold, garnish with border of salad greens sprinkled with French dressing.

Yield: 6 servings

The easiest way to get onion juice is to cut an onion in half and place over a lemon juicer and twist as you would for lemon juice.

Water Chestnut and Tomato Salad

3 tomatoes, sliced, then cut in
   half
1 (8½ ounce) can water
   chestnuts, drained and
   sliced
¼ cup salad oil
4½ teaspoons cider vinegar

1 teaspoon soy sauce
Dash Tabasco
½ teaspoon sugar
2 teaspoons lemon juice
Fresh spinach, washed in salt
   water and torn into pieces

To serve: Make a bed of the spinach on salad plate. Arrange tomato slices in ring around edge of plate. Place water chestnuts in center. Mix remaining ingredients in a screw-top jar and shake well. Pour over salad. Cover and refrigerate until serving time.

Yield: 6 servings

Fish Salad with Lemon Dressing

This is a delicious main dish salad. Garnish with fresh tomato wedges if you wish.

2	cups water	2	pounds cod, halibut or any
1	teaspoon salt		white fish, in 1 piece
1	tablespoon lemon juice		

In a medium skillet, bring water, lemon juice and salt to a boil. Add fish and simmer, covered, about 15 minutes or just until fish flakes. Remove from pan to a bowl, cover, and refrigerate, several hours or overnight in liquid. Next day, remove fish from liquid, discard any skin or bones. and break fish into bite-size pieces. Mix with dressing and put in refrigerator at least an hour. Drain and arrange on four spinach-lined plates. Spoon dressing over and garnish with tomato wedges, if desired.

Lemon Dressing:

1	tablespoon vegetable oil	⅛	teaspoon pepper
¼	cup lemon juice	½	teaspoon sugar
1	tablespoon Dijon-style	1	tablespoon water
	mustard	¼	cup mayonnaise
½	teaspoon salt		

In a small bowl, combine the oil, lemon juice, mustard. salt. pepper, sugar and water; mix well with wire whisk, then whisk in mayonnaise. Set in refrigerator overnight.

Yield: 4 to 6 servings

Red Wine Dressing

1	cup salad oil	½	teaspoon dried oregano,
⅓	cup cider vinegar		crumbled
⅓	cup dry red wine	¼	teaspoon salt
1	teaspoon sugar	1	clove garlic
1	teaspoon dried leaf thyme,		
	crumbled		

Combine all ingredients in a jar and shake well to mix. Remove garlic; shake again just before serving.

Yield: 1⅔ cups

Apricot Ring Mold

First and third layers:

2   envelopes unflavored
    gelatin
1   cup cold water
2   cups apricot nectar

¼   cup lemon juice
8   ounces drained crushed
    pineapple (1 cup)
Dash salt

Middle layer:

2   teaspoons unflavored
    gelatin
¼   cup cold water
½   cup mayonnaise
8   ounces Philadelphia cream
    cheese, room temperature

1   cup finely chopped celery
½   cup chopped pecans
Leaf lettuce

This salad has 3 layers. The first list of ingredients make the first and third layers, the second list makes the second layer. Soften the 2 envelopes of gelatin in ¼ cup cold water. Heat the remaining ¾ cup of water to boiling, pour over the softened gelatin and stir until dissolved. Add nectar and lemon juice and chill until slightly thickened. Stir in pineapple, then pour half of mixture into an oiled 1½ quart ring mold. Set mold in refrigerator, leave rest of mixture in a cool place, but do not let it congeal.

Soften the 2 teaspoons of gelatin in ¼ cup cold water, dissolve over hot water. Gradually add the mayonnaise to the cream cheese, blending until smooth. Add the gelatin, celery and pecans. Remove mold from refrigerator and pour mixture over congealed layer. Replace in refrigerator. Chill until firm, then add the rest of the apricot mixture to mold and chill until firm. To serve: unmold onto leaf lettuce. Cut in wedges. Garnish with apricots, if desired.

Yield: 8 servings

Creamy Orange Salad

This salad could also be garnished with strawberries or any fresh fruit or fresh fruit combination.

2 packages orange jello	4 tablespoons lemon juice
2 cups hot water	⅛ teaspoon salt
12 ounces cream cheese, softened and cut into small cubes	Fresh orange sections or mandarin oranges
½ cup frozen orange juice, thawed but undiluted	

Dissolve the jello in hot water. Gradually add to the cream cheese, blending until smooth. Add the orange juice, lemon juice and salt. Mix well with wire whip. Pour into 10 individual salad molds that have been rinsed in cold water and drained upside down. Serve on lettuce and garnish with orange sections or Mandarin oranges.

Yield: 10 (4 ounce) molds

Recipe may be halved.

Jellied Cucumber Salad

1 envelope unflavored gelatin	2 teaspoons lemon juice
½ cup cold water	1 tablespoon vinegar
½ cup boiling water	3 ounces cream cheese, room temperature
2 cups finely shredded cucumber, seeds removed before shredding	Milk
½ teaspoon salt	Watercress or spinach

Soften gelatin in cold water, then dissolve in boiling water. Cool slightly, then add cucumber, lemon juice, vinegar and salt. Chill until slightly thickened, then pour into a fancy 1 quart mold that has either been lightly oiled or rinsed with cold water and drained. Chill until firm. Unmold and garnish with cream cheese which has been whipped with a small amount of milk and forced through a pastry tube.

Yield: 6 to 8 servings

Sauces

Barbecue Sauce

½   cup cider vinegar
1   cup Worcestershire sauce
2   cups water
1   cup melted butter or
      margarine
1½ cups light brown sugar,
      packed

1½ cups ketchup
3   teaspoons salt
3   teaspoons chili powder
1   teaspoon prepared mustard
Dash Tabasco

Heat all ingredients to boiling and boil for 5 minutes. This sauce will keep in the refrigerator for weeks. Good on chicken or any meat.

Yield: About 6 cups

Cream Cheese Sauce

This is a delicious smooth, rich sauce that can be used over vegetables or combined with other ingredients in casseroles.

1   stick butter or margarine
6   tablespoons flour
½   teaspoon salt or to taste
3   cups whole milk or light
      cream

4   ounces cream cheese,
      softened, broken into pieces

Melt butter or margarine in heavy saucepan, add flour and cook until foamy. Remove from heat and gradually add milk or cream, stirring constantly. Return to heat and cook, stirring, until mixture thickens. Remove from heat and mix in cream cheese, stirring until smooth. Taste for seasoning.

Yield: About 4 cups

Shrimp Sauce for Vegetables

1   tablespoon flour
1   tablespoon butter
¼   teaspoon salt
⅛   teaspoon dried tarragon,
      crushed

⅔   cup cream or milk
3   ounces frozen tiny cooked
      shrimp, thawed and drained
2   tablespoons vermouth
Paprika

In a medium heavy saucepan, melt butter, then stir in flour, salt, tarragon and a dash of pepper. Remove from heat and stir in cream or milk all at once. Return to heat and cook until thick and bubbly. Cook 2 minutes more then add shrimp and wine. Heat through, then pour over cooked broccoli, asparagus or cauliflower. Sprinkle with paprika.

Stir-Fry Sauce

This sauce is used in several recipes in this book. It is useful to keep on hand as it keeps for 2 weeks in the refrigerator. You may freeze it in 1 cup portions for up to 3 months.

3 tablespoons dark brown sugar, packed	½ cup dry sherry
3½ tablespoons cornstarch	¼ teaspoon Tabasco sauce
2 teaspoons ground ginger	3 tablespoons red wine vinegar
4 garlic cloves, crushed	2½ cups chicken or beef broth
½ cup soy sauce	

Put all ingredients except broth in a blender. Blend well and pour into a large jar, add broth and shake well. Refrigerate.

Yield: About 5 cups

Cream Sauce Mix

More butter may be added, if a richer sauce is desired, adding at saucemaking time. Sauce may be glamorized by adding a beaten egg yolk, toasted almonds or lemon juice.

2 cups non-fat dry milk	1 cup softened butter or margarine
1 cup flour	

Mix flour and dry milk, cut in margarine or butter with pastry cutter or 2 knives. Store in covered container in refrigerator.

1 cup cream sauce:

¼ cup mix to 1 cup water for thin cream sauce	¾ cup mix to 1 cup water for thick cream sauce
½ cup mix to 1 cup water for medium cream sauce	

Mix together and cook in a heavy saucepan, stirring, over medium heat until thickened.

Creme Fraiche

These are 3 recipes for Creme Fraiche used in France instead of sour cream. It does not break down when used in sauces as sour cream does. It can also be whipped and used in salad dressings instead of whipped cream.

For 1 cup:

1 cup heavy cream	1 tablespoon buttermilk

For 3 cups:

2   cups heavy cream
1   (8 ounce) container sour
      cream

For 4 cups:

1 quart heavy cream	2 tablespoons buttermilk

Bring cream to room temperature, then combine with buttermilk or sour cream, according to which recipe you are using. Stir well and place in a glass jar, cover loosely and let set at room temperature for 6 to 8 hours on a warm day, up to 24 hours on a cold day; or until mixture thickens. Stir well, then place jar cover on top and place in refrigerator for at least 4 hours. Stir before using as a topping for fresh fruit, or in a sauce.

Yield: 1 cup, 3 cups, 4 cups

Creme Fraiche will keep 4 to 6 weeks in refrigerator. To make another batch, follow directions similar to sour dough. Remove 1 tablespoon of Creme Fraiche and add to cream and proceed per directions.

Winter Pesto Sauce

Fresh basil is almost impossible to obtain during some of the winter months. I love Pesto sauce at any time of the year, so this recipe is the answer.

¾   cup olive oil
2   cups fresh parsley leaves,
      preferably flat-leaf, packed
      to measure
3   tablespoons dried sweet
      basil leaves

1   tablespoon pine nuts or
      walnuts
2   cloves garlic, peeled
¼   teaspoon salt
⅛   teaspoon freshly ground
      black pepper

Place all ingredients in blender, cover and blend 40 to 50 seconds, stopping several times to scrape down sides with rubber spatula. Blend until well puréed. Store in covered container in refrigerator. Stir before using.

Yield: About 1⅓ cups

Garlic Spinach and Parsley Pesto

Since the ingredients are different, but the directions for making each of these recipes is the same, I am combining them.

Parsley Pesto:

1   cup flat leaved parsley, packed to measure
1   tablespoon dried sweet basil leaves, packed
½   teaspoon salt
2   tablespoons walnuts or pine nuts

¼   cup freshly grated Parmesan cheese
2   cloves garlic, peeled
½ to ¾ cup olive oil
2   tablespoons lemon juice

In blender, combine fresh and dried leaves with salt, pepper if stated, Parmesan cheese, garlic, nuts and half the olive oil. Blend at high speed until ingredients are smooth, stopping several times to scrape down sides with a rubber spatula. Add rest of olive oil by driblets and blend well. Sauce should be thin enough to run off spatula easily, if too thick, add a little more oil.

Garlic-Spinach Pesto:

1   cup, packed measure, torn spinach that has been washed in salt water and rinsed.
4   cloves garlic, peeled
1   cup parsley leaves
½   cup freshly grated Parmesan cheese

¼   cup walnuts or pine nuts
1   teaspoon dried whole tarragon
1   teaspoon dried whole sweet basil
½   teaspoon salt
½   teaspoon pepper
1   cup olive oil, divided

Follow above directions.

Yield: ⅔ cup each recipe

Buerre Manié in sauce

I use this method of making cream sauces, particularly if in large quantity. It is the easiest way I know of.

For medium cream sauce:

4   tablespoons flour
4   tablespoons butter or
     margarine

2   cups milk
Salt and pepper to taste

Mix flour and butter or margarine to a paste. Heat milk in heavy saucepan. Remove from heat and add the flour-butter mixture in small chunks, stirring constantly with a wire whisk, until all is combined. Return to heat and cook over medium heat, stirring constantly, until thickened. Taste for seasoning.

For a thin sauce, use 2 tablespoons flour and butter to 2 cups milk, for a thick sauce, use 6 tablespoons flour and butter to the 2 cups milk. Recipe can be increased to whatever quantity of sauce you require.

Cheese Sauce for Vegetables

1   green onion, thinly sliced,
     green stems included
1   tablespoon butter or
     margarine
1   tablespoon flour
Dash white pepper
⅔   cup whole milk

½   cup grated Gruyere, Swiss
     or cheddar cheese
1   tablespoon diced pimiento
Salt to taste
1   tablespoon vermouth or
     lemon juice

In heavy saucepan, cook onion in butter until limp, Stir in flour and white pepper, blending well. Remove from heat and add milk, gradually, beating with a wire whisk. Return to heat and cook, stirring constantly, until thickened. Cook 1 minute more, then, over low heat add cheese and cook just until cheese is melted. Add vermouth or lemon juice and pimiento.

Yield: About 1 cup

Raleigh House Au Gratin Sauce

Raleigh House was open only in the summer months so I always gave recipes to my patrons to use during the winter. This recipe was one of the ones most often requested.

3 cups milk
1½ sticks margarine
1 pound Velveeta cheese, broken into chunks

6 level tablespoons cornstarch
Additional ¾ cup milk

Put milk and margarine in top of a double boiler, place over boiling water and let margarine melt. Add cheese and stir until cheese is melted. Dissolve cornstarch in ¾ cup milk and add slowly to cheese mixture, stirring constantly, until sauce thickens. Either combine with potatoes or whatever you want to use it for, or pour into a container with a cover. Place in refrigerator. This sauce does not need any salt.

Yield: About 5 cups

Herb Sauce

This is versatile pesto-like mixture. Use small amounts to season stews, cooked vegetables or pasta.

3 cups snipped parsley
1 cup lightly mixed basil, oregano and or thyme
2 tablespoons Dijon mustard

2 cloves garlic, minced
⅓ to ½ cup olive oil
½ cup grated Parmesan cheese

In a blender container or food processor, combine parsley, herb leaves, mustard, garlic, and ⅓ cup olive oil. Cover and blend or process until nearly smooth. If mixture is thick, add more oil, a teaspoonful at a time, and continue blending or processing until mixture is the consistency of mayonnaise. Stir in Parmesan cheese.

Yield: About 1 cup

Freeze, if desired, in ⅓ cup containers. Will freeze up to 6 months.

Blender Hollandaise Sauce

3	egg yolks	½	teaspoon salt
2	tablespoons fresh lemon juice	2	dashes cayenne pepper
		1	stick butter, melted

In blender container, mix egg yolks, lemon juice, salt and cayenne pepper at low speed. With controls set at "blend", pour in hot melted butter in a steady stream. If not using immediately, place container in hot, but not boiling, water. If water is too hot, sauce will be apt to curdle. Any leftover sauce can be frozen satisfactorily in a tightly covered container.

Yield: about 16 tablespoons

Blender Bearnaise Sauce

This is a delicious sauce to serve with roast beef or steak

2	tablespoons dry white wine	¼	teaspoon pepper
1	tablespoon tarragon vinegar		
2	teaspoons chopped shallots		
1	teaspoon dried tarragon, crumbled between palms of hands to bring out the flavor		

Combine all ingredients in a heavy small saucepan. Reduce mixture over high heat, stirring, until almost all the liquid has evaporated. Pour into ¾ cup Hollandaise sauce and transfer to a blender. Cover and blend at high speed for 5 seconds.

Yield: ¾ cup

Chambord Melba Sauce

Chambord is a liqueur made with raspberries, and is one of my favorites

10	ounce package frozen raspberries	1	teaspoon cornstarch
½	cup currant jelly	1	tablespoon cold water
⅓	cup sugar	⅓	cup Chambord
		½	teaspoon fresh lemon juice

Combine raspberries, jelly and sugar in a heavy saucepan. Stir over medium heat until boiling. Dissolve cornstarch in the water and add to mixture, stirring constantly. Let barely simmer for 10 minutes. Remove from heat and add Chambord and lemon juice. Strain and chill before using.

Yield: 1½ cups

For Peach Melba, place a fresh or frozen peach half, cut-side up, in a stemmed crystal sherbet glass. Place a ball of vanilla ice cream on top and spoon Melba sauce over for an elegant dessert.

Creamy Mushroom Sauce

1	(8 ounce) package cream cheese, cubed	¼	teaspoon garlic salt
½	cup milk	4	ounce can sliced mushrooms
¼	cup grated Parmesan cheese	¾	teaspoon chopped parsley

Gradually add milk to cream cheese, blend well; then cook over low heat, stirring, until smooth. Add remaining ingredients. Heat and serve over vegetables or chicken.

Yield: 1¾ cups

Praline Liqueur Sauce

This is delicious, rich sauce. It can be used over ice cream and sprinkled with toasted almonds or pecans. You can also roll a ball of ice cream in chopped nuts. Spoon some of the sauce on a dessert plate and place nut ball on top .

8	ounces white chocolate	⅓	cup whipping cream
¼	cup Praline Liqueur		

Melt chocolate over simmering, not boiling water, in top of a double boiler. Combine with liqueur and cream, blending well. Cool and use as you desire.

Yield: 1¼ cups

Praline Pudding or Cake Sauce

1 stick butter, do not substitute	2 tablespoons heavy cream
1½ cups powdered sugar, sifted after measuring	½ cup toasted pecans or almonds, chopped
	2 teaspoons Praline Liqueur

Cream butter until smooth, then beat in sugar. Add cream and liqueur, mix well, then fold in toasted nuts. Refrigerate or freeze in a covered container. Bring to room temperature and stir well before serving on warm cake or steamed puddings.

Yield: 2 cups

Mother's Vanilla Sauce

This is a not too rich sauce to be served warm over cakes or puddings. I particularly like it over fresh warm spice cake or gingerbread.

1 cup sugar	4 tablespoons butter (½ stick)
2 tablespoons cornstarch	2 teaspoons vanilla
2 cups boiling water	

Mix sugar and cornstarch in a heavy saucepan, gradually stir in boiling water. Set over medium heat and cook, stirring constantly, for 2 minutes or until thickened. Remove from heat and add vanilla and butter. Mix well until butter is melted. Serve warm or cold.

Yield: 2½ cups

A lemon sauce may be made by this same recipe. Use 2 teaspoons lemon juice and 1 tablespoon grated lemon rind instead of the vanilla.

Butterscotch Sauce

This was a frequently used sauce for cakes and puddings in our home when I was growing up.

1 cup brown sugar, packed	½ cup half and half
½ cup white corn syrup	
¼ cup butter or margarine, cut into bits	

Mix all ingredients in a heavy saucepan. Cook over low heat, stirring, until thickened. Serve warm over cakes and puddings, cold over ice cream.

Yield: 2 cups

Milk may be substituted for the cream but add 2 teaspoons cornstarch to the brown sugar, then proceed.

Dad's Vanilla Sauce

My father liked to cook, too. He even made delicious pies, crust and all. This sauce is a little richer than mother's.

½ cup sugar	1 stick butter, cut into bits
2 teaspoons cornstarch	1 teaspoon vanilla
½ cup whole milk	

Mix sugar and cornstarch, then add milk and cook over medium heat, stirring constantly, until thickened. Add butter and vanilla and heat until butter is melted.

Yield: 1½ cups

Soft Custard Sauce

This can be used as a sauce or as a pudding on it's own. Just put it in your prettiest dessert dishes and serve with a dollop of whipped cream on top.

2	whole eggs	1½	cups milk
¼	cup sugar	1	teaspoon vanilla or any
¼	teaspoon salt		flavoring you prefer

Beat eggs and sugar together in the top of a double boiler, then blend in salt. Add milk and mix well. Cook over simmering, not boiling, water. Do not let water touch bottom of top pan. Cook, stirring constantly, until custard coats the back of the spoon. This is when your finger leaves a path when drawn across the back of the spoon. Remove from heat and add vanilla. If mixture starts to curdle, beat with a wire whisk. Cool and refrigerate in a tightly covered container.

Yield: About 2 cups

My mother used to dip a teaspoon into almond extract and then measure the vanilla. Try it sometime.

Bobby's Rum Sauce

This is delicious served over pound cake.

½	cup butter	1	teaspoon vanilla extract
1	cup granulated sugar	¼	cup light rum or to your
½	cup half and half		taste

Cook butter, sugar and cream in top of a double boiler over boiling water, stirring, until thickened; about 10 minutes. Cool and refrigerate. About 20 minutes before serving, remove from refrigerator and add the vanilla and rum and reheat in double boiler.

Yield: 1½ cups

Amaretto Custard Sauce

5	large egg yolks	2	tablespoons Amaretto or to
½	cup sugar		taste
¾	cup hot milk		

Beat egg yolks and sugar until light and fluffy. Add hot milk gradually, stirring constantly with a wire whisk. Cook in a double boiler until thickened. Remove from heat and add Amaretto. Cool and refrigerate until using.

Yield: 1 cup

Be sure to save the whites of the eggs for future use. I usually freeze them, 2 or 3 each, in small jars. Just thaw and use as you would fresh ones. They whip up beautifully at room temperature.

Instant Teriyaki Sauce

2	cups French dressing	⅛	teaspoon garlic powder, not
2	cups soy sauce		garlic salt
¾	teaspoon ground ginger		

Combine all ingredients. Mix well and brush on steak, chicken, shrimp, ribs, burgers, or shishkebabs before broiling. Will keep almost indefinitely refrigerated.

Yield: 1 quart

Cranberry Sauce with Chambord

4	cups cranberries, washed	2	cups water
¾	cup sugar		
2	tablespoons Chambord		
	liqueur or to your taste		

Combine cranberries, sugar and water in a saucepan, bring to a boil and simmer the mixture, stirring occasionally, for 45 minutes. Pour mixture into a sieve over a bowl and let drain for 20 minutes. Measure the liquid and discard the solids. You should have 1⅓ cups. If there is less, add water; if there is more, boil the liquid down to amount required. Add the chambord and chill, covered, until it is cold. Serve over ice cream or cake.

Yield: 1½ cups

Grand Marnier Strawberry Sauce

Serve over ice cream, pound cake or fresh fruit of your choice

¼	cup sugar	2 pints strawberries, sliced
Rind of 1 small orange removed	1½ tablespoons lemon juice
in thin julienne strips	1½ tablespoons Grand Marnier
½	cup water	or to your taste

Combine sugar, orange rind and water in saucepan, bring to a boil, covered, then uncover and boil for 5 minutes. Remove rind with a slotted spoon and discard.Cool syrup. Place strawberries in a blender or food processor and purée, then force purée through a sieve, pressing hard on solids. Add to cooled syrup along with the lemon juice and Grand Marnier. Chill, covered. When serving, add more Grand Marnier, if you wish.

Yield: About 2 cups

Hot Fudge Sauce

This is made in the microwave, and can be served as a fondue.

⅓	cup water	2 tablespoons light corn
2	ounces unsweetened	syrup
	chocolate	1 teaspoon vanilla
1	cup sugar	½ stick of butter

Microwave the water, chocolate and butter in a 2 cup glass measure on high power until melted, about 2 minutes. Stir in sugar and corn syrup, microwave on medium power, stirring once, for 2 minutes. Then microwave on medium-low power, stirring twice, for 2 or 3 minutes. Stir well. Let stand, uncovered, stirring once in a while, until cool. Add vanilla and mix.

Yield: 1 cup

Apricot Brandy Sauce

This is made in the microwave.

1	cup apricot nectar	1 teaspoon grated lemon peel
½	cup sugar	3 tablespoons apricot brandy
1	tablespoon cornstarch	or to taste

Mix sugar, nectar, cornstarch and lemon peel in 2 cup glass measure. Microwave on high, stirring occasionally, until thick and clear, about 3 minutes. Let stand 6 minutes. Stir in brandy to taste. Serve warm or cold.

Yield: 1 cup

Brandy Sauce

¾   cup sugar
3   tablespoons cornstarch
¼   teaspoon salt
2   cups boiling water

½   stick butter or margarine
2   tablespoons brandy or to
    your taste

Combine sugar, cornstarch and salt in a heavy saucepan. Add boiling water in a stream, stirring until well blended. Simmer the sauce over low heat until it is thickened and translucent. Remove from heat and stir in the butter until it is melted. Cool 10 minutes, then add the brandy. Serve over steamed puddings or whatever you wish.

Yield: 2½ cups

Raleigh House Chocolate Sauce

This sauce keeps almost indefinitely in the refrigerator. This sauce is thick. You may add a little more milk or water to thin it, if you like.

2½   cups granulated sugar
1   cup cocoa
2   cups white corn syrup
½   teaspoon salt

1½   sticks margarine
1   (12 ounce) can evaporated
     milk
2   teaspoons vanilla

In heavy large saucepan, mix sugar and cocoa together well, add corn syrup, salt and margarine. Mix well, then place over medium heat and bring to a boil, stirring constantly, to keep from sticking. Turn heat to low and let simmer, stirring occasionally, until a little dropped into ice water makes a soft ball. Remove from heat and add vanilla and evaporated milk. Mix well, then place in container with a cover or in jars. Let cool, then place in refrigerator.

Yield: About 6 cups

Raleigh House Butterscotch Sauce

⅔ cup very firmly packed
    light brown sugar
¼ cup white corn syrup
4 tablespoons butter or
    margarine

¼ teaspoon salt
⅓ cup evaporated milk
½ teaspoon vanilla

Combine the brown sugar, corn syrup, butter and salt in heavy saucepan. Bring the mixture to a boil over medium heat, stirring constantly, lower heat and simmer until a half teaspoonful of the syrup forms a soft ball when dropped into a cup of ice water. Remove from heat and add the evaporated milk and vanilla. Store in refrigerator in a covered container. Stir before serving.

Yield: About 1 cup

Blueberry Sauce

We used to serve blueberry sauce for the ice cream at Raleigh House until blueberries became unattainable in the large commercial cans.

¼ cup sugar
2 teaspoons cornstarch
Pinch salt
¾ cup water

2   teaspoons lemon juice
3   tablespoons softened butter
    or margarine
10 ounces frozen blueberries

Combine the sugar, cornstarch and salt . Mix well, then add water and lemon juice. Bring mixture to a boil over medium heat, then reduce heat and simmer, stirring occasionally, for 4 minutes. Add the blueberries and cook for 3 minutes, stirring with a wooden spoon so as not to break up the blueberries. Add softened butter and stir until butter is melted. Cool and refrigerate in covered non-metallic container or jar.

Yield: 1¼ cups

Creamy Coconut Sauce

2   eggs, beaten
2   tablespoons sugar
1⅓ cup whole milk

1 teaspoon vanilla
5 tablespoons flaked coconut,
   toasted

Beat eggs in a small heavy saucepan, add sugar and mix well. Gradually add milk, beating with a wire whisk. Cook over low heat, stirring constantly, until thickened. Remove from heat and stir in vanilla. Cool, then add coconut.

Yield: 1¾ cups

Apple Cinnamon Sauce

This sauce is good, too, on waffles or pancakes

2	cups apple juice	¼	teaspoon salt
½	teaspoon ground cinnamon	2	tablespoons sugar
1½	tablespoons cornstarch	⅓	cup raisins (optional)

Mix apple juice, sugar, salt, cornstarch and cinnamon in a heavy saucepan. Cook over medium heat, stirring constantly until thickened. Add raisins, if desired. Good over gingerbread.

Yield: 2 cups

Mother's Hard Sauce

This sauce is especially for steamed puddings. My mother was a teetotaler even in cooking, so she used vanilla as flavoring. I always use brandy.

½	cup butter, softened	1	egg yolk
1½	cups powdered sugar, sifted after measuring	2	teaspoons vanilla

Beat butter until fluffy. Add egg yolk and beat again, then slowly add powdered sugar and beat well, Add vanilla or brandy.

Yield: 2 cups

If you double this recipe, just use a whole egg, not 2 egg yolks.

Easy Chocolate Sauce

1	cup heavy cream		Pinch salt
6	ounces chocolate chips (1 cup)	½	teaspoon vanilla

Bring cream or evaporated milk to a boil in heavy saucepan over medium heat. Remove from heat and stir in chocolate chips, salt and vanilla. Stir until mixture is smooth.

Yield: 1¾ cups

Wine Marinade

½ cup oil
½ cup dry white wine
¼ cup lime or lemon juice
2 tablespoons snipped parsley

½ teaspoon salt
Dash Tabasco
1 small onion, very thinly sliced

Combine ingredients, separating onion into rings. Place 3 pounds fish, chicken or meat in a plastic bag set in a deep bowl. Pour mixture over meat, fish or chicken.Press in sides to distribute marinade. Close bag and set in refrigerator for 4 to 6 hours or overnight, occasionally turning bag over. Bake as directed in recipe you are using.

Yield: 1½ cups

Dill Sauce

2 tablespoons margarine
1 tablespoon flour
1 cup chicken broth or clam broth

1 egg yolk, beaten
¼ cup sour cream or creme fraiche
2 teaspoons dried dill weed

Melt margarine in heavy saucepan over low heat; add flour and cook until foamy. Gradually add chicken broth or clam broth and cook over medium heat, stirring constantly, until thickened. Pour a little of the hot mixture over the beaten egg yolk, mix, then add to rest of hot mixture. Cook, stirring constantly, for 5 minutes. Remove from heat, stir in sour cream or creme fraiche and dill weed. Warm and serve over seafood.

Yield: 1¼ cups

Vegetables

Carrots and Zucchini, Julienne

4   medium carrots, scraped
    and cut into julienne strips
2   medium zucchini, cut into
    julienne strips
3   tablespoons butter, melted

⅛   teaspoon salt
⅛   teaspoon pepper
2   tablespoons fresh parsley,
    chopped

Wash zucchini in salt water, then rinse, to remove the grit. Arrange carrots in a small saucepan with only an inch of water. Bring to a boil and cook for 5 minutes, covered, until barely tender. Drain. Melt butter in skillet and sauté carrots and zucchini for 5 minutes. Add seasonings and serve immediately with chopped parsley sprinkled on top.

Yield: 4 servings

Mushrooms and Water Chestnuts

5   tablespoons butter, melted
3   tablespoons flour
½   teaspoon salt
Dash pepper
1½   cups half and half
1   pound fresh mushrooms,
     quartered, if large

¼   cup butter
15   ounces water chestnuts,
     drained and sliced
1   tablespoon chopped parsley

Wash mushrooms or wipe off. If they are small button ones, leave whole. Melt butter in saucepan, add flour, salt and pepper. Add half and half and blend. Put over medium heat and cook, stirring, until thickened. Sauté mushrooms in the ¼ cup butter for 3 minutes. Avoid overcooking. Add water chestnuts and mushrooms to sauce. Cook 3-4 minutes. Taste for seasoning. Garnish with parsley. Note: if sauce is too thick, thin with a little cream.

Yield: 8 servings

Creamed Mushrooms and Raw Peanuts

This was a very popular side dish served at a restaurant in San Antonio many years ago on their Sunday buffet. It is really good and a conversation piece for any party.

½	pound small mushrooms	⅛	teaspoon paprika
1	cup raw peanuts		Dash Worcestershire sauce
3	tablespoons butter		Salt and pepper to taste
2	tablespoons flour		
1¼	cup cold milk or half and half		

Wash mushrooms, dry, then sauté them in the butter for only 3 minutes. Avoid overcooking. Add flour, paprika and Worcestershire. Blend milk or cream in slowly. Place over heat and stir until thickened. Add peanuts and cook 3 more minutes. Season to taste with salt and pepper.

Yield: 4 servings

Mushroom Pie

This is delicious as an entree for a luncheon or, cut in smaller pieces for an appetizer.

1	10 inch pie shell, baked 10 minutes in a 350° oven	1	tablespoon chopped parsley
½	pound mushrooms, sliced	3	eggs, slightly beaten
1	tablespoon grated onion	1½	cups milk
½	cup grated Swiss cheese		Salt and pepper to taste

Sauté mushrooms and onion in 2 tablespoons butter about 3 minutes, drain. Place layer of mushroom mixture in bottom of pie shell. Top with grated cheese. Mix the remaining ingredients and gently pour over mushrooms. Bake at 350° about 40 minutes or until firm in center. Let cool 10 minutes before cutting into wedges.

Yield: 6 to 8 servings

Zucchini, Carrot, Squash Casserole

This casserole makes an attractive plate when served with potatoes and, perhaps, roast beef.

1   pound zucchini, scrubbed in salt water, and coarsely grated
1   pound yellow summer squash, washed and coarsely grated
1   teaspoon salt
1   small onion, coarsely grated
½   teaspoon nutmeg
1   large carrot, scraped and coarsely grated
8   ounces (2 sticks) of butter, divided

Toss the zucchini and squash with the salt in a colander and let them drain. weighted down with a large bowl and 2 pound weight, for 30 minutes. In a large skillet, sauté the onion in 4 ounces of butter, covered, over low heat, and stirring occasionally, until onion is softened. Add the carrots and cook the mixture, covered, stirring occasionally, for 10 minutes. Add the remaining vegetables, the other 4 ounces butter, the nutmeg, salt and pepper to taste. Cook the mixture, uncovered, over high heat just until the vegetables are well heated. Serve at once.

Yield: serves 6

Corn and Cheese Pudding

1   (16 ounce) can whole kernel corn
2   ounce jar pimiento, drained and chopped
1   cup grated cheddar cheese
2   eggs, beaten
½   cup milk
1   tablespoon flour
1   tablespoon sugar
2   tablespoons melted butter or margarine
1   teaspoon salt

Combine all ingredients in bowl; mix well. Pour into a buttered 1½ quart casserole. Bake at 350° for 45 or 50 minutes or until bubbly and lightly browned.

Yield: 4 to 6 servings

Ratatouille in Tomatoes

This could be served also as a first course as well as a vegetable.

3	medium zucchini		Salt and pepper
1	medium eggplant		Chopped parsley for garnish
4	medium tomatoes, peeled and diced	3	large tomatoes cut into 3 thick slices, each
2	green peppers, thinly sliced	10	ounces fresh spinach, Washed and torn into bite-sized pieces
1	cup thinly sliced onion		
¼	cup olive oil		
1	clove garlic, minced		

Sauté onion in oil until soft. Add diced tomatoes, cook 1 minute. Mix in garlic, salt and pepper, zucchini, sliced thin and eggplant, peeled and diced,and green peppers. Sauté, covered, for 5 minutes. Remove cover and simmer until all liquid has evaporated. Watch carefully to see that mixture does not scorch. Correct seasoning. Chill. Marinate tomato slices in red wine and vinegar dressing or in Italian dressing. Place spinach on salad plates, place a tomato slice on the spinach and top with the ratatouille, or place leaves of spinach on dinner plate, top with tomato slice and serve as a vegetable.

Yield: serves 8

Carrot Puff

This dish tastes like a cross between carrots and sweet potatoes.

1	pound carrots, peeled and sliced	⅔	cup sugar
1	stick margarine, melted	3	tablespoons flour
3	eggs	1	teaspoon baking powder
		1	teaspoon vanilla

Cook carrots until tender in a small amount of water; drain. Combine carrots and melted margarine in blender container, blend until smooth. Add eggs, sugar. flour, baking powder and vanilla. Blend well. Spoon mixture into a well-greased 1 quart souffle dish or casserole. Bake at 350° 45 minutes or until firm. Serve immediately.

Yield: serves 8

Cynthia's Zesty Carrots

This is my granddaughter's recipe. It is very good. Even guests who do not like carrots comment on it.

6 to 8 medium carrots	½ teaspoon salt
¼ cup water or carrot liquid	¼ teaspoon pepper
2 tablespoon grated onion	½ cup fine bread crumbs
2 tablespoons prepared horseradish	2 tablespoon butter, melted
½ cup mayonnaise	Dash paprika

Peel and cut carrots into slender lengthwise strips. Cook in a small amount of water until just tender. Spread in shallow baking dish. Mix rest of ingredients and pour over. Top with the bread crumbs mixed with melted butter and a dash of paprika. Bake at 350° about 25 minutes or until bubbly.

Yield: 6 to 8 servings

Creamy Squash Casserole

This is the squash casserole we served for many years at Raleigh House. We had many requests for the recipe after we discontinued serving it. It is exceptionally good.

2½ pounds yellow or zucchini squash or a combination of the two. Wash well in salt water and slice.	3 eggs, beaten
	¼ cup cream or evaporated milk
1 medium onion, sliced	Salt and pepper to taste
¼ cup butter or margarine, melted	24 Ritz crackers, crushed
	½ cup butter or margarine, softened

Cook squash and onion in a small amount of water until tender. Drain well. Put in mixer bowl with eggs, ¼ cup melted butter, cream and a little salt and pepper. Mix well, then correct seasoning. Place in a buttered rectangular baking dish and cover with the cracker crumbs mixed with the softened margarine. Bake at 350° about 25 minutes or until firm in center.

Yield: 8 servings

Rice Spinach Casserole

I like this casserole as it combines a starchy and a green vegetable and is pretty on a buffet table.

3	cups cooked rice	¼	cup butter
1	(10 ounce) package frozen chopped spinach	2	tablespoons lemon juice
		1	teaspoon salt
¾	cup chopped green onion with tops		Dash garlic powder, not garlic salt
½	cup minced parsley	1	egg
½	cup slivered almonds	1	cup milk

Combine rice, spinach, onion, parsley, almonds, butter, lemon juice, salt and garlic powder in 2 quart casserole. Beat egg with milk. Stir into rice mixture. Cover and refrigerate until ready to cook. Bake about 45 minutes at 350° or until hot.

Yield: 8 servings

Rice and Vegetables

I served this at a church dinner. It served as a vegetable and starch. The menu was complete with entree, salad, and, of course, dessert.

2	carrots, finely diced	½	cup boiling water
1	onion,sliced	½	teaspoon salt
2	ribs celery, diced	¼	cup blanched almonds, halved,(optional)
1	large zucchini or yellow squash, diced	4	cups cooked brown or white rice
½	green pepper, diced		
1	tomato, seeded and chopped		Salt to taste

Put first 6 ingredients in sauce pan with boiling water. Cover tightly and simmer until carrots are tender. Drain. Stir in almonds, then add rice. Mix lightly with a fork. Add more salt, if needed. Place mixture in a casserole and heat in 350° oven.

Yield: 8 servings

I cooked the rice in chicken boullion for more flavor. You could also use well-flavored chicken broth. You may use any vegetables you wish. I used only carrots, celery, onion and green pepper as we were having tomatoes in the salad.

Wild Rice and Cheese Casserole

Be sure to follow the "quick-soak" method of preparing wild rice for the final cooking.

1	cup wild rice	½	cup butter or margarine
¼	teaspoon salt	1	cup grated sharp Cheddar
3	cups boiling water		cheese
½	pound mushrooms, sliced, about 3 cups	1	(16 ounce) can tomatoes
		1	teaspoon salt
½	cup onion, finely chopped	1	cup hot water

Follow the "quick-soak" method to prepare rice for cooking. Then cook rice, covered, in boiling, salted water until nearly tender, 30 minutes. Drain rice, if necessary. Sauté mushrooms and onion in butter, for about 5 minutes. Toss rice with all ingredients. Place in a buttered 2 quart casserole; cover and bake for 1 hour at 350°.

Yield: 6 to 8 servings

This may be prepared the day before and baked just before serving. Serve as a vegetable with pork, poultry or game.

Wild Rice—Quick Soak

This quick-soaking method cuts the cooking time considerably and produces a good product every time. Follow directions in each recipe for final cooking.

1	cup wild rice	3	cups boiling water

Wash rice under cold, running water, in a colander or sieve. Then place in large saucepan, add 3 cups boiling water. Parboil for 5 minutes only. Remove from heat. Cover and let soak in same water for 1 hour. Drain, wash and cook as directed in recipe. Amount can be increased, of course, according to how much cooked rice you need for your recipe.

Yield: 4 cups

Wild rice is very versatile and can be combined with shrimp, poultry or whatever you wish.

Wild Rice and Mushroom Casserole

Be sure to follow the "quick-soaking" method of preparing rice for final cooking.

⅔ cup wild rice, uncooked
½ teaspoon salt
3 cups boiling water
¼ cup finely chopped onion
1 cup fresh mushrooms, sliced
2 tablespoons butter
1 tablespoon flour

1 cup beef boullion or 1 beef boullion cube dissolved in 1 cup hot water
½ teaspoon salt or to taste
⅛ teaspoon pepper
¼ cup slivered or sliced almonds

Cook rice in boiling water and ½ teaspoon salt until nearly tender, about 30 minutes. Drain, if necessary. Set aside.In a large skillet, sauté onions and mushrooms in butter about 5 minutes. Blend in flour, then add boullion; cook over medium heat, stirring, until thickened. Add salt and pepper and cooked rice. Mix well. Turn into buttered casserole. Sprinkle with the almonds. Cover and bake at 350° for 30 minutes or until heated through.

Yield: 4 servings

Tomato Broccoli Casserole

This is very easy to prepare and delicious as well.

3 (10 ounce) packages frozen broccoli spears
3 large fresh ripe tomatoes, sliced

1 cup mayonnaise
3 ounce container grated Parmesan cheese

Thaw broccoli and drain. Put half in a buttered rectangular casserole, sprinkle a little salt and pepper over. Then layer half of the tomato slices. Spread half of the mayonnaise and half the cheese. Top with another layer of broccoli, tomatoes, mayonnaise, and cheese.Bake in a 350° oven until hot and bubbly.

Yield: 6 to 8 servings

Baked Celery

This recipe came from a friend of mine. The crispness of the celery and almonds makes it unusual and delicious.

1   bunch celery, sliced in ½ inch slices
½   cup slivered, blanched almonds
½   cup grated sharp cheese
¼   teaspoon salt
¼   teaspoon pepper
¾   cup fine bread crumbs or cracker crumbs

⅓   cup softened butter
1½   cups thin white sauce (1½ tablespoons flour, 1½ tablespoons butter, ¼ teaspoon salt, 1½ cups milk) cooked the usual way

Wash celery and cut into ½ inch slices. Place in a well-buttered 9″ × 12″ casserole. Cover with almonds, then cheese. Season white sauce to taste and pour over. Top with crumbs mixed with the softened butter. Put in refrigerator for at least 3 hours. Remove and bake at 375° for 25 minutes. Celery will still be crisp.

Yield: 6 servings

It must be made at least 3 hours in advance and refrigerated. This is the secret of it.

Oriental Green Peas

¼   cup olive oil
¼   cup peanut oil
1½   cups celery, cut diagonally
3   packages frozen green peas
1   (8½ ounce) can sliced water chestnuts, drained

4   teaspoons cornstarch
1   cup canned beef broth
1   teaspoon soy sauce
Salt to taste
½   cup chopped onion

Heat oil in a large skillet over medium heat, add celery and onion and sauté for 5 minutes, then add peas and water chestnuts. Cook only a few minutes until peas are barely heated. Vegetables should be crisp. Dissolve cornstarch in ¼ cup beef broth and the soy sauce. Combine with rest of broth, stirring well. Pour over vegetables and cook over medium heat, stirring, until thickened. Taste for seasoning.

Yield: serves 12 to 14

Dumpling Squash with Cream Cheese

3   (10 to 12 ounce) dumpling
     or acorn squash
1   (3 ounce) package cream
     cheese, room temperature
2   tablespoons milk
3   beaten eggs

2   tablespoons thinly sliced
     green onions
¼   teaspoons salt
⅛   teaspoon pepper
6   tablespoons pecans, toasted
     and chopped, divided

Cut off top of squash. Scoop out seeds, trim off bottom so squash will stand up. Place them, cut-side down, in baking pan with 1″ boiling water in bottom. Cover tightly with foil and bake at 375° until almost tender. Beat cream cheese until softened, add milk and beat until fluffy, add eggs, green onions, salt and pepper. Beat until well combined. Turn squash, cut-side up. Divide egg mixture in squash. Sprinkle with 3 tablespoons of the pecans. Bake at 375° 20 minutes or more until center is set. Let stand 5 minutes before serving. Cut squash in half and sprinkle with remaining 3 tablespoons pecans.

Yield: 6 servings

Mushroom Casserole

1½   pounds fresh mushrooms,
     quartered
1   tablespoon butter, melted
1   beef boullion cube
⅓   cup hot water
¼   cup butter

2   tablespoons flour
Dash pepper
½   cup whipping cream
¼   cup fine,dry bread crumbs
¼   cup grated Parmesan
     cheese

Sauté mushrooms in 1 tablespoon butter over medium heat for only 3 minutes, Do not overcook. Dissolve boullion cube in hot water and set aside. Melt the ¼ cup butter in a large skillet, add flour and stir until smooth. Blend in pepper, whipping cream and boullion. Stir in mushrooms with juice, if any. Pour mixture into a buttered 1½ quart casserole. Top with bread crumbs and cheese. Bake, uncovered, at 350° for 30 minutes.

Yield: 4 to 6 servings

Armenian Beans

These were served at one of my family reunions. It is a nice change from pork and beans.

1   pound can kidney beans, drained

1   pound can pinto beans, drained

1   pound can French cut green beans, drained

1   can baked beans, undrained

1   bunch green onions, chopped

1   large green pepper, chopped

4   strips lean bacon cut and cooked until crisp

Mix all ingredients in casserole and bake at 350° until bubbly. Recipe can be doubled for a crowd.

Yield: 8 to 12 servings

Irene's Spinach on Artichoke Bottoms

This dish was very popular at many of Irene's dinner parties.

3   large cans artichoke bottoms, drained

8   ounces cream cheese, room temperature

1   stick butter, divided, room temperature

¼   teaspoon nutmeg

Salt and pepper to taste

Dash Tabasco

2   (10 ounce) packages frozen chopped spinach, thawed and squeezed dry

Place spinach in heavy saucepan and heat over very low heat until no moisture remains. While spinach is still warm, add cream cheese which has been cut into small squares. Blend with spinach, then add ¼ of the stick of butter, salt, pepper, nutmeg and Tabasco. Let mixture cool and thicken. Wash and drain artichoke bottoms, place on oiled baking pan. Divide spinach mixture between artichoke bottoms. Dot with rest of butter. Bake at 350° for 20 minutes.

Yield: 14 to 16 servings

Tomatoes Jacque

This is a pretty, as well as delicious, addition to a dinner plate.

¼   cup fresh parsley, chopped
½   teaspoon dried basil,
     crumbled
2   tablespoons snipped chives,
     frozen or fresh
2   teaspoons minced garlic
1½ teaspoons salt
¾   cup soft bread crumbs,
     about 1½ slices bread

¼   cup olive oil, divided
2   cups finely chopped onions,
     about 3 medium
8   large tomatoes, sliced,
     about 3½ pounds
Freshly ground pepper

Mix parsley, basil, chives, salt and bread crumbs. In large skillet, heat 2 tablespoons of the olive oil over moderate heat. Add onions and garlic and cook 5 minutes or until soft but not brown. Heat oven to 350°. Spread onion mixture evenly in a glass baking dish about 13″×9″. Top with sliced tomatoes. Sprinkle with bread crumb mixture and drizzle with remaining 2 tablespoons of oil and bake 25 minutes, until tomatoes are tender and crumbs are lightly browned.

Yield: 8 servings

Wild Rice with Vegetables

Follow the quick-soaked method of preparation before finishing the cooking of the wild rice in this recipe.

2   cups wild rice, quick-soaked
3   cups chicken broth
3   cups water
4   medium carrots, coarsely
     chopped
1   large onion, coarsely
     chopped

1   large clove garlic. minced
1   stick butter
1   cup fresh parsley, chopped
Additional butter, if needed

Cook rice in chicken broth and water about 30 minutes or until done. In a large skillet, sauté carrots. onion and garlic in butter until barely tender. Drain rice and stir into vegetables in skillet. Add parsley with salt and pepper. Gently heat, stirring occasionally, until heated through.

Yield: 8 to 10 servings

Snow Peas, Mushrooms and Rice

1 cup wild rice and white rice mixture
2 scallions
1 tablespoon butter
1 teaspoon salt
2½ cups chicken broth
2 tablespoons oil

1 package frozen snow peas
4 large mushrooms, sliced
1 (5 ounce) can water chestnuts, drained and sliced
½ teaspoon salt
¼ teaspoon pepper

Wash rice thoroughly. Cut green scallion stems diagonally into 2 inch lengths. Chop the white part of the scallions fine. Keep green and white parts of scallions separate.Melt butter in a large saucepan. Add minced white of scallions and sauté until tender. Add rice, 1 teaspoon salt and the chicken broth. Bring to a boil, stir once and reduce heat. Cover tightly and cook over low heat. Meanwhile, heat oil in large skillet. Add scallion stems, snow peas, mushrooms and water chestnuts; Sauté until mushrooms are barely tender. Transfer cooked rice and vegetable mixture to a 2 quart casserole, add salt and pepper to taste. Heat casserole in 325° oven, for about 15 minutes or until piping hot

Yield: 4 to 6 servings

Snow Peas with Water Chestnuts

4 (7 ounce) packages frozen snow peas
1 teaspoon salt
¼ teaspoon pepper

1 cup water chestnuts, drained and sliced
2 tablespoons butter, softened

Place snow peas in saucepan. Add 1 cup cold water and salt and pepper. Bring to a boil and cook 2 minutes. Drain well. Add water chestnuts. Heat over very low heat, then toss with butter.

Yield: 6 servings

Green Beans Scandia

We served this recipe at several church dinners over 30 years ago in a much larger quantity,of course. This is a delicious way to prepare canned beans. The chicken base, vinegar and dill make an unusual vegetable dish.

1	(1 pound) can cut green beans	1	tablespoon sugar
1	tablespoon chicken base (not boullion cubes)	½	teaspoon dried dill weed
		Dash pepper	
2	tablespoon butter or margarine	1	tablespoon cornstarch
		1	tablespoon cold water
3	tablespoons vinegar	2	cups finely shredded cabbage, packed

Drain liquid from beans into saucepan. Add next 6 ingredients and heat to boiling. Stir cornstarch into water. Add to liquid and cook, stirring, until mixture thickens. Add cabbage and heat to boiling. Simmer, covered, for 3 to 5 minutes. Add beans, heat and serve.

Yield: 6 servings

You may use frozen or fresh beans but cook them first.and save ¾ cup of the water they are cooked in for the sauce. Sexton and Minor Foods make the chicken base. It has a true chicken flavor and little salt.

Baked Beets

I like this recipe as it is easy to make and easy to serve.

5	cups sliced canned beets	2	tablespoons vinegar
½	cup thinly sliced onion	⅔	cup beet juice
½	cup sugar	6	tablespoons butter
1½	teaspoon salt		

Place a layer of beets in buttered casserole, then the onion, then top with the rest of the beets. Mix sugar, salt, vinegar and beet juice and pour over beets. Top with bits of the butter. Bake at 350° about 30 minutes or until onion is soft, stirring frequently.

Yield: 12 servings

Spinach Squash Casserole

Chicken base is much more flavorful than boullion with less salt. Sexton and Minor Foods are two brands I know of.

8   medium yellow or zucchini
     squash
1   teaspoon chicken base, not
     boullion
1   (10 ounce) package of
     frozen chopped spinach,
     defrosted and squeezed dry
¼   cup creamed small curd
     cottage cheese
1   tablespoon grated Parmesan
     cheese

1   large egg, beaten
¼   teaspoon Lawry's seasoned
     salt
¼   teaspoon onion salt
¼   teaspoon freshly ground
     pepper
3   tablespoons dry bread
     crumbs
Paprika

Wash whole squash in salted water. This makes the grit roll off. Drop in boiling water; cover and simmer about 8 minutes, until tender but still firm. Drain and cool. Cut off stems, then cut lengthwise in half. Carefully scoop out pulp, leaving shells. Mash pulp and add spinach along with cottage cheese. Mix well, then add seasonings, cheese and egg. Spoon into squash shells and top with bread crumbs then a sprinkling of paprika. Place on baking sheet that has been either buttered or sprayed with vegetable spray; cover with foil and bake at 300° for 30 minutes.

Yield: 8 servings

Marinated Green Beans and Broccoli

You may use any combination of vegetables you wish.

1   (10 ounce) package frozen
     broccoli florets
1   (10 ounce) package frozen
     French cut green beans
2   tablespoons olive oil
2   tablespoons red wine
     vinegar

1   teaspoon dill seed
1   clove garlic, crushed
¹⁄₁₆ teaspoon freshly ground
     black pepper
Salt to taste

Thaw and drain broccoli florets. Cook green beans in 2 " water until crisp-tender, drain. Combine oil, vinegar, dill seed, crushed garlic, salt and pepper. Pour over vegetables, toss gently. Let marinate a few hours or overnight in the refrigerator. Serve either hot or cold, garnished with crisp bacon bits.

Yield: 6 servings

Spinach Tarts

You may buy tart shells or make them with your favorite pie crust recipe. Bake them with centers weighed down with foil filled with dried beans or uncooked rice. Bake at 375° for 5 minutes, remove foil and beans and bake until very light brown.

2   (10 ounce) packages frozen, chopped spinach, thawed, and squeezed dry
2   tablespoons frozen or fresh chives, chopped

Salt and pepper to taste
1   cup grated cheddar cheese
1   (8 ounce) package cream cheese, room temperature
8   baked 3″ tart shells

Heat spinach in saucepan with a little water for only 3 minutes, drain. While spinach is still warm, blend in cream cheese, chives, salt and pepper until smooth. Place in tart shells. Top with cheddar cheese and bake at 375° 10 to 15 minutes or until piping hot.

Yield: 8 servings

Rice Florentine

This is another way to serve 2 vegetables in one dish.

1   (10 ounce) package frozen leaf spinach, thawed
1⅓ cups uncooked rice
3   cups water
2   tablespoons butter or margarine
1   teaspoon salt

⅛   teaspoon white pepper
2   cloves garlic , minced
¼   cup snipped fresh parsley
½   stick butter, melted
¼   cup grated parmesan cheese

Squeeze spinach until dry, then chop coarsely. Set aside. Bring water to a boil in medium saucepan, reduce heat to simmer and add butter, salt, pepper and garlic. Add uncooked rice, bring water to a boil and cook, covered, about 15 minutes or until rice is tender and liquid is absorbed. Add spinach and parsley and pour ½ stick butter, melted, over mixture. Toss with ¼ cup grated Parmesan cheese and serve.

Yield: 6 servings

Brussels Sprouts with Baby Carrots

2   (10 ounce) packages frozen
    brussels sprouts
1   cup chicken broth
¼   cup butter
1   (16 ounce) can baby carrots,
    drained

⅛   teaspoon ground ginger
½   teaspoon seasoned salt or
    to taste

Cook brussels sprouts in chicken broth in a large, covered saucepan for 10 minutes or until barely tender; drain. Meanwhile, in large skillet, melt butter and sauté carrots with ginger about 5 minutes, add cooked brussels sprouts and sauté a few minutes longer. Sprinkle with seasoned salt.

Yield: 8 to 10 servings

Brussels Sprouts and Celery

I like to use celery in combination with other vegetables. We served green beans with diagonally sliced celery sautéed in butter at Raleigh House for many years.

4   cups fresh Brussels sprouts
     or frozen ones, thawed
1½   cups chopped celery
1½   cups boiling water
1   teaspoon salt

4   tablespoons butter (½ stick)
4   tablespoons flour
Milk
Dash nutmeg
½   cup grated Cheddar cheese

Wash Brussels sprouts in salted water to remove grit; remove any wilted outside leaves. Cut off ends. Cook sprouts and celery in boiling water in covered pan about 8 minutes or until barely tender, drain, saving liquid for sauce. Blend butter and flour in small saucepan. Measure cooking liquid; add enough whole milk to make 1¾ cups. Stir gradually into flour mixture. Cook over medium heat, stirring, until sauce thickens,add nutmeg. Combine vegetables and sauce in a 1½ quart casserole. Sprinkle with the cheese. Bake in a 350° oven just until heated through. Serve at once.

Yield: 6 servings

Spinach Crepe Cups

This is an easy way to make cups out of crepes. Takes the place of patty shells.

Crepes:
3 eggs, beaten	½ teaspoon salt
⅔ cup flour	1 cup whole milk

For crepes, combine eggs, flour,salt and milk in blender, blend until smooth. Let stand 1 hour in refrigerator. Then make the crepes by pouring 2 tablespoons batter into hot lightly oiled 7 inch skillet or crepe pan. Cook until under side is lightly browned. Dump out on a clean towel. Proceed to make the 12 crepes. Cover with another towel and set aside.

Filling:
1½ cup grated sharp cheddar cheese	4 ounce can sliced mushrooms, drained
3 tablespoons flour	½ teaspoon salt
3 eggs, slightly beaten	Dash pepper
⅔ cup mayonnaise	6 crisply cooked slices of bacon broken into bits
10 ounce package chopped spinach, thawed and squeezed dry	

Toss cheese with flour; add remaining ingredients, except bacon. Mix well. Fit 2 crepes into each of 6 greased muffin cups. Fill with cheese-spinach mixture. Bake at 350° for 30 to 35 minutes or until center is firm. Garnish with crisp bacon bits, if desired.

Yield: 6 servings

These shells can be filled with any filling you choose, chicken, ham etc.

Glazed Carrots

1 pound small carrots, cut on the diagonal into ¼ inch slices	¾ cup water
4 tablespoons butter	4 teaspoons honey
½ teaspoon grated lemon rind	2 teaspoons lemon juice or to taste

Melt butter in a skillet, add carrots, rind, honey and ¾ cup water and boil the mixture, shaking the skillet occasionally, until almost all the liquid is evaporated. Add the lemon juice and salt to taste and cook the mixture over low heat. stirring, for 30 seconds, or until carrots are coated with the glaze.

Yield: 4 servings

Gruyere Potato Casserole

This is a rich but delicious way to serve potatoes.

1½ pounds boiling potatoes	Nutmeg to taste
1⅓ cups milk	Pepper to taste
1 cup heavy cream	⅔ cup grated Gruyere or
1½ teaspoon salt	Swiss cheese
1 teaspoon minced garlic	

Peel the potatoes and grate them coarsely, transfer them to a large bowl of cold water to keep them from turning brown. Stir the potatoes, briefly, to rinse off some of the starch. Drain them well in a colander. Combine the potatoes, milk, cream,salt, garlic, nutmeg and pepper in a saucepan. Bring just to a boil, stirring,and pour the mixture into a buttered 12" oval au gratin dish. Sprinkle cheese on top. Bake in a preheated 375° oven until brown and bubbly.

Yield: 4 generous servings

Rice-Noodle Pilaf

My great grandchildren love this casserole and so do grown ups. The ease of preparation is another plus. I have a Corning Ware casserole I use for this dish.

¼ cup butter	4 ounces medium noodles
2 onions, chopped	1½ teaspoon salt
2 cups uncooked Uncle Ben's rice	5½ cups canned or homemade chicken broth
1 (8 ounce) can sliced mushrooms, drained, or ½ pound fresh, sliced	¼ cup butter

1½ hours before dinner, start heating oven to 375°. Sauté onions in the butter in a heavy skillet or saucepan, until crisp-tender; add rice and mushrooms and sauté until rice is golden. Add noodles and salt, toss. Add chicken broth and ¼ cup butter and heat until butter melts. Transfer mixture to a casserole, 7"×11"×2". Bake, covered, 25 minutes, then with a fork, turn rice from the bottom to the top of pan and cook 20 more minutes, covered, or until rice is tender. Uncover casserole and fluff up rice. Serve immediately. If mixture seems dry before rice is cooked add about ½ cup more of broth or hot water.

Yield: 12 servings

If you do not have chicken broth on hand, get some chicken necks, about a pound and a half,cover them well with cold water and simmer until tender. Then add enough water to make the 5½ cups needed. Salt to taste.

Raleigh House Wild Rice Dressing

This recipe was given to me by my sister-in-law. I always served it with roast duck as well as other fowl. It makes a pretty as well as delicious entree when combined with either steamed or boiled jumbo shrimp.

1 cup wild rice	2 ounce can pimientos,
2½ cups Uncle Ben's converted	drained and chopped
white rice	1 (8 ounce) can sliced
2 large onions, chopped	mushrooms, undrained, or 1
½ of a large bunch celery,	pound fresh mushrooms,
chopped	sliced
2 sticks margarine or butter,	
melted	

Sauté celery and onions in margarine until crisp tender. Do not overcook as celery should still be green. If fresh mushrooms are used, add them last and let them sauté for only 3 minutes. Cook wild rice according to the Quick-Soak method elsewhere in this book. Cook white rice according to directions on box. Drain wild rice and finish cooking it with 3 cups water and ¼ teaspoon salt for 30 minutes, drain, if necessary, and combine rices in large bowl. Add vegetables,with the margarine used to sauté them, to the rice. Add pimientos. If mixture seems dry, add more margarine, melted. Taste for seasoning, add salt and pepper. Pour into either 1 large or 2 smaller casseroles. Heat in a 325° oven, covered, until hot.

Yield: About 20 servings

Another way I have used this dressing is with Cornish Game hens, halved and roasted glazed with butter. To serve: place the dressing in center of platter, then game hens and border with broccoli or asparagus spears.

Marinated Broccoli and Carrots

¼ cup water	2 cups broccoli florets
1 teaspoon salt	3 tablespoons vegetable oil
2 cups thinly sliced peeled	1 tablespoon cider vinegar
carrots	¼ teaspoon dried basil leaves

Place carrots in a saucepan of boiling water. Add salt, cover and steam about 5 minutes or until carrots are crisp tender. Add broccoli, cover and steam 5 minutes. Drain and toss with oil and vinegar, mixed. Sprinkle with basil, crushed between palms of hands. Serve warm.

Yield: 4 cups

Easy Spinach Souffle

The beauty of this is that it is so uncomplicated to prepare as well as very good.

2	eggs	½	teaspoon salt (optional)
1	(10¾ ounce) can cream of mushroom soup	1	(10 ounce) package frozen chopped spinach, thawed and drained well
1	small onion, thinly sliced	Dash nutmeg	
⅛	teaspoon garlic powder, not garlic salt		

Into blender container, put eggs, soup, onion, garlic powder and salt. Cover and blend 30 seconds. Add spinach and nutmeg and blend 30 seconds more. Pour into 1 quart ungreased casserole or souffle dish. Bake at 350° until set, about 50 minutes to an hour.

Yield: 4 servings

Spinach Lasagna

This is an original recipe of mine, a version of a dish I ate in Venice, Italy many years ago. It is a family favorite and is another good way of serving both a starchy and green vegetable in one dish.

6	lasagna noodles. cooked according to package directions, drained and cut in half crosswise	1	cup evaporated milk, undiluted
1	(10 ounce) package frozen chopped spinach, thawed and drained thoroughly by pressing down in colander or sieve	2	tablespoons flour
		2	tablespoons butter or margarine
		½	cup chicken stock or ½ cup more milk
3	eggs, beaten	¼	teaspoon salt
		Dash pepper	

Melt butter in saucepan, add flour; mix, then slowly add milk, chicken stock, salt and pepper, Cook, stirring, until thickened. Mix a little of the hot sauce into the beaten eggs, then add to the rest of sauce. Mix with spinach and place in 11″ × 7″ × 2″ buttered baking pan. Bake in a pre-heated 350° oven about 20 minutes or until just firm in center. Cool, then cut into 12 "fingers" making one cut down and six across.

Continued on next page

Sauce:

1⅓ sticks butter or margarine
½ cup plus 1 tablespoon flour
4 cups milk

6 ounces cream cheese, room
temperature
Salt to taste

Cream the butter and flour together in a small bowl. This is a buerre manié or kneaded butter. It is the easiest way I know of to make cream sauce in quantity. Heat milk in top of a double boiler over hot water. Gradually add pieces of the buerre manie' to the hot milk, stirring constantly with a wire whisk until thickened and smooth. Remove from hot water and add cream cheese in pieces, whisking again until sauce is smooth. Taste for seasoning. Sauce will probably need more salt. To assemble: Butter a 9″×13″×2″ baking pan. Wrap a "finger" of spinach in each of the halves of the noodles; lay, seam-side down, in pan; placing 3 rolls at one end, lengthwise, then continuing making 4 rolls of three each. Pour hot sauce over and sprinkle generously with grated Parmesan cheese. Serve each guest one roll with sauce. You may fix this in individual casseroles, but you may need to make more sauce, one-half the recipe should be enough.

Yield: 12 servings

I usually make twice this recipe as it freezes well. However, place in a 350° oven to reheat before it is completely thawed, to keep sauce from separating

Cynthia's Spinach Casserole

This a pretty dish to serve around the holidays with its red and green vegetables

4 (10 ounce) packages of
frozen leaf spinach, thawed
and drained
2 cups cottage cheese
2 cups crushed saltine
crackers
2 cups grated sharp cheese
4 eggs, beaten
1 teaspoon salt

½ teaspoon pepper
1 stick margarine
2 onions, chopped
2 tablespoons flour
4 small cans tomato paste
½ cup boiling water
Additional salt and pepper, if
needed

Combine spinach, cottage cheese, crackers, eggs and salt and pepper. Melt the margarine in a saucepan and sauté the onion until limp. Add flour, tomato paste and boiling water. Place over medium heat and cook, stirring constantly, until thickened. Taste for seasoning. Divide the spinach mixture into two 7″×11″×2″ baking pans that have been buttered. Pour tomato sauce mixture on top., and sprinkle with the grated sharp cheese. Bake for about 25 minutes in a 350° oven or until bubbly.

Yield: 20 servings

Potato-Cheese Balls

The cream cheese or Monterey Jack cheese in the center makes this dish. The balls are baked, not fried, which is another plus.

3	cups mashed potatoes, about 2 pounds	1	teaspoon chili powder (optional)
¼ to ½	cup milk, warmed	6	ounces cream cheese or Monterey Jack cheese
2	teaspoons salt	1	egg beaten with 1 tablespoon water
½	stick butter or margarine, softened		Dry bread crumbs
2	egg yolks		

Pare potatoes and cut into cubes, place in saucepan with 3 inches of boiling water in bottom. Cook until tender. Drain well in colander. Place potatoes in mixer bowl and beat until smooth. Add butter, salt, ¼ cup of the milk, chili powder and eggs. Beat well. Potatoes should be firm enough to roll into a ball, but moist enough to hold together when rolled between the palms of the hands. Add part or rest of milk, as needed.

Divide potatoes into 12 balls. Divide cheese into 12 portions. Make an indentation in middle of each ball and insert cheese, enclosing with potato. Roll balls in beaten egg, then in crumbs. Place on well buttered cookie sheet and bake at 350° until brown.

Yield: 12 balls

These can be made a day ahead and refrigerated, covered. Cheddar cheese may be used for the center, also.

Jimmy's Spinach Puff

6	eggs		Dash pepper
1	cup frozen chopped spinach, thawed and squeezed dry	1	teaspoon MSG (optional)
		3	tablespoons melted butter, or margarine
½	cup milk	¼	cup flour
⅓	cup grated Parmesan cheese	1¼	cups milk
½	teaspoon salt	¾	cup grated Velveeta cheese

Place first 7 ingredients in blender; blend 1 minute on high speed. Grease a 1½ quart souffle dish and dust with fine dry bread crumbs. Shake out excess. Pour souffle in and bake in a pre-heated 375° oven for 20 minutes or until firm 2" from sides. While puff is cooking, combine melted butter and flour in a saucepan, add milk and cook, stirring constantly, until thickened. Stir in cheese, then taste for seasoning, adding salt and pepper, if needed. Turn out puff on serving dish and spoon sauce over.

Yield: about 4 servings

Individual Crepe Casseroles

This is another version of spinach-filled crepes without the cheese or bacon.

Spinach Custard:

3	eggs	1	teaspoon flour
¼	teaspoon salt	1½	cups milk
¼	teaspoon onion salt	1	(10 ounce) package frozen chopped spinach, thawed and drained well.
⅛	teaspoon dried savory leaves, crumbled		
	Few grains pepper	12	(8") crepes

Beat eggs with seasonings and flour, then add milk, then spinach. Mix well. Fit 2 crepes into buttered round individual 4" or 5" × 1¼" deep casseroles, 6 in all. Divide spinach mixture between them. Bake, uncovered, in a pre-heated 350° oven about 20 to 25 minutes or until a knife inserted in center comes out clean.

Yield: 6 servings

Crepes are very versatile. The crepe-lined casseroles may also be filled with creamed chicken and mushrooms or ham and ripe olives or with the popular ratatouille.

Make Ahead Spinach Souffle

This can be prepared as much as a day ahead, refrigerated, and baked just before serving. If refrigerated, allow 10 minutes more baking time.

1	stick butter	4	heaping cups chopped fresh
½	cup flour		spinach, stems removed
3	cups half and half	2	teaspoons grated onion
2	teaspoons salt	7	eggs, beaten
½	cup grated sharp cheddar cheese		

In a large saucepan or skillet, melt butter, then add flour and mix well until blended and smooth. Slowly add cream, stirring constantly. When it comes to a boil, cook for 3 minutes, stirring constantly. Add salt and cheese. Mix well. Fold in spinach and onion; then fold in eggs. Pour into a 2 quart souffle dish or straight-sided casserole that has been buttered and dusted with fine, dry bread crumbs. Bake in a pre-heated 350° oven for 30 minutes.

Yield: 8 servings

If you wash the spinach in salted water, the grit will just roll off. Lift it out and rinse again under running water.

Broccoli and Corn Pudding

4	tablespoons butter (½ stick), softened		Freshly ground black pepper
4	cups broccoli florets, fresh or frozen	5	tablespoons flour
		1	teaspoon salt
4	cups raw corn kernels, fresh or frozen	1	teaspoon sugar
		4	eggs, beaten
	Grated rind of a lemon	2	cups milk

Butter a 9" × 13" baking dish. Place broccoli florets at each end. Put corn in center. Sprinkle the lemon rind over the broccoli and pepper over corn. Mix the flour, salt, sugar and butter in a bowl. Mix eggs and milk and gradually stir into flour mixture, mix well to make a thin batter. Pour over vegetables. Bake in a preheated 350° oven for one hour or until a silver knife inserted in the center, comes out clean.

Yield: 6 servings

Snow Peas and Tomatoes

1 pound fresh snow peas	½ teaspoon salt
2 tablespoons butter	2 medium tomatoes, coarsely
2 teaspoons soy sauce	chopped
½ teaspoon dried whole basil, crushed between palms of hands	

String snow peas and remove ends. Put butter in shallow 2½ quart casserole. Microwave on high 45 seconds or until melted. Add snow peas, soy sauce, basil and salt; toss. Sprinkle tomatoes over top. Cover and microwave at high 3 minutes or until snow peas are crisp tender.

Yield: 6 to 8 servings

Dilled Carrots and Zucchini

4 large carrots	3 tablespoons butter
4 medium zucchini	½ teaspoon dried dill weed
1½ cups chicken broth	

Cut both the carrots and zucchini in julienned strips. In saucepan, combine carrots and chicken broth. Bring to a boil and cook about 5 minutes or until barely tender, add zucchini and cook only 5 minutes. Broth should be almost gone. Add butter and dill weed and pepper and salt to taste.

Yield: 6 servings

Artichoke Bottoms with Cheese

When I was in Stuttgart many years ago, I was served artichoke bottoms with a generous topping of cheddar cheese. So simple to make and so delicious. They were served piping hot.

Fried Rice

This is expertly seasoned to go with oriental food, but will not be good if cold rice is not used.

1	quart cold cooked rice	2	tablespoons cooking oil
1	green onion, finely chopped	2	tablespoons soy sauce
3	finely sliced mushrooms	1	egg
½	cup finely diced cooked chicken, ham or pork		

Sauté meat in oil, add mushrooms, rice, green onion and soy sauce. Continue to cook over low heat for 10 minutes, then add well beaten egg and stir until egg is cooked. If a darker color is desired, add more soy sauce.

Yield: 6 servings

Spinach Casserole

This may be baked in a large casserole or in individual custard cups.

3	(10 ounce) packages frozen chopped spinach, thawed and squeezed dry	Salt and pepper to taste
1½	tablespoons flour	½ cup mayonnaise
1½	tablespoons butter	1 tablespoon onion juice
½	cup milk	3 eggs, well beaten
		½ teaspoon salt
		½ teaspoon pepper

Melt butter in small saucepan, add flour. Mix, then add milk. Cook, stirring, until thickened. Add salt and pepper to taste. Add mayonnaise, onion juice and the well beaten eggs. Mix well, then add spinach. Taste for seasoning. Pour into a well buttered 1½ quart casserole or individual baking dishes. Set in pan with 1 inch hot water. Bake at 350° for 35 to 40 minutes or until firm in center.

Yield: 10 servings

Baked Acorn Squash

3	medium acorn squash, cut in half and seeds removed	½	cup crushed pineapple, drained
3	tablespoons brown sugar, packed	3	tablespoons pineapple juice
3	tablespoons butter	1	egg, beaten
		½	teaspoon salt

Place squash, cut side down in baking pan with an inch of hot water. Bake at 350° until squash is tender. Scoop out pulp and place in bowl, add brown sugar, butter, pineapple, pineapple juice, egg and salt. Mix well, then place in well buttered casserole. Bake at 350° for 30 to 40 minutes or until lightly browned.

Yield: 6 servings

Chinese Fried Rice

3	cups cold cooked rice	½	cup frozen peas, thawed and drained
4	large eggs, beaten		
½	teaspoon salt	1	tablespoon chopped green onions
3	tablespoons salad oil, divided		
¼	pound cooked ham, diced	1	tablespoon soy sauce

In non-stick skillet or wok, heat 2 tablespoons oil over medium heat. Add cooked rice and gently stir until it is coated with oil. Push to one side of skillet or wok. In same skillet or wok over medium-high heat, heat 1 tablespoon oil until very hot; pour in eggs and cook, stirring constantly with a wooden spoon, until eggs are the size of peas and leave the sides of the pan. Mix eggs with rice, then stir in ham, green peas and soy sauce and heat through. Sprinkle with green onions when serving. Check for seasoning.

Yield: 4 main dish servings

Raisin Almond Rice

1 cup finely minced onion	¼ cup blanched almonds, sliced or slivered
1 tablespoon butter or margarine	2 cups chicken broth
1 cup uncooked rice	Salt to taste
2 teaspoons raisins	Freshly ground pepper to taste

In small saucepan, cook onion in butter until wilted. Stir in rice, raisins and almonds. Add broth, salt and pepper. Bring to a boil, Reduce heat, cover, and simmer 20 minutes or until rice is tender and all liquid is absorbed.

For microwave oven: Cook butter and onion 5 minutes at high in 2 quart casserole. Add remaining ingredients, cover, and cook 13 to 15 minutes on high or until broth is absorbed and rice is done.

Yield: 4 servings

Mexican Rice

3 tablespoons bacon drippings	½ cup skinned and diced fresh tomatoes
1 onion, chopped	1 teaspoon salt
1 cup uncooked rice	Boiling water
1 bell pepper, chopped	
1 teaspoon chili powder or to taste	

Sauté onion in bacon drippings. Add rice; stir constantly until brown. Add rest of ingredients except water. Mix, then cover well with boiling water. Cover and simmer very slowly without stirring, until rice is tender and flaky. Liquid should be absorbed.

Yield: 6 servings

Noodles with Water Chestnuts

6   cups medium size noodles
3   tablespoons butter
1½ cups milk
Salt
Pepper
1   (5 ounce) can water
     chestnuts, coarsely chopped

10   ounces frozen snow peas
     (optional)
3   additional tablespoons
     butter
½   cup slivered, toasted
     almonds

Cook noodles until almost tender. Drain and place in casserole with butter, milk, salt, pepper and water chestnuts. Mix well, cover, and refrigerate several hours or overnight.

About an hour before serving time, add snow peas with additional 3 tablespoons butter, if desired. Mix, place in a buttered casserole or souffle dish, 8" in diameter and 4" deep, then bake at 350° until hot, stirring gently once or twice. Before serving, sprinkle with toasted almonds. If noodles seem dry before they are done, add about ¼ to ⅓ cup more milk. Sprinkle with toasted almonds before serving.

Yield: 8 servings

Simple Wild Rice Casserole

1 pound of wild rice will yield 20 to 25 servings, 1 cup wild rice yields 3 to 4 cups cooked; when blending with white rice, use 50% wild rice. Chicken broth may be used in the cooking for rice pilaf.

1   cup uncooked wild rice,
     rinsed well and drained
1   cup canned sliced
     mushrooms

¼   cup finely diced onion
½   cup sliced water chestnuts
3   cups chicken broth, heated
¼   cup butter

Mix rice, onion, water chestnuts and mushrooms in a 2 quart casserole. Add heated broth and butter. Cover and bake at 325° for about 1½ hours, or until rice is tender and liquid is absorbed.

Yield: 6 to 8 servings

Never throw away remains of wild rice, use it in soups or casseroles. It freezes well.

Macaroni, Cheese, Bacon Casserole

During World War I, everyone was asked to have one meatless meal a week. My father felt a meal was not complete without meat, so my mother compromised by adding the bacon to this casserole.

½ pound macaroni	3 cups grated sharp cheese, divided
1 tablespoon butter	
1 egg, beaten	1 cup milk
1 teaspoon salt	6 strips bacon
1 teaspoon dry mustard	

Boil the macaroni in salted water until just tender; drain thoroughly. Stir in butter, milk and egg; Mix the mustard and salt with 1 tablespoon hot water and add to macaroni, then add 2 cups of the cheese. Pour into buttered 2 quart casserole. Sprinkle remaining cheese on casserole, place bacon on top. Bake at 350° about 40 minutes or until custard is set and top is light brown.

If you are using a shallow rather than a deep casserole, use enough bacon to cover top.

Yield: 8 servings

She always served this with a Waldorf salad of red unpeeled apples, celery and nuts plus a generous sprinkling of quartered candied cherries. It makes a pretty salad and the cherries add a pleasant texture to the otherwise crisp salad.

Feathered Rice

1½ cups uncooked rice	3½ cups boiling water
1½ teaspoons salt	

Heat oven to 400°. Spread rice in shallow baking pan. Add salt and pour boiling water over. Stir with a fork. then cover tightly with foil. Bake for about 20 to 25 minutes or until rice is done and water is absorbed. Fluff up with a fork before serving.

Yield: 6 cups

Spanish Rice

½	cup uncooked Uncle Ben's rice	1	(number 2) can of tomatoes, 2½ cups
2	tablespoons butter or margarine	3	tablespoons minced green pepper
1	cup thinly sliced onions	1	small bay leaf
1⅛	teaspoons salt		Pepper

Cook rice according to package directions. In hot butter in skillet, cook onions until golden and tender. Add salt and rest of ingredients except rice. Simmer, uncovered, 15 minutes; remove bay leaf. Add rice and mix well; turn into a buttered 1 quart casserole. Bake, uncovered, at 375° for 30 minutes.

Yield: 4 servings

Asparagus with Creme Fraiche

1½	pounds fresh asparagus, peeled and trimmed	½	cup mayonnaise
½	cup creme fraiche or sour cream		Pinch cayenne pepper
			Lemon juice to taste

Cook asparagus in boiling, salted water for 4 minutes or until just tender. Drain in a colander and refresh under cold water. Return to pan and reheat a few minutes, then place on a platter or individual serving dishes and place the mixture of last 4 ingredients over the top. This may also be served at room temperature, if you wish.

Yield: 6 servings

Carrot-Zucchini Casserole

6 medium carrots, cut into thin strips	10 ounce package frozen small green peas, thawed
3 small zucchini, sliced very thin	

Cook carrots in boiling, salted water for 5 minutes, drain. In buttered shallow 1 quart casserole, mix the vegetables together.

Sauce:

2 tablespoons cornstarch	1 teaspoon salt
1½ cup milk	¼ teaspoon pepper
½ stick butter or margarine	

In a small, heavy saucepan, mix cornstarch and cold milk together, add the margarine or butter, salt and pepper and bring to a boil. Boil 1 minute, taste for seasoning and pour over vegetables. Sprinkle with a scant teaspoon sweet basil that has been crumbled between the palms of the hands to bring out the flavor. Bake in a 350° oven for 25 minutes. Top with 1 cup croutons.

Yield: 4 to 6 servings

Equivalents:

1 cup quick-cooking oats makes 1¾ cups, cooked.

1 cup rice makes 3 to 3½ cups, cooked.

1 cup cornmeal makes 4 cups, cooked.

9 to 12 graham crackers make 1 cup crumbs.

18 to 20 saltine crackers make 1 cup crumbs.

1 slice bread makes ½ cup fine crumbs.

1 pound apples make 3 cups, peeled and sliced.

1 pound grapes make 2¾ cups, seeded.

1 average lemon makes 2 to 3 tablespoons juice.

1 orange makes ½ cup juice.

1 pound fresh cranberries make 3½ cups sauce.

½ pound butter equals 1 cup butter.

1 square chocolate equals 1 ounce.

1 pound all-purpose flour equals 4 cups.

1 pound chopped nuts equals 4 cups.

1 pound confectioners sugar equals 3½ cups.

2 cups water equals 1 pound.

5 large Grade A eggs equals 1 cup.

Substitutions:

1 cup sugar for 2 cups corn syrup. Note: Never substitute more than half the sugar called for in a recipe with corn syrup.

1 cup sugar for ½ cup honey for pudding, custards and pie fillings. 1 cup for bread and rolls. ⅞ cup honey for cookies and cakes. Reduce liquid by 3 tablespoons for each cup sugar.

1 teaspoon sugar for ⅛ teaspoon artificial sweetener. Do not bake with saccharine, as it becomes bitter.

7 small eggs for 6 medium eggs, or 4 large eggs.

1 tablespoon flour for thickening for 1½ teaspoons cornstarch or 1 teaspoon quick-cooking tapioca.

1 tablespoon lemon juice for ½ teaspoon vinegar.

½ cup evaporated milk plus ½ cup water. 1 quart whole milk for 1 quart skim milk plus 3 tablespoons cream.

1¾ cups confectioners sugar for 1 cup granulated sugar.

1 cup cake flour for ⅞ cup all-purpose flour.

1⅓ cup rolled oats for 1 cup all-purpose flour.

1 whole egg for 2 yolks plus 1 tablespoon water.

1 small garlic clove for ⅛ teaspoon garlic powder.

1 cup canned tomatoes for 1½ cups fresh, chopped tomatoes, simmered 10 minutes.

1 tablespoon fresh herbs for ⅓ to ½ teaspoon dried.

Note: Do not substitute liquid oil for solid butter or margarine in a recipe for cake. Texture will be poor because air will not be beaten in with the adding of the fat.

Index

Index

RALEIGH HOUSE
P.O. Box 2182
Kerrville, TX 78029-2182

Please send me _____ copies of Raleigh House Cookbook   @ $19.95 each _____

Texas residents add 8¼% sales tax   @   1.65 each _____

Postage and handling   @   2.00 each _____

Total Enclosed _____

Name _____

Address _____

City _____ State _____ Zip _____

Make checks payable to Raleigh House.

- -

RALEIGH HOUSE
P.O. Box 2182
Kerrville, TX 78029-2182

Please send me _____ copies of Raleigh House Cookbook   @ $19.95 each _____

Texas residents add 8¼% sales tax   @   1.65 each _____

Postage and handling   @   2.00 each _____

Total Enclosed _____

Name _____

Address _____

City _____ State _____ Zip _____

Make checks payable to Raleigh House.

- -

RALEIGH HOUSE
P.O. Box 2182
Kerrville, TX 78029-2182

Please send me _____ copies of Raleigh House Cookbook   @ $19.95 each _____

Texas residents add 8¼% sales tax   @   1.65 each _____

Postage and handling   @   2.00 each _____

Total Enclosed _____

Name _____

Address _____

City _____ State _____ Zip _____

Make checks payable to Raleigh House.

If you would like to see Raleigh House Cookbook in your area, please send the names and addresses of your local gift or book stores

If you would like to see Raleigh House Cookbook in your area, please send the names and addresses of your local gift or book stores

If you would like to see Raleigh House Cookbook in your area, please send the names and addresses of your local gift or book stores